READINGS IN MORAL THEOLOGY NO. 4:
THE USE OF SCRIPTURE IN MORAL THEOLOGY

READINGS IN MORAL THEOLOGY

No. 4:

The Use of Scripture in Moral Theology

Edited by
Charles E. Curran
and
Richard A. McCormick, S.J.

PAULIST PRESS
New York/Ramsey

Library of Congress
Catalog Card Number: 83-62465

ISBN: 0-8091-2563-3

Published by Paulist Press
545 Island Road, Ramsey, N.J. 07446

Printed and bound in the
United States of America

Contents

FOREWORD

This fourth volume of our series *Readings In Moral Theology* deals with the use of the Scriptures in Christian ethics. The ecumenical and methodological aspects of this topic are obvious.

Protestant ethics has consistently appealed to the Bible, but as the essays in this volume show there has been a significant development in the twentieth century in the way in which Protestant ethics has utilized the Scriptures in trying to develop a systematic Christian ethics. Today there remains much diversity in the way in which different Protestant ethicists use the Bible. The Second Vatican Council called for all Catholic theology, including moral theology, to be nourished by the Scriptures. In the last two decades Catholic moral theology has given much more importance to the Scriputres, but there is no general agreement about exactly how the Bible should be used in a systematic moral theology. Thus both Protestant ethics and Catholic moral theology continue to grapple with this fundamental methodological question.

The complex question of the use of the Scriptures in Christian ethics or moral theology involves at least four different aspects. The first aspect is the determination of the meaning of the particular scriptural text as it is found in the Bible itself. In this process one must employ all the tools of contemporary biblical exegesis, including textual, source, form, redaction and literary criticism. Generally speaking, the ethicist will be heavily dependent on the professional exegete for help on this level. In addition, the particular text must be seen in its relation to the whole Bible.

The second aspect of the question involves the meaning of the text for today in our different historical, cultural, and sociological situation. We are also living today with an understanding of eschatology and the relationship of the world to the kingdom which differs especially from the eschatology of the New Testament. This level of the problem is often expressed in terms of the relevance and meaning of the Scriptures for today.

A third aspect of the question discussed in this book concerns the different levels within moral theology itself. Christian ethics deals with many different levels—the general perspective of Christian ethics, the ethical model, the person as both subject and agent, the fundamental call to conversion or change of heart, the values and goals of the Christian life, the attitudes, character, and dispositions of the Christian person, norms and concrete decision making. The Scriptures will function somewhat differently on each of these different levels of moral theology.

A fourth aspect is the relationship between the Bible and the other sources of ethical wisdom and knowledge for the discipline of moral theology. Most Christian ethicists would agree that in addition to the Scriptures, some importance must also be given to tradition, Church teaching, human experience, and reason. However, the exact relationship among all these different sources continues to be a matter of discussion.

This volume follows the format and purpose of the previous volumes in this series. The articles have been selected from the existing literature on the subject. Although both of us have our opinions, our purpose is not to advocate any one position but rather to give a representative sampling of the different issues and approaches involved in the use of the Scriptures in Christian ethics. Hopefully, this volume will also stimulate further interest in and research on this very important and complex topic.

Charles E. Curran
Richard A. McCormick, S.J.

Jesus, Ethics and the Present Situation

Richard H. Hiers

This article originally appeared in Richard H. Hiers' *Jesus and Ethics: Four Interpretations,* 1968.

Not even the most radical literary and form critics doubt that it is possible to obtain from the Synoptic sources a probable account of the character and content of Jesus' teaching/preaching. The central problem is that Jesus' message appears in connection with his expectation that history was in its last days, that the Kingdom of God, Son of Man, and time of judgment would soon come.

THE PROBLEM OF UNREALIZED ESCHATOLOGY

It has been difficult for most interpreters both to believe that Jesus actually expected these events and intended his message for his contemporaries living in the interim before their occurrence, and at the same time to believe that Jesus' message can be relevant and authoritative for the moral life in the modern world. These writers are generally convinced that Jesus and his teaching do have some such relevance and authority. Rather than sacrifice this conviction at the altar of historical criticism, many of them prefer to believe that Jesus must have *meant* his message for all times, or for us, or to look for some way to detach Jesus' message from its eschatological context. Harnack and Schweitzer adopt the latter strategy. Bultmann and Dodd, on the other hand, attempt to translate the eschatological world view into some more congenial philosophy, respectively, existentialism and Platonism.

2 / *Richard H. Hiers*

Dodd also maintains that Jesus thought that the Kingdom of God had already come. Many, especially Anglo-Saxon, writers concur, though with the reservation that Jesus *also* expected it to come in the future. The dogmatic interest of many such interpreters is evident in their tendency to stress the present aspect of the kingdom and to deemphasize, or even ignore, its future coming. It seems, generally, to be feared that if Jesus really expected the imminent arrival of the Kingdom, his teaching could have no more meaning for us since (1) he would not, then, have *intended* his teaching "for us"; (2) he would have been mistaken, and his authority would thus be placed in doubt; and (3) we in the twentieth century do not share this expectation, and thus his message would be irrelevant to our situation. Like Harnack, many recent writers have also attempted to circumvent these difficulties by discounting the evidence with respect to Jesus' eschatological perspective "in an effort to identify completely the historical Jesus with the interpretation of his teaching held to be ethically and religiously valid for our time."[1] What can be said about these "difficulties"?

First, it must simply be recognized that Jesus did not, so far as we can tell from the Synoptic evidence, intend his message for later generations, centuries, or us. This does not, however, mean automatically that his message can have no meaning for us. If what Jesus had to say about the character of God and man and their mutual or triadic relationship (God-self-neighbor) was true in the first century, it is not invalidated by the fact that God, man, and neighbor have continued to confront one another in succeeding centuries, unless the nature of God or the nature of man has changed substantially. There is no evidence that such change has occurred. Jesus may not have intended his sayings and parables for us, but we are not precluded from seeing in them examples or "dramatic pictures of action in concrete situations" arising out of a "consistent understanding of God, man, and the world" which "appeal to the conscience by way of imagination."[2] As H. R. Niebuhr pointed out, Jesus' words echo in our memories as we perceive analogies between the concrete situations in which we encounter our neighbors and the situations, actions, and admonitions presented in the traditions attributed to Jesus. It is interesting to notice, for instance, how many interpreters find meaning and authority in Jesus' words from Matt. 25:40, "As you did it to one of the least of these my brethren, you did it to me," or in his story of the Samaritan who "proved neighbor" to the injured traveler (Luke 10:25–37).

With respect to the second point, it must be admitted without reservation that Jesus was mistaken. The Kingdom of God simply did not come, certainly not in the form that he expected and announced that it would. Even if it could be shown, exegetically, that Jesus did think that the Kingdom had come, we would still have to conclude that he was mistaken, for there is no evidence that it did come, either in or during his ministry, or subsequently. Attempts have been made to locate its immanence in the world. Harnack thought that is was present as God's rule in men's hearts. The "social gospel" theologians saw it present (if only partially realized) in social progress. Dodd suggests that it is present in recurrent celebrations of the Eucharist.[3] Bultmann thinks it present in every recurrent existential crisis of decision in response to preaching (the Protestant sacrament). It is clear, however, if the historical experience of the past twenty centuries has any weight, that the Kingdom of God has not yet come on earth. History reveals the ambivalent character of human nature and destiny. At every level of achievement, as Reinhold Niebuhr puts it, man may and does actualize both his creative and his destructive vitalities. The history of twenty centuries does not justify complete pessimism or moral cynicism and paralysis, of which Reinhold Niebuhr is sometimes, inaccurately, accused.[4] On the other hand, history does not justify the naïve optimism of those who think that the Kingdom of God can be made to appear if only we put Reinhold Niebuhr back on the shelf unopened, half read, or forgotten, and think only positive thoughts about man's nature and destiny, as in the case of Altizer, Cox, Fletcher, and Hamilton.

Jesus was mistaken in believing that the ambiguities of historical existence were about to be resolved in ultimate judgment and redemption. But his understanding as to what God requires and desires of man is not thereby discredited.

The third difficulty needs to be taken seriously: we do not share Jesus' (and the early church's) expectation that the arrival of the Kingdom and Messiah are imminent. If we visualize the end of history in the form of man-made cataclysm, it has more the appearance of Amos' "day of Yahweh" than Jesus' "good news" of the coming of the Kingdom. Our optimism takes the form of hoping that the world as we know it—improved, perhaps, by temporary "proximate" solutions—will be permitted to continue indefinitely into the future. In that case, however, the radical sayings of Jesus about selling all and giving to the poor, or taking no thought for the morrow, however "sublime," cannot be followed responsibly, even if he meant them to be obeyed literally. Furthermore, our historical-political situation is now different from that of Jesus' hearers, who lacked the freedom and responsibility of participating in making the policy decisions of the Roman government. Democracy has given us responsibility for the decisions and indecisions of government which affect the well-being of fellow citizens and fellow humans of other nations. We can no longer hide behind the Pauline-Lutheran illusion that God governs directly and unambiguously through the imperial or national regime. Furthermore, through our natural resources and technology we have become, in David Potter's phrase, a "people of plenty." Now we find not only the local Lazarus sitting at our gate but also the traditionally ignored or exploited "peasant village masses" of the world.[5] Our meager paternalistic interest in both draws us increasingly into a quandary, because of our gradually awakening consciousness that they, most ungratefully, suppose that there is some correlation between their plight and our prosperity. If Jesus did not have us and our complicated situation in view, he cannot have meant his teaching for us, or even understood our problems. How, then, could his message be relevant to our modern situation?

II
THE SIGNIFICANCE OF JESUS' ETHICS IN THE MODERN SITUATION

All the modern interpreters except Dodd, who does not discuss the subject, maintain on the one hand that Jesus did not intend his teaching as a program of social reform, and on the other, that his teaching is, nevertheless, relevant to the conditions of human life in society. Harnack and Bultmann agreed that Jesus' commandment of love is "profoundly socialistic," or, at least, "may have far-reaching implications for national and social life." Both, however, tended to stress the God-soul relationship to the exclusion of the self-neighbor-world dimension. Harnack's description of the Kingdom as "God and the soul, the soul and its God" includes no mention of the neighbor. Bultmann considers the basic moral question to be, "How can I achieve my true self?"[6] In this view of ethics, as in the medieval quest for the *visio Dei,* the neighbor comes only incidentally or instrumentally into view. Schweitzer has little to say about the social relevance of Jesus' ethic; yet more than the others, he was explicitly concerned for the fate of society, indeed, of civilization. In his two-volume *Philosophy of Civilization,* he undertook to elaborate a world-affirming philosophy, "reverence for life," which could serve to redeem civilization from the doom toward which it was evidently bound. He did not attempt, however, to base "reverence for life" on Jesus' message, though twice, in passing, he attributed it to Jesus. Rather, he sought its basis in mysticism and/or "elemental thinking." In his work as a physician, Schweitzer undertook to do what one man could for the well-being of thousands of diseased men, women, and children in the Congo. Obedience to Jesus' ethic of love or "active self-devotion to others" was not only something Schweitzer wrote about; he "reduplicated" it in his own life.

None of these men, however, develops a social ethic or strategy for resolving, either ultimately or proximately, the problems of man's life in society. Perhaps this fact is no accident. It is not possible to devise a theory of social ethics from Jesus' teaching or commands alone. Each of the four major interpreters does make a distinctive contribution toward an understanding of the significance of Jesus and his ethics for the moral life, but in each case that contribution needs to be supplemented by other considerations.

Harnack offers, as one expression of the "essence of Christianity" Jesus' discovery and proclamation of the "infinite value of the human soul." Man's value is derived from the fact that he was created by God, who continues to care about him. Bultmann, on the other hand, insists that man has value only when he decides for God in the "crisis of decision." Bultmann's position corresponds to a characteristic Lutheran tendency to regard "faith" as the greatest of works, as, indeed, the sole basis for human value in the eyes of God. Harnack and Bultmann are both touching part of the truth. Bultmann is correct in that faith is inextricably correlated to the perception of value.

As H. R. Niebuhr has shown, faith is the bond of confidence and loyalty between the self and the object of faith which is, as such, at the same time the source or center of meaning and of value. Harnack did not recognize that the "Fatherhood of God" and the "infinite value of the human soul" are faith statements, not objective truths. Furthermore, man's value is not, from the standpoint of Jesus' own radically monotheistic faith, an "independent" or "infinite" value, but, as Harnack himself seemed to understand when he associated this value with the Fatherhood of God, it is a *relational* value. Man has value in relation to the source of all value, God. He may have, to God, more value than many sparrows or sheep, but he does not have absolute value: e.g., more than *all* sparrows or sheep or other "lesser" forms of being. Schweitzer and H. R. Niebuhr correctly point out that an ethic which is concerned only with man as the locus of all value is, from the standpoint of radical monotheism or reverence for life, a tribalistic or henotheistic ethic. Futhermore, man does not have absolute value in relation either to other men or to God, who alone is absolutely "good." The neighbor whom I encounter in this particular situation does not have absolute value over against other neighbors in the present or other situations.[7] But Bultmann is wrong in restricting value to those who decide correctly in the "Now" of decision. The God of radical monotheistic faith—as such was incarnate both in the men of faith in ancient Israel and in Jesus of Nazareth—is the universal Creator, Sovereign, and Redeemer, not a tribal god who is concerned only for men of the tribe of faith. The Synoptic Jesus admonished his followers to be concerned not only for one another, as in the of the Johannine Jesus' restrictive "love of the brethren"—the love of fellow clansmen practiced by the Gentiles—but to love all men, including their enemies and persecutors, after the pattern of God's love which is not reserved for the "good" and "just," but also bestowed on the "evil and unjust."[8]

The recognition in faith that all men (indeed, all existent beings) have value in relation to God is an ever-relevant corrective against the ever-present tendency on the part of men to find relatively greater—and even exclusive—value in those who in nation, race, culture, time, class, sex, or thought are so blessed as to resemble themselves most closely. To such faith there is no longer any distinction in value between "chosen people" and "barbarians," male and female, East and West, Negroid, Oriental, and Caucasian, Communist and capitalist, believer and "infidel."

Schweitzer's several theories by way of explaining Jesus' significance for us are of interest, but the two most important are his conception of the significance of Jesus' will for "our" will, and his characterization of Jesus' ethic as an ethic of "self-devotion to others." The first expresses the sense of authority that Schweitzer found in the person as well as the words of Jesus. It is not just because the sayings of Jesus were imaginatively or "beautifully" spoken and written that they have had meaning in later times. These sayings express the understanding of a particular authoritative and perceptive person (whom the Christian church, for want of a better title, has designated "the Christ") with respect to the nature and demand or will of God. That person took God so seriously as to undertake in his life and message to exemplify and inform his contemporaries as to His will, and of their ultimate situation in relation to God. The person as well as the message of Jesus present the claim of God upon man. God not only values all being, he also wills that it be ordered in such a way as to realize the well-being of all the particular beings in the realm of being.[9] The message of Jesus has to do not only with values but with the will of the Valuer. The will of Jesus, his will to will the will of God, is both norm and authority for the wills of his followers. Schweitzer did not spell out the content of Jesus' will. He did describe the will of God as his "will of love," which Jesus taught that men were to "help carry out in this world." In his later descriptions of Jesus' ethics as the "ethics of love" or "self-devotion to others," Schweitzer made it clear what he understood the content of Jesus' will to be: that his followers love, i.e., be devoted to the well-being of others.

Ethics may be described as the aspect of a person's faith in the object of faith as center of value, in which the person commits or devotes himself to that object as the cause which he desires and wills to serve. When the object of faith is God, the center of value for all that is, ethics, as devotion to God, entails devotion to the concrete manifestations of being which one encounters, thus other human beings (and nonhuman beings as well). Schweitzer did not indicate explicitly that devotion to God is the ground of the self's devotion to others, but this understanding seems implicit in his references to God's will of love. In any case, the conception of Jesus' ethics as the ethics of self-devotion to others illumines the relational character of love as concern for others, expressed in appropriate action with respect to their well-being. The relational nature of the love has not always been so clearly understood. Though Jesus spoke very little about love or loving, a great many of his sayings and parables have to do with attitudes and actions relating to the well-being of others.

Bultmann's conception of Jesus' (and also Christian) ethics as the ethics of radical obedience contains two focuses. In relation to God, it means complete surrender of my will to God's will. But (as with Schweitzer), what God wills is that I love my neighbor. This does not mean the surrender of the will to arbitrary external authority, as in Orthodox Judaism and Islam. But it does mean obedience to God, not merely going about business as usual, as if ethics were no more than a refinement of man's quest for pleasure. "Which God will you serve, the Lord or Baal?" thundered Elijah at Mt. Carmel. Jesus, who also came to cast fire upon the earth, presented his generation with a similar choice: No one can serve two masters; you cannot serve God and mammon. Baal and mammon represent the gods that men have always served gladly, for these gods—so their adherents suppose—can be made to serve the purposes of their worshipers. Bultmann correctly perceives that in every moral decision it must be decided anew, Do I choose to serve myself, or to serve God and my neighbor? Unless this question is decided, all talk about "values," "rules," "the situation," or even "love" is likely to be no more than a smoke screen behind which we maneuver so as to serve ourselves. "Repentance" or "conversion" has to do with this fundamental moral decision. Jesus summoned his hearers to turn from their self-centered concerns and toward God, to cease taking themselves with absolute seriousness and to begin to take God seriously as the One who has always manifested his sovereignty in nature and soon would assert it in history. Only when faith has turned from the small gods who serve the self to the One whose cause is the whole realm of being can one begin to affirm and serve one's companions in being in the same way that one otherwise affirms and serves one's own well-being. Conversion is that turning of faith from one god to another. With the redirection of faith, there comes a redirection of ethics: from the self-serving ethics of faith as confidence in and loyalty to self, to the neighbor-serving ethics of faith as confidence in and loyalty to God, whose will is love, i.e., whose cause is the well-being of all his children and creatures.

The ethics of radical obedience or conversion involves the recognition and affirmation of value in the neighbor. The neighbor is not loved because one is commanded to love him: I am going to be nice to you because I have to, even though I despise you. Rather, the neighbor is perceived as one whose well-being is important to God, and received, in H. R. Niebuhr's phrase, as a "companion in being," as a member of one's own family in the family of being. Sometimes we love our brothers and sisters because we know we ought to do so. These are moments of obedience. But in those too uncommon moments when we respond to our brother and sister in being as one whose life and joy or sorrow touch our own, as one whom, in fact, we do love, we experience the meaning of *radical* obedience.

Other terms have also been used to describe this difference: the ethics of grace of "the higher righteousness," as against law; or of inwardness or disposition, as against outward act; or of spirit, against flesh; or of the "new being" or "new creation." Like the phrase "radical obedience," all these terms unfortunately point to the condition of the self, rather than to the relationship between the self and the neighbor. For this reason, the term "love" or some other relational category, such as "self-devotion to others," is necessary in order to complete the meaning. Otherwise, the perversion of ethics lies at hand in the form of pretension to "virtue." Paul's unruly Corinthians prided themselves on their "spirituality," instead of concerning themselves with the well-being of the weaker brethren and the edification and upbuilding of the church. Likewise, the saints of all ages have stood on precarious ground when they began to think of their saintliness, humility, or even faith, hope, and love as virtues or "qualities" they meritoriously possessed, rather than of the needs and well-being of others.

C. H. Dodd's contribution has already been noted: the manner in which Jesus' sayings and parables in fact (even if not so intended) appeal to our imagination, as we find ourselves in situations analogous to those of his hearers or of the persons in his stories. There is always some degree of analogy in any situation wherever two (or more) persons come together, for in any situation, there is the possibility of discovering the other as neighbor and of being neighbor to the other, and there is always the temptation to treat the neighbor as if he were someone else's brother, as if he were not even one of the least of Jesus' brethren, and to pass by on the other side of the road.

III

THE MEANING OF LOVE AS A RELATIONAL TERM

The relevance of Jesus and his ethics is not confined, then, to the "commandment" or "principle" of love. Nevertheless, love is certainly a central category, even when expressed in other terms, such as "self-devotion to others," "the higher righteousness," or "radical obedience." It is important to try to understand the meaning of love. Love is often construed as a subjective phenomenon, as feeling of some sort. Love can appear in sentimentality or romanticism as affection, or in eroticism as desire or lust. Love is also often represented objectively, as a hypostasis or predicate, for instance, by Fletcher. Understood relationally, love has both subjective and objective elements.

Love involves the subject or self, both as one knows oneself to be under requirement, and as one who experiences concern for the other person. Love is not simply obedience to requirement: in love as *radical* obedience, one *desires* well-being of the other person, and at the same time knows that this is what God desires, wills, and requires. Thus, love includes but is not confined to the performance of acts or "doing good." It also includes affection or "goodwill." There is such a thing as loveless love. The performance of "good deeds" or "acts of charity" may be without love, i.e., without genuine desire for the good of the other person. Paternalistic love is likely to suffer from this defect. Genuine love includes compassion, suffering with the neighbor in his distress, and rejoicing in his joy. It includes, as Buber has pointed out so effectively against Heidegger, the fulfillment of one's own being in the relationship of being with the neighbor, the other self, the thou.[10] Love includes liking, enjoying being together with one's neighbor. But already, it is clear that love is not subjective feelings alone; rather, it is to be found in the relationship of the self with other selves.

The objective aspect of love is not love itself, but the objective well-being of the other person, or of the totality of persons involved in "the situation." The peril of subjective love, whether as sentimentality, eroticism, or paternalism, is that the objective (as well as subjective) well-being of the other person is ignored. The sentimentalist indulges in the enjoyment of his feelings, but does not translate these into actions beneficial to his companions in being. The "playboy" seeks the satisfaction of his own erotic desires, but regards his partner of the moment as "disposable."[11] The paternalist also ignores the objective needs of his beneficiaries: because he thinks he knows already what is good for them, he does not bother to listen to them or otherwise exert himself to discover their actual situation. He quiets any suspicion he may have that something more or different may be needed with the pleasant feeling that he has, after all, done something good. In exchange, he expects gratitude, a clue to the self-serving function of his ethics. Love cannot be guided entirely by the subjectivity of the other person however. Permissiveness results—if not from indifference or even hostility to the other person—from the supposition that what the other person *wants* is *good for* him. Such, of course, is not always the case. Love understood as a relational category, however, is neither paternalistic nor permissive: it means devotion to the other person in both attitude and action. Love, understood relationally, is both subjective and objective. Love is subjective in that it involves the subject's concern or desire, but this desire relates to the objective well-being of the other person, and is expressed concretely in appropriate action. But what is appropriate? To answer that question, it is necessary to examine the meaning of "the situation."

IV
THE NATURE AND DIMENSION OF "THE SITUATION"

Bultmann describes the situation of encounter and moral decision as taking place in "empty space." Here, without reference to any "standard," "past experience," or "rational deductions" one will, if obedient to God, recognize the "one command" that is "the divine requirement," and thereby know what to do.[12] Bultmann seems to understand, however, that in every situation, what God requires is "radical obedience," i.e., love of neighbor. Fletcher, who also supposes that in every situation there is *one* "right" or "good" thing to do, is more explicit as to the centrality of love: "Love decides there and then."[13] His description of the functioning of love in the situation is not particularly edifying, however, because of his objectification of love as "good in and of itself." In Fletcher's confused account of the situation, love serves love: anything is right "if in *this* circumstance love gains the balance" or love is served.[14] What he means, of course, or should mean, is that love exists relationally in the situation as persons affirm and serve the well-being of other persons. Bishop Robinson is clearer on this point than Fletcher. Love is not "the highest good." Neither, however, are the neighbor's *needs.*[15] Rather, the neighbor himself, thus his well-being, is the focus of concern. Love, then, is not an entity, but functions in the situation, perhaps along with other related relational values, such as humility, forgiveness, prudence (or good sense), justice, and courage, all of which have to do with one's relationship with the other persons involved. Courage, for instance, means the willingness to risk one's own well-being for the sake of the neighbor's.

But how is the situation to be defined? Bultmann and Fletcher both tend to view each situation as discrete in time: past and future are unimportant; now alone matters. Paul Ramsey correctly recognizes that the past is part of the situation after all. One brings to the situation certain "summary rules" or "summary principles," i.e., what Bishop Robinson calls "the cumulative experience of one's own and other people's obedience."[16] The past of the other person or persons is also a part of the situation. The physician reviews the medical history as well as the present symptoms of his patient. The past emotional, spiritual, and moral histories of persons are ingredients in the situation. One can respond with understanding and effectiveness to the individual and collective Negro reactions of alienation and frustration that appear in the summer riots only when their past, and the past of their ancestors, is recognized for what it was: slavery, repression, brutality, segregation, and exploitation at the hands of whites, whose own guilty past is also an ingredient in the present. Thus humility and contrition are relevant modes of response, as well as love, forgiveness, and justice.

The situation also extends into the future. What we do now not only will have consequences for ourselves but for others, some of whom do not appear when we take only a narrow view of the situation. The unwanted child of pleasure-seeking lovers (whether married or not) suffers though he was not yet present in the earlier now of decision. The costs of war include not only the soldiers and civilians killed and bereaved but the loss of infinite human lives not yet conceived, as France and Britain know too well. The consequences for the persons in the situation also extend indeterminately into the future. Emotional and physical breakdown may result in the future from doing what now seems "right," for instance, when the college girl who thought that "this" was real love discovers that her erstwhile sexual partner no longer cares for her (if he ever did), or when the boy who experimented with psychedelic drugs finds that he cannot return from the realm of confusion. The situation extends backward and forward in time.

It also extends laterally into space. In nearly every situation there are more than two people. Ramsey proposes that by Jesus' eschatological outlook, all other neighbors "except the one actually present were apocalyptically removed from view and taken care of by God." But as he points out, "There is no such situation in a nonapocalyptic world."[17] Even a literalistic reading of Jesus' radical sayings does not support Ramsey's interpretation. Jesus did not say, for example, "Give everything you have to the first man who wants to borrow from you," or "When you give a feast, invite one poor, maimed, lame and blind man." Jesus evidently expected his disciples to respond helpfully to more than one neighbor. Ramsey is correct, however, in pointing out the tendency on the part of latter-day disciples to hide their own security and well-being behind a cloak of multiple and conflicting neighbor claims. The fact is, as Ramsey points out, whether Jesus recognized it or not, in our world, we find a number of neighbors in the situation.

Fletcher generally tries to reduce the number of persons involved in the situation to the fewest possible. Thus, in various examples, he glibly states that under certain circumstances "even killing 'innocent' people might be right."[18] It might be less evil than the suffering and death of a still greater number of people, but it can hardly be "right." It would not be plausible to argue that it is right or good for those who are killed! In order to avoid recognizing the ambiguous and tragic character of many a situation, Fletcher prefers to draw a gerrymandered border around it, thus excluding the victims of one's "right" act from consideration, and thus also sparing the "righteous" any sense of guilt.[19] As Schweitzer points out in his chapter on the ethics of reverence of life, a sense of guilt serves an essential purpose, in that it makes one aware of the evil in the situation and keeps one alert to the possibilities of reducing that evil.[20] Otherwise, one can accept tragic consequences (especially for others) with complacency. The consolation that one has done the "right" thing when one has acted harmfully toward even one person in order to help others is a dangerous illusion. As Schweitzer says in the sentence Fletcher himself twice quotes: "The good conscience is an invention of the devil."[21]

The "others" cannot be excluded from the situation by waving a wand. It is likely to include, for instance, not only the boy and the girl who now wish to make each other (and themselves) happy, but also a parent or two who may suffer deep anguish when they learn of their child's "innocent" frolic. Those who take psychedelic drugs without, apparently, damaging themselves or their posterity nevertheless may by their example contribute to the downfall of "weaker brethren." Obviously, the casualty statistics from Vietnam only begin to measure the losses incurred by wives (and some husbands), children, parents, brothers, sisters, and loved ones on both (or all) "sides" of the conflict. It is, in fact, nearly impossible to circumscribe most situations. In many areas of life now the situation is worldwide. It is in our power to destroy the lives of millions of humans and other creatures. It is in our power to provide medicine, technological aid, jobs, and food to millions of diseased, unemployed, and hungry people.

Because there are so many others whose existence complicates the situation, it is tempting to retreat behind intuition or magic: to suppose, with Bultmann and Fletcher, that God, the situation, or love will tell us what to do. The difficulty with this approach is that it does not take the actual situation seriously enough. If the situation, or, more precisely, the combination or structure of factors operating helpfully and harmfully upon the persons in the situation is decisive, there is then a moral responsibility to gain what knowledge one can about the situation. The morally responsible person cannot decide on the basis of intuition or in empty space. He must seek to know the facts of the situation as these affect persons. He will need to learn what he can from history, sociology, psychology, politics, technology, and all other areas of understanding that may have some bearing on the well-being of the persons involved. He may even have to become involved in the situation himself, or recognize that he is already involved in it! When the situation is taken seriously, situation ethics becomes social ethics.

V

ESCHATOLOGY AS A DIMENSION OF "THE SITUATION"

Were the Kingdom of God now present, there would be no need for ethics or teachers of ethics, for then, says the prophet Jeremiah, in the name of the Lord:

> I will put my law within them,
>   And I will write it upon their hearts;
> and I will be their God,
>   and they shall be my people.
> And no longer shall each man teach his neighbor and each his
>   brother,
>   saying, "Know the LORD,"
> for they shall all know me,
>   from the least of them to the greatest, says the Lord.[22]

Those writers who, following Paul, describe the Christian life as a "new creation," or a life in grace, in Christ, or in the Spirit, are testifying to the experience of forgiveness or reconciliation which is based, in the Christian tradition, upon the ministry, suffering, death, and resurrection of Jesus. This past event—though not the arrival of the Kingdom of God—is a decisive part of the present situation. The Christian experiences himself, as Bultmann puts it, as one who has been freed from himself, so that he can be unreservedly for his neighbor.[23] This experience may be related to the experience of conversion or repentance—turning from self to God and neighbor—which Jesus evidently considered to be an existential possibility and necessity for his hearers who wished to enter the Kingdom of God when it came. Jesus apparently understood that God would accept the repentant sinner (with "joy," in fact)[24] apart from the necessity of his own death,[25] belief in himself as the Christ, participation in the sacraments or other later Christian doctrines and institutions.

The future advent of the Kingdom was clearly a matter of consequence to Jesus. Its coming, though still future, was a decisive factor in the present situation. Soon it would be too late to repent. Those found unprepared—having exploited their fellows, or failed to respond to them in times of distress, in short, those who were indifferent to God and neighbor—would be judged adversely. God, himself, would take charge of history, possibly through the Son of Man or Messiah; in any case, it would be God, no longer Satan, the demons, and the "rulers of this age" who ruled the earth. The message that God's Kingdom was coming was "good news" to those who had been faithful to him, who had sought righteousness and reconciliation, and had been humble and pure of heart even at the cost of persecution and physical privation, for they would inherit the Kingdom on earth. It is unlikely that Jesus understood this gospel as "myth." Yet even if we do so regard it, its meaning for us is not thereby dissipated.

There are at least two features of the eschatological hope that are relevant for our moral situations. As in the case of Jesus' hearers, so for us also, time is short. Not only does our own life come to an end soon—we know not when, but surely within the span of a normal lifetime—but also the lifetime of others is similarly limited. We do not have an infinity of time in which to respond to our neighbor who now needs our help. He may not be there tomorrow. Or perhaps we will not be. Many encounters or situations are highly limited in time, at least so far as the time when we can act responsibly is concerned. We and those who come after us will have to live (or suffer) for generations with the consequences of our actions or failures to act now, but we do not have forever in which to act. It is now too late already, for instance, to avert the scar of racial hatred in our country. We have tried to heal the wounds of our people lightly by saying "peace, peace" when there was no peace. When we became aware in earlier decades that educational and job opportunities, housing and justice, were manifestly unequally apportioned between races, we could have acted with contrition and concern to atone for the sins of the fathers (and some of our own complicity). Our response, such as it was, came in the form of tokenism. What is done now is not likely to be done out of contrition, but because the self-interest of the white majority and the national interest are in jeopardy. By the time our nation officially recognizes the existence of Communist China, it will be too late to do so with good grace in quest of a basis of coexistence if not reconciliation. We will be forced to it by Chinese power (as China was forced to recognize the existence of the West somewhat over a century ago). By then it may be too late for coexistence. In history, a people normally pay for the sins of the past: the whirlwind will be reaped. Tomorrow it may be too late to make and effect the moral decision that is called for today. Some damage cannot be undone. The Negro children who, since 1954, have continued to be recipients of a separate but unequal education have been permanently damaged. The victims of war in Vietnam have already paid for our decisions, and more will pay tomorrow for our decisions and indecisions of yesterday and today. All ethics are interim ethics.

Eschatology is relevant to the contemporary moral life in yet another way: as hope. God is no *deus ex machina* who can be depended upon to deliver his chosen people from catastrophe in the last act. Eschatology includes judgment, and those who imagine themselves heirs to the promise do well to ponder Amos' declaration:

You only have I known
    of all the families of the earth;
therefore I will punish you
    for all your iniquities. (Amos 3:2)

It may be that America and Western civilization, as we have known them, must go under. And yet, this is not "the end" if God is the one who is at work in and against history to bring his purpose to fulfillment. We no longer look for the Kingdom of God to appear in history as the end result of natural evolution or of moral effort. If history is to be redeemed, it will be as in the case of our own little individual histories: a miracle of his grace.

We do not spend our time profitably in trying to visualize the architecture and city plan for the "new Jerusalem." As with all symbols of the ultimate, our images and formulas are inevitably crude and pretentious if not idolatrous. Yet the understanding that God will ultimately reveal and actualize his Lordship over history, however expressed symbolically, means that the present historical situation has meaning. Historical, material existence is not viewed as a mistake, or as a consequence of a "fall" from pure spirituality. Nor is salvation perceived in terms of immortal, ethereal life in a realm beyond space and time. Space and time are sanctified by the prospect of God's redeeming activity in space and time. The ambiguities of history will be resolved. The principalities and powers, including our own will to power, will be judged. The cruelties and pretensions of our past and present will be recognized as such. In redemption there will be contrition and judgment:

> A new heart I will give you,
>   and a new spirit I will put within you;
> and I will take out of your flesh the heart of stone
>   and give you a heart of flesh.
>
> *   *   *
>
> You shall dwell in the land I gave to your fathers;
>   and you shall be my people, and I will be your God.
>
> *   *   *
>
> Then you will remember your evil ways,
>   and your deeds that were not good;
> and you will loathe yourselves for your iniquities
>   and your abominable deeds.[26]

Perhaps the most terrible kind of judgment is that which comes with the recognition of what we have done. There is nothing arbitrary or external about that judgment. In any case, the expectation of judgment, as this may be experienced in, and ultimately at the end of, our individual and collective histories, gives meaning to the present situation in which we encounter concretely our various neighbors. We readily come under the illusion that what we do as individuals or as a people makes no difference: there seems to be so little that we can do, so why bother? We cannot save mankind, so why should we worry about those few whom we can help? The prospect of judgment gives expression to the realization that our actions and inactions are of ultimate importance, for by them we sustain or fail to sustain our fellow beings, each of whom is important to the Ultimate Source of being, who wills the being and well-being of each.

The prospect of salvation does not render less serious our moral situation. But it gives the hope that God can overrule our at best partly adequate, but often guilty responses, and accomplish his purposes for men and all of creation despite, as well as with, our help. The prospect of forgiveness makes it possible for us to acknowledge our guilt and begin, even now, in our continuing historical existence to experience that grace or forgiveness which liberates us from bondage not only to our sins but to our illusions of virtue. Thereby we begin to be liberated for our neighbors.

Notes

1. Cynthia L. Smith, "Synoptic Eschatology." Unpublished paper, University of Florida, 1966.

2. Dodd, *Gospel and Law,* pp. 55, 61, 76.

3. Dodd, *Apostolic Preaching,* pp. 162 f.

4. E.g., Oden, *op. cit.,* pp. 14–24. But see, e.g., Reinhold Niebuhr, *The Irony of American History* (Charles Scribner's Sons, 1952), pp. 157 ff.

5. The term was coined and emphasized by Prof. Ralph Turner of Yale.

6. Hiers, *Jesus and Ethics,* p. 95.

7. Ramsey and Fletcher to the contrary. See below, pp. 161 f.

8. Matt. 5:43–48; cf. John 13:34 f. Christians have found it difficult enough to love one another, let alone their enemies: I John 2:1–11; 3:10–24.

9. Cf. Schweitzer, *Philosophy of Civilization,* pp. 299, 305.

10. Martin Buber, *Between Man and Man* (Beacon Press, Inc., 1955), pp. 167 ff.

11. Cox, *Secular City,* p. 202.

12. Hiers, *Jesus and Ethics,* pp. 87 f.

13. Fletcher, *Situation Ethics,* pp. 125, 135 f.

14. *Ibid.,* pp. 71, 126, 132.

15. Cf. Ramsey, *Basic Christian Ethics,* p. 59: "Jesus' actions and teaching may be described as flowing from an orientation which valued the needs of the neighbor above all else." Love does not cease in the Messianic age when there will be no more unfulfilled needs! (Cf. I Cor. 13:8 ff.)

16. Ramsey, *Deeds,* p. 159; Robinson, *Honest,* p. 119.

17. Ramsey, *Basic Christian Ethics,* pp. 40, 42.

18. Fletcher, *Situation Ethics,* pp. 75, 124 f., 135 f.

19. Fletcher explicitly denies that guilt is involved (*ibid.,* p. 124).

20. Schweitzer, *Philosophy of Civilization,* esp. pp. 316–327.

21. *Ibid.,* p. 318. Fletcher acknowledges that he had not read these words in their original context (*Situation Ethics,* p. 83).

22. Jer. 31:33 f. See also Hos. 2:18–20; Isa. 11:9; I Cor. 13:8–13.

23. Bultmann, *History and Eschatology,* p. 152.

24. Luke 15:7, 10, 23, 32.

25. There is no evidence that Jesus himself understood his death as necessary in order to induce God to reconcile himself to the world, or to grant forgiveness to sinners. He did, evidently, expect that shortly after his death the Kingdom of God would come.

26. Ezek. 36:26, 28, 31; cf. 16:59–63.

Biblical Revelation
and Social Existence

James H. Cone

This article originally appeared in *Interpretations* in 1974.

> Any point of departure for exegesis which ignores God in
> Christ as the liberator of the oppressed or makes salvation
> as liberation secondary is invalid. The test of validity lies
> not only in the particularity of the oppressed culture, but in
> the One who freely grants us freedom when we were
> doomed to slavery.

Theologians are becoming increasingly aware of the influence of
social context upon their work. The sociologists of knowledge, such
as Karl Mannheim, Werner Stark, Thomas Luckmann, and Peter
Berger, have persuaded us that all theology, past and present, is
shaped by socially determined values. Werner Stark speaks of an
"axiological grid," which every person develops in childhood before
the age of reflection.

> We see the broad and deep acres of history
> through a mental grid . . . through a system of values which
> is established in our minds *before* we look out on to it—and
> it is this grid which decides . . . what will fall into our
> field of perception.[1]

Stark and the others were not contending for social determinism but
for the reciprocity between ideas and social existence. Thought is not
pure and autonomous; it is an expression of life. Accordingly, the

consideration of any system of ideas is not complete without an investigation of the social context in which the system arose.

While all this may bring sorrow to some who would elevate ideas to an ethereal realm, it is a fact of life and, I contend, not a regrettable fact. In fact, for those who take seriously the doctrine of creation, it has a friendly, earthy feel. Furthermore, because creation entails revelation, we recognize that revelation itself, the radiant point of contact between God and people, has its own social context or (since it occurred at different times) contexts. Unlike the God of Greek philosophy, who is removed from history, the God of the Bible is involved in history. His revelation is inseparable from the social and political affairs of Israel. The God of Peter, James, and John is not an eternal idea nor an absolute ethical principle. Yahweh is known and worshipped as the Lord who brought Israel out of Egypt and raised Jesus from the dead. He is the active God, the political God, the Protector of the poor and the Establisher of right for those who are oppressed. To know him is to experience his acts in the concrete affairs and relationships of people, liberating the weak and helpless from pain and humiliation.

Theological language, therefore, is necessarily social language, not only because of what people are but also because of who God is. The purpose of this article is to examine the social context of divine revelation and to set forth the implications of that context for the theologian's task.

I

THE SOCIAL CONTEXT OF DIVINE REVELATION
IN THE OLD TESTAMENT

The Old Testament is a history book. To understand it and the divine revelation to which it testifies, we must think of the Old Testament as the drama of God's mighty acts in history. It tells the story of God's acts of grace and of judgment as he calls the people of Israel into a free, liberated existence.

Historically, the story began with the Exodus. The Exodus was the decisive event in Israel's history, because through it Yahweh revealed himself as the Savior of an oppressed people. The Israelites were slaves of Egypt; thus, their future was closed. But Yahweh "heard their groaning, and remembered his covenant with Abraham, Isaac and Jacob; he saw the plight of Israel, he took heed of it" (Exodus 2:24–25 NEB). Yahweh, therefore, took Israel's history into his own hands, and gave this people a divine future, thereby doing for Israel what she could not do for herself. "With arm outstretched and with mighty acts of judgments" (Exodus 6:6 NEB), he delivered Israel out of Egypt and across the Red Sea. And "when Israel saw the great power which the Lord had put forth against Egypt, . . . they put their faith in him," responding with a song to the Lord:

> I will sing to the Lord, for he has risen up in triumph;
> the horse and his rider he has hurled into the sea
> (Exodus 15:1 NEB)

In the Exodus-event, God is revealed by means of his acts on behalf of a weak and defenseless people. He is the God of power and of strength, able to destroy the enslaving power of the mighty Pharaoh.

> The Lord is my refuge and my defence,
> he has shown himself my deliverer.
> (Exodus 15:2 NEB)

The centrality of the Exodus for Israel's consciousness, seen first through the people's recognition of deliverance, was further developed at Sinai, as the Exodus became the basis for Israel's covenant with Yahweh.

> You have seen with your own eyes what I did to Egypt,
> and how I carried you on eagles' wings and brought you
> here to me. If only you will now listen to me and keep
> my covenant, then out of all peoples you shall become
> my special possession; for the whole earth is mine. You
> shall be my kingdom of priests, my holy nation.
> (Exodus 19:4–5 NEB)

This passage connects the Exodus, the revelation of Yahweh through his acts ("You have seen . . . what I did"), with the covenant, which is the foundation of Yahweh's revelation through his Word ("If only you will listen to me and keep my covenant"). The Exodus is the point of departure of Israel's existence, the foundation of her peoplehood established at Sinai. This is the meaning of the preface to the Ten Commandments in Exodus 20:2: "I am the Lord your God who brought you out of Egypt, out of the land of slavery." *Therefore,* "you shall have no other god to set against me" (20:3 NEB).

The covenant is an invitation to Israel to enter into a responsible relationship with the God of the Exodus wherein he will be her God and she his "special possession." This invitation places Israel in a situation of decision, because the covenant requires obedience to the will of Yahweh. To accept the covenant means that Israel must now live as Yahweh's liberated people, becoming the embodiment of freedom made possible through his freeing presence. The covenant not only places upon Israel the responsibility of accepting the absolute sovereignty of Yahweh as defined in the first commandment; it also requires Israel to treat the weak in her midst as Yahweh has treated her. That is the significance of the apodictic laws in the Covenant Code:

> You shall not wrong a stranger or oppress him;
> for you were strangers in the land of Egypt.
> > (Exodus 22:21; see also 23:9
> > RSV)

> You shall not ill-treat any widow or fatherless child.
> If you do, be sure that I will listen if they appeal to me;
> My anger will be roused and I will kill you with the sword.
> > (Exodus 22:23–24 NEB)

In the Exodus-Sinai tradition Yahweh is disclosed as the God of history, whose revelation is identical with his power to liberate the oppressed. There is no knowledge of Yahweh except through his political activity on behalf of the weak and helpless of the land. This is the significance of Yahweh's contest with Pharaoh, the plagues against Egypt, and the "hardening" of Pharaoh's heart. The biblical writer wishes to emphasize that Israel's liberation came not from her own strength but solely from the power of Yahweh, who completely controls history.

God's election of oppressed Israelites has unavoidable implications for the doing of theology. If God had chosen as his "holy nation" the Egyptian slavemasters instead of the Israelite slaves, then a completely different kind of God would have been revealed. Thus Israel's election cannot be separated from her servitude and liberation. Here God discloses that he is the God of history whose will is identical with the liberation of the oppressed from social and political bondage. The doing of theology, therefore, on the basis of the revelation of Yahweh, must involve the politics which takes its stand with the poor and against the rich. Indeed, theology ceases to be a theology of the Exodus-Sinai tradition when it fails to see Yahweh as unquestionably in control of history, vindicating the weak against the strong.

The Old Testament story does not end with the Exodus and the gift of the covenant. Yahweh does not withdraw from his people's history. On the contrary, the covenant means that Yahweh's liberating presence continues to sustain the people through the wilderness to the Promised Land. And when Israel failed to keep her side of the covenant by running after the gods of Canaan, Yahweh did not reject his people. His will to save and to make them free was a constituent of his being with them. God's grace could not be destroyed by Israel's disobedience.

The conflict between grace and disobedience was escalated when Israel became a monarchy, for the rulers often forgot the Exodus-Sinai experience and the function of the King in Israel. It is within this social and political context that we ought to understand the rise of prophecy. The prophets were messengers of Yahweh who gave God's Word to the people, reminding them of God's deliverance and covenant which brought the community into existence. They also proclaimed Yahweh's future activity of judgment and renewal that was about to burst into the present.

The prophets gave a large measure of their addresses to proclaiming the emptiness and tragedy of Israel's present existence. The tragedy of Israel is due to her failure to remember the Exodus-Sinai tradition. As Amos said,

> It was I who brought you up from the land of Egypt,
> I who led you in the wilderness forty years,
>> to take possession of the land of the Amorites.
>> (2:10 NEB)

Because Israel often failed to live on the basis of God's saving-event of the Exodus, she also failed to understand the significance of Yahweh's imminent eschatological judgment. Amos proclaimed the connection between the past and the future as they both invaded Israel's present moment.

> For you alone have I cared
> among all the nations of the world;
> therefore I will punish you
>> for all your iniquities.
>> (Amos 3:2 NEB)

What was Israel's sin? What did the people do to rouse the anger of their Lord? The prophets were almost unanimous in their contention that Israel disobeyed the first commandment. The people failed to recognize Yahweh's sovereignty in history, and thus began to trust their own power and the power of political alliances with other nations (Isa. 31:1). But that was not all! The disobedience of the first commandment always has consequences in the social life of the community. Israel, therefore, began to oppress the weak and the poor in their own community. That was why Amos said that "the Lord has sworn by his holiness that your time is coming," because you "grind the destitute and plunder the humble" (4:2; 8:4 NEB). Even though Yahweh "cared for you in the wilderness, in a land of burning heat, as if you were in a pasture," you "forgot [him]," becoming "an oppressor trampling on justice, doggedly pursuing what is worthless" (Hosea 13:5–6; 5:11 NEB). Because Yahweh will not permit the triumph of evil, Israelites must be punished for their wrong doings.

According to Amos and Hosea, Israel will be punished because the people do not "practice loyalty and justice" (Hosea 12:6 NEB), but rather "have turned into venom the process of the law and justice itself into poison" (Amos 6:12 NEB). They " 'buy the poor for silver

and the destitute for a pair of shoes[.]' The Lord has sworn by the
pride of Jacob: I will never forget any of their doings."

> Shall not the earth shake for this?
>   Shall not all who live on it grieve?
> All earth shall surge and seethe like the Nile
>   and subside like the river of Egypt.
>
> Did I not bring Israel up from Egypt,
> the Philistines from Captor, the Aramaeans from Kir?
>   Behold, I, the Lord God,
>   Have my eyes on this sinful kingdom,
> and I will wipe it off the face of the earth.
>
>   (Amos 8:6–8; 9:7–8 NEB)

We may shudder at the anger of Yahweh as voiced in the prophecy of Amos and say that the latter lacks tender mercy found in Hosea. Nevertheless God's mercy can never invalidate his will for
justice. There is no divine grace in the Old Testament (or in the New
Testament) that is bestowed on oppressors at the expense of the suffering of the poor. The theme of justice and Yahweh's special concern for the poor and the widows have a central place in Israelite
prophecy. Thus Jeremiah:

> For among my people there are wicked men, . . .
> Their houses are full of fraud,
>   as a cage is full of birds.
> They grow rich and grand,
>   bloated and rancorous;
> their thoughts are all of evil,
>   and they refuse to do justice,
> the claims of the orphan they do not put right
> nor do they grant justice to the poor.
>
>   (5:26–28 NEB)

And Micah:

> God has told you what is good;
>   and what is it that the Lord asks of you?

> Only to act justly, to love loyalty,
> to walk wisely before your God
> (6:8 NEB)

The emphasis upon justice for the poor is present even in a prophet like Isaiah of Jerusalem, for whom the David's reign, rather than the Exodus, is the significant act of deliverance. According to Isaiah, "Yahweh bound himself by a covenant oath to David, promising to preserve the Davidic line to the Davidic kingdom 'for the sake of my servant David' . . . (Isaiah 37:35; see II Sam. 7)."[2] Isaiah thus represents what scholars designate as the David-Zion tradition. Yet Isaiah, in prefect solidarity with the prophets of the Mosaic tradition, proclaimed that Yahweh is the God of justice who sides with the weak against the strong.

> Put away the evil of your deeds,
> away out of my sight.
> Cease to do evil and learn to do right,
> pursue justice and champion the oppressed;
> give the orphan his rights, plead the widow's cause.
> (1:16–17 NEB)

In Israel, only Yahweh is King:

> For the Lord our judge, the Lord our law-giver,
> the Lord our king—he himself will save us.
> (Isaiah 33:22 (NEB)

The function of the human king in Israel is to be Yahweh's servant, executing justice in his name. "The King is God's son . . . He is commissioned to rule by God himself, he governs with perfect justice and wisdom, he is the great benefactor and shepherd of his people. . . ."[3] As Yahweh's son by adoption (Ps. 2:7), the king is enthroned to rescue the needy from their rich oppressors, the distressed who have no protector.

> May he have pity on the needy and the poor,
> deliver the poor from death;

> may he redeem them from oppression and violence
> and may their blood be precious in his eyes.
>
> (Psalm 72:12–14 NEB)

The poor are Yahweh's own, his special possession. These are the people the divine has called into being for freedom. Therefore as the sovereign King of Israel whose existence is dependent upon God's saving power, Yahweh judges Israel in the light of their treatment of the poor. The indictment is severe.

> The Lord comes forward to argue his case
> and stands to judge his people.
> The Lord opens the indictment
> against the elders of his people and their officers:
> They have ravaged the vineyard,
>   and the spoils of the poor are in your houses.
> Is it nothing to you that you crush my people
>   and grind the faces of the poor?
>
> (Isaiah 3:13–15 NEB)

It is a fact: In almost every scene of the Old Testament drama of salvation, the poor are defended against the rich, the weak against the strong. Yahweh is the God of the oppressed whose revelation is identical with their liberation from bondage. Even in the wisdom literature where the sages seem to be unaware of Israel's saving history, God's concern for the poor is nonetheless emphasized.

> He who is generous to the poor lends to the Lord.
>
> (Proverbs 19:17 NEB)

> He who oppresses the poor insults his Maker;
> he who is generous to the needy honours him.
>
> (Proverbs 14:13 NEB)

Like Moses and the prophets, the wise man is concerned for the orphan:

> Do not move the ancient boundary-stone
> or encroach on the land of orphans:

> they have a powerful guardian
> who will take their cause against you.
>
>   (Proverbs 23:10–11 NEB)

If theological speech is based on the traditions of the Old Testament, then it must heed their unanimous testimony to Yahweh's commitment to justice for the poor and the weak. Accordingly it cannot avoid the risk of taking sides in politics, and the side that theology must take is disclosed in the side that Yahweh has already taken. Any other side, whether it be with the oppressors or the side of neutrality (which is nothing but a camouflaged identification with the rulers), is unbiblical. If theology does not side with the poor, then it cannot speak for Yahweh who is the God of the poor.

As the Old Testament story continues, we see that the people of Israel did not listen to the voice of prophecy. Thus they went into exile—the Northern Kingdom in 722 B.C. and the Southern Kingdom of Judah in 597 B.C. and 587 B.C. The experience of exile was a shattering event for Israel. "They believed that Yahweh had manifested his lordship in Palestine; but could he be worshipped in a strange land where other gods seemed to be in control?"[4]

> By the rivers of Babylon we sat down and wept
>   when we remembered Zion.
> There on the willow-trees
>   we hung up our harps,
> for there those who carried us off
>   demanded music and singing,
> and our captors called on us to be merry:
>   'Sing us one of the songs of Zion.'
> How could we sing the Lord's song
>   in a foreign land?
>
>   (Psalm 137 NEB)

It was in the midst of Israel's despair that prophecy began to strike a new note. Jeremiah began to speak of the covenant (31:31–34) and Ezekiel of a new heart and a new spirit (36:26). And then there was the voice of the unknown prophet who began by proclaiming:

> Comfort, comfort my people;
>   —it is the voice of your God;
> speak tenderly to Jerusalem
>   and tell her this,
> that she has fulfilled her term of bondage,
>   and that her penalty is paid:
> she has received at the Lord's hand
>   double measure for all her sins.
>
> (Isaiah 40:1–2 NEB)

Again Yahweh revealed himself as the deliverer of the weak and defenseless Israel. This was Israel's second Exodus, and like the first it was due exclusively to the power of Yahweh overwhelming those who asserted their power against his people.

On the people's return to their homeland there was the rebuilding of the Temple and the rededication of the community to the obedience of the Law. But Israel's story logically does not end with the Old Testament. If Yahweh is to keep his promise to bring freedom, then the Old Testament cannot be the end of Yahweh's drama with Israel. The Old Testament pushes beyond itself to an expected future event which Christians say happened in Jesus Christ.

II
THE SOCIAL CONTEXT OF DIVINE REVELATION IN THE NEW TESTAMENT

Christians believe that the Old Testament story of salvation is continued in the New Testament. Indeed, they affirm that the New Testament is the witness to the fulfillment of God's drama of salvation begun with Israel's liberation from Egypt. This view is expressed in the New Testament itself: "Do not suppose that I have come to abolish the Law and the prophets," says the Matthean Jesus. "I did not come to abolish, but to complete" (5:17 NEB). Without exception, the New Testament writers believe that the God present in Jesus is none other than the God of Abraham, Isaac, and Jacob, and that through the divine act in the man from Nazareth something radically new has happened. On the one hand, Jesus is the continuation of the Law and the prophets; but on the other, he is the inauguration of a completely new age, and his words and deeds are signs of its imminent coming.

The Gospels according to Matthew and Luke begin the Jesus-story with his birth in Bethlehem. Although most New Testament scholars rightly question the historicity of these two apparently independent accounts, both sources (often designated "L" and "M") nonetheless reflect accurately the character of the early church's memory of the historical Jesus. Continuing the Exodus-Sinai and David-Zion traditions in which there is a special connection between divine revelation and the poor, the early church remembered Jesus' historical person as exemplifying the same character. That character, they concluded, *must* have been present in his birth. This is the significance of the birth stories in Matthew and Luke, the Son of God Christology in Mark, and the Fourth Gospel's contention that "When all things began, the Word already was" (1:1 NEB). The four Gospels intend to express divine purpose; and the content of the purpose is disclosed clearly in the Magnificat:

> His name is Holy;
> his mercy sure from generation to generation
>   toward those who fear him;
> the deeds his own right arm has done
>   disclose his might
> the arrogant of heart and mind he has put to rout,
> he has brought down monarchs from their thrones,
>   but the humble have been lifted high.
> The hungry he has satisfied with good things,
>   the rich sent empty away.
>
> (Luke 1:49–53 NEB)

From the outset, the Gospels wish to convey that the Jesus-story is not simply a story about a good man who met an unfortunate fate.

Rather, in Jesus, God is at work, telling his story and disclosing the divine plan of salvation.

The first historical reference to Jesus is his baptism by John the Baptist.[5] Whatever may be said about the messianic consciousness of Jesus at this stage in his ministry, it seems clear from the evidence of the Synoptic Gospels that something happened between Jesus and God wherein the former became aware of a special calling. The clue to the meaning of his divine election is found in "the Spirit . . . descending upon him" (Mark 1:10 NEB; cf. Matt. 3:16f.; Luke 3:21f.) and the much discussed proclamation: "Thou art my Son, my Beloved; on thee my favour rests" (Mark 1:11 NEB; cf. Matt. 3:17; Luke 3:22). The saying about the descent of the Spirit suggests Jesus' awareness of the prophetic character of his vocation as well as the presence of something entirely new in his person. This new thing was Jesus' recognition that the dawn of the time of salvation, inaugurated by the return of the Spirit, was inseparable from his person and also that this new age was identical with the liberation of the poor and the afflicted. Apparently Jesus in his own eyes was not merely a prophetic messenger like John the Baptist, who, proclaiming the advent of the coming age, stood between the old age and the new.[6] Rather through his words and deeds he became the *inaugurator* of the Kingdom, which is bound up with his person as disclosed in his identification with the poor.

The proclamation (Mark 1:11; Matt. 3:17; Luke 3:22) following the baptism supports the contention that Jesus saw a connection between his person and the dawning of the Kingdom. This proclamation is reminiscent of Psalm 2:7 and Isaiah 42:1, and it suggests Jesus' awareness of a kingship role in the context of servanthood.

> 'You are my son,' he said;
> 'this day I become your father.'
>
> (Psalm 2:7 NEB)

> Here is my servant, whom I upheld,
> my chosen one in whom I delight,
> I have bestowed my spirit upon him,
> and he will make justice shine on the nations.
>
> (Isaiah 42:1 NEB)

If we take this echo of Psalm 2:7 and Isaiah 42:1 as a clue to Jesus' self-understanding at baptism, then his subsequent words and deeds also become clearer. Psalm 2:7, a coronation hymn, emphasizes his role as King, who is God's representative to bring justice to the nation. Here the political note emerges in Jesus' consciousness. Isaiah 42:1 refers to the Servant of Yahweh, who brings justice by his own suffering. Jesus' synthesis of these two themes produced a new messianic image. Servanthood provides the context for exercising kingship or lordship. The King is a *Servant* who suffers on behalf of the people. He takes their pain and affliction upon himself, thereby redeeming them *from* oppression and *for* freedom. Here, then, we have the key to Jesus' understanding of his mission: *Lordship and Servanthood together, that is, the establishment of justice through suffering.*

This same theme is connected with the temptation story which follows (Luke 4:1f.; Matt. 4:1f.; cf. also Mark 1:12–13). The chief point in this narrative is not so much Jesus' rejection of the role of a "political," revolutionary messiahship (as defined by the Zealots), though that may be partly involved. Most New Testament interpreters are so quick to make that point that they miss the heart of the matter,[7] namely, *Jesus' rejection of any role that would separate him from the poor.* This story affirms that Jesus rejected such roles as wonder worker or political king, because they would separate him form the suffering of the poor, the very people he had come to liberate.

The theme of God's liberation of the poor is continued in the story of Jesus' reading in the Nazareth synagogue from the Book of Isaiah.

> The spirit of the Lord is upon me because he has anointed me,
> he has sent me to announce good news to the poor,
> to proclaim release for prisoners and recovery of sight for the
>   blind;
> to let the broken victims go free,
> to proclaim the year of the Lord's favour.
>
> (Luke 4:18–19, Isaiah 61:1–2 NEB)

After the reading, Jesus commented, "Today in your very hearing this text has come true," thus tying the promised deliverance to his own mission.

The theme appears again when John the Baptist sent his disciples to Jesus to ask of him, "Are you the one who is to come, or shall we expect another." And Jesus replied: "Go and tell John what you have seen and heard: how the blind recover their sight, the lame walk, the lepers are made clean, the deaf hear, the dead are raised to life, the poor are hearing the good news . . ." (Luke 7:22f. NEB; cf. Matt. 11:5f.). This reply echoes Isaiah 61:1–2 (the passage read at Nazareth) in combination with Isaiah 35:5ff. and 29:18f., which depict the day of salvation.[8]

> Then shall blind men's eyes be opened,
> and the ears of the deaf unstopped.
> Then shall the lame man leap like a deer,
> and the tongue of the dumb shout aloud;
> for water springs up in the wilderness,
> and torrents flow in dry land.
> The mirage becomes a pool,
> the thirsty land bubbling springs . . .
> (Isaiah 35:5f. NEB)

> On that day deaf men shall hear
> when a book is read,
> and the eyes of the blind shall see
> out of impenetrable darkness.
> The lowly shall once again rejoice in the Lord,
> and the poorest of men exult in the Holy One of Israel.
> The ruthless shall be no more, the arrogant shall cease to be;
> those who are quick to see mischief,
> those who charge others with a sin
> or lay traps for him who brings the wrongdoer into court
> or by falsehood deny justice to the righteous—
> all these shall be exterminated.
> (Isaiah 29:18–21 NEB)

The reply to John's disciples, like the saying in Nazareth synagogue, shows that Jesus understood his person and work as the inauguration of the new age, which is identical with the freedom for the oppressed and health for the sick. Accordingly any understanding of the Kingdom in Jesus' teachings that fails to make the poor and their liberation its point of departure is a contradiction of Jesus' presence.

Jesus' conquest of Satan and the demons also carries out the theme of the liberation of the poor. "If it is by the finger of God that I drive out the devils, then be sure that the kingdom of God has already come upon you" (Luke 11:20 NEB). Jesus' power to exorcise demons is the *sine qua non* of the appearance of the Kingdom, because freedom for the oppressed can come about only by overcoming the forces of evil. Jesus saw this victory already in hand after his disciples returned from the mission of the Seventy: "I watched how Satan fell, like lightning, out of the sky" (Luke 10:18 NEB).

The reference to Satan and demons is not simply an outmoded first century world-view that is objectionable to twentieth century science. The issue is much more complex than that! Bultmann and his program of demythologization notwithstanding, the *offense* of the gospel is and ought to be located precisely at the point where our confidence in modern knowledge encounters the New Testament message, namely, in Jesus' liberating exorcisms. Unlike the fundamentalists, I am not contending that the biblical cosmology ought to replace contemporary science in college classrooms. Rather I intend to make the *theological* point that the "scandal" (*skandalon*, stumbling-block) is not different for us today than for the people who encountered Jesus in the first century. It is that the exorcisms disclose that God in Jesus has brought liberation to the poor and the wretched of the land, and that liberation is none other than the overthrow of everything that is against the fulfillment of their humanity. The scandal is that the gospel means liberation, that this liberation comes to the poor, and that it gives them the strength and the courage to break the conditions of servitude. This is what the Incarnation means. God in Christ comes to the weak and helpless, and becomes one with them, taking their condition of oppression as his own and thus transforms their slave-existence into a liberated existence.

To locate the scandal of the Jesus-story at the point of God's liberation of the poor and in opposition to Rudolf Bultmann's emphasis on human self-understanding, means that the gospel comes not only as a gift but that the acceptance of the gift of freedom transforms our perception of our social and political existence. The New Testament gospel of liberation turns our priority system upside down and demands that we fight for the freedom of those in captivity. This message of liberation cannot appeal to those who profit from the imprisonment of others but only to slaves who strive against unauthorized power. The gospel of liberation is *bad news* to all oppressors, because they have defined their "freedom" in terms of the slavery of others. Only the poor and the wretched who have been victims of evil and injustice can understand what Jesus meant when he said: "Come to me, all whose work is hard, whose load is heavy; and I will give you relief. Bend your neck to my yoke, and learn from me, for I am gentle and humble-hearted; and your souls will find relief. For my yoke is good to bear, my load is light" (Matt. 11:28–30 NEB).

The gospel will always be an offense to the rich and the powerful, because it is the death of their riches and power. That was why the man from the ruling class could not follow Jesus. The price was too high: "Sell everything you have and distribute it to the poor, and you will have riches in heaven; and come, follow me" (Luke 18:22 NEB). This man was incapable of separating himself from his commitment to his possessions. There were others who had similar problems. They could not follow Jesus because they had priorities higher than the gospel of liberation for the poor. There was the person who wanted to bury his father and another who wanted to say good-bye to the people at home (Luke 9:59f). They, like the five foolish girls in the parable of Matthew 25:1f., did not recognize the *urgency* of the hour nor the *priority* inherent in the acceptance of the coming kingdom. Jesus expressed the claim of the kingdom in radical terms: "If anyone comes to me and does not hate his father and mother, wife and children, brothers and sisters, even his own life, he cannot be a disciple of mine" (Luke 14:26 NEB).

Because most biblical scholars are the descendants of the advantaged class, it is to be expected that they would minimize Jesus' gospel of liberation for the poor by interpreting poverty as a spiritual condition unrelated to social and political phenomena. But a careful reading of the New Testament shows that the poor of whom Jesus spoke were not primarily (if at all) those who are spiritually poor as suggested in Matthew 5:3. Rather, as the Lukan tradition shows, these people are "those who are really poor, . . . those who are really hungry, who really weep and are persecuted."⁹ The poor are the oppressed and the afflicted, those who cannot defend themselves against the powerful. They are the least and the last, the hungry and the thirsty, the unclothed and the strangers, the sick and the captives. It is for these little ones that the gospel is preached and for whom liberation has come in the words and deeds of Jesus.

It is important to point out that Jesus does not promise to include the poor in the kingdom *along with* others who may be rich and learned. His promise is that the kingdom belongs to the poor *alone.* This is the significance of his baptism with and life among the poor, and his contention that he "did not come to invite virtuous people, but sinners" (Mark 2:17 NEB). The first beatitude has the same emphasis: "How blest are you who are in need; the kingdom of God is yours" (Luke 6:20 NEB). Another dimension of the same theme is stressed in Luke 10:21 (cf. Matt. 11:25 NEB): "I thank thee, Father, Lord of heaven and earth, for hiding these things from the learned and wise and revealing them to the simple." In the words of Joachim Jeremias, "God does not give his revelation to learned theologians, but to the uneducated . . . ; he opens the *basileia* (kingdom) to children (Mark 10:14) and to those who can say '*Abbā* like a child (Matthew 10:3)."¹⁰ God's kingdom is for the bad characters, the outcasts, and the weak, but not for the self-designated righteous people. "Publicans and prostitutes will enter the *basileia* of God, and not you" (Matt. 21:31).¹¹ Here the gospel, by the very definition of its liberating character, *excludes* those who stand outside the social existence of the poor.

The centrality of the New Testament emphasis on God's liberation of the poor is the key to its continuity and discontinuity with the Old Testament message. The continuity is obvious: Just as the Mosaic and David-Zion traditions, the prophetic and the wisdom literature focus on the divine right of the poor to be free, Jesus also defines himself as the helper and the healer of the oppressed. "Never despise one of these little ones; I tell you, they have their guardian angels in heaven, who look continually on the face of my heavenly Father" (Matt. 18:10 NEB). Jesus' life was a historical demonstration that the God of Israel wills salvation for the weak and the helpless. God hates injustice and will not tolerate the humiliation of the outcasts.

If Jesus' life with the poor reveals that the continuity between the Old and New Testaments is found in the divine will to liberate the oppressed from sociopolitical slavery, what then is the discontinuity? Or, more appropriately, in what sense does the New Testament witness take us beyond the Old and fulfill it? The new element is this: The divine freedom revealed in Jesus, as that freedom is disclosed in the cross and resurrection, is more than the freedom made possible in history. While God's freedom for the poor is not *less than* the liberation of slaves from bondage (Exodus), yet it is *more than* that historical freedom. And it is this *more* which separates the exodus from the Incarnation, the Old Testament view of the Savior as the victor in the battle and the New Testament view of the Savior as the One who "give[s] up his life as a ransom for many" (Mark 10:45 NEB). While both stress the historical freedom of the unfree, the latter transcends history and affirms a freedom not dependent on sociopolitical limitations.

The cross and the resurrection of Jesus stand at the center of the New Testament story, without which nothing is revealed that was not already known in the Old Testament. In the light of Jesus' death and resurrection, his earthly life achieves a radical significance not otherwise possible. The cross-resurrection events mean that we now know that Jesus' ministry with the poor and the wretched was God himself effecting his will to liberate the oppressed. The Jesus story is the poor person's story, because God in Christ becomes poor and weak in order that the oppressed might become liberated from poverty and powerlessness. God becomes the victim in their place and thus transforms the condition of slavery into the battle ground for the struggle of freedom. This is what Christ's resurrection means. The oppressed are freed for struggle, for battle in the pursuit of humanity.

Jesus was not simply a nice fellow who happened to like the poor. Rather his actions have their origin in God's eternal being. They represent a new vision of divine freedom, climaxed with the cross and the resurrection, wherein God breaks into history for the liberation of slaves from societal oppression. Jesus' actions represent

God's will not to let his creation be destroyed by noncreative powers. The cross and the resurrection show that the freedom promised is now fully available in Jesus Christ. This is the essence of the New Testament story without which Christian theology is impossible.

III
CHRISTIAN THEOLOGY AND THE BIBLICAL STORY

If, as suggested above, Christian theology exists only as its language arises out of an encounter with the biblical story, what then is the meaning of this encounter? Since the Bible consists of many traditions woven together, how does a theologian use the Bible as a source for the expression of truth without being arbitrary in selecting some traditions while ignoring others? Some critics have accused Black Theology of just that: a decided bias towards the Mosaic tradition in contrast to the David-Zion tradition, towards the Old Testament in relation to the New, and towards the prophets with little reference to the sages of Israel. These critics have a right to ask what is the hermeneutical principle of selection involved here, and how is its validity tested. What is valid and invalid hermeneutics, and how is one distinguishable from the other?

Black Theology's answer to the question of heremeneutics can be stated briefly: *The hermeneutical principle for an exegesis of the scriptures is the revelation of God in Christ as the liberator of the oppressed from social oppression and to political struggle, wherein the poor recognize that their fight against poverty and injustice is not only consistent with the gospel but is the gospel of Jesus Christ.* Jesus Christ the liberator, the helper and the healer of the wounded, is the point of departure for valid exegesis of the scriptures from a Christian perspective. Any starting point that ignores God in Christ as the liberator of the oppressed or that makes salvation as liberation secondary is *ipso facto* invalid and thus heretical. The test of the validity of this starting point, although dialectically related to Black cultural experience, is not found in the particularity of the oppressed culture alone. It is found in the One who freely grants us freedom when we were doomed to slavery. In God's revelation in Scripture we come to the recognition that the divine liberation of the oppressed is not determined by our perceptions but by the God of the Exodus, the prophets, and Jesus Christ who calls the oppressed into a liberated existence. Divine revelation *alone* is the test of the validity of this starting point. And if it can be shown that God as witnessed in the Scriptures is not the liberator of the oppressed, then Black Theology would have to either drop the "Christian" designation or choose another starting point.

The biblical emphasis on the social and the political character of God's revelation in history for the weak and the helpless has important implications for the task of theology today. (1) There can be no Christian theology that is not social and political. If theology is to speak about the God of Jesus who reveals himself in the struggle of the oppressed for freedom, then theology *must* also become political, speaking for the God of the poor and the oppressed.

(2) The biblical emphasis on God's continuing act of liberation in the present and future means that theology cannot merely repeat what the Bible says or what is found in a particular theological tradition. Theology must be prophetic, recognizing the *relativity* of human speech, but also that God can use human speech at a particular time for the proclamation of his Word to the suffering poor. As theologians, therefore, we must take the risk to be prophetic by doing theology in the light of those who are helpless and voiceless in the society.

(3) Theology cannot ignore the tradition. While the tradition is not the gospel, it is the bearer of an interpretation of the gospel at a particular point in time. By studying the tradition, we not only gain insight into a particular time but also into our time as the past and present meet dialectically. For only through this dialectical encounter with the tradition are we given the freedom to move beyond it.

(4) Theology is always a word about the liberation of the oppressed and the humiliated. It is a word of judgment for the oppressors and the rulers. Whenever theologians fail to make this point unmistakably clear, they are not doing Christian theology but the theology of the antichrist.

Notes

1. *The Sociology of Knowledge* (London, Routledge and Kegan Paul, 1958), pp. 16, 7–8. For other important works in the field see Mannheim, *Ideology and Utopia,* trans. Louis Wirth and E. Shils (New York, Harcourt Brace and World, 1936); Berger and Luckmann, *The Social Construction of Reality* (New York, Doubleday Anchor Books, 1967); and Berger, *The Sacred Canopy* (New York, Doubleday Anchor Books, 1969).

2. Bernard W. Anderson, *Understanding the Old Testament* (Englewood Cliffs, N.J., Prentice-Hall, Inc., 1957), pp. 289f.

3. Gerhard von Rad, *Old Testament Theology,* Vol. I, trans. by D. M. G. Stalker (New York, Harper & Row Publishers, 1962), p. 41.

4. Anderson, *Understanding The Old Testament,* p. 377.

5. Although few New Testament scholars question the historical validity of Jesus' baptism by John, yet the question of the accessibility of the historical Jesus has undergone much discussion in the 20th century. Since the publication of Albert Schweitzer's *The Quest of the Historical Jesus* (1906) and the rise of Form Criticism shortly thereafter, it was commonplace to hear distinctions drawn between the Jesus of history and the Christ of faith. The former referred to the person accessible to the tools of historical scholarship, and the latter to the proclamation and teachings of the early church. It was generally assumed by Rudolf Bultmann that practically nothing can be known of the Jesus of history (cf. his *Jesus and the Word,* trans. by L. P. Smith and E. H. Lantera, [New York, Charles Scribner's Sons, 1934] where he says: "I do indeed think that we can now know almost nothing concerning the personality of Jesus" [p. 8].) That view tended to dominate New Testament scholarship in Germany until the 1950's when many of Bultmann's followers began to speak of the new quest for the historical Jesus. These persons (who included Ernst Käsemann, Günther Bornkamm, Hans Conzelmann and Ernst Fuchs) recognized that Bultmann's historical skepticism not only had scientific flaws but also, and more importantly, threatened the foundation of the faith itself. Käsemann expressed it well: "Only if Jesus' proclamation decisively coincides with the proclamation about Jesus is it understandable, reasonable, and necessary that the Christian kerygma in the New Testament conceals the message of Jesus; only then is the resurrected Jesus the historical Jesus. From this perspective we are required, precisely as theologians, to inquire behind Easter. . . . By this means we shall learn whether he stands behind the word of his church or not, whether the Christian kerygma is a myth that can be detached from his word and from himself or whether it binds us historically and insolubly to

him" (cited in Wolfhart Pannenberg, *Jesus—God and Man,* trans. by L. L. Wilkins and D. A. Priebe [Philadelphia, The Westminster Press, 1968], p. 56.). For a detailed discussion of this problem, see James Robinson, *The New Quest of the Historical Jesus* (London, SCM Press, Ltd., 1959); also Hugh Anderson, *Jesus and Christian Origins* (New York, Oxford University Press, 1964).

It should be made clear that this essay is being written on the assumption that there is no radical distinction between the Jesus of history and the Christ of faith. I have discussed elsewhere this issue and have located the indispensable historical datum (without which the gospel is no longer valid) as Jesus' identification with the oppressed (*A Black Theology of Liberation,* Chapter VI). The key, therefore, to the baptism incident (and with others reported in the Gospels) for our purposes is not only "Did it really happen?" but rather "What is the theological meaning embedded in it?" Although history *qua* is the place where revelation happens, it is not revelation. Revelation is the disclosure of God in the social context of history but is not identical with it. Since I contend that the Jesus of the Gospels cannot be separated from the "real" Jesus and have discussed the reasons for this conclusion elsewhere, there is no need here to enter into the critical discussion about the old and new quests for the historical Jesus. The text of the New Testament serves not only as a theological check on what we theologians are permitted to do with Jesus; but it also serves as a *historical* check against contemporary historians.

6. There has been much discussion about Jesus' probable attitude toward John the Baptist. Jesus certainly saw his ministry connected with John's and there is evidence from the Fourth Gospel that he received his first disciples from John (1:35–39). For a discussion of John's relation to Jesus, see Joachim Jeremias, *New Testament Theology,* trans. by John Bowden (New York, Charles Scribner's Sons, 1971), pp. 43ff.

7. One of the few exceptions is Ernst Käsemann whose writings disclose an unusual sensitivity to the use of the gospel as an opiate of the oppressed. "Every word, every deed, every demonstration is a denial of our Lord and ourselves, unless we test them from the point of view of whether they are opium of the people, or can be regarded and abused as such." *Jesus Means Freedom,* trans. by Frank Clarke (London, SCM Press, 1969), p. 13. See also his *New Testament Questions of Today,* trans. by W. J. Montague (Philadelphia, Fortress Press, 1969); *Perspectives on Paul,* trans. by Margaret Kohl (Philadelphia, Fortress Press, 1971).

8. See Jeremias, *New Testament Theology,* p. 103.f.

9. *Ibid.,* p. 112.

10. *Ibid.,* p. 116.

11. For the exegetical support of the exclusive interpretation of Matthew 21:31, see Jeremias, *New Testament Theology,* p. 117. "The *proagousin 'umas* . . . does not denote a priority in time, but an exclusive displacement of the others."

The Question of
the Relevance of Jesus
for Ethics Today

Jack T. Sanders

This article originally appeared in the *Journal of the American Academy of Religion* in 1970.

The relation of Church (or Christian) to world is a perennial theological problem that is particularly pressing today. This paper will investigate, in part, one aspect of that problem: the significance of Jesus for its solution. Specifically, the question is whether and in what degree an American Christian of the modern day may in any way gain from Jesus guidance or clues for behavior, for existence "in the world."

In order to seek an adequate answer, we must realize that everyone lives in a highly complex ethical situation. This ethical situation requires both individual and corporate response—the two sometimes separate, sometimes overlapping, sometimes conflicting. Further, what we have come to call our "pluralistic society" confuses ethical issues to a still greater degree, especially on the corporate level, since the possibility is immediately raised that "Christian" ethics may not be appropriate to such a society, composed, as it is, of a variety of non-Christian groups and individuals. Because of this complex ethical situation, our inquiry regarding Jesus will have to raise—at least in passing—the question whether Jesus may be valid for individual ethics, corporate ethics, or both; and whether this validity may extend to a pluralistic society. To be sure, there is hardly any hope of finding individual instructions that will still be valid after nearly 2000 years; but whether Jesus provides a general ethical validity—

middle axioms, norms or even a mere direction of response—will be the question.

In fact, a considerable number of Christian theologians (including pastors and theological students), although not all, assume and will argue that Jesus left an ethical *teaching* which all Christians should attempt to follow. An example of this view is to be found in the *Interpreter's Dictionary of the Bible,* where it is stated that the Golden Rule (Matt. 7:12) is "a climactic summary of the Sermon on the Mount," and that this, along with the commandment to love God and one's neighbor as oneself, "justifies the conclusion that love (*agapē*) was of the essence of Jesus' ethical teaching." The discussion of Jesus' ethical teaching is then concluded with the affirmation that "the ethics of Jesus is best thought of as the demands which are placed upon those who have accepted God's rule, as Jesus proclaimed and lived it."[1] Yet such a position is not without problems.

I

One always runs a risk in finding in Jesus, in his teachings or his life, a guide for ethics in one's own day. This risk is what Henry Cadbury, at the height of the Social Gospel, labeled "the peril of modernizing Jesus."[2] In expanding on that theme, Cadbury consciously avoided arguing from *konsequente Eschatologie* ("thoroughgoing" or, in Cadbury's more accurate English, "consistent eschatology"). He thought that this view might not win the day—as indeed it did not—and that it was better to argue from specific texts, i.e., that a certain saying of Jesus could not have meant what those appropriating it on behalf of the Social Gospel took it to mean (for this purpose, Cadbury also found it expedient to accept most such sayings of Jesus as authentic).

To argue from the individual sayings, however, is always precarious, for the possibility always exists that one may have misinterpreted a saying, or that both sides may have overlooked a significant saying; or Jesus may be modernized in some other way, and then one must go through all the material again. Ultimately, any such argument against "modernizing" Jesus can be conclusive only when it deals with the foundation of his teachings—that is, with his basic re-

ligious orientation. It was in fact thoroughgoing eschatology that
had done this.

In his justly famous book, *The Quest of the Historical Jesus,* Albert Schweitzer had sought to show the general invalidity of modernizing Jesus' teaching.[3] Thus he made it clear that Jesus intended
only, in his opinion, an interim ethic. "There is for Jesus no ethic of
the Kingdom of God, for in the Kingdom of God all natural relationships . . . are abolished. Temptation and sin no longer exist. . . .
To serve, to humble oneself, to incur persecution and death, belong
to 'the ethic of the interim' just as much as does penitence."[4] This
view that Jesus' ministry was primarily determined by his imminent
eschatology (an insight which Schweitzer, to be sure, inherited and
expanded upon) has found quite a large following among New Testament scholars, although presumably no one today accepts his analysis of the eschatological historicity of Mark. There have been, of
course, those who have rejected such a view of Jesus' ministry.
Among the most prominent of such "dissenters" from the eschatological consensus has been C. H. Dodd, whose "realized eschatology" is presented most clearly in his book, *The Parables of the
Kingdom*[5] However, any view that holds that Jesus did not proclaim
an imminent eschatology will have to be considered erroneous.

That Jesus held an imminent eschatology will have to be considered a fact. This is most clearly seen in his endorsement of the ministry of John the Baptist (Matt. 11:7–11*a*, 16–19 & par.), an
endorsement that is surely to be viewed as authentic in view of the
fact that it proved an embarrassment to the church, as Matt. 11:11*b*,
a Christian attempt to alter the first saying, attests. The saying found
in Matt. 11:12 f., the more original form of which is probably maintained in Luke 16:16, probably also signifies the imminence involved
in Jesus' proclamation of the Kingdom, although the exact meaning
of this logion is uncertain. Clearer, however, are the parable of the
fig tree (Mark 13:28 f.), which implies that God's eschatological
summer, i.e., the Kingdom of God, is near; and the saying about seeing Satan falling like lightning (Luke 10:18). Finally, a number of
sayings about "entering the Kingdom" will almost certainly be authentic sayings of Jesus, even if the early Church could make use of
this phrase for its own purposes (e.g., Matt. 5:20; 7:21). These are
Mark 9:43–47; 10:15; Matt. 21:31*b;* Luke 11:52. Thus, on this evi-

dence alone, any view that does not treat Jesus as espousing a view of imminent eschatology will have to be considered self-apocopating.

A third alternative, therefore, immediately suggests itself: the possibility that, although Jesus did expect the Kingdom of God to come soon, his significance for ethics may endure beyond the disappointing of that expectation. Such a possibility is presented most adequately by Amos Wilder in his book, *Eschatology and Ethics in the Teaching of Jesus.*[6] In this work, Wilder quite readily accepts not only Jesus' eschatological orientation, but also the fact that the imminent eschatology, by its emphasis on "reward and penalty," provided "sanctions" for Jesus' ethics.[7] Such eschatologically oriented sanctions, however, he considers to have been only "formal" sanctions, the "fundamental sanctions" being given by Jesus' proclamation of the "nature of God" and his appeal to the scriptures, and by the "authority and example of Jesus."[8]

The problems begin, however, when Wilder attempts to keep the eschatology as a constitutive element of Jesus' teaching. He writes, "We do not wish to rule out entirely the place of such sanctions in the teaching.... But these formal sanctions should be looked upon as supplementary rather than as compromising the fundamental sanctions."[9]

Two things are problematical in that statement. One is the supposition that the eschatology is related to ethics only in terms of future reward and punishment. That is really not to understand the role of imminence in Jesus' thinking. The Jesus who called John the Baptist the greatest man on earth (Matt. 11:11*a*) and who saw "Satan falling like lightning from heaven" (Luke 10:18) was convinced that God's final action in world history was beginning. Hence, in agreement with the Baptist, he saw the present moment as the final moment for repentance. Indeed, it is correctly observed by Wilder that repentance was necessary in the face of God's righteousness, but that is because God's righteousness was considered to be *at hand.* The other problem with Wilder's solution is the contemporary problem of the loss of transcendence, i.e., the death of God. This problem is clearly expressed by Rabbi Richard Rubenstein, who writes, "The death of God *as a cultural event* is irrefutable. . . .What Hegel, Nietzsche, and Dostoevsky understood by the death of God—the absence of any sense of meaning, direction, or value derived from a transcendent theistic source—is certainly an accurate description of the way we experience the world."[10] In this sense, Christianity must realize that it indeed lives in the time of the death of God. (Where Christians still recognize a "Christian" ethical imperative—and there are quite a variety of these—such is for the most part simply the maintaining of a traditional heteronomy; and one would have to lay emphasis on the *heteros.*) Wilder is apparently arguing that Jesus' view of transcendence is essentially qualitative rather than temporal; but the historical progression from temporal to spatial to qualitative transcendence is now in the process of being resolved into a view of absolute immanence. Thus, even if Wilder's view of the role of imminent eschatology in Jesus' teaching could be vindicated, he would still not have demonstrated that Jesus provides a valid ethic for today, since the nearness of transcendent righteousness, which he does hold to be essential in Jesus' ethical teaching, can no longer be assumed.

In the last analysis, if God's righteousness is the basic reality behind the call to righteousness, must not God's judgment also be included within the horizon of the "fundamental sanctions"? If judgment is thus inseparably connected, as it seems, with divine righteousness, then the eschatology is not ultimately overcome in Wilder's reconstruction. This being the case, we may now turn to an examination of views—in the development of theology following Schweitzer—in which imminent eschatology is seen to be constitutive for Jesus, while at the same time an ethical significance or validity of Jesus is asserted.

II

In his book on Jesus,[11] Rudolf Bultmann apparently attempted to hold the two alternatives for understanding Jesus that Schweitzer had so clearly delineated. That is to say, Bultmann recognized as well as anyone else Jesus' apocalyptic orientation but nevertheless sought relevance in his teachings. Of course, Bultmann later wrote, *"The message of Jesus* is a presupposition for the theology of the

New Testament rather than a part of that theology itself."[12] Here, however, he states equally plainly that "The investigation concerns the content, meaning, and validity for us of what is taught in the gospels."[13] This is, of course, a famous problem in Bultmann's system, but it is of no purpose to attempt to resolve it here; rather, the question to be asked is whether Bultmann's Jesus book has provided any justification for considering Jesus' teachings to be relevant for modern ethics. Bultmann at first seems to deny any such significance by affirming that "*Jesus teaches no ethics at all* in the sense of an intelligible theory valid for all men." Such a theory would have to presuppose an anthropology, and would make man "the measure of human action."[14] Jesus calls instead for a radical obedience to God's will,[15] and Bultmann clearly understands this to imply a contextual ethic. "This moment of decision contains all that is necessary for the decision, since in it the whole of life is at stake. . . . *Now* must man know what to do and leave undone, and no standard whatsoever from the past or from the universal is available."[16] Love (*agapē*) may be another way of expressing the radicality of this existential contextualism,[17] yet Bultmann rejects the notion that *agapē* can "be regarded as an ethical principle from which particular concrete requirements can be derived."[18] It would never be possible to say, "Because I love, I must do such and such"—neither in advance of a situation, nor in the situation itself. As Bultmann understands Jesus' command to love, it would be impossible ever to calculate from love to action; *agapē* rather means doing what *must* be done *now*—that is, letting the context provide even what must substitute for norms.

Bultmann was, of course, employing *Sachkritik* here (a critical anlaysis that seeks the true subject matter), just as he saw Jesus to have made use of *Sachkritik* with respect to the Jewish law.[19] There can be no doubt that Jesus himself would be surprised to see what was, in his mind, probably a purifying of that law in prospect of the dawning Kingdom cast in such existential terms. Yet some of his radical commands surely in fact imply what Bultmann has explicated. Can a modern Christian, then, appeal to Jesus for a contextualism valid for today? The problem, unfortunately, lies again in the eschatological orientation, just as Albert Schweitzer made clear; for, as Bultmann recognized, the radicality of Jesus' ethical imperatives was *based in his belief that the Kingdom was about to dawn.* Bultmann would not agree with Schweitzer that Jesus proclaimed an "interim ethic,"[20] yet he did agree that "Jesus' demands are in one point to be understood in the light of the eschatological message—namely that in them 'Now' appears as the decisive hour."[21] But existentialism cannot maintain itself as the demythologized form of imminence, for imminence means that *God* is coming, or, as it soon became for Christianity, that the *parousia* is about to occur. But was not Schweitzer right about the parousia? Is not the "whole history of Christianity . . . based on the . . . non-occurrence of the parousia"?[22] Can the (existential) imminence of my own future, even if that future is understood as opening the possibility of transcendence to me, really be the modern equivalent of Jesus' belief that God was about to judge the world? For modern man knows that, however imminent his own judgment may always be, the world and its problems will continue.[23] Thus it is precisely the fact that the modern Christian recognizes himself to be a part of an ongoing world that creates the insurmountable problem for demythologizing at this point, and that forces one to the conclusion that Schweitzer was more correct than Bultmann: Jesus' view of imminence, upon which his ethical preaching was based, was and must remain an eschatological view.

In his *Theology of the New Testament,*[24] Bultmann offered, less extensively, the same interpretation of Jesus' ethical teaching as in *Jesus and the Word,* with the alteration that *agapē* was elevated in importance to be the heading under which radical obedience was discussed.[25]

Bultmann's explanation of the validity of Jesus' ethical teaching again brings to attention two related problems. The first is that Jesus' eschatological orientation is so related to his ethical imperative that the two cannot be separated, even by demythologizing. The other is the problem of the death of God. If transcendence be lost, can Jesus' ethical teaching be maintained in any sense, even if the problem of the barrier of the eschatology could be overcome, as for example in demythologizing? The remainder of this paper will examine significant interpretations of Jesus since Bultmann with regard to the validity of Jesus for modern ethics, and will seek particularly to see how recent interpreters of Jesus deal with the two problems just mentioned.

III

In spite of some aspects of Bultmann's work that pointed the other way, the overall impact of his work was to focus the attention of a large segment of the New Testament community away from Jesus. By 1953, however, a call was heard from among the Bultmannians to take up the "question of the historical Jesus" again,[26] and the first Bultmannian to answer this challenge was Günther Bornkamm, whose *Jesus of Nazareth* appeared for the first time in Germany in 1956.[27] Unfortunately, this work represents something of a reversion to a pre-cited stage of New Testament scholarship, so that Bornkamm, especially with regard to the ethical question, accepts most of the Sermon on the Mount as authentically spoken by Jesus, and apparently accepts the basic original unity of the passage. To be sure, he acknowledges that Chapters 5–7 were "put together by Matthew," but the Sermon on the Mount is nevertheless *the* passage which contains "Jesus' proclamation of the divine will."[28] Quite surprisingly, even Bornkamm takes two statements in Matthew 5, which almost certainly stem originally from the community lying behind the Gospel of Matthew, or from Matthew himself, to be the keynotes of the whole passage. These are Matt. 5:17: "Think not that I have come to abolish the law and the prophets: I have not come to abolish them but to fulfill them," and Matt. 5:20: "Unless your righteousness exceeds that of the scribes and Pharisees, you will never enter the kingdom of heaven."[29] Bultmann had noted that Matt. 5:17–19 stems from "the discussions between the more conservative (Palestinian) communities and those that were free from the law (Hellenistic)," and that v. 20 "is most probably a heading or introduction by Matthew to 5:21–48."[30] Once this is stated, it is difficult to see how these two verses could be interpreted otherwise.[31]

Accepting this Matthean call to "righteousness" as being from Jesus, Bornkamm sees in the Sermon on the Mount the same existential aspect that Bultmann saw in the "radical demand" of God enunciated by Jesus, i.e., that "the claims of Jesus carry in themselves 'the last things,' without having to borrow validity and urgency from the blaze of the fire in apocalyptic scenes. They themselves lead to the boundaries of the world, but do not paint a picture of its end."[32] Bornkamm thus drops the apocalypticism entirely from Jesus' ethical teaching, thereby presumably avoiding the problem of making Jesus' ethics valid for another day; yet, precisely in this attempt to show the insignificance of the apocalypticism and thus the present validity of Jesus' ethical teaching, eschatology is again seen to be the insurmountable problem, for Bornkamm recognizes that Jesus' ethic is an impossible ethics! He characterizes it as a lofty ideal "that again and again . . . has quickened man's conscience"; but this does not render it invalid, for "just because it leads so often to a hopeless tension between God's will and man's ability, it also wakens the hunger and thirst after righteousness which receives Jesus' promise."[33] But where in the Sermon on the Mount itself is any indication that this is what it was intended to do? Is not the higher righteousness called for in Matt. 5:20 then given content in considerable detail in what follows? And is not the conclusion of the chapter, "You shall be perfect!" (Matt. 5:48), the summation of what has been indicated before?[34] Is there here any indication that this passage—even taken uncritically, as Bornkamm for the most part does—reveals that Jesus expected anything less than total (radical) obedience?

Such obedience, however, is possible only if the end has drawn near. Once the pressure of imminence begins to be released, the command must be relaxed. This is normally done by understanding it as an ideal; whereas, even Matthew does not create the Sermon on the Mount as an ideal, but rather as a paradigm for Christian piety (cf. especially Matt. 5:13–20). Thus those sayings in the Sermon on the Mount authentically from Jesus can be considered an impossible ethics only if one is to go on living in the world. If the end of the world has drawn nigh, bringing with it God's righteousness and judgment, the "impossible" ethics becomes both possible and consistent.

Bornkamm sees the commandment to love, however, as overcoming the tension involved in the Sermon on the Mount. As in Bultmann's *Theology of the New Testament,* so for Bornkamm love (*agapē*) is primary and central in Jesus' ethical teaching.[35] The commandment to love means "the renunciation of self-love, the willingness for and the act of surrender. . . . In this way and no other, God's call comes to us, and in this way the love of God and the love of our neighbor become one."[36] The parable of the Good Samaritan is taken to give clear expression to this commandment.[37] Thus the commandment to love becomes for Bornkamm Jesus' "real" demand, whereas the ethics of the Sermon on the Mount present a presently unrealizable ideal. "Jesus never calls [man] to his ideal destiny, but lays hold of him in what in what he already is and does."[38] Bornkamm thus seems to hold that love overcomes the impossible ethics of Jesus. Yet the love commandment itself is not at all free of serious difficulties.

In a lengthy criticism and evaluation of Bornkamm's book, in which his own views are of course presented,[39] Ernst Fuchs takes issue precisely with the view that "again and again man can only be referred to what he knows already," i.e., that he can no longer "stand back from the request."[40] The command to love one's neighbor as oneself "betrays," argues Fuchs, "precisely *as* demand an *insurmountable* 'last effort' of the individual 'to stand back' from the demand, thus from love."[41] "Love is never fulfilled," continues Fuchs, "as long as it remains demand."[42] Fuchs had in fact argued in an earlier article that the problem of a commandment to love, by its nature unfulfillable, is overcome Christologically. Fuchs reminds there that "Jesus was given for our sins." "Precisely for this reason," he then adds, "the . . . saying of John 3:16 stands as it were written over the New Testament. That means that the sending of Jesus was an act of God's love in word and deed, which we may and must hold onto as long as we are in the situation of struggling with our own will, with our own natural self love."[43] Thus, *because* of our standing in this way in God's love, we are both commanded and made capable of loving God and neighbor, as in the Pauline imperative in the indicative.[44] This being in God's love, which is the result of Jesus' having come, is thus the fulfillment of the commandment. But if the commandment is fulfilled, then the Christian must ask, *"what remains to be done."*[45] The answer to this question involves what Fuchs calls "something like a Christian ethics." And that something is that the Christian must always "make his behavior, in continual struggle with self-love, into a witness of faith for Jesus Christ."[46] It may thus be observed that Fuchs is attempting to give a doctrinal answer to the problem of the commandment of love, and this is further obvious when he concludes that the commandment "possesses true validity only for the believers."[47] This would only mean, however, that, *doctrinally stated,* the Christian says that Jesus himself fulfilled the commandment to love on behalf of the believer. If Fuchs now still wishes to derive from this doctrinal position "something like a Christian ethics," that is all very well, but one must be clear—as regards our present problem—that such a "something" is in no way a guide to moral action. Rather, it becomes a mode of proclamation. To be sure, this is still an ethics in the broader sense of the term, precisely in the same way that Paul was proposing an ethics when he called the celebration of the Lord's Supper proclaiming "the Lord's death until he comes" (I Cor. 11:26 f.); but this is little help to the modern Christian who would like to derive from Jesus some guidance or direction—however general or fundamental—for his personal or corporate behavior in a world presenting him with ethical problems.

In his criticism of Bornkamm's book, then, Fuchs argues with sharp insight that love can proceed only from love, not from demand—that is, that the problem one encounters in the commandment to love is that one does not believe in the *power* of love. What the commandment to love really intends to elicit is not obedience to itself as demand, but rather belief in the power of love! But that can occur only where there is love. Only *in* love can one realize "that love really masters our life."[48] Here, therefore, Fuchs seems to move away from the statement of his earlier article that the commandment to love presents "something like a Christian ethics" to the more thoroughly consistent position that this commandment calls Christian existence into being—that is, in fact calls one to recognize, in faith, that *agapē* is the supremely powerful reality.

In the context of the "new quest of the historical Jesus," Fuchs now distinguishes between present and future aspects of *agapē*. The historical Jesus whom one, in faith, encounters in the proclamation of the gospel is of course the *resurrected* Jesus, the Jesus who takes the burden of the commandment on himself, thus the Jesus in whom one has hope that love will conquer; this is the eschatological aspect of Jesus' preaching. But Jesus also risks everything to his disciples— that is, on them depends the validity of the claim that the Kingdom of God is breaking in at the present in the ministry of Jesus; thus, this Jesus, the *crucified* one, commands his disciples to love because he counts on their loving.[49] Thus Fuchs still does consider the command to love to be valid, and to be the command of Jesus; but, even though he uses the term "ethical" as the antithesis to "eschatological,"[50] it would seem that he is no longer speaking even of "something like a Christian ethics" but is rather—by speaking of Jesus' counting on his disciples to love—bringing the Pauline (eschatologically oriented) "imperative in the indicative" into a more general discussion of the place of present and future in Christian existence; and that he is doing this in terms of the historical Jesus—that is, the Jesus encountered by hearers of the gospel as giving and commanding love. In other words, the historical Jesus—by the love commandment—designates Christian existence, which is both imputed and entrusted to the believer in the present in prospect of what is yet to be. If this understanding of *agapē,* however, succeeds in rendering invalid Bornkamm's direct relationship between the commandment and what is expected of the believer, it still cannot be seen to have offered assistance in the formation of valid and consistent ethics for today, since the orientation toward a future of fulfillment cannot be given up (and that is just the point!). It goes almost without saying that any attempt to build an ethics on such an understanding of Jesus would have to have as its goal a strictly Christian ethics (by Fuchs' affirmation), one which would realize at the outset that it was irrelevant for non-Christians. Perhaps such an ethics would have provided no problem to "Christendom"; but "Christendom" is now a thing of the past, and one would probably have to say that an ethics requiring solid commitment to *one* religion has become unusable in modern American society. It will have to be added that it would be difficult to envisage any way in which love understood as the proclamation involved in the living of the crucifixion side of the gospel could be related to corporate behavior.

James M. Robinson's book, *A New Quest of the Historical Jesus,*[51] summarizes the whole problem of the historical Jesus, the recent debate, and suggests direction for further discussion. The point Robinson himself comes down on most sharply is what he calls "A New Concept of History and the Self." Because "historicism" and "psychologism" are no longer the central concerns respectively of historiography and biography, "the kind of history and biography attempted unsuccessfully for Jesus by the nineteenth century is now seen to be based upon a false understanding of the nature of history and the self." He explains this statement at greater length: "Nineteenth-century historiography and biography were modelled after the natural sciences, e.g., in their effort to establish causal relationships and to classify the particular in terms of the general." This method, however, bypassed "the distinctively historical and human, where transcendence, if at all, is to be found. . . . Today history is increasingly understood as essentially the unique and creative, whose reality would not *be* apart from the event in which it becomes." Thus history should be viewed as "the act of intention, the commitment, the meaning for the participants, behind the external occurrence."[52]

With this definition of history in hand, Robinson believes that a new quest of this *historical* Jesus is possible, in which *historical* would not mean what *historical* meant to all those reviewed in Schweitzer's book, whose historical quest Schweitzer brought to so decisive an end, but rather something like the "historic" Jesus. This historical Jesus would be identifiable with the kerygmatic Christ since "the *kerygma*," in its decision-invoking function, would presumably continue "Jesus' message; and if the decision called for by Jesus as well as by the *kerygma* was at the basis of his own selfhood, then it is apparent that his person corresponds to its christology."[53]

To be sure, Robinson has not envisioned here practical consequences or a practical application of this theological endeavor, yet the *content* which the new quest of the historical Jesus uncovers is essentially an ethical content! Robinson defines the unity between Jesus' proclamation and the church's proclamation, hence the new selfhood called for by both Jesus and the *kerygma,* in this way:

> Jesus called upon his hearer to break radically with the present evil aeon, and to rebuild his life in commitment to the inbreaking kingdom. Paul called upon his hearer to die and rise with Christ. Yet when one moves beyond such an initial comparison to the deeper level of meaning, the underlying similarity becomes increasingly clear. To break categorically with the present evil aeon is to cut the ground from under one's feet, to open oneself physically to death by breaking with the power structure of an evil society, and to open oneself spiritually to death by renouncing self-seeking as a motivation and giving oneself radically to the needs of one's neighbour, as one's real freedom and love. To do this because of faith in the inbreaking kingdom is to do it in faith that such total death is ultimately meaningful; in it lies transcendence, resurrection. . . . It is this existential

meaning latent in Jesus' message which is constitutive of his selfhood, expresses itself in his action, and is finally codified in the Church's *kerygma.*[54]

This understanding of Jesus avoids modernizing Jesus as well as avoiding asking modern man to subscribe to ancient views. It further avoids the problems posed by a belief in God's imminent judgment, and it speaks of transcendence not in the sense of a heteronomous God, which is still the category to which Bultmann's God belongs, but rather in the sense of one's own transcendence. Can this new understanding of Jesus provide a valid ethics for today? Can my acceptance in faith, in response to the Jesus who confronts me in the *kerygma,* of my own death—understood as a death on behalf of others—now be the basis of a consistent and meaningful ethics? To be sure, as in the case of Fuchs, one would have to realize that the ethics implied here is dependent on acceptance of the *kerygma.* It is not applicable to the non-Christian.

Asking me as a Christian to accept my own death as an existential reality seems in effect to solve the problem of eschatology. If the problem is that I have to anticipate the end of the world, I may now do so existentially, since accepting my death on behalf of others of course entails accepting the death of *my* world and its values. What was significant about the eschatology of Jesus and his followers was that it anticipated the *imminent* end of the world. Eschatology is in any case no problem if it only anticipates the *ultimate* end of the world. Astronomy may do the same. But the acceptance of my death means my death *now,* and this must mean also the destruction of my world now. Both these events may be existentially accepted. Yet eventually the ardor with which one embraces such a viewpoint must begin to pale; for existentialism is out of step with the times. My life with its problems goes on; my world and its problems continue. For a few days or weeks, perhaps for a few years, I can accept my own death; but the endurance of the problem-fraught world must finally begin to weigh upon this outlook. Ultimately, I must either give up the death of the world and cling only to my own death—in which case I understand myself to be a derelict—or I must give up the existential stance altogether. It is after all, then, the continual pressure of the *continuous existence of the world and its problems* that finally breaks apart an existential approach to Christian ethics. Eschatology has turned out to be a hydra that rears another head even here. In other words, the ethical implications of the new quest of the historical Jesus would appear to be inappropriate to the modern understanding of "world."

One final possibility to be considered, for an ethics that surmounts the problems we have dealing with, is provided by the Bultmannian who has translated theology into anthropology, Herbert Braun. In his article, "The Problem of a New Testament Theology,"[55] Braun demonstrates that various aspects of New Testament theology involve an understanding of God that is beyond the reach of modern man, and which even created problems in the early church before the later books of the New Testament were written. Thus, whereas Jesus viewed the Torah, more specifically its ethical rules, as "entirely binding," Paul distinguished clearly between law and faith as alternate paths to salvation—the latter, of course, being for him the authentic path.[56] Contemporary with Paul, however, Jewish Christianity emphasized the importance of the Torah, as in Matthew, especially in the Sermon on the Mount; and after Paul the early catholic church no longer saw the distinction he had maintained, as is seen, e. g., in the Pastoral Epistles.[57] This means that the church could understand theonomy only as heteronomy, could understand God's rule only as expressed in definite commands, frequently subject to casuistic interpretation, and ofttimes simply arbitrary. Jesus, however, in Braun's view, had in reality given the ground rules for overcoming this situation—that is, for Jesus "love toward God is interpreted as love toward one's neighbor."[58] This, of course, refers to the "Great Commandment," but Braun sees the same principle at work when "the help and kindness demonstrated or not demonstrated to the oppressed neighbor is in fact demonstrated or not demonstrated to Jesus (Matt. 25:31 ff.)."[59] Both Paul and John then take up this same theme.

With Jesus, therefore, we have, according to Braun, *theonomy as autonomy*. Braun refers to the saying about man's being lord of the sabbath and concludes, "Such words of Jesus certainly do not mean that their contents are valid because of Jesus' authority; rather they count on the conscientious Yes of the hearer simply on the basis of their content. In fact, therefore, we have theonomy as autonomy, not as heteronomy."[60] One must not overlook the radicality of this statement for theology. Braun has in effect said that what is valid in the teaching of Jesus has its validity because it is recognized to be valid in and of itself—not because Jesus said it! Thus he can conclude the article with the following words:

> The word of proclamation and the act of love reach me—if they really do reach me—from my fellow man. God is the whence of my being taken care of and of my being obliged, which comes to me from my fellow man. To abide in God would therefore mean to abide in the concrete act of devoting onself to the other; whoever abides in *agapan* abides in God (I John 4:16). I can speak of God only where I speak of man, and hence anthropologically. . . . That would mean then, however, that man as man, man in relation with his fellow man, implies God. That would always have to be discovered anew from the New Testament. God would then be a definite type of relation with one's fellow man. The atheist misses *man*.[61]

One will not be surprised that this same article has recently been reprinted in an anthology edited by Thomas J. J. Altizer as one of several essays dealing with the phenomenon of the death of God.[62] Thus Braun's Christian ethics, which seems to be at least ultimately derived from Jesus, would clearly move beyond the contemporary problem of the loss of transcendence. If it thus escapes this problem, then of course it also escapes the problem of the eschatological orientation, since, as we saw, the problem there lay primarily in the anticipation of God's imminent judgment. Braun's ethical interpretation of Jesus is, in fact, highly appropriate to reality today in that it lays down no norms, no middle axioms, hence allows no possibility of casuistry and, although expressed in terms of person-to-person relationships, may be at least theoretically relevant for the corporate level of ethical activity (although it must be admitted that the possibility of defining the corporate ethical situation in these terms is uncertain). It says simply, "I must respond to the need of the other," and it says no more than that. It is, to be brief, an absolutely contextual ethics. Braun's ethics, presumably, remains Christian, it should be pointed out, inasmuch as he states that one is freed to this kind of ethical responsibility in what he calls simply the "I may"; but that is, of course, simply the de-transcendentalized version of forgiveness of sins. Where Bultmann would have said that one's knowldge of having received forgiveness freed one to respond to God, and this response took the form of love of neighbor, Braun prefers to say that the "I may" and the "I ought" come to me from my fellow man.[63] Both my being freed and the claim laid upon me come in the context of interpersonal relationships, and the latter comes in terms of the former! Yet such an understanding of the validity of Jesus for ethics is not exclusively Christian since, because of the autonomy of the ethical demand, it lays its claim on one not in the context of Christian proclamation but rather in the human situation itself.

Has this approach thus succeeded in bringing Jesus' ethics into the modern world? In a certain sense it has, but in such a way that Jesus becomes altogether irrelevant for the ethics. By emphasizing that theonomy appeared in Jesus' proclamation as *autonomy* and not as *heteronomy,* Braun has suggested that any ethical principle coming from Jesus will stand on its own. It does not need Jesus, which means that it possesses its own authority. To turn to Jesus for ethical guidance would be to ask for the imposition of a heteronomy; and Braun makes it clear that the ethical situation is not such that one asks what Jesus said, or what he did, or even to what existence he calls. One asks rather what one's fellow man needs. And one does not ask this question because one has learned from Jesus that one *should* ask it; rather one asks it simply because the human situation frees one to ask it. That is all. Thus where the best attempt is made to present Jesus as offering a Christian ethics valid for the modern world, Jesus himself is ultimately unimportant.

One will, of course, have to say that Braun has learned this ethics from Jesus, i. e., from the Great Commandment, the parable of the Last Judgment, and probably the parable of the Good Samaritan.[64] The only question is whether he has thereby done violence to Jesus' teaching. For Jesus, as we have seen, the imminence of God's kingdom made righteousness a pressing matter. This seems to have been because he understood the proclamation of God's nearness to mean not only that one was now freed from self-seeking (Braun's "I may") but that one must also accept the righteousness of the (future) kingdom as already determinitive for existence now (Braun's "I ought"). For Braun, however, both freedom and responsibility arise from the ethical situation itself, i. e., autonomously. In the case of the "I ought," one can probably draw a straight line from the parable of the Good Samaritan to this point; that will present no problem. But the "I may"? Is freedom for selfless ethical behavior the equivalent of the freedom from self-seeking provided by God's imminence? Does not the "I may" arise for Jesus out of the conviction that my destiny—and that of my world—is now for all practical purposes in God's hands? This would seem to be the implication of at least the parables of the Pharisee and Publican and the Laborers in the Vineyard (Matt. 20:1–16)—and certainly of the parable of the Last Judgment. If we are thus correct in attributing the freedom involved in the ethical demand that stems from Jesus to his awareness of the imminence of the righteous God, then we will have to say that the removal of the eschatological orientation from Jesus' ethical teaching would leave a truncated obligation, but *not* the organic unity of freedom and obligation Braun finds in the ethical situations. For Jesus, eschatology is constitutive for ethics. To disengage the one is to remove the ground for the other. The ethics proposed by Herbert Braun has much to commend it, but it is not Jesus' ethics, not even Jesus' ethics demythologized.

To put the matter now most sharply, Jesus does not provide a valid ethics for today. His ethical teaching is interwoven with his imminent eschatology to such a degree that every attempt to separate the two and to draw out only the ethical thread invariably and inevitably pulls loose strands of the eschatology, so that both yarns are ruined. Better to leave the tapestry intact, to let Jesus, as Albert Schweitzer appealed to us to do, return to his own time. As Cadbury warned, we should avoid the peril of modernizing him. We should let him be a Jew of Palestine of nearly 2000 years ago; let him have his eschatological hopes that were crushed, as Schweitzer said, on the wheel of fate that was his cross; let him believe in the imminent end of the world and God's imminent judgment and, in prospect of that, call his hearers to a radical surrender to God. In doing so, we may even learn to appreciate him more.

Notes

1. W. D. Davies, "Ethics in the NT," in *Interpreter's Dictionary of the Bible,* Vol. II, 1962, pp. 168, 170.

2. Henry J. Cadbury, *The Peril of Modernizing Jesus,* New York: The Macmillan Company, 1937.

3. Albert Schweitzer, *The Quest of the Historical Jesus,* trans. W. Montgomery, 3rd. ed., London: Adam & Charles Black, 1954. The first German edition was published in 1906.

4. *Ibid.,* p. 364.

5. C. H. Dodd, *The Parables of the Kingdom,* New York: Charles Scribner's Sons, 1961.

6. Amos N. Wilder, *Eschatology and Ethics in the Teaching of Jesus,* New York: Harper & Brothers, 1950.

7. *Ibid.,* pp. 73–115.

8. *Ibid.,* pp. 116–32.

9. *Ibid.,* p. 141.

10. Richard L. Rubenstein, "Thomas Altizer's Apocalypse," in *America and the Future of Theology,* ed. William A. Beardslee, Philadelphia: The Westminster Press, 1967, p. 32.

11. Rudolf Bultmann, *Jesus and the Word,* trans. Louis Pettibone Smith and Erminie Huntress Lantero, New York: Charles Scribner's Sons, 1958. The first German edition was published in 1926.

12. Bultmann, *Theology of the New Testament,* Vol. 1, trans. Kendrik Grobel, New York: Charles Scribner's Sons, 1951, p. 3.

13. Bultmann, *Jesus and the Word,* p. 123.

14. *Ibid.,* pp. 84 f.

15. *Ibid., passim,* part. pp. 64–84.

16. *Ibid.,* pp. 87 f.

17. *Ibid.,* pp. 110 f.

18. *Ibid.,* p. 112.

19. Cf. the discussion of Jesus' sovereignty over against the law based on his understanding of the true content and purpose of the law, *ibid.,* p. 75.

20. *Ibid.,* pp. 126–29.

21. *Ibid.,* p. 129.

22. Schweitzer, p. 358.

23. In another context, Bultmann (*The Presence of Eternity,* New York: Harper & Brothers, 1957, p. 153) explicitly recognizes this fact, but without seeing that it makes a demythologizing of the judgment of the world impossible.

24. Bultmann, *op. cit.*

64 / *Jack T. Sanders*

25. *Ibid.,* p. 18.

26. Ernst Käsemann, "Das Problem des historischen Jesus," in *Exegetische Versuche und Besinnungen,* Vol. 1, Göttingen: Vandenhoeck & Ruprecht, 1960, pp. 187–214. The lecture was first delivered in October of 1953 at the Gathering of Former Marburgers.

27. Günther Bornkamm, *Jesus of Nazareth,* trans. Irene and Fraser McLuskey with James M. Robinson, London: Hodder & Stoughton, 1960.

28. *Ibid.,* p. 100.

29. *Ibid.*

30. Bultmann, *The History of the Synoptic Tradition,* trans. John Marsh, New York: Harper & Row, 1962, p. 138.

31. Cf. further Georg Strecker, *Der Weg der Gerechtigkeit* (FRLANT, 82), Göttingen: Vandenhoeck & Ruprecht, 1962, pp. 144, 151 f. and Ernst Fuchs, in the volume discussed below, pp. 100-25, part. p. 100. Bornkamm elsewhere made it plain, at about the same time, that he agreed with Bultmann's statement on the origin of Matt. 5:17–19; cf. p. 24 of his "End-Expectation and Church in Matthew," in Bornkamm, Gerhard Barth, and Heinz Joachim Held, *Tradition and Interpretation in Matthew,* trans. Percy Scott (The New Testament Library), Philadelphia: Westminster Press, 1963. This article first appeared in German in *The Background of the New Testament and Its Eschatology. In Honour of Charles Harold Dodd,* Cambridge: Cambridge University Press, 1956, pp. 222–69. Bornkamm's discussion of Matt. 5:20 is ambiguous here, however; cf. *ibid.,* pp. 16, 17 and part. p. 25, where he understands the antitheses as representing Jesus' teaching in spite of Matthew.

32. Bornkamm, p. 109.

33. *Ibid.,*

34. Cf. Ernst Lohmeyer, *Das Evangelium des Matthäus,* ed. Werner Schmauch (Meyers Kommentar), Göttingen: Vandenhoeck & Ruprecht, 1958, p. 7*; Strecker, *op. cit.,* p. 141, n. 2.

35. Bornkamm, p. 110.

36. *Ibid.,* p. 111.

37. *Ibid.,* pp. 112 f.

38. *Ibid.,* p. 117

39. Ernst Fuchs, "Glaube und Geschichte im Blick auf die Frage nach dem historischen Jesus. Eine Auseinandersetzung mit G. Bornkamms Buch über 'Jesus von Nazareth,'" in *Zur Frage nach dem historischen Jesus,* Tübingen: J. C. B. Mohr (Paul Siebeck), 1960, pp. 168–218.

40. Bornkamm, p. 117.

41. Fuchs, p. 204.

42. *Ibid.,* p. 205.

43. Fuchs, "Was heisst: 'Du sollst deinen Nächsten lieben wie dich selbst'?" *op. cit.,* p. 12.

44. *Ibid.,* p. 13.

45. *Ibid.,* p. 15.

46. *Ibid.*

47. *Ibid., p. 16*

48. *Ibid.,* p. 205.

49. *Ibid.,* p. 211. Fuchs, *ibid.,* p. 214, rightly accuses Bornkamm of "falling back into positivism" by trying to handle the commandment to love only from the point of view of Jesus' earthly ministry.

50. *Ibid.,* p. 207

51. James M. Robinson, *A New Quest of the Historical Jesus* (SBT, 25), Naperville: Alec R. Allenson, 1959.

52. *Ibid.,* pp. 66 f.

53. *Ibid.,* p. 112.

54. *Ibid.,* pp. 122 f.

55. Herbert Braun, "The Problem of a New Testament Theology," trans. Jack T. Sanders, *Journal for Theology and the Church,* I (1965), 169–83.

56. *Ibid.,* p. 171.

57. *Ibid.,* pp. 181 f.

58. *Ibid.,* p. 179.

59. *Ibid.*

60. *Ibid.,* p. 180.

61. *Ibid.,* p. 183.

62. Braun, "The Problem of a New Testament Theology," in *Toward A New Christianity: Readings in the Death of God Theology,* ed. Thomas J. J. Altizer, New York: Harcourt, Brace & World, 1967, pp. 201–15.

63. *Ibid.,* p. 183.

64. In conversation, Braun was recently willing to have himself described as a humanist who had learned something essential from Jesus.

Commands for Grown-Ups

Richard J. Mouw

This article originally appeared in *Worldview* in 1972.

I

"Modern theologians no longer explain strange Revelations about the ordinary world but tend to seek strange realms in which those Revelations will be ordinary truths." Thus Ernest Gellner in a parenthetical aside from his controversial attack on recent "linguistic philosophy" in *Words and Things*. While his judgment may apply to much that goes on in Protestant theology today, there are other contemporary Christians, those who think of themselves as "evangelicals" or traditional "confessionalists." Insisting—to toy with William of Occam's well-known dictum—that worlds are not to be created beyond necessity, evangelicals refuse to accept the "strange realms" proposed by many contemporary theologians.

They insist the Bible is more than a record from, and of, the past. In it God addresses us today with *information,* i.e., claims to be believed, truths about God and man and about *this* world, as it is, was and shall be. Those who reject this view of revelation commonly charge that it leads to consequences simply unacceptable to the reflective twentieth-century mind.

More particularly, they charge that anyone who sees the Bible as providing reliable, often specific, commands or directives for the moral life fails to understand the requirements for moral decision-making. I believe the reasoning behind the charge is hardly convincing, often being based on great confusion about what those of us who appeal to divine moral authority are really saying.

But first some preliminary comments: Defenders of the Bible's authority regularly counter caricatures and literalistic abuses of their position with a reminder that the Bible is not a textbook of natural science; neither, we must add, it is a textbook of moral science. The Bible, in the view I shall defend, is the authoritative record and vehicle of God's address to, and dealings with, man in all of his activities, projects and relationships—including those which are properly called *moral.* The Bible offers no theory of moral obligations nor a theory of moral justification; it does call man to obedience in the moral sphere as in all other spheres, and points him to the grace which empowers us to do the right and avoid the evil.

The moral philosopher, on the other hand, critically reflects upon the moral sphere, pondering the nature and foundations of moral obligation and how men ought to go about deciding what is the right thing to do. The *Christian* moral philosopher deals with the same questions but with a conscious recognition of his membership in a community to which God has spoken a word on, among other things, moral matters. The Christian moral philosopher concerns himself with the *status* of divine directives in Christian moral reasonings. He puzzles about what it means that these directives were first addressed to people in cultural and political settings quite different from our own. On occasion, he engages in apologetics, spelling out what he sees as a plausible moral perspective, in response to critics. The apologist may answer charges directly or, as I will attempt, he may challenge his critics' assumptions.

Talk about divine moral commands is extremely unpopular. The belief that there is something fundamentally wrong about people submitting to moral direction "imposed" upon them from "above" or "without" seems to be one of the few beliefs capable of uniting thinkers of otherwise divergent philosophies. Whether it be Bertrand Russell articulating the *credo* of the "free man," or Jean-Paul Sartre denouncing "bad faith," or Julian Huxley preaching a "religion without revelation," or Herbert Marcuse envisioning man's final "liberation"—all agree that submission to "external" moral authority is incompatible with a proper understanding of "the good life."

Agreement on this score is not limited to intellectuals; it even seems capable of bridging the "generation gap." Compare the counter-culture's "do your own thing" with Frank Sinatra's musical *apologia:* that, granted all the mistakes and hurts, at least this much is true, and that is what really matters—"I did it *my* way."

The arguments given for rejecting moral "heteronomy," especially as they relate to the traditional understanding of Christian morality, deserve a closer examination. Patrick Nowell-Smith, for example, has recently attacked the whole enterprise of Christian ethics on the grounds that it promotes an "infantile" morality with the "characteristics of deontology, heteronomy, and realism, which are proper and indeed necessary in the development of a child, but not proper to an adult" ("Morality: Religious and Secular" in *Christian Ethics and Contemporary Philosophy,* edited by Ian Ramsey). And, in the professed service of Christian ethics, Graeme de Graaff insists that "there is no room in morality for commands, whether they are the father's, the schoolmaster's or the priest's. There is still no room for them when they are God's commands" ("God and Morality" in *Christian Ethics and Contemporary Philosophy*).

DeGraaff's charge, as stated, is simply false. There is at least one condition under which an adult moral agent might have a clear moral obligation to obey commands; for instance, when he made an intelligent *promise* to do so and has no overriding reason to break the promise. If, for example, when Mother Mary told the servants at the Cana wedding feast, "Do whatsoever he commands you," they had answered by promising to do so, then they had at least a *prima facie* moral obligation to *Mary* to obey the Lord's commands.

But those who are suspicious of commands in morality surely have something more basic in mind than this; they are skeptical of a moral system in which "externally" imposed commands have a *central* place. This skepticism is closely related to ideas about psychological development, as is obvious in Nowell-Smith's comments.

The work of the Swiss psychologist Jean Piaget (whom, incidentally, Nowell-Smith cites in support of his position) is important to their argument. In outlining the stages of the moral development of the child, Piaget describes a "heteronomous" stage, characterized by "the primitive consciousness of duty" and in which "duty is nothing more than the acceptance of commands received from without." This stage precedes that of "autonomy," in which a rigid sense of duty is replaced by a "morality of goodness." The child begins to reflect on the point of moral rules and begins "to appeal to reason in order to bring unity into the moral material."

Perhaps Christian morality, of the sort that stresses obedience to commands, results from inadequate moral development, a "freezing" at the heteronomous stage. This arrested development might be compared with Piaget's account of a *normal* transition from the heteronomous stage to the autonomous one:

> It seems to us an undeniable fact that in the course of the child's mental development, unilateral respect or the respect felt by the small for the great plays an essential part: it is what makes the child accept all the commands transmitted to him by his parents and is thus the great factor of continuity between different generations. But it seems to us no less undeniable . . . that as the child grows in years the nature of his respect changes. In so far as individuals decide questions on an equal footing—no matter whether subjectively or objectively—the pressure they exercise upon each other becomes collateral [this and other quotations from Piaget's *The Moral Judgment of the Child*].

The normal transition from heteronomy to autonomy, then, is intimately related to a change in the child's attitude toward the one who issues commands: the more the child sees the commander as a person like himself, that is, the more the respect between the commander and the commandee becomes mutual, the less the child will look outside himself for moral authority. A person whose moral development is arrested at the heteronomous stage has failed to come to see a particular moral commander as an equal, or near equal, to himself.

II

Critics of Christian morality, however, do not accuse Christians of assigning an undeserved role to the moral commands of human beings, of parents, for example, but of God. Piaget's theory might be extended in this way: A person whose heteronomy is frozen at the level of the God-Man relationship is one who has failed to come to see *God* as an equal, or near equal, to himself. Put this way, the proposition hardly seems worthy of serious consideration. For "mature" morality also involves, surely, the sincere desire to be faithful to the facts as one sees them. A Christian who outgrows a morality because it fails to see the equality, or near equality, of God and Man, or because it involves the sort of "respect felt by the small for the great," would be in rather direct conflict with some central Christian beliefs, among them the belief that God and Man are *not* equal, nor even nearly equal, with respect to greatness, moral or otherwise.

Appeals to the type of psychological developmental theory espoused by Piaget are irrelevant to the question of whether a moral system can legitimately emphasize obedience to *divine* commands; at least the relevance of such appeals is not obvious without some subsidiary arguments, such as attempting to demonstrate God's moral non-supremacy.

The case can be put another way. Imagine a person who undergoes a normal transition from the heteronomous stage to the autonomous one. Imagine further that the spirit of autonomy inspires him to reflect much on moral questions. Questions about the nature and grounds of the moral life occupy his mind to the extent that in his conversation, reading and study he concentrates on man's moral relationships, finally earning a Ph.D. or two in the process, even spending some time studying under Piaget at the University of Geneva. Suppose that as a result of all of this he concludes: (a) men are capable of, even prone to, considerable self-deceptions and confusion regarding moral matters; (b) the moral state of mankind is so sorry that any reliable moral guidance from "the outside" would be welcome.

Christians are committed to views very similar to those arrived at by our hypothetical seeker. They hold that sin has affected human capacity for moral deliberation to the degree that we are desperately in need of moral guidance, and that such guidance is available: for an omniscient, omnibenevolent moral agent has publicly spoken on moral matters.

If a person can reasonably believe Christian teachings about human sinfulness and about God's moral nature, then it is also reasonable to accept the implications of such beliefs for the moral life and

Christian moral decision-making. A proper challenge to the Christian notion of obedience must go beyond basically psychological claims about the "maturity" of Christian morality and question the existence and nature of God and/or the existence and nature of sin.

III

The Christian brand of heteronomy, as distinct from the heteronomy discussed by Piaget, might be termed a *mature* heteronomy. Here the attitude of commandee to commander is one of mature trust, legitimate respect and responsible obedience. In the Scriptures God calls humanity to enter into convenant with Him, a relationship based upon a proper understanding of God's authority and the human condition, and a free, responsible acceptance of the covenantal obligations.

Often criticisms of the Christian ethic of obedience to divine commands presuppose that the Christian view of the God-Man relationship must be understood in terms of the "despotic" model (Bertrand Russell's favorite charge). Thus, Erich Fromm presents the bibilical story of the fall into sin:

> Acting aganist God's orders means freeing himself from coercion, emerging from the unconscious existence of prehuman life to the level of man. Acting against the command of authority, committing a sin, is in its positive human aspect the first act of freedom, that is, the first *human* act. In the myth the sin in its formal aspect is the eating of the tree of knowledge. The act of disobedience as an act of freedom is the beginning of reason [*Escape From Freedom*].

Fromm sees two options open to us in our attempt to relate to the rest of reality: "submission" to some external power or authority, thereby sacrificing one's individuality, or engaging in a "spontaneous relationship to man and nature" in such a way that one's individuality is kept intact. Obedience to divine commands is obviously, for him, the first kind or relationship. But note how he describes the second relationship: its expressions "are rooted in the integration and strength of the total personality and are therefore subject to the very limits that exist for the growth of the self." The Christian, faced with the choice, might well *choose* this second option as Fromm describes it. For the Christian understands his relationship to God not in terms of the despotic model which characterizes Fromm's "submission" but as an involvement in a "growth process" which, as Fromm puts it, recognizes that the process is "subject to" (must *submit* to?) certain "limits." The rub comes, of course, when we ask questions such as: *what* limits? from what *source*? in what sorts of *activity* does the "total personality" derive its "strength"? Here the Christian insists that the debate over the "reasonableness" of divine commands cannot be carried on apart from a discussion of differing views of the nature of man. The fact that Christians *do* have a view on that subject, one intimately related to their account of moral values, is not enough to distinguish the Christian's position from Fromm's or from anyone else's.

In spelling out the way in which his view of human nature affects his understanding of our moral situation, the Christian cannot avoid speaking of the *sin* which, as he sees it, characterizes our present, fallen condition. Two aspects of that condition are important to the present discussion. The first is the role that *self-deception* plays in human life. In the biblical account of man's fall, Eve deliberately chose to pretend to a role, or office, which she knew full well she could not fill: she succumbed to the Tempter's challenge that she "be like God." This primal act of self-deception extends itself into all areas of human activity. In the moral realm it shows up in the form of *rationalization,* the "inventing" of reasons for doing what ought not to be done.

Christians are not alone in recognizing the pervasive force of self-deception in human affairs. In recent years the intellectual community has been sensitized to its presence on the corporate level, especially as *national* self-deception about race relations and foreign policy. This sensitivity, however, is not always as acute in dealing with self-deception on the intimate, personal level. Jean-Paul Sartre, in *Being and Nothingness,* does present a fairly comprehensive picture of the role of self-deception in "bad faith projects," although Sartre isn't very clear in proposing an antidote to that condition.

The Christian insists that the self-understanding necessary to being freed from self-deception can only come in the light of some external, transcendent *standard*. As John Calvin put it:

> It is certain that man never achieves a clear knowledge of himself unless he has first looked upon God's face, and then descends from contemplating him to scrutinize himself. For we always seem to ourselves righteous and upright and wise and holy—this pride is innate in all of us—unless by clear proofs we stand convinced of our own unrighteousness, foulness, folly, and impurity [*Institutes of the Christian Religion,* Book I].

A second, and related aspect is the Christian attitude toward *vulnerability*. Paul Goodman describes the fear of being vulnerable in this way:

> If a man is not continually proving his potency, his mastery of others and of himself, he becomes prey to a panic of being defeated and victimized. Every vital function must therefore be used as a means of proving or it is felt as a symptom of weakness. Simply to enjoy, produce, learn, give or take, love or be angry (rather than cool), is to be vulnerable [*People or Personnel and Like a Conquered Province*].

Goodman suggests that this fear of vulnerability stems from our accepting the "top-down management" model, first expressed in the modern era in the external forms of political and social organization, and gradually "internalized," producing the internal strife he describes. He proposes a de-structuring of the present modes of social/political life which will result in corresponding benefits for the individual psyche.

Theologically conservative Christians see the development of this model differently but agree with Goodman on the *fundamental* nature of one's attitude toward vulnerability. This is the question addressed by St. Paul when he speaks of "bondage" and "liberty" in a way that seems, to the secular mind, to have things reversed. For in the Christian view, the life dedicated to the "proving" of one's sovereign mastery over men and things is a life of fearful "bondage"; to be made capable of obedience when that is the proper response, of self-less service when that is required, of recognizing and submitting to expertise and correction when that is what is being offered—that is "liberation."

IV

In arguing for the position that God has commanded us to act in certain ways, I would distinguish between a *direct moral justification* and an *indirect moral justification* for a given course of action. A person has a *direct* justification for a course of action if he reasonably believes it to be supported, in the light of all relevant factual information, by what he takes to be the correct moral criteria. A utilitarian, for example, would offer as justification for a specific act of, say, physically harming another person the consideration that, in the light of all available relevant factual information, the act will produce more good consequences than bad. A deontologist, on the other hand, might offer as a justification for the same act the consideration that, while the act, as an act of harming another person, is *prima facie* wrong, the act has additional moral features, the presence of which overrides the *prima facie* wrongness of the act *qua* act of harming another person.

An *indirect* moral justification for a course of action is different. Suppose one holds that an act is morally justified if, and only if, it possesses property p (for instance, being productive of the greatest good, or being one's actual duty); suppose also that p is not directly accessible with respect to a given course of action. But there might be some other distinct, and accessible, property q (for instance, that the action is recommended by someone with an expert grasp of the matter), the possession of which makes the possession of p either logically certain or inductively probable (other things being equal). In such a case, one could accept the presence of q as reason for believing that the action also possesses p—that is, as reason for believing the action is justified.

As we can distinguish between direct and indirect justification, so we can make a further distinction in the question itself: "What *makes* something right?" is different from "How do *we* go about *deciding* what is right?" A moral system *may* offer the same answer to both questions; but it *need* not, for they are different questions.

I am not saying here that because God commands something we have a *direct* justification for considering it to be right. (Thus, my arguments here are not in support of the view that "such-and-such is right" *means* "God commands such-and such"—although I suspect some variation on that statement might plausibly be defended). Here I maintain the minimal view that God's commanding something provides at least an indirect justification for believing that course of action to be morally right.

Failure to make this sort of distinction can lead to confusion in discussing morality and God's commands. For example, this by Wolfhart Pannenberg:

> The proclamation of imperatives backed by divine authority is not very persuasive today. No doubt some people do not steal or commit adultery because God has forbidden such behavior. But presumably their number is fast declining. In a rationally organized world people are accustomed to act according to reasons, even if they do frequently fail to follow their better insights. To disobey an imperative that is proclaimed without clear reasons and effective sanctions will appear wrong to fewer and fewer people [*Theology and the Kingdom of God*].

The comment is puzzling for several reasons, not least because it is *sociological* in nature—how people today are "accustomed to act" and what "will appear to be wrong" to them—and most thinkers since Hume have been somewhat embarrassed to derive normative conclusions from such premises. (That Pannenberg *intends* a normative conclusion is apparent in the sentence immediately following these remarks: "Neither can the appeal to conscience provide absolute norms for behavior.")

Furthermore, if appeals to the way in which the contemporary world is "organized" *are* legitimate, one could as well argue that we live in an age of *specialization,* in which it is often impossible for individuals to possess "clear reasons" for the guidelines and claims they act upon. I might, for example, be perfectly justified (in the indirect sense) in reporting to my wife that I have an ulcer, and acting upon the belief that my report is true, if I had received the diagnosis from a physician whom I know to possess the proper credentials—even though I could not explain precisely what an ulcer is, or intelligently refute the claim that I have a hiatal hernia instead.

It would perhaps be nice if we could personally explain and provide (direct) justifications for all the directives we act upon. But in the absence of such personal expertise it is not *unreasonable* to trust authorities whose credentials have been reasonably established. Of course it may be that people today are not, for the most part, *interested* in God's credentials. But to have one's credentials ignored is not the same as losing them.

V

A morality based on obedience to divine commands cannot be attacked, it should be clear by now, without also challenging a complex of beliefs with which it is intimately associated. To attack such a morality on pscychological grounds is to enter into a discussion of issues which go far beyond questions of psychological development. Appeals to "maturity," or "freedom," or "rationality," open up legitimate questions about the theoretical framework in which those terms are understood. Ultimately, one is led to issues relating to the existence and nature of the deity, and of man's condition, and to fundamental questions concerning the *locus* of moral authority.

Yet another frequent criticism of the sort of morality I have been defending is that it makes things too *easy,* that in the final analysis it must be judged to be, if not incoherent, then at least *stultifying* in its effects on human beings. There is an element of plausibility in this charge, for the attitudes and behavior of Christians who profess to be living in obedience to God's moral directives have often been marked by a lack of moral concern and struggle.

This syndrome, howver, is due more to an indifference to the complex world in which we live than to some intrinsic fault in the Christian moral posture. Anyone who seriously commits himself to passionate involvement in human struggles soon realizes that it is impossible to remain morally "pure." The Christian faces many situations in which he must violate at least one of God's commands. This suggests, I think, that divine moral commands inform us of our *prima facie* duties. A *prima facie* duty is one which we ought to perform "all else being equal"; that is, we must do it unless it is overridden by some "weightier" duty.

The difficulty comes in the weighing, of course, but this is a difficulty for *any* morality that recognizes the binding-ness of more than one duty. His claim to be a recipient of divine moral directives does not free the Christian from the complexity and agony of moral decision-making. For man—to generalize upon an ancient teaching—was not made for the Law; rather, the moral Law was made for man. The commands of God are no pattern for a life of isolated "purity," but directives for following the way of service and self-sacrificing love.

In this light one recognizes the unfairness of Joseph Fletcher's charge that a morality based on specific Scriptural guidelines is a "prefab morality" which serves as "a kind of neurotic security device to simplify moral decisions" (in *Situation Ethics*). The position I have outlined involves struggles which might differ from those experienced by Fletcher and others, but it does not necessarily simplify the moral life; in addition to the dilemmas described above, there is the ongoing and difficult hermeneutical and theological work necessary to getting the directives themselves straight.

What this morality offers, then, is not simplicity; it does offer *hope*. While the One who first gave those directives did so on a mountain, He meant them as guidelines for travel in the wilderness. Knowing well the gap between the sketchiness of the guidelines and the rough places in the wilderness, He added a promise: "Behold, I send an Angel before thee, to keep thee in the way, and to bring thee into the place I have prepared" (Ex. 23:20).

The Actual Impact
of the Moral Norms
of the New Testament:
Report from the
International Theological
Commission

Text by Hans Schürmann
Introduction and Commentary
by Philippe Delhaye

This article originally appeared in *Esprit et Vie* in 1975.

A. INTRODUCTION

1. Framework for the Research

We hear with some frequency nowadays that there are three major types of morality. And as the world moves from conformity to a return to sources and to a questioning of all things, it is necessary to take due note of the fact that all these moral codes, in seeking to provide the individual with a valid life scheme and society with a few rules for peaceful coexistence or cooperation, do not have a great variety of options open to them. One is tempted to sum up the possible ethical bases in these three words: God, man, society.

The state, or society, will give priority to the group, and will demand sacrifices in its name. It is the will or the views of a strong leader, of a privileged oligarchy, or, conversely, of the republic of comrades that will determine what is to be done or not done.

Man is the basis and criterion for another type of moral code, which we find in Kant and also in Aristotle and the Stoics. The foundation of this code of ethics consists of knowing the nature of man. It is by acting in the sense intended by Nature (which, for some, is God or a creature of God) that man himself finds his dignity and attains happiness.

A theological type of morality stresses the relationship (of subject, of creature, of salvation) between man and God in a pact, a covenant, which, at its peak, means revelation and grace. In all religious moralities there are sacred books. These books have an impact on life, because they contain a history of salvation that is manifested in facts and in words, some of which imply intellectual faith in a dogma and others a life pursuant to that faith and to the standards that it entails. In this spirit, Christian morality is called "the law of faith" (Rom 3:28).

It is clearly within the context of giving priority to this religious morality that, from its very first five-year term (1969–1974), the International Theological Commission (I.T.C.)[1] undertook research on the "criteria of Christian moral knowledge." This involved an inquiry into both the methodology of morality and its criteriology. In the abstract, the two questions are not the same. To ask "how one distinguishes moral good from moral evil" is not the same as to try to find out what authority one appeals to to determine the criteria. But, in point of fact, it is nearly impossible to separate these two types of research, both because of the haste of non-experts pressed to come up with practical conclusions and because of the scruples of the experts who are afraid to force the meaning of scriptural texts in trying to fit them into our intellectual categories.

The sub-commission that worked from 1969 to 1974 was fortunate to have among its members two top-ranking exegetes: Fr. Feuillet, P.S.S., one of the most dependable professors at the Faculty of Theology of Paris[2] and Fr. Schürmann, professor at the Erfurt Regional Seminary (East Germany). Both of these men have accumulated a vast documentation whose importance and impact scholars have been able to evaluate in a number of publications.

At the same time, groups of *periti* were expanding the inquiry to other fields and to other aspects of the question. We shall mention only the group headed by Fr. Gilbert, which will shortly be giving us a volume on the Christian morality of the Old Testament, the group headed by Msgr. Descamps who, as early as the 1950's, was attempting to identify the moral directives of the Synoptics.[3]

2. The Meaning of the Schürmann Text

The second phase of the I.T.C.'s work began with the second five-year term, in the summer of 1974. The poor state of health of Fr. Feuillet had forced him to indicate a desire not to be reappointed. Prof. Schürmann continued on alone, but with a major effort and great power of synthesis.[4] He had just presented a particularly remarkable paper to the XII Congress of Polish Biblical Scholars, held in Breslau in September.[5]

At the same time, Prof. Schürmann had followed very closely the development of attempts to reduce scriptural moral norms to the status of superstructure for a particular age and milieu. He was especially familiar with Paul's writings. But—as all those who have attempted to venture a moral theology based on biblical sources have discovered—the Pauline writings abound in admonitory passages, in directives that at times are general, at times specific. Paul settles cases of conscience and sets forth principles for doing so. He freely provides lists of moral acts (the fruits of the Spirit in Galatians 5; the practical directives of charity in 1 Corinthians 13). To speak accurately and precisely, it is to Paul that we must address ourselves, not exclusively but in a privileged manner. It is to him that the currently debated questions must be posed. The profound unity of his New Testament morality makes it possible to resort to this process of pedagogical simplification (no. 2 in the Schürmann text; subsequent references in parentheses will also be to the Schürmann text which is found at the end of this chapter).

If one wishes therefore to understand Prof. Schürmann's text with profit and to do justice to it, it is necessary to take into consideration the impact of a certain number of literary "reduction" processes. Underlying this text, one must be mindful of the more complete Breslau text, and not overlook the work by Fr. Feuillet or the *periti* which the author, the morality sub-commission and the Commission itself took into consideration, in varying degrees, of course, depending on varying degrees of commitment to an active project. In any event, the I.T.C. called upon one of its people to formulate some initial conclusions, which it then approved by a wide margin, asking him also to publish his work.

There was also a "reduction" process as regards the object of the inquiry. The Old Testament always attracts the attention of the Christian moralist and/or the Christian faithful. But it poses its own special problems and, in any event, its essential values are captured in the New Testament (no. 2, no. 11a).

Among the authors of the Christian Bible, Paul was a particularly forceful figure, as we have just recalled, following the lead of the author himself (no. 3). While Paul did not know Christ in the flesh, he did receive the mandate to preach his faith and his morality. He is capable of making a clear distinction between the orders of the Lord and those that he himself formulates (no. 3). Through him, today's reader goes back to the very sources of revelation, in conjunction with the ageless Church, but more particularly with the Church that still had in its midst those who had retained the memory of the words of the Lord, garnered from his mouth or rapidly crystallized into early catechetical teachings. These *apostoli,* these *viri apostolici* (D.V. 18) were marked by the Spirit (no. 3).

Special note should be made of the texts of nos. 7 and 12. The latter, which is a conclusion, speaks of "requirements and admonitions . . . that seek to bind unconditionally, and that transcend all historical diversity." No. 7 summarizes the various reasons for this permanence of the Christian requirement:

(a) the attitudes and words of Jesus:
(b) the conduct and teaching of the apostles and other "spirituals" of the Christian beginnings;
(c) the life style and tradition of the early communities, at a time when the nascent Church was still marked in a very special way by the Spirit of truth;
(d) the action of this Spirit, announced by the Lord Jesus: "Many things yet I have to say to you, but you cannot bear them now. But when he, the Spirit of truth, has come, he will teach you all the truth" (Jn 16:12–13)

This does not mean that reflection or Christian life is locked into a mere repetition pattern and that it is alien to the signs of the

times. But, as Prof. Schürmann also says (no. 12): "It is only by being attentive to the Word of God (*Verbum Dei audiens*) (cf. D.V. 1)
that it is possible to interpret without danger the signs of the times.
The work of discernment must be undertaken within the community
of God's people, in the unity of the *sensus fidelium* and of the magisterium, aided by theology."

It is in this spirit that the author of the report will attempt to
solve the problem of the impact of early Christian moral standards
on the life of today's faithful. In terms of exegesis (no. 2), the question arises as to what St. Paul, and in general all the New Testament
authors, meant to say in transmitting the Christian message. On the
hermeneutical level (no. 2 and no. 12), he analyzes this question: Did
the sacred authors, and, earlier, Jesus himself, formulate rules for living that transcend history and require permanent attitudes, or did
they only present and set forth "models" and "paradigms"?

These terms may seem surprising, particularly since they have
acquired new meanings in the human sciences in recent years. It is
not possible to avoid using them, since it is often in terms of this vocabulary that the question of the permanence of the moral teachings
of Jesus and the apostles is often posed nowadays. It is important to
see that the paradigm in question, then, does not involve a rule of
grammar, but rather a declension: *rosa, rosae, rosam,* which indeed
retains a language pattern, but can also be applied to some very different words. The first declension also applies to *regina* or to *auriga.*
Therefore, the paradigm is the element that can vary without any
variation in the linguistic structure of the syntagma.

In applying this approach to the morality of the New Testament, some will say that the content of the norms may change according to historical circumstances, but that faithfulness to Jesus
implies only that one act out of radical obedience to an ideal (Bultmann), or seek the liberation of man (J.-B. Metz). The "model" referred to here is not the miniature model carefully copied from the
object reproduced, nor even a person one chooses to imitate. According to the vocabulary of structuralism, it is "a simplifying mental image interposed between reality and structure, the observer and the
object of his observation."[6]

Expressing these concepts in a different way, one might think of
the difference intended when a present-day American speaker uses

the optative "should" or the imperative "must." The optative is the interpretation proposed by those for whom the Pauline models and paradigms represented real values in his time but that cannot be retained as such for our times. These ideals can be explained by the circumstances of the time, but are not suited to our own situation. It is in this connection that some bring up the prohibition on premarital relations.

In the other interpretation, that of a permanent norm, premarital relations are prohibited today as they were yesterday because, in God's creative and redemptive idea, marital relations are co-extensive with the commitment and sacrament of marriage. There are, therefore, some permanent obligations in the imperative mood even if, obviously, prudence must always intervene when it is a question of reflecting them correctly in life.

The first response is in terms of reason and experience, enlightened, to be sure, by the *memoria Christi* (memory of Christ). The second response feels that Christ calls us, and *obligates us,* always in the same way, though without dispensing us from responding to him with discernment. If I may be permitted a curious blending of two formulations; one by St. Anselm, the other from Vatican II, I might suggest: *fides moribus applicanda et quaerens intellectum* (faith applied to morality and seeking understanding).

B. COMMENTARY

1. The Mystery of Christ as Moral Standard

The mistake made in early attempts at a Bible-based morality may have been the almost exclusive search for formulas set forth by Christ that could be transformed into strict and precise rules. But formulating a law is an eminently more difficult task than people once imagined it to be. Think for a moment of the obstacles encountered by highly competent experts trying to translate the rich and nuanced teachings of Vatican II into the precise pronouncements of canon law. If that was true of the Council, how much more difficult a task when the New Testament is involved.

To get around this problem, a number of theologians have proposed that a distinction be made in Christian morality between a "transcendental" aspect and another "categorical" aspect. The first would deal with the foundations of morality and with an overall orientation, and the second with attitudes in the various "categories" of concrete actions. Schürmann, for his part, rejected this distinction which, while "operational," is nevertheless a return to Kantianism, where fundamental options encounter nothing but empty categories. He retains, however, that which had drawn certain recent moral theologians toward these formulations by distinguishing various degrees of Christian commitment (no. 6 and no. 11). We will come back to this point.

But first, we must point out in particular how Schürmann refuses to distinguish specific words and acts of Christ from a profound attitude of Christ. The Lord in his entire personality is our law. His words are to be interpreted on the basis of the person of the dead and risen Christ continuing his action through the light and grace of the Spirit (no. 6). And so, for us, the law of Christ is essentially assimilation with him, so that this morality has an external element, words, and an internal element, the grace of the Holy Spirit given to each believer (no. 4). "I am not without the law of God but am under the law of Christ. . . . Be imitators of me as I am of Christ" writes St. Paul to the Corinthians (1 Cor 9:21; 11:1).

To live as a Christian, St. Paul says to the Galatians, is essentially to "walk in the Spirit" (5:16), which produces in us, with our collaboration, "his fruit" which is "charity, joy, peace, patience, kindness, goodness, faith, modesty, continency" (5:22–23). Therefore, we will avoid the "works of the flesh: immorality, uncleanness, licentiousness, idolatry, witchcraft, enmities, contentions, jealousies, anger, quarrels, factions, envy, murders, drunkenness, carousings, and suchlike" which prevent those who do them from "attaining the kingdom of God" (5:19–21). St. Thomas would later say, in a very beautiful text that is very much underutilized in teaching: "There is a twofold element in the law of the Gospel. The principal element is the grace of the Holy Spirit that is given to us internally. Another, secondary, element, consists of the documents of the faith and the precepts that govern human attitudes and acts."[7]

The morality of Christ is therefore a vast complex whole in which one finds the grace of the Spirit, pre-paschal directives (no. 4), words and examples rethought in terms of the mystery of life and death, as well as in terms of the divinity of Christ (no. 4 and no. 5 of Schürmann's text).

This morality has, to be sure, an eschatological orientation, and Schürmann recalls it (no. 10): "We must act in love and in faith in accordance . . . with the advent of eschatological salvation. . . . We must allow ourselves to be conditioned in hope by the proximity of the kingdom, that is, the second coming, in continuing vigilance and readiness."

But entering into the paschal sacrifice of Christ, his life in the love of the Father and of the brethren is "even more characteristic of New Testament morality than its eschatological orientation" (no. 5).

More than ever, then, it is necessary to grasp the meaning of the incarnation and redemptive work of Christ, as well as, for the Christian, of a life with Christ (no. 5). Christ's life is essentially the manifestation of God's love. "But God commends his charity toward us, because when as yet we were sinners, Christ died for us" (Rom 5:8). In Christ, this implies kenosis, self-emptying, service, humility, obedience unto the death of the cross. *Cum in forma Dei esset . . . semetipsum exinanivit . . . humiliavit semetipsum factus oboediens usque ad mortem, mortem autem crucis* (Phil. 2:6–11).

This implies a similar attitude among Christians: *Hoc enim sentite in vobis quod est in Christo Jesu* (Phil 2:5). "Behave among yourselves as one behaves in Jesus Christ" is the version of the Ecumenical Bible, whereas Osty prefers: "Have you the same thought that was in Christ Jesus." The apostle immediately attaches to this fundamental attitude certain concrete forms of praxis which are, above all, the concrete expression of this attitude: to live in full harmony, with one heart, to do nothing out of contentiousness or out of vainglory, but in humility (Phil 2:1–4).

Schürmann certainly did not find his interpretation of St. Paul in Nygren, but how can we fail to note the resemblance, through reference to the same sources, between this I.T.C. document and Nygren's book *Eros et Agapé.*[8] This book was a shock for many people in the 1950's because it pointed out the disguised Pelagianism of a certain moralism and because of its perception of the novelty of Christian love. To love is no longer to desire, as in Plato, Aristotle or Epicurus, it is to give. And it is to give not because of the merits of the one to whom one is doing good, for sinners had no more claim on

God's goodness than our enemies or those who are indifferent to us have on ours.

Of course, there has to be reciprocity and response so that morality can reach its normal level in the other also, just as the Father awaits the return of the prodigal son (Lk 15:11–32) in order to reestablish with him the bonds of friendship. But the Christian is equally obligated to love the one who ignores and neglects him, like the heavenly Father who does good even to the ungrateful and the wicked. "If you love those who love you, what merit have you? For even sinners love those who love them. . . . But love your enemies and do good . . . and your reward shall be great, and you shall be the children of the Most High, for God is kind toward the ungrateful and evil. Be merciful, therefore, even as your Father is merciful" (Lk 6:32–36).

The Christian is a new creature who lives no longer for self but for God and for others (no. 5). One's concrete daily contacts with the world itself are changed (no. 5). This requirement of love, radical but real, is truly the characteristic feature of Christian morality (no. 5).

"*In finem dilexit eos . . .*" (Jn 13:4). This text, to which Schürmann twice makes reference in speaking of precepts that go to the very end (no. 11), is truly "the law" of the New Testament: the central requirement of the New Testament writings (no. 10) which, as a precept that "goes to the very end," demands an absolutely binding form, consists of an exhortation to make a total gift of self in Christ to the Father: faith, hope and charity are truly the essential points of Pauline morality (no. 10). But charity is pre-eminent: it is with regard to charity that the apostle of the Gentiles speaks of "the law of Christ" (Gal 6:2). John presents it as the "new commandment" (Jn 13:14; 15:12; 1 Jn 2:7ff). In it is "fulfilled" the law of the Old Testament (Gal 5:14; Rom 13:6; Mt 7:13; 22:40) (no. 11).

2. The Various Degrees of Christian Commitment in the Divine Mystery

Every word of God, every Christian norm that tends toward a radical giving, is, in and of itself, a rule of life that transcends differences of time and place (no. 6). This, however, does not mean that every word of Christ is to be taken literally, or that all Christian precepts are of equal standing. Certain casuists have been justifiably reprimanded for not distinguishing between levels of importance of different laws or between the various degrees of commitment to or against Christ, disregarding, for instance, the part played in Christian life by the fundamental option and high points of conversion.

In connection with the need for interpretation, Schürmann aptly makes reference to certain passages from the early catechesis of the Sermon on the Mount and to certain Pauline applications of the Lord's precepts.

Some passages of the Sermon on the Mount have, indeed, always been taken by commentators in a spiritual sense, in the sense that, in our present-day vocabulary, corresponds to what is called a model or paradigm (no. 6). Let us cite here Matthew 6:17: "But you, when you fast, anoint your head and wash your face"; Matthew 6:35: "Do not be anxious for your life, what you shall eat; nor yet for your body, what you shall put on"; and, finally, the famous saying of Matthew 5:39 harshly criticized by Kruschchev during his visit to the United States: "If someone strikes you on the right cheek, turn to him the other also." St. Thomas,[9] for instance, sees these as vivid ways of expressing the danger of transforming mortification into ostentation, the rejection of absolutized material concerns, and not a rejection of work and advance planning, the promotion of a willingness to forgive that does not extend to eliminating essential defense. Or these texts might be considered as counsels for the perfect. It would hardly have been necessary to repeat this here if, in the current advocacy of relativism, people did not use these paradoxical texts to eliminate every norm, even one based on the essential norm of love-as-giving.

Perhaps more noteworthy is the passage where Schürmann (no. 6) considers the interpretation that Paul gives to some words of Jesus.[10] Jesus counsels those he has sent to live without bad conscience on what their hearers will furnish or provide them, for "the laborer deserves his wages" (Lk 10:7). But Paul tells the Corinthians (1 Cor 9:14–15) that, while he has this right, he does not exercise it and prefers to support himself by his own labor. Was St. Paul not pastorally justified in renouncing this right that he reaffirms?

In the case of the "Pauline privilege" (1 Cor 7:12–16), one may see a weakening of the indissolubility of marriage proclaimed by Christ; and this clearly shows that before applying a Gospel dictum, one must be sure of avoiding the legalism (no. 6) and "biblicism" of the *Scriptura sola,* ignoring the tradition of the Church (no. 3 and no. 12). It took a long time for the Church to make it clear that this indissolubility applied only to a consummated sacramental marriage, but from the outset St. Paul understood, as Allo says in his *Commentaire de la Première aux Corinthiens,*[11] that the "sacramental bond was not established by the mere fact that the converted spouse gave his or her consent to continuance of the relationship, so long as the consent of the other party remained in abeyance." How could such a union have been inserted into the *mysterion* of Christ and into his own love as a spouse (Eph 5:33)?

While it is necessary, therefore, to distinguish different types of Christian norms, it is necessary to establish criteria that remain as far removed from biblicist literalism or fundamentalism as they are from the rationalism that judges Scripture in the name of purely human intelligence and experience (no. 12). Schürmann, along with some Bible scholars or moralists of our own time, lists some of these criteria for determining the actual impact of New Testament norms (no. 8 and no. 9).

The first criterion is, of course, the link with the Christian moral condition itself, which is the response of radical love to God. To the extent that a word of Christ or a text of the apostles speaks about this life with God and for God, it cannot be the subject of any modification. When St. Paul says to the Romans (6:10–11): "Thus consider yourselves also as dead to sin, but alive to God in Christ Jesus," he draws the unavoidable conclusions of their insertion through baptism into the mystery of the dead and resurrected Christ: "For the death that he died, he died to sin once for all, but the life that he lives, he lives unto God."

A second criterion is found in the intensity and frequency of parenetic statements: St. Paul mentions on twenty occasions the three great "gifts" (1 Cor 12:31) of faith, hope and charity. On some thirty occasions, he uses the theme of conscience, the meeting place between God and the human person: it is necessary to consider this in a different light than the two calls to silence addressed to women (1 Cor 14:34; 1 Tim 2:11).[12]

Finally, an analysis will be made of the purpose for which certain rules of conduct were formulated. It is important to know whether the apostles were thinking of the essential union with Christ or only of good order and discipline at gatherings (cf. 1 Cor 14:26–29).

These criteria make perfect sense when we see how Schürmann applies them to arrive at a hierarchy of norms.[13] And we can now look more closely at the degrees of applicability of the rules of conduct and the Christian standards expressed in Holy Scripture. This list may initially seem long to some, but it is the only means of avoiding the kind of simplification that would lead on the one hand to rigidity, and on the other to relativism.

(a) *General Attitudes*

A first type of Christian requirements has to do with general attitudes of praxis at both the intentional and action levels. There are, essentially, two aspects to this (no. 10):

* the central and radical requirement of total giving of self to the Father in Christ. This is an absolute obligation.
* formal principles of behavior that express the requirement of baptismal life, the response to the eschatological call. This applies primarily but not exclusively to faith, hope and charity. Here, too, one must speak of an unconditional and binding value.

(b) *Special Attitudes*

In the light of these general principles, New Testament morality demands certain attitudes that govern special areas of concrete existence. The obligation is just as permanent and transhistorical, but it is modified according to the content of the norms (no. 11). The Schürmann report presents three major types of special obligations.

(1) New Testament moral rules concerning concrete forms of love of neighbor. Along with Chapter 2 of the Epistle to the Philippians cited above, we might mention Chapter 4 of 1 Thessalonians, in which St. Paul distinguishes a fundamental will of God pertaining to a holy life (haec est enim voluntas Dei: "Thelema tou theou" v. 3), from precepts given by the Lord Jesus (quae precepta dederim vobis, "paraggelias," v. 2), including a warning against any behavior that would be detrimental to a brother or sister (v. 6).

One can also recall the final discourses of the Lord, with the exhortation to wash the feet of the brothers and sisters (13:14): "If, therefore, I the Lord and Master have washed your feet, you also ought to wash the feet of one another," along with the new commandment (Jn 13:34), also based on the Lord's example: "As I have loved you, you also should love one another." Washing the feet of the brethren had a meaning when everybody walked around in sandals or barefoot. Today, as the Church has readily understood, this can now only be a symbolic ceremony accomplished out of fidelity to the memory of the Lord. But what remains is the spirit of this directive: one must humble oneself before others; to render them the humblest of services, one must assume the attitude of a slave.

It is therefore possible to speak of an "analogical, closely related, adapted, intentional" application (no. 11) without in any way denying the unconditional and permanent value of the fundamental law of love. Judgments of prudence and spiritual discernment conditioned by special historical circumstances take nothing away from the absolute obligation, to the extent that concrete acts are the expression of a rule divine in its origin (no. 11). Let us note, in passing, that even those who hold to the distinction between "transcendental" and "categorical" aspects are always more or less obligated to make an exception for the practice of Christian agape.

(2) Other special precepts do not directly concern brotherly love. The fundamental Christian rule of life of acting out of love for God, for others and for oneself remains at the intentional level,[14] but "love does not do away with the substance of the other virtues and of different patterns of behavior" (no. 11). It is good to reread the texts to which Schürmann refers, sometimes too succinctly, as he himself regrets (no. 3 and no. 11).

Some precepts are particular in themselves and refer to the mentality of Christians and communities. Christians must live in a spirit of joy, of prayer and of thanksgiving (1 Thess 5:16 and parallel texts, Phil 1:4; Eph 5:20): "Rejoice always. Pray without ceasing. In all things give thanks; for this is the will of God in Christ Jesus regarding you all." Giving thanks is even a moral criterion, because an action whereby we recall the divine origin of things implies rules of spiritual conduct (1 Tim 4:1–5).

Even if the will of God seems to be foolishness as compared with human wisdom (1 Cor 3:18), the Christian knows the ambivalence of certain circumstances such as riches, success, failure (1 Cor 7:29–31). What matters here is an essential and ineluctable spiritual attitude, rising above changes in events in the history of mankind and of individuals (the condition of slaves, for instance) (1 Cor 7:17–24) (no. 11).

"A number of these spiritual directives are formulated in very concrete terms and cannot be carried out literally today in the context of present-day community relations. Still, they retain some of their original normative authority and demand an adapted or similar form of implementation" (no. 11).

Schürmann also refers his readers "to the lists of virtues" that express abiding values (no. 11). Let us reread these texts. Galatians 5:22 mentions, over and above the fruits of the Spirit already mentioned, peace, patience, goodness, kindness, self-control. 2 Corinthians 6:6 invites us to purity, knowledge of God, patience, goodness. "The fruit of the light, according to Ephesians 5:9, is called: goodness, justice, truth." 1 Thessalonians 4 enumerates certain requirements of the work of sanctification: a marriage that is not dominated by the sole instinct of pleasure (vv 5–7), calm, concern for one's own affairs, work (vv 11–13). Even if these directives can have a bearing outside the Christian calling (v 12), it is out of obedience to the Lord that these good works are to be practiced. "Therefore, whoever rejects these things rejects not man but God, who has also given his Holy Spirit to us" (v 8).

The permanence of these moral values and standards is therefore backed by the divine origin of the precepts, by insertion into the Christian vocation, by the expectation of the kingdom, as well as by the requirements of the dignity of the human person.[15] Some moral theologians will stress the later aspect, which is based on the nature of things. They cannot be faulted, at least provided that they avoid a kind of secularization that cuts these moral principles off from any insertion into Christ (no. 11).

As a counterpoint to the lists of virtues, New Testament writings, and, in particular, the writings of Paul, contain lists of sins. This is not indicative of a negative frame of mind, but is rather just another way of indicating the attitudes that are demanded on an ongoing basis by the Christian calling. To know whether a form of behavior is bad, one must essentially see the extent to which it is opposed to "fundamental theological-eschatological requirements." This, says Schürmann (no. 11), "applies to the baptismal pareneses (cf Eph 4:17–31), where catechumens are confronted with the principal vices of the pagans." We have already cited Galatians 5:19–21. Let us look again at other texts: "No fornicator, or unclean person, or covetous one—for that is idolatry—has any inheritance in the kingdom of Christ and God" (1 Cor 6:10–11).

(3) Finally, a very special case, among the various interpersonal relationships, is represented by what the ecumenical Bible calls "new relationships" and what the exegetes more usually refer to as "the domestic tablets." In the exegetical style of the "tablets of the law" (Ex 31:18; Dt 9:17; 2 Chr 5:10), they constitute a very specific species that formulates husband-wife, parent-children, master-slave relations (no. 11).

Schürmann is very sensitive to the fact that, in these precepts, elements are conditioned by the historical circumstances of the first century. This is true in particular for the situation of women, which has come to be seen in a new light through the life of the Church and the evolution of civilization. The same could be said, of course, for slaves. There is, therefore, an element of flexibility here that must be determined by hermeneutics. This is in response to the apostle's own effort at reflection because, as the note of the ecumenical Bible to the text of Colossians 3:18 says, "while Paul is repeating here the moral precepts set forth by current philosophy, his constant reference to the Lord profoundly modifies them." The note stresses, in particular, "the reciprocity introduced into the duties of members considered as strong (husbands, parents, masters) and members considered as weak (wives, children, slaves). The strong-weak opposition may perhaps not apply any more nowadays to husband-wife relationships. Psychological and legal developments will cause some doubt as to the exact meaning of the text: "Let wives be subject to their husbands as to the Lord" (Eph 5:22). But can the permanent and profound significance of this statement not be found by returning to the preceding verse (v 21): "Be subject to one another in the fear of Christ"?

In short, even where there is historical and cultural growth, we must appeal to the spirit of the Lord, to the spiritual sense of the Church.

Clearly, then, Schürmann's report, as approved by the I.T.C., is important for a biblically-based Christian morality. It deserves our attention and should serve as a guide for a good deal of future research. It is characterized essentially by a desire for unfailing fidelity to the moral teachings of Christ and his apostles, and especially St. Paul. Though using a different vocabulary and working from a dissimilar perspective, it embodies the concern of the Fathers for interpreting the Scriptures "according to the Spirit." It permits a reply to those who, preoccupied with social developments and assailed by the objections of a constantly renascent sociologism, wonder how they can continue to follow Christ and want to retain of him more than just a vague "memoria."

The Question of the Binding Nature of the Value Judgments and Moral Directives of the New Testament

(Translation from the German text of Fr. Schürmann)[16]

I

THE PROBLEM

No. 1.—Vatican II presented to the faithful "with greater fullness of riches the table of God's Word" and "opened up more broadly to them the treasures of the Bible." (*Sac. Conc.* 51; D.V. 22). Consequently, the Council was desirous that "in their homilies, priests explain the mysteries of faith and the rules of Christian life on the basis of the sacred text" (*ibid.,* 52; D.V. 24). However, a difficulty arises: is it not true that we find here and there in the Old Testament (cf. D.V. 15) and even in the New, certain moral judgments that are conditioned and determined by the times in which these books were written? Does this authorize us to affirm in a general way, as is so often heard these days, that it is necessary to question the binding nature of all the value judgments and of all the directives of the Scriptures because they are all conditioned by time? Or should it at least be admitted that moral teachings pertaining to specific questions may not lay claim to a permanent value precisely because of their dependence upon a given age? Would human reason then be the final criterion for evaluating biblical value judgments and directives? Cannot the value judgments and directives of Holy Scripture claim to have, in and of themselves, any abiding value, or, in any event, any normative value whatsoever? Were the Christians of another age obligated merely in the manner of "patterns" or "models" of behavior?

No. 2.—While the "books of the Old Testament retain, as inspired texts, an imperishable value" (D.V. 14; cf. Rom 15:4), and since God willed in his wisdom that "the New Covenant be hidden in the Old and that the Old be explained by the New" (Aug., *Quaest. in Hept.* 2, 73, PL 34, 623), we shall nevertheless, in the following pages, limit our analysis to the New Testament writings. Indeed, the "books of the Old Testament, fully recaptured in the Gospel message, attain and reveal their complete significance in the New Testament" (D.V. 16). As a result, the question as to the binding nature of the value judgments and directives of the Bible arises particularly with respect to the writings of the New Testament.

The matter of determining the nature of the obligation that attaches to New Testament value judgments and directives is a function of hermeneutics in moral theology. It includes, however, an exegetical question as to the type and degree of obligation that these New Testament evaluations and directives claim for themselves. We shall concentrate especially on examining this problem with regard to Paulinian value judgments and directives, because this moral question is particularly reflected in the Pauline corpus. Also, despite a surprising diversity (for instance, in Paul, John, Matthew, James, etc.) New Testament writings show unusual convergence in the area of moral teaching.

No. 3.—As regards value judgments and directives in the matter of morality, the writings of the New Testament can claim a particular value, since it is in these writings that the moral judgment of the early Church is crystallized. Like the "nascent Church" itself, it is still present at the sources of revelation and is marked in an exceptional manner by the Spirit of the glorified Lord. Consequently, the behavior and the word of Jesus, as the ultimate criterion of moral obligation, could be manifested in a particularly valid manner in the value judgments and directives formulated in the Spirit and with authority by the apostle, as well as by the other "spiritual people" of the early Church, and in the *paradosis* and *paratheke* of the primitive Christian communities as immediate standards of action.

The nature and mode of the obligatory—but analogical—character of these two criteria on which the moral directives of the New Testament are based (compare 1 Cor 7:10–25 and 7:12–40), as well as the various value judgments and directives based on these two criteria (in other words, the various moral rules and pareneses) will be briefly formulated in concise theses in the following sections. It should be noted, however, that the New Testament proofs can be given here only allusively and succinctly, and that a certain sketchiness in classification is inevitable.

II
THE CONDUCT AND WORDS OF JESUS
AS THE ULTIMATE CRITERION OF JUDGMENT
IN MORAL MATTERS

No. 4.—For the authors of the New Testament, the conduct and words of Jesus serve as a normative standard of judgment and as supreme moral rule insofar as they are the "law of Christ" (*ennomos*) "written" in the hearts of the faithful (Gal 6:2; cf 1 Cor 9:21). Furthermore, for the New Testament writers, the directives of Jesus handed down during the pre-paschal period have decisive value and binding force in a context of imitation of the example given by the earthly Jesus and even more by the pre-existing Son of God.

Thesis 1: The conduct of Jesus is the example and standard for a love that serves and gives itself.

No. 5.—Already in the Synoptics, the "coming" of Jesus, his life and his action are understood as a service (Lk 22:27ff) which attains its ultimate fulfillment in death (Mk 10:25). At the pre-Paulinian and Paulinian stages, this love is designated in terms of *kenosis,* as a love that is fulfilled in the incarnation and in the death on the cross of the Son (Phil 2:6ff; 2 Cor 8:9). In John's view, this love attains its "fulfillment" (Jn 19:28–30) in the "coming down" of the Son of Man through his incarnation and death (Jn 6:41ff, 48–51, etc.), in the giving of the self on the cross (Jn 13:1–11); this therefore represents the "work" par excellence of Jesus (Jn 17:4; cf 4:34). The conduct of Jesus is therefore characterized ultimately as love that serves and gives itself "for us" and which makes visible for us the love of God (Rom 5:8; 8:31ff; Jn 3:16; 1 Jn 4:9). The entire moral behavior of the faithful is summed up basically in the acceptance and imitation of this divine love: it is therefore love with Christ and in Christ.

(a) In the New Testament writings—especially in Paul and John—the *demands of love* are motivated and, at the same time, given their own character, by that radicalism that causes love to go beyond itself, and perhaps even given a *special content* by the behavior of the Son who strips himself of himself (Paul), or who "comes down" (John). This love giving itself over to human existence and death represents and brings to light the love of God. This trait is even more characteristic of New Testament morality than its eschatological orientation.

(b) The "Sequela Jesu" and his imitation, "association" with the incarnate and crucified Son and the life of the baptized person in Christ, also determine in a specific way the concrete moral attitude of the believer as regards the world.

Thesis II: The Word of Jesus is the ultimate moral norm.

No. 6.—The words of the Lord make explicit the attitude of the love of Jesus, he who came and was crucified. They must be interpreted on the basis of his person. Thus, seen in the light of the paschal mystery and "brought to mind" in the Spirit (Jn 14:26), these words constitute the ultimate norm of moral conduct for believers (cf 1 Cor 7:10–25).

(a) Certain words of Jesus, based on their very literary genre, do not present themselves properly speaking as laws; they are to be understood as *behavior models* and should be considered as paradigms.

(b) For Paul, the words of the Lord have a definitive and permanent binding force. However, in two passages where he expressly cites directives of Jesus (cf Lk 10:7b and par.; Mk 10:11 and par.) he advises that they be observed as to their deep-down intent, and as faithfully as possible, given situations that have changed or become more difficult (1 Cor 9:14; 7:12–16). He therefore moves away from a legalistic interpretation in the manner of late Judaism.

III
THE JUDGMENTS AND DIRECTIVES
OF THE APOSTLES AND OF EARLY
CHRISTIANITY ARE ENDOWED WITH
A BINDING FORCE

No. 7.—The binding nature of these directives set forth in the New Testament is based on a number of things: the attitudes and words of Jesus, the conduct and teaching of the apostles and other "spiritual persons" of the Christian beginnings, the life style and tradition of the primitive communities, to the extent that the nascent Church was still marked in a special way by the Spirit of the risen Lord. In this context, it must not be forgotten that the Spirit of truth, especially as regards moral knowledge, "will teach" the disciples "all the truth" (Jn 16:13ff).

No. 8.—It should be noted that in terms of the various value judgments and directives of early Christianity, considered either in their form or in their content, the claim of binding authority differed greatly from case to case, and that these directives, in rather broad fields, were marked by a practical-pastoral goal orientation.

Thesis III: Certain value judgments and certain directives are permanent by reason of their theological and eschatological foundations.

No. 9.—In the New Testament writings, the chief parenetic value and, consequently, the importance relative to intensity and frequency of the statements involves the value judgments and directives (essentially formal) that require, as a response to the love of God in Christ, surrender in total love to Christ, that is, to the Father, and behavior in keeping with the reality of eschatological time, that is, the saving action of Christ and the baptized state.

No. 10.—The status of permanent obligation must be assigned to the value judgments and to these directives thus defined, to the extent they are unconditionally based on the eschatological reality of salvation and motivated by the Gospel.

(a) The central requirement of the New Testament writings which, as a precept "unto the very end," claims an absolute binding form consists in the call to total giving of self in Christ to the Father.

(b) An unconditional binding value is also claimed by numerous counsels and eschatological imperatives of the New Testament writings which, for the most part, remain at the level of formal morality. These imperatives call upon us, on the one hand, to conduct ourselves in faith and in love, in accordance with reality and with the situation in the light of the coming of eschatological salvation; they also call upon us to insert ourselves actively into the redemptive work of Christ, in other words, into the baptized state. At the same time, they warn us that we must allow ourselves to be conditioned in hope by the proximity of the kingdom, that is, of the second coming, in continuous vigilance and readiness.

Thesis IV: Individual value judgments and directives entail a diversity of obligations.

No. 11.—Alongside the value judgments and directives already mentioned above, the New Testament writings also present value judgments and directives that relate to particular areas of life, in other words, to specific actions which, though in a different manner, also have permanent binding force.

(a) One encounters frequently, and in a particularly marked way in the New Testament writings, directives and duties involving *brotherly love* and *love of one's neighbor,* which are often related to the conduct of the Son of God (e.g., Phil 2:6ff; 2 Cor 8:2–9), or which make reference to words of the Lord. These requirements—to the extent they remain general—assume an unconditional value as "law of Christ" (Gal 6:2) and as "new commandment" (Jn 13:14; 15:12; 1 Jn 2:7ff). In them is "fulfilled" the law of the Old Testament (Gal 5:15; cf Rom 13:8ff; also Mt 7:12; 22:40), that is to say, they are concentrated in the commandment of love and find their final objective in that commandment.

However, where the commandment of love "takes flesh" in specific and concrete directives, it is necessary to determine whether and how judgments conditioned by a particular time or by particular historical circumstances color the fundamental requirement to the point that, in different circumstances, one might require only an analogical, closely-related, adapted or intentional application.

(b) Alongside the commandment of love—but very often within the context of the requirement of love—the New Testament writings present other moral value judgments and directives that pertain to particular areas of life. The "fulfillment" of the law by love (Gal 5:14; cf Rom 13:8ff) is found especially at the intentional level; but love does not take away the substance of the other virtues or behavior patterns. It is expressed through different ways of acting and virtues that are not fully identified with love. One finds, for instance, in 1 Cor 13:4–7; Rom 12:9ff, in the moral teachings of the pastorals and of the Epistle of St. James, catalogues of virtues and vices and the domestic tables of the New Testament writings.

(aa) It should be remembered that a large part of these special value judgments and special directives have a very marked "spiritual" character, and, as such, determine the life of the community from that perspective. Exhortations to rejoice (Phil 3:1; 12:5), to pray without ceasing (cf 1 Thess 5:17), to give thanks (1 Thess 5:16; Col 3, 17), to "foolishness before God" as opposed to the "wisdom of this world" (1 Cor 3:18ff), and indifference (1 Cor 7:29ff) are certainly permanent Christian precepts that "go all the way"—in other words, "fruits of the Spirit" (cf Gal 5:22). Others are counsels (1 Cor 7:12–27ff). Many spiritual directives are formulated in very concrete terms and cannot be carried out literally in the context of present-day community relations (see only 1 Cor 11:5–14; Col 3:16; Eph 5:19). Still, they retain something of their original normative authority and require adapted or analogous "fulfillment."

(bb) As regards value judgments and individual—in the special sense of concrete—norms of moral behavior, their binding nature will be established on the basis of how they are motivated by basic theological-eschatological requirements or requirements of universally binding moral scope, or of the "Sitz-im-leben" they have in various communities. This applies, for instance, to the baptismal pareneses (cf Eph 4:17–21), where the catechumens are confronted with the principal vices of the pagans such as uncleanness (1 Thess 4:7ff) and dishonesty (1 Thess 4:6). Such requirements, along with the warning against idolatry (Gal 6:20ff), are strongly highlighted by their very nature.

Still, one cannot ignore the fact that in the case of many concrete moral value judgments pertaining to special areas of life, value judgments and real judgments conditioned by the times can condition moral perspectives or make them relative. While, for instance, the New Testament writers consider women as subordinated to men (cf 1 Cor 11:2–16; 14:33–36ff)—which is understandable given the times—it nevertheless seems to us that, on this point, the Holy Spirit has led contemporary Christianity, together with the whole modern world, to a better understanding within the moral requirements of the world of persons. Even if this were the only example that could be found in New Testament writings, it would suffice to demonstrate that, as regards value judgments and directives in particular areas, the question of hermeneutic interpretation of the New Testament may not be avoided.

IV
CONCLUSION

No. 12.—The majority of the value judgments and directives of the New Testament call for concrete behavior toward the Father who reveals himself in Christ, and therefore are placed in a theological-eschatological context. This applies in particular to the demands of Christ, but also to most apostolic directives; requirements and admonitions of this kind intend to bind unconditionally and transcend historical diversity. Even value judgments and directives that pertain to individual sectors of life share in large part in this perspective, at least insofar as they postulate more generally a love of neighbor perceived in its union with the love of God and Christ. Furthermore, the vast domain of the "spiritual" counsels of the New Testament is suffused with this theological-eschatological context and is determined by it. It is only in the relatively narrow area of concrete and particular directives and operating norms that the moral judgments and counsels of the New Testament must be capable of being rethought.

Our presentation therefore in no way supports the view according to which all the value judgments and directives of the New Testament are conditioned by time. This "relativization" does not apply even generally for particular judgments which, for the most part, cannot in any way be hermeneutically understood as pure "models" or "paradigms" of behavior. Only a small proportion of them can be considered as being subject to conditions of time and circumstance. Yet there are some that can. This means that, in the face of these value judgments and directives, human experience, the judgment of reason and theological-moral hermeneutics all have roles to play.

If this hermeneutics takes seriously the moral scope of the Scriptures, it cannot operate either in a purely "biblicist" manner, or from a purely rationalistic standpoint, in its search for the criteria of a moral theology, for instance in establishing the moral criteria of acts. It will achieve positive results only in a spirit of "encounter," in other words, in a continuing comparison of today's critical knowledge with the moral givens of Scripture. It is only by listening to the Word of God—*Verbum Dei audiens* (cf. DV 1)—that the signs of the times can be interpreted without danger. This work of discernment must be undertaken within the community of God's people, in the unity of the *sensus fidelium* and of the magisterium, aided by theology.

Notes

1. It is unnecessary to repeat here the information provided regarding the work of the I.T.C. at the time of the publication of Urs von Balthasar's

"Neuf thèses pour une morale chrétienne" in *Esprit et Vie* for April 24, 1975, p. 257. Let us add merely that the German text of the nine theses has just been published in a small volume released by Johannes-Verlag, Einsiedeln, 1975: J. Ratzinger, *Prinzipien christlicher Moral. Uber Mitarbeit von Heinz Schürmann und Hans Urs von Balthasar.*

2. Fr. Feuillet has published in *Esprit et Vie* a substantial part of the work he did as part of this inquiry.

3. Cf. *Morale chrétienne et requêtes contemporaines,* Coll. "Cahier de l'actualité religieuse", Paris, Casterman, 1954. A. Descamps, *La morale des Synoptiques,* pp. 27–46. At around the same time, Professor Descamps was publishing numerous articles on biblical morality in *Revue diocésaine de Tournai.*

4. Professor Heinz Schürmann was born in Bochum (Germany) on January 18, 1913. He was ordained a priest in 1938. His studies and research led to a doctorate in theology at Münster. He also received his teaching license in New Testament exegesis in 1952 at Münster. He began teaching New Testament exegesis the following year at the regional seminary at Erfurt (East Germany).

5. The complete text of this communication was published in Poland and in *Gregorianum,* 1975, pp. 237–281: *Haben die paulinischen Wertungen und Weisungen Modelkarakter? Boebachtungen und Anmerkungen zur Frage nach ihrer formalen Eigenart und inhaltlichen Verbindlichkeit.*

6. J. Giraud, P. Pamart, J. Riverain, *Les mots "dans le vent,"* Paris, Larousse, 1971. The *Dictionnaire général des Sciences Humaines* by G. Thines and A. Lempereur, Paris, 1975, presents the paradigm based on terminology as a "provisional hypothesis in the research and development of the facts" (p. 696) and linguistically as "a category of elements that can be substituted within a given context" (p. 697). The cultural model (pp. 603–607) is described as "an integrated complex of socio-cultural standards characterizing a society" . . . "an aspect of historicity."

7. St. Thomas, *Summa Theol.* Ia-IIae, q. 106, art. 2. Concl.: "Ad legem Evangelii duo pertinent. Unum, quidem principaliter, scilicet ipsa gratia Spiritus Sancti interius data. . . . Aliud pertinent ad legem Evangelii secundario, scilicet documenta fidei et pracecepta ordinantia affectum humanum et humanos actus."

8. A. Nygren, *Erôs et Agapé. La notion chrétienne de l'amour et ses transformations,* translation by P. Jundt, 3 vols., Paris, Aubier, 1944, 1952. Nor is it a question of forgetting—as Nygren himself seems to do—that this love brought by God to humans implies a response on our part. But it is a question of the second moment of the theological virtue of charity, which St. Thomas so brilliantly analyzed in the categories of friendship. The first mo-

ment is that of the gratuitous gift: "In this is the love: not that we have loved God but that he has first loved us, and sent his Son a propitiation for our sins" (1 Jn 4:10). The Latin text of the Vulgate even said *prior dilext nos,* but the neo-Vulgate eliminated the redundancy.

9. The reader of *Esprit et Vie* can refer to the article I published January 16 and 23, 1975, pp. 33–43, 49–58: *Les normes particulières du Sermon sur la Montagne d'après les commentaires de S. Thomas.* In *Super Evangelium S. Matthaei lectura,* one can refer to numbers 609, 622, 542. The patristic texts cited in *Catena aurea,* chap. VI, no. 13, 17 and chap. V, no. 20, demonstrate the traditional backdrop for this type of spiritual interpretation.

10. St. Paul apparently cited the words of the Lord in a literal manner only on four occasions: the right of the servant of the Gospel to subsistence (1 Cor 9:14 referring to Lk 10:7), the institution of the Eucharist (1 Cor 11:23), the censure of divorce (1 Cor 7:10) and the otherwise unknown logion which has some connection with Paul's desire to waive the livelihood he could have expected from his followers: "I have coveted no one's silver or gold or apparel. You yourselves know that these hands of mine have provided for my needs. . . . You ought . . . to remember the word of the Lord Jesus, that he himself said, 'It is more blessed to give than to receive' " (Acts 20:33–35). This text would seem to provide a valid reason for waiving this right to subsistence: to avoid the scandal caused by the greed of some (1 Pet 5:23).

11. E.-B. Allo, *Saint Paul, Première épitre aux Corinthiens,* Coll. "Etudes Bibliques," 1934, pp. 168–169.

12. Some good exegetes wonder whether 1 Corinthians 14:34 may not be a gloss that ended up as part of the text. In any event, these words must be understood as allowing for the possibility that women can "prophesy" in the meeting.

13. In this connection, one might recall the text—which is admittedly not at all ambiguous—in which *Unitatis Redintegratio* (no. 11) speaks of a "hierarchy of the truths of Catholic doctrine based on their differing relationship to the foundations of the Christian faith."

14. Cf. Ph. Delhaye, *L'orientation religieuse des actes moraux d'après la Sainte Ecriture et la théologie,* in *"A la rencontre de Dieu," Mémorial A. Gelin,* Lyon, 1960, pp. 415–428.

15. One is reminded of the vast area common to Christian morality and to human moral codes. St. Thomas explains how the revelation of Christ assumes these natural truths. The apostles and the Lord himself, in accepting them, give them new dimensions through their insertion into charity, the "queen of virtues" and in the life of grace.

16. This translation was made in three stages. During the December

1974 session, Fr. Elders, S.V.D. (of the University of St. Thomas, Angelicum) lent his assistance to Fr. Hamel, S.J. (Gregorianum) who was working on the same sub-commission as Schürmann. Later, Fr. Hamel redid the translation. Finally, the Secretariat of the I.T.C. polished up the text to make it easier to read for French-speaking readers.

Scripture,
The Soul of Moral Theology?

Edouard Hamel

This article originally appeared in *Gregorianum* in 1973.

Vatican II spoke, though very briefly, of the relationship between Scripture and moral theology. After formulating the general
hope that "the study of Holy Scripture should be the soul of theology" (D.V. ["Dei verbum"], 24; O.T. ["Optatam totius"], 16), the
Council uses, as regards moral theology, this rather more shaded,
possibly more timid, formula: "Special care will be given to the perfecting of moral theology, whose scientific presentation, more richly
nourished by the teaching of Holy Scripture, will bring to light the
greatness of the vocation in Christ of the faithful and their obligation
to bear fruit in charity for the life of the world" (O.T. 16).

Scripture poses a series of problems for moral theology which
are not so readily solved.

To begin with, why go back to the Bible in moral theology?
Why must Scripture be its soul? Is the Gospel of salvation not written by the Spirit in the heart of Christians (Jer 31:33)? Have not moral standards been "impressed" by the Creator on the conscience of
human beings (Rom. 2:15)? Would recourse to the Bible to find moral standards not constitute pointless redundancy? Would it not be inspired by a more or less neurotic need for security, a need to go from
one authority to another, from the theology of Denzinger to the theology of the Bible?

A second set of questions deals with the manner of referring to
the Bible. What will the moral theologian look for in the Bible? Is
the moral message of the New Testament not found exclusively at a

deep intentional level, at the level of motivation and not of behavior? Must we look there for only a transcendental type of morality, or also for rules of a categorial type? And what value will the concrete moral standards contained in the New Testament actually have? A permanent value, or just an historical value? Are they binding norms or just an ideal to which one should strive?

We do not pretend, within the limits of this short analysis, to deal exhaustively with each of these problems, some of which are indeed thorny. We simply wish to focus somewhat more closely on the reality represented by the metaphors "soul" and "nourishment" used by Vatican II and to indicate which roles, out of a large variety of possible applications, Scripture can play in moral theology.[1]

I
WHY GO BACK TO THE SCRIPTURES IN MORAL THEOLOGY?

1. Scripture and the Law of the Spirit

What is the relationship between Scripture and the Gospel written in men's hearts? Jeremiah had announced the new covenant in these terms: "I will put my law in the depths of their being and will write it on their heart" (Jer 31:33). And Ezekiel said: "I will give you a new heart and put a new spirit within you; and I will take away the stony heart out of your flesh and will give you a heart of flesh. And I will put my spirit in the midst of you, and I will cause you to walk in my commandments" (Ez 36:26–27).

In the Epistle to the Romans, Paul combines these two images from the prophets and affirms that the great novelty of the new covenant in terms of morality is the presence within the heart of the Christian of the "law of the Spirit of life," a new operating principle that enables the Christian to act "not according to the flesh but according to the spirit" (Rom 8:2–4).[2]

Jeremiah had promised that, at the time of the new covenant, the faithful would no longer have to teach one another, saying to one another: "Know the Lord. For all shall know me . . ." (Jer 31:24).

And Paul, in the First Epistle to the Thessalonians where, for the first time, he sets forth his moral teaching, paraphrases the oracle of Jeremiah in these terms: "Concerning brotherly love, there is no need for us to write to you, for you yourselves have learned from God to love one another. For indeed you practice it ..." (1 Thess 4:9–10). In his First Epistle, John also alludes to this promise of Jeremiah: " ... let the anointing which you have received from him dwell in you, and you have no need that anyone teach you, but ... his anointing teaches you concerning all things" (1 Jn 2:27).

Jeremiah, Ezekiel, Paul and John therefore affirm that, under the new covenant, Christians will no longer need to be taught by others, because they have received the Holy Spirit as an interior teacher. Why then still go back to the Scriptures? Is not the interior law sufficient? Could Scripture give us a moral message other than the one given us by the Spirit?

Even justified, the Christian remains a *homo viator* subject to the tension of the *already* and of the *not yet.* The Holy Spirit received in baptism does not illuminate conscience in such a way that the Christian no longer has to resort to Scripture. For the moment, the Christian has received only the warrant, the pledge (2 Cor 1:22), of the Spirit. The prophecy of Jeremiah is fulfilled in the baptized only gradually. Paul, for his part, was not prepared to canonize the judgments of conscience of any individual Christian. The initial gift of the Spirit merely inaugurates the transformation of the Christian. The metamorphosis must continue throughout one's life.

This is why the evangelists, while aware of the prophecies of Jeremiah and Ezekiel, nevertheless left behind a moral message. There is therefore not opposition but complementarity between the two Gospels. The Gospel in Christian hearts, because of human weakness, runs the risk of being altered, so that it is Scripture that will faithfully remind the believer of its content. Since Scripture by itself is just the written word—it states the message of salvation without providing the strength to carry it out—it is the Gospel written in the heart that will give the Christian the strength to produce the fruits of justice.

The same Holy Spirit, who reminds us from the inside of "whatever I have said to you" (Jn 14:26), has also reminded us from the outside by inspiring the sacred authors who have reported to us "everything that Christ taught" (Mt 28:30). The testimony of the Scriptures is also the testimony of the Holy Spirit (Heb 10:15). This is why, by referring to the moral message set forth in writing under the inspiration of the Spirit, the Christian will have a better chance of being faithful to the voice of the same Spirit who speaks from within one's own heart.

It was left to St. Thomas to provide more specifics and to formulate in an almost definitive manner what constitutes this interrelationship between Scripture and interior law. In his classic treatise on the new law, he writes: "What is primary in the law of the New Testament, and it is in this that its entire virtue consists, is the grace of the Holy Spirit that is given through faith in Christ. It then follows that what is primary in the new law is the very grace of the Holy Spirit that is given to Christ's faithful."[3]

For him, the written Gospel is part of what he calls the *quasi secundaria* of the new law: "The new law also includes certain things that are like pre-dispositions to the grace of the Holy Spirit, or like conditions for its utilization, constituting as it were the secondary portion of the new law, in which it was necessary for Christ's faithful to be instructed. . . . It must therefore be said that the new law is chiefly an interior law, but that it is, secondarily, a written law."[4] The law of love diffused in our hearts is therefore objectivized, as a consequence or condition, in precepts: the Lord's commandments written in the Gospel.

2. Scripture or Reason?

In what manner does God's law reach man? Through reason or through the Scriptures? Would the voice of conscience not suffice to teach us what is right or wrong, what is worthy or unworthy of a human being? Are not *recta ratio* and conscience the privileged theological places where we can learn the will of God? By consulting his conscience, does a person not already know what God wants? According to St. Thomas, the New Testament gives us no moral precepts other than those which the person can normally discover through personal reflection or spontaneous moral judgment. The

God of revelation is the same as the God of creation. The new creation does not destroy the first creation but makes reference to it. Moreover, on a number of specific points, Scripture gives us no concrete solution (which does not mean that it has no "answer" to give us). And there is nothing in this to be astonished about, since the writings of the New Testament, at least in detail, are occasional texts which do not constitute a complete moral treatise.

Why then insist on returning to Scripture in order to learn moral rules if conscience and reflection, on the one hand, are often the only sources of answers, and if, on the other, they can already *anticipate,* so to speak, the responses of the Bible? Why did God take care to reveal positively the precepts of the Decalogue if humankind could discover them by itself, if it had already discovered a number of them, as we are told nowadays by biblical science.?[5] Paul did not hesitate to borrow many moral categories and rules from Stoicism and inserted into his teaching virtues esteemed by the Greeks. Since they had already been discovered by human reason, what advantage is there to *reread* them in the Bible?

The reply to this serious question will be found in part in this Vatican II text which, in turn, repeats the teaching of Vatican I: "We must attribute to revelation the fact that things which, in the divine order, are not in themselves inaccessible to human reason, can also, in the present condition of humankind, be known by all, easily, with a firm certitude and without any admixture of error" (D.V. 6; *D.- Sch.* 3005).

Human reason is not infallible in its efforts to know and to formulate moral standards. Human beings are constantly tempted to relive for themselves the experience of Adam and Eve and to decide for themselves what is good or evil (Gen 3:5). In the matter of morality, some would like to be able to "demonstrate" the falsity of rules that they would prefer were not true. Vatican II reminds us—a reminder that is not always welcome—that, in the present condition of humankind, we will always find it difficult to read in all its perfection the law of our being inscribed in the depths of our conscience, especially when it deals with points that go to the very heart of our predilections. Passion can take away from reason a portion of its facility, its lucidity, its objectivity. It is not easy to be both judge and party to the action.

In the area of sexual morality, for example, conscience, left to its own reflections, can easily become clouded over. On this point, Judaism was brought back to a knowledge of the true moral standards only by the word of God. Indeed, it is in the matter of idolatry and sexuality that the moral code of Israel was the farthest removed from that of surrounding peoples. And in the Epistle to the Romans, Paul reminds us that paganism had, particularly on this point, lost the meaning of what human reason ought to have indicated to it.

Because it is guaranteed by Revelation,[6] biblical morality will be the faithful and abiding mirror of human morality and it will, if necessary, correct the indications that come from reason. At times it will merely *confirm* what conscience or scientific reflection had already discovered in the way of standards, but this confirmation will offer a certitude that no other monitoring instrument could provide, because it comes from the word of God. What human reason has found out, God confirms. The Christian knows that there is an identity of views between the Creator and human reason.

Not only will biblical morality help us to defend ourselves against ourselves, but it will provide us with a sure light to illuminate so many complex human problems where it is sometimes so difficult to see clearly. The light provided by Scripture will be added to the light of human reason, supporting it, guiding its reflections, keeping it out of impasses and indicating to it the sure paths to be followed.

What is more, biblical morality will reveal to the Christian the profound meaning of the indications that come from one's own conscience. Left to one's own lights, the human being remains an enigma to oneself. Only revelation enlightens us as to the ultimate meaning of our life, of our activity and of our destiny. Only revelation provides the full meaning of human moral rules, of all human values.

Biblical morality will also serve as a *developer:* moral norms, still in the embryonic stage in everyday morality, will appear in their fullness only in contact with transcendental Christian morality. Let us think, for instance, of love for one's enemies. There are, in non-Christian morality, some hidden elements that will be brought into the fullness of light, that will be, so to speak, "revealed," only in contact with the Scriptures.[7] It is in this way that biblical morality reminds human beings of their incomparable dignity.

II
GOING BACK TO SCRIPTURE IN MORAL THEOLOGY

1. Voice from the Past, Always Current

Speaking of the Scriptures, Vatican II says that they are the "supreme rule of the Church's faith because, inspired by God and consigned *once and for all* in writing, they *immutably* communicate the word of God himself and cause *the voice of the Holy Spirit* (D.V. 21) to reverberate in the words of the prophets and of the apostles. Scripture is therefore both a voice from the past and a voice from the present. It is history subject to the rules common to any historical text, but it is also history of salvation written "once and for all." While conditioned by history, Scripture remains eminently current.

But how can a text written in the past and marked by history continue to talk to, and have meaning for, people today? Will the New Testament have an answer to questions raised by modern man? How can its application to today's world be assured?

Both exegesis and theology have a number of tasks to perform here:

1. The Word of God is expressed in human words and not in dictates coming directly from God. It is transmitted to us under the wrapper of history, in forms that are necessarily dependent upon culture. It is therefore essential to use all possible means to make the text itself speak, to allow ourselves to be guided by its contents without trying to project into it our own patterns of thought.

2. The biblical text must *speak to today's reader.* Its explanation must lead the reader to a better understanding of self, to a solution of the questions that arise, which are often quite different from those that arose at the time the sacred writer was drafting the text. It is therefore necessary to seek to establish a point of contact between the sacred text of earlier origin and our contemporary era which approaches it with our own questions, our own mentality and our own problems.

Such a meeting ground is possible because the text is both history and history of salvation, written for a very specific purpose and for a particular audience, but at the same time intended to offer to the world a permanent and immutable light. To accomplish this, however, will require a serious hermeneutic effort.

Let us take sexuality as an example. It is possible to study this problem in the Bible strictly from an historical, sociological or archeological standpoint, to see how the Hebrews saw sexuality, what their problems were, what solutions they brought to these problems, or to study the Pauline concept of sexuality, to find out what responses Paul gave to the questions that were asked in his time. But if one stays there, the lessons to be drawn for our own time will not go beyond the lessons we can glean from the study of any chapter of secular or ecclesiastical history. Thus reduced to pure history, the Bible has practically nothing to say today either to theology or to the world.

But if we consider the Bible insofar as it contains a permanent message of salvation for humankind we will try to draw, from the biblical view of sexuality, a message that can enlighten humankind today and tell it what God thinks of human sexuality, a light that can serve as the basis for, that can monitor, correct if necessary, and above all integrate into a more integral framework, its own concept of sexuality.

It is a matter of setting up a dialogue or dialectical relationship between two concepts of sexuality marked by different cultures, that of the Bible and that of contemporary humanity, between two historically different perspectives, in order to find a *common perspective*. And because the text in question is the word of God and because, therefore, it is not for the reader to call the word to account but for the word to challenge the reader, the latter will have to make an effort to penetrate the sacred text and reach that precise point where the wall separating the time of the biblical text and one's own time has finally disappeared, until a "merger of perspectives" (H.G. Gadamer) takes place, until the dialogue between the text and the reader is established at that transcendental level where the latter finally grasps the message that God is addressing to the reader, where the Word of God tells the reader something.

Moreover, this hermeneutic effort applies not merely to the understanding of a sacred text. It is required in order to set up any dialogue whatsoever between two persons who start off from different points of view. They must remain in contact until they manage to understand and to encounter the vision of the other, until they have established that common perspective that we have mentioned. This is the same process that permits us, while studying a classical work, for instance, to find a universal human experience based on a human experience marked by time. Universal does not mean cosmopolitan.

However, when the text studied is not just history but also history of salvation, the human universal attained through hermeneutic effort is the human universal as God sees it and tells it to us; it is a permanent message of salvation. It is this vision, at once profoundly human and divine, that will aid modern people in achieving a better understanding of themselves and their problems. Getting back to sexuality, this means that we are able to find in the Bible, based on the standards that are given to us there, a fundamental sexual anthropology that will tell us, if the hermeneutic effort is properly carried out, what God thinks of human sexuality. The "answer" that the Bible gives will not necessarily be at the level of concrete rules, but it will always correspond at least to the fundamental significance of sexuality. It will provide us with an integral vision that will enable us to find more concrete answers with greater certainty. In that sense, it is fair to say that there is no moral problem on which the Bible is totally silent.

2. Truth of Salvation and Updating Exegesis

What kind of truth must be looked for in the Bible?[8] Biblical truth is quite different from Greek truth. It is not pure doctrine but experimental knowledge. To know God means to enter into a close relationship with him, communicate with his wishes and carry them out. Biblical religion is a religion of action rather than of knowledge.

The Bible contains "the truth that God has deigned to teach with a view to our salvation" (D.V. 2, 6). Inspiration was given for the purpose of a revelation that is our salvation. Unceasingly animated by the living breath of the Spirit, the Bible communicates to us a message of salvation that goes beyond the ability of the text itself to express: "In the Holy Books, Vatican II tells us, the Father who is in heaven comes with tenderness to meet his children and enters into conversation with them; and the power and force concealed by the word of God are so great that they constitute, for the Church, its support and its vigor, and for the children of the Church, the strength of their faith, the nourishment of their souls, the pure and abiding source of their spiritual life" (D.V. 21).

The Scriptures are made to be read in faith; their role is to transmit to the believer the reality of the mystery of Christ that surpasses the potential for expression of all human tongues. What the believer receives when one studies the Bible is more than what the letter itself can offer. The person who reads the Bible in faith finds oneself linked to the very source from which the Scriptures emanated, the Holy Spirit. The Scriptures are the word of God spoken in the heart of believers, who must welcome it and wrap themselves in it, because it links up with the Gospel already written in their heart.

The truth of salvation contained in the Scriptures does not concern only personal and free usages such as the *lectio divina,* the liturgy and meditation. It also has its repercussions at the level of biblical and theological science. It is not intended solely for the moral life but also for moral science.

Thus, in order to make correct use of the Bible in moral theology, a *twofold* type of exegesis is necessary. First, there is needed a scientific and philological type of exegesis which consists in making a rigorous analysis of the texts in order to determine with maximum possible accuracy the original sense as intended by their author. But this first type is not enough. It is necessary to add to it an *updating exegesis,* based on the model of the interpretations given by the sacred writers themselves. One finds in the Scriptures, as a matter of fact, a continuing process of interpretation and updating. The ancient traditions are *reread;* the words of Jesus are "applied" by Paul and John to the new situations in the community. The exegete and the theologian must remain open to the call that comes forth from Scripture. To be faithful to the authentic and profound meaning of the Bible, scientific study will be backed by an effort to comprehend and to update the text in order to discover the message of salvation that God wants to give us. Without this updating exegesis, the Bible has practically nothing to say to the world of today; it is scientifically established history, nothing more. It does not challenge. Could a Bible thus made ineffectual, that no longer calls us to account, still truly be a message of salvation for humankind?[9]

This updating exegesis will therefore not be confined to seeing whether the texts that formulate moral rules are applicable as such at the categorial level that is specific to the current situation. Very rarely will the transfer from the biblical text to the present situation occur directly at the categorial level. A hermeneutic updating effort will be required to attain, through the historical concrete reality, the transcendental and metahistorical level that has permanent value. In discovering the permanent and transcendental within and beyond the categorial, theologians simultaneously leave themselves open to the revelation of a message of salvation whose value is eminently current. At the conclusion of such a hermeneutic effort, one discovers the salvific will of God.

And since a moral message is involved, the moral theologian knows that this truth of salvation that is found thanks to the hermeneutic effort made must of necessity be at the same time a permanent requirement of reason and of human dignity. The paths of revelation and of reason come together. God wants what is good for humankind. But what God wants is also what is good for humankind. The divine will known by revelation is one of the elements that enables us to know in what our true good consists. It will at times be the only means of making this known to someone who has not as yet recognized it on one's own.

Two passages from the Acts of the Apostles will furnish us with some concrete examples of this updating exegesis.

Summaries of Christian Life (Acts 2:44–46; 4:32)

These summaries of Christian life stress two aspects of the life of the early Church community: the communion of hearts and the communication of property, the latter being presented as the natural fruit of the former. Luke shows us how, under the influence of the Spirit, the community moves almost spontaneously and necessarily from the union of hearts to the pooling of assets.

These pictures presented to us by Luke seem indeed to constitute generalizations and amplifications of individual cases. Various attempts were freely made in the various communities which, clearly, did not all have one single form of common life.[10] Some felt spontaneously impelled to sell a part of their property to benefit the indigent, in order to ensure greater equality and equity in their community.

These summaries are therefore not models to be merely reproduced in an absolute and universal manner. Luke wants to demonstrate the extraordinary power of the breath of the Spirit within the early community which is manifested in the special fruits of a spontaneous sharing of property. Thus is attained, in full freedom, that ideal of sharing and equality desired by Deuteronomy: "There should be no one of you in need" (Dt 15:4), but which the most beautiful social laws of the Old Testament had been unable to achieve. To the impotence of the law, Luke opposes the power of the Spirit. It is at this level that the summaries constitute an ideal that must never stop providing inspiration for the Christian. Agape will normally impel the Christian to put a portion of one's property spontaneously at the disposal of the community either in the form of a donation for the poor, or in a socially useful manner.

This is the permanent message that emerges for us from these experiments of the early Church, somewhat naive perhaps and not always equally productive, depicted for us by Luke. In this respect, they have value as a permanent witness. On the one hand, they are not to be taken literally as rigid models applicable as such to each situation, nor, at the same time, are they the fruit of some speculative construct without any relationship to concrete reality.

Christianity condemns selfish attachment to personal property. Christian communion is not limited to the spiritual sphere alone but must also extend to all other areas of human life. It is not evangelical to claim to be in communion with Christ without sharing one's goods with the "poor" who call on his name. "By her example, the Church of the early days teaches that where Christianity is alive, the communion of the faithful normally extends to worldly goods. The heart of the faithful, in effect, is elsewhere than in these goods. The Gospel detaches them from these goods as it unites them to Jesus Christ."[11] These experiments also bear witness to the high quality of the communitarian and social life of the early Church (1 Jn 4:20). A community born of the Spirit will spontaneously seek to express the grace received in social fruits.

The Decree of the Council of Jerusalem (Acts 15)

The disputed question was the following: What is to be required on the part of the Greco-Christians so that the Judeo-Christians can have dealings with them without becoming legally contaminated? The problem clearly arose in the *mixed* communities where contacts between Judeo-Christians and converted pagans risked becoming strained because of these rules of legal purity still observed by the Jews who had converted from Judaism. Of all the laws of legal purity reported in Leviticus 17 and 18, the apostles decided to impose on the pagans only the three laws that seemed to them to be the most basic: abstention from meats offered to idols, illicit unions considered here as a source of legal contamination, and strangled flesh.

This decree, which seemed so essential at least for certain mixed communities of the early Church, later fell into disuse. What value does this episode that Luke insists on relating to us still have for us now? Can we find in it a permanent message of salvation?

James begins by posing the fundamental principle of the total freedom of converted pagans with regard to Jewish observances: "My judgment is not to disquiet those who from among the Gentiles are turning to the Lord" (Acts 15:19). In spite of this, a number of basic laws of Judaism were imposed on them. For some time, they had to bear the burden of obligations unnecesary in themselves. Why? In order to save the *koinonia,* to ensure peace and unity between the two groups within mixed communities. A categorical rule is imposed in specific historic circumstances in order to guarantee the observance of the transcendental norm of agape. It had no purpose other than to serve agape within the community. Luke is offering us here a model for a practical solution to a conflict of values between Christian freedom and love. In principle, the pagans are free of any legal observance. Yet, in order to protect the supreme requirement of unity and love within the community, they are asked to make a temporary sacrifice of freedom.[12] This is the permanent message that God is sending us in this episode which, at first blush, seemed to be but a matter of anecdotal history.

3. Different Types of Biblical Morality

In the New Testament, it is easy to distinguish several types of moral law.[13] This diversity in presentation and emphasis in moral matters seems to correspond roughly to the major phases that mark the history of the infant Church.

1. Initially the Church, conscious of its resources of grace, unceasingly experiencing the power of the Spirit, and encompassing as yet only a small number of faithful, attempted to live fully the absolutes proclaimed by Jesus: faith, hope and charity. At this level, an *eschatological type* of moral law was developed, found above all in the Synoptic Gospels. Everything is reduced to essentials: "Convert; the kingdom of God has arrived." Very few concrete precepts are found. The differentiation between theory and practice is barely touched upon.

2. In a second phase of development, the Church had to organize, set up structures, get involved in the concrete and give some response to the cases of conscience that arose. It recognized the need for a certain dose of casuistry in order to refine the relationship between Christian intentionality and daily life. Thus, a categorical type of moral law developed, found especially in Paul. Indeed, one notes in him the tendency to multiply concrete admonitions, prohibitions and casuistic applications. He did not hestitate to borrow from current moral law, whether Judaic or Stoic, the concrete precepts that seemed to him to be compatible with the fundamental kerygma. By thus resorting to sources outside Christianity, Paul was already establishing the continuity between Christian and non-Christian moral law in the area of categorical precepts.

3. With John a third type of moral law would arise, one which could be called *transcendental*. It is a return to essentials. Everything is unified and reduced, in practice, to faith and to love; this is the quintessence of Christian morality.

Must one choose among these various types of moral law?

Where is the specific element of Christian morality? The tension that exists among them must be resolved in complementarity and not in opposition. All three types are equally inspired and are part of the canon. We cannot favor one to the detriment of the others: this would be tantamount to setting up one's own canon within the single canon of the Church.

To be sure, that which is unique to Christian moral law resides rather in the eschatological and transcendental types, but we cannot omit the categorical type of morality given to us by Paul. The presence of concrete moral rules demonstrates the legitimacy of introducing into moral theology certain more detailed prescriptions. Of course, these do not constitute the specific element of Christian morality, because a number of them come from the non-Christian world. But they do serve to incarnate and to translate into daily life the two great commandments of agape. Without them, there is a danger that the transcendental might remain too much in the air and that the force of agape might remain purely verbal, without effect on everyday life. The importance of these concrete rules derives less from their material content than from the profound reality that they seek to express, and which we will be helped to discover through our hermeneutic effort.

An Hypothesis

Protestant theologians have generally always found it very difficult to admit that the law is linked to the Gospel as it was to the Old Testament. Paul's polemic against the Judaizing tendencies of early Christianity has always appeared to them to be the only key for interpreting the Gospels. They extend Paul's criticisms of certain interpretations of the law to the very structure of Mosaic law. This is why they are so hesitant to admit that the law is as much an integral part of the New Testament as it was of the Old. For them, there is no continuity between the two covenants. The new covenant has nothing to do with the old. The new announces to the Christian an interior law of liberty. The morality of the New Testament is more indicative than imperative, more revealed truth than revealed moral law. Whoever is under grace is no longer under the law.

In opposition to this excessively one-sided view which claims to be based on certain texts of Paul, the Council of Trent had already specified that the New Testament was not reduced to the sole precept of faith, and that the Gospel contained something other than a pure promise of eternal life without the observance of the commandments (D.-Sch. 1569). It was perhaps as a reaction to the too-exclusive exploitation of Paul by the Protestants that Catholic theology, at least for a certain period of time, turned to the teachings of the Jesus of the Gospels, in order to prove that the Christian, according to Christ's own will, is still required to observe the Commandments of God. Thanks especially to the Sermon on the Mount, it was possible to show that Jesus had upheld the requirements of the Decalogue. But since the Ten Commandments confirmed by Jesus, with one exception, merely repeated the basic requirements of natural law, it is quite possible that Catholic moral theology could have found there the opportunity for committing itself resolutely to the path of natural law, which seemed evangelical enough since Jesus had restated, and deepened, the requirements of the Decalogue.

If our hypothesis is correct, we come to the following conclusion. Protestant theology, as a whole, has developed a transcendental type of moral theology not based on the moral law of the Synoptics, but rather on the criticisms that Paul had made of certain concepts of Jewish law. Leaving aside Paul's categorical morality, it has exclusively exploited Paul's fundamental kerygma. On the other hand, Catholic moral theology was, for a long time, of the categorial type, based not on the moral law of Paul, but working from the standpoint of the doctrine of natural law which lent itself well to a casuistic-type moral law.

Catholic moralists probably did not see clearly as yet how the Scriptures could be the soul of moral theology. The magisterium and natural law seemed to be privileged theological places preceding, if not in practice superior to, the Scriptures, which served above all to confirm the theses established elsewhere.

To be sure, the limited influence of the Bible on the development and organization of Catholic moral theology is not due only to the reason that we have just formulated by way of a hypothesis. It is also necessary to take into account the fact that Catholic exegetes had not as yet demonstrated to the moralists the possibilities for using Scrupture in moral theology. Monographs on moral themes did not exist.

III

THE CATEGORICAL MORALITY OF PAUL

In the morality of Paul, one can identify three levels.[14]

1. A *kerygma* of a Christological and interpersonal nature centered on the communion of the Christian with Christ and on the communion of Christians with one another.

2. A *transcendental moral law:* from Paul's kerygma flows a series of specific transcendental moral guidelines, the life of faith, hope and charity, life in Christ and in the Spirit.

3. The transcendental moral law flowing from the kerygma then encounters the then current moral law of the Jewish, sapiential and Greek worlds. From this synthesis of the transcendental elements of the kerygma and the rational elements derived from the non-Christian morality of the time was to arise the *categorical moral law* of Paul. Linked to the transcendental dynamics of faith, hope and charity and influenced by it—Paul finds therein standards for discernment—it comes in large part from the current moral law.

Obviously, it is necessary to stress the link that ties together these three types of morality. This simultaneous presence in Paul of a transcendental and categorical moral law makes it possible to demonstrate the extent to which the moral aspirations of the Old Testament and of Judaism, the prophets and the law, were not abrogated but accomplished in the Christian dispensation. The early Church did not reject the moral concerns of Israel; it made them its own, though clarified and completed in the light of the life, death and resurrection of Christ. The major Old Testament themes—the exodus, Sinai, Moses, the convenant—are picked up in the New, but linked now to the person of Jesus. In Paul, everything centers on Christ, but on the Christ who comes to perfect, not to abolish. There is continuity between the two covenants, but this continuity is guaranteed and measured by the person of Jesus which remains, in Paul, the central theme of his theology and of his moral law.[15] The key to a proper understanding of New Testament morality is, therefore, not Paul's criticisms of the law but the person of Jesus, heart of the Pauline and Christian kerygma.

Paul's categorical morality does raise some problems. What value does it retain for today's Christians? Because it is far more conditioned by culture than was heretofore thought, must one conclude that it has hardly any value now? Might the message of salvation not be limited only to the transcendental which flows directly from the kerygma, all the rest flowing from pure history? Does the categorical morality of Paul contain, along with elements that are clearly inapplicable, certain permanent elements? And if it does include some, how are we to know? How are we to distinguish between what is transient and what is abiding? This, we believe, is one of the most difficult problems that arise in connection with the relationship between Scripture and moral theology. What are the standards of current validity of Paul's categorical standards?[16]

We have spoken of permanent content and not of absolute value. It is a question of determining whether some of Paul's categorical moral precepts have permanent value. The question as to whether this permanent value is absolute (that is, allowing of no exceptions whatsoever) is a different one. We shall not discuss it here.

The presiding genius of Pauline moral law certainly does not lie in its specific directives. The most important element is the *path,* the *spirit,* the intentionality that we are given by his transcendental morality. But what would the Pauline transcendental be without a concrete prescriptive component that gives it flesh and introduces it into daily life? This is why Paul's categorical morality cannot be lightly dismissed. This does not mean that one must assign the same value to each of his precepts, or take them literally. One cannot give the same weight to what Paul says about the veil for women, fornication or homosexuality.

On the other hand, to refuse *a priori* to assign any permanent value to the categorical norms established by Paul because they are all more or less dependent upon the culture of his time and that, consequently, the problems are not posed in the same way today, would be tantamount to considering only the transcendental dynamic moral law of faith, hope and charity as a message of salvation and reducing categorical moral law to a status of pure historical interest. It would no longer be history of salvation but Church history. But in the Bible, everything is inspired, everything is God's Word, even if it does not all have the same importance. One cannot cut away what is religious from what is not.

Because of the very nature of the inspiration given to the sacred author for a message of salvation, as well as because of the nature of the Scriptures which unchangeably communicate to us the word of God, might there not be a way to identify, by means of hermeneutics, and starting with concrete moral rules, but going beyond their historic and cultural trappings, a part of this permanent saving truth that God wishes to communicate to us through the Scriptures? Reflecting in and with the light of God, aided by his whole theological and human culture but always guided by the Spirit, Paul thought it proper to specify in writing some rules in the matter of sexuality. It is difficult to believe that all of this represents for us just a chapter of history. It must be possible to draw from it, at one level or another, a message of salvation that is valid for us.

What might be the criteria for such a hermeneutic effort?

1. How Tight or Loose is the Link to the Kerygma?

It is necessary, first of all, to see how Paul links this concrete moral standard to the kerygma. The more a moral rule goes to the heart of the Pauline message, the more independent it will be of historic and cultural conditions, and the more valid it will be for us. When Paul tells us that a particular way of acting runs counter to the fundamental kerygma, that a particular behavior of the baptized person—fornication, for instance—is incompatible with one's union in Christ, that those who act in this manner are excluded from the heavenly kingdom, then it seems that we are dealing with rules that are still valid today. Sometimes there remains the difficulty of determining the precise nature of the moral actions of which Paul speaks. Some are clear in and of themselves, others less so. It may even be said that the "Christian specificity" of a precept whose verbal formulation might very well be found to exist as is in the Stoic moral codes of the time is precisely its link with the Pauline kerygma.[17]

An analysis of the link that Paul establishes between a specific concrete action and the motivation for same which is tied more or less closely to the kerygma will make it possible for us to make a judgment as to the permanent value, or lack of permanent value, of the condemnation of the action. This analysis must be pressed until the links that tie this action to salvation are clearly apparent. Only in this way will it be possible to understand that certain actions which, from the standpoint of human dignity alone, do not clearly seem to deserve censure will be censurable for a Christian conscience illuminated by the mystery of the death and resurrection of Christ, and enriched by the presence in that conscience of the Holy Spirit. That which provides guidance for the Christian in one's actions will also be valid for the moral theologian's reflections. The moral theologian can redo for one's own time what Paul did for his, using the same "filters" as the apostle. It is fidelity to the fundamental kerygma that will provide the moral theologian with the ultimate criteria for selection and verfication, in order to declare "new" forms of action introduced and proposed by current moral codes to be Christian or not.

2. An Argument That Goes Beyond the Concrete Case

Paul's arguments are sometimes more useful and more enlightening than the concrete solution itself because, upon occasion, they *go beyond* the case in point. In dealing with specific problems that perhaps no longer arise today, Paul establishes a line of reasoning that goes beyond the situation that he contemplated and that can be applied to other concrete cases. This is, in our view, the case with homosexuality.

In the Epistle to the Romans (1:25–32), Paul condemns not homosexual tendencies but homosexual activity. Evidence of this is the series of action verbs contained in the passage: exchanging, abandoning, doing, perpetrating, committing. He explicitly envisages only the forms of homosexual activity practiced in the pagan world of that time: pederasty, lesbian and sapphic love.

Paul has no intention of providing in this brief passage a complete teaching on homosexuality. He is judging the pagan world of his time and not persons, whose intentions are God's business only.

While the Greeks, thanks to their concept of erotic love in which fertility was absent, living in a world where woman was reduced to the role of mother or object of lust, celebrated homosexuality as the most noble form of pleasure, the Hebrews condemned homosexual relations as being contrary to the commandment of the Creator: "Increase and multiply" (Gen 1:28).

Paul is therefore looking at homosexuality from a Jewish standpoint. He shares the severe judgments made by his contemporaries. If homosexuality was particularly repugnant in the Jewish world, it was because of the fundamental orientation toward fertility emphasized thoroughout the Old Testament. What struck the Jews was the absolute sterility of this type of sexual relationship. It is, moreover, partly for this reason than contemporary Judaism did not accept consecrated celibacy without some reluctance. This state of life seemed to be contrary to the Old Testatment orientation, against Genesis in particular.

Paul's criticism has its parallels in Judaic literature. But he is the only one who gives the problem a theological emphasis. For him, the homosexual relations of the pagan world of his time are the consequence of a disorder of a religious nature. They are the symptom of the decadence of the pagan world. The voluntary and conscious exchanging of the Creator for the creature is followed by the exchanging of sexes. An error on the religious plane leads to an error on the level of morals. One perversion is punished by another. The cause that Paul indicates surely remains valid: even today, homosexual activity may be a sign of religious and moral decadence. But one cannot conclude from this that it is true in all cases. Homosexual tendencies will often not be culpable, either in themselves, or *in causa*. But what would Paul say about attempts among homosexuals, whose tendency is not culpable, to justify the outright acting out of their tendency? God loves them as they are, it is said. And this is true. It has perhaps been too readily overlooked in pastoral practice. Paul had, however, reminded us of this in proclaiming that redemption is offered to all, Jews and pagans alike. But can we as readily conclude that God loves what they do? This does not mean that one must, today, share the severity of judgment of the Jewish world of Paul's day.

Paul affirms that homosexual activity is "against nature" (Rom 1:26). What does he mean by this? The expression is Greek but he gives it a biblico-theological content. It is used in a sapiential type of reasoning that goes back to the Old Testament idea of a single God, Creator of all. Paul means that, in homosexual activity, the body is not being used in accordance with the design of the Creator God as this design was positively revealed in the twofold account of creation. While the first chapter of Genesis speaks of fruitfulness (Gen 1:28), the second presents the complementary nature and the polarity of the sexes as the law that underlies their mutual relations (Gen 2:18–24).

Paul applies to both sexes the idea of a divine order positively revealed by God (Genesis) and accessible to the human conscience (otherwise he could not blame the pagans). If it is possible to have behavior that is against nature, it is because there is a "natural" use for the sexes, pursuant to the will of the Creator.[18] There are, in the sexed human person, basic structures that already provide us with an indication of the Creator's will and that at the same time trace out for us the limits and the possibilities of sexual activity. In modern terms, Paul would say that we are anatomically and theologically *preceded beings.* Our basic structures are already, in and of themselves, a destiny.

We believe we can conclude that the line of argument used by the apostle truly goes beyond the concrete cases that he was contemplating. In connection with certain homosexual practices, he argues in such a way as to condemn homosexual activity in general.

As for using the expression "have exchanged the natural use for that which is against nature" (Rom 1:26) to support the affirmation that Paul is condemning here only true heterosexuals who engage in homosexual acts (this would be the only perversion that he is discussing) and not acts between true homosexuals (the latter would not be "exchanging" anything but merely following and acting upon their "natural" tendencies), we believe that this is a perfect example of fundamentalist type of exegesis.

3. *Arguments Along the Lines of Pauline Thought*

In his First Letter to the Corinthians, Paul declares fornication to be contrary to the Christian kerygma (1 Cor 6:12–20). But he is explicitly discussing sexual relations between a Christian and a prostitute. May one invoke his authority in connection with the question, so widely discussed today, of premarital relations between engaged people? If one can, then how, in what measure, and with what degree of certainty?

The Old Testament did not distinguish engagement from marriage. There was never any question, in Jewish law, of bethrothal in the current sense of the term. According to Jewish customs, engaged couples had practically the same rights and duties as married people. Sexual relations between them were not recommended but were not absolutely prohibited. In dealing with fornication, Paul could certainly not have been thinking of the situation created by our modern engagements between two people who are promised to one another, but not as yet permanently and irrevocably so. This is why it is difficult to apply directly and explicitly to the case of premarital relations between engaged persons the line of argument used by Paul to condemn relations with a prostitute. One cannot put on the same level relations between an engaged couple who love one another and are already promised to one another, and the profoundly degrading abuse of prostitution.

Yet, would it not be possible to try to demonstrate the illicit nature of premarital relations by resorting to Pauline anthropology?

It might be possible to argue on the basis of: (a) the *total* nature of all sexual experience, so strongly underlined by the surprising application that Paul makes to the transient relationship with a prostitute of the text from Genesis: "the two become one flesh" (Gen 2:24).[19] (b) the nature of *total giving* involved in virginity and marriage. For Paul, the Christian has a choice of only two alternatives: either the unconditional gift of self to Christ in consecrated celibacy, or the unconditional total and permanent gift of self to the spouse in marriage, a gift practically speaking already made in the Jewish betrothals. There seems to be no room for any other alternative. For those who are not called to consecrated celibacy, marriage offers the sole possibility of sexual union that is compatible with the union to Christ and that does not run counter to baptismal consecration. In the matter of sexual union, the Pauline anthropology seems to preclude a mere loan, experimentation, and even *anticipation*. For Paul, sexual union between Christians presupposes the total and permanent giving *in Christo* of the two partners, following the example of Christ and his Church. Thus the radical seriousness of any sexual union. It serves to express the total and permanent gift of self. But in modern engagements, this type of gift has not as yet been made.

On the Pauline view of chastity: After having applied the image of the temple, or better yet of the sanctuary, to the body of the baptized person (1 Cor 6:19), Paul enjoins the Corinthians to "glorify" God in their own bodies (v 20). The Christian must give glory to God even in the use of one's own body, sanctified by the presence of the Holy Spirit. For Paul, baptismal consecration acts even in the flesh, which itself becomes consecrated. This almost liturgical (so to speak) view of Christian chastity[20] which extends even to the body is certainly more fully respected by two engaged people who recognize that their human love, no matter how true and sincere, has not as yet attained that quality of total and permanent gift that would enable it to be expressed by the mutual gift of their bodies, an act which has the significance of incarnating and sealing in the flesh the total and permanent gift of themselves.

This series of arguments would seem to allow us to conclude that premarital relations between engaged persons are not in keeping with Paul's sexual anthropology. But while the Pauline arguments regarding homosexuality covered all possible cases, here we must argue on the basis of the Pauline view of sexuality and draw conclusions from that. While in the case of homosexuality we felt that we were able to use Paul's own arguments, here we have had to construct an argument *ad mentem Pauli* (according to the mind of Paul). We no longer have the same certitude as in the preceding case, nor the same guarantee of as strict a dependence upon revelation. We are, so to speak, in the area of *theologice certum.*

4. Pauline Casuistry

It is useful to see how Paul resolved cases of conscience.[21] He provides us with models of moral reasoning and shows us how to find a solution that is at once Christian and human. Let us take as an example the case of idol offerings. Could Christians eat meat sacrificed to the idols? Paul's balanced solution reveals to us his thinking and his methodology in the matter of practical morality.

He posits first of all the principle of Christian freedom (1 Cor 8:4–8). If the idol is nothing, then the idol offerings are nothing either. In principle, the Christian is therefore free to eat the sacrificed meats.

Paul then examines the matter more closely, taking all circumstances into consideration. In concrete situations, Christian liberty is limited. It is limited first of all by *agape:* Christians are not alone; they are brothers and sisters living in the same community. In exercising one's freedom, therefore, it will be necessary to consider one's neighbor. The Christian cannot abstract from the possibility of *scandalizing* a brother or sister (1 Cor 8:7–9:23). Freedom may also be restricted by *prudence*; what in itself is perfectly licit may become dangerous. In specific cases, the use of one's freedom is not without danger (1 Cor 9:24–10:22).[22]

Paul resorts to basic theological affirmations involving agape and Christian liberty in order to resolve a specific case that in practice no longer arises today. But the disappearance of the case does not entail the invalidity of the theological principles used to solve it. These principles, once separated from the sociological circumstances that made them specific, retain a permanent value. In some concrete circumstances quite different from those of Paul's time, I might be asked to renounce certain prerogatives and liberties because of the weakness of my brother or sister and out of the respect for the other's conscience. This is true fidelity to Paul: to find, in historically different situations, the corresponding modern attitude.

In terminating these few reflections on Paul's categorical morality, it is necessary to repeat that Paul was not a practical moralist interested only in the concrete problems of his Christians. He was concerned, it is true, with the specific moral conduct of his people. In this, he was merely carrying on a constant concern of the early Church: "What shall we do?" the converts of Pentecost day ask Peter (Acts 2:37). But Pauline casuistry is inseparable from the central themes of the kerygma. Paul's categorical morality is essentially based on convictions that are theological (human beings depend entirely on God's creative and redemptive power), eschatological (this world as we see it is passing away: 1 Cor 7:31), and Christological (plunged into death with Christ, the Christian must continuously rise again to a new life). In the final analysis, it is the "in Christo" aspect that gives it its entire meaning.[23]

IV
CONCLUSION

Thanks to the progress of biblical science, we know now better than in pre-critical days how the texts of the New Testament have been given to us in an historical wrapper: God spoke the language of human beings. We can defend ourselves more effectively against a too facile transposition of the language of the early centuries, with its metaphors and its historical context, into contemporary social life. A literal use of the Bible tends toward Tolstoyian Utopia or toward a fundamentalist-type concordism.

On the other hand, the hermeneutic effort to update that we have mentioned allows us to protect ourselves from an excessively restrictive exegesis that would, on the pretext of historical accuracy, reduce biblical standards to inoffensive sociological dicta. It reminds us that Scripture is a rendezvous with God who in it, through it and in each part of it speaks to people of all ages. It is not just history, but history of salvation. We must therefore listen to it and examine it carefully until it can "speak" to modern people, until it has, so to speak, delivered the permanent message that God addressed to us through these norms and standards written in human language. Thanks to this exegetical updating, moral theology will be able to rise above the impasse between *unilateral supernaturalism* that rejects all philosphical reflection and appeals solely to the Bible to know the will of God, and *unilateral rationalism* that ignores recourse to the Bible and, in practice, makes *recta ratio* the soul of moral theology.

Notes

1. This study constitutes the complete text of a lecture given at the University of Sydney (Australia) in August 1972. It follows another study

entitled "La legge morale e i problemi che pone al biblista," published in *Fondamenti biblici della Teologia morale,* Brescia, Paideia, 1973. On this point of the relationship between Scripture and moral theology, it would be helpful to consult the very complete bibliography published by L. Di Pinto under the title *Dossier bibliografico Bibbia-morale,* in *Rassegna di Teologia,* 14 (1973), 32–62.

2. S. Lyonnet, *Il Nuovo Testamento alla luce dell'Antico,* Brescia, Paideia, pp. 110–112.

3. *Sum. Theol.* 1–2, q. 106, a. 1, in c.

4. *Ibid.* Melchior Cano wrote regarding the apostolic tradition: "It would have been very unlikely for evangelical doctrine, which is the law of the spirit of life, to be set forth entirely in a dead text, and for no part of it to have been impressed in human hearts, as Jeremiah has especially promised." Thomas More, for his part, wrote: "Even if no Gospel had been written, there would still be the Gospel written in human hearts, which preceded all the Gospels." Texts cited by Y. Congar in *La Tradition et les traditions,* Vol. II, Paris, 1963, p. 249 and 251.

5. The moral principles given us in the Bible can be considered from a number of standpoints: (a) in their materiality; (b) insofar as they attain the conscience that understands their exigency and their humanizing value; we cannot "respond" to Scripture which calls to us if we do not first understand ourselves, with ontological priority, as moral subjects obligated in conscience to respond to God if ever he speaks to us; (c) insofar as they are part of a written text; (d) insofar as they are God's word written in the heart of the believer: Scripture as message of salvation.

6. Revelation has expressed itself in a special manner in Scripture (D.V. 81), because only there was it fixed in writing once and for all. The writings of the New Testament put us in touch directly with the apostolic tradition which is the *sole source* of the Church's faith. As an infallible codification of the apostolic tradition, they play a unique and irreplaceable role in the life of the Church and particularly in theology. As a higher example of tradition, the voice of the apostolic tradition in the midst of human tradition, Scripture is the sure rule, the test of the Church's faithfulness to the apostolic trust. Being as close as possible to the event of revelation in Christ, sanctioned by the authority of the apostles and fixed in writing for all time, Scripture constitutes, within the Church, an objective, permanent and unerring presence. It is the place where the apostolic kerygma has been preserved without alteration, it is the safeguard of the origins, the rule that prevents the tradition from going astray and allows it to be unfailingly sure of the correctness of its path. Recourse to Scripture will permit the Church to correct faults, oversights, excessively unilateral emphases such as, for instance, a

132 / Edouard Hamel

morality that is too casuitic, too legalistic, not concerned enough with the good news of salvation. It will cast a very sure light on a great many difficult problems of special morality.

7. P. Rossano, *Morale ellenistica e morale neotestamentaria,* in *Fondamenti biblici della teologia morale,* Brescia, Paideia, 1973; W.D. Davies, *The Relevance of the Moral Teaching of the Early Church,* in *Neotestamentica et Semitica,* Edinburgh, 1969, pp. 30–49; *idem, Ethics in the New Testament,* in *The Interpreter's Dictionary of the Bible,* New York, 1962, pp. 167–176.

8. P. Benoit, *La vérité dans la Bible,* in *Vie Sprituelle,* 114 (1966), 387–416.

9. L. Alonso Schökel, *La Bibbia come primo momento ermeneutico,* in *Esegesi ed Ermeneutica,* Brescia, Paideia, 1972, pp. 145–148.

10. E. Rasco, *Actus Apostolorum,* II, Romae, 1968, pp. 296, 299, 327–328.

11. P.H. Menoud, *La vie de l'Eglise naissante,* Neuchâtel, Delachaux et Niestlé, 1969, pp. 65–66.

12. C. Martini, *Caratteristiche relative e assolute nella morale neotestamentaria,* in *Fondamenti biblici della teologia morale,* Brescia, Paideia, 1973.

13. I. de la Potterie, *Le problème oecuménique du Canon et le Protocatholicisme,* in *Axes 4* (1972), no. 4, pp. 7–20.

14. P. Rossano, *Morale ellenistica e morale neotestamentaria* (cf. note 7).

15. W.D. Davies, *The Moral Teaching of the Early Church,* in *The Use of the Old Testament in the New, and Other Essays,* Studies in Honor of W.F. Stinespring (ed. J.M. Efird), Durham, 1972, pp. 310–332; V. Furnish, *Theology and Ethics in Paul,* New York, 1968.

16. See J. Fuchs, *The Absoluteness of Moral Terms,* in *Gregorianum,* 52 (1971) 418–422; B. Schüller, *Zur Rede von der radikalen sittlichen Forderung,* in *Theol. und Phil.* 46 (1971) 321–342; K. Demmer, *Sein und Gebot,* Paderborn, 1971, pp. 190–234.

17. C. Martini, *Fondamenti biblici della morale,* in *Rassegna di Teologia,* 14 (1973) 4.

18. P. Grelot, *L'idée de nature en théologie morale: le témoignage de l'Ecriture,* in *Suppl. Vie Spir.* (1967), no. 81, pp. 217–218, 223.

19. B. Schlegelberger, *Vor-und ausserhelicher Geschlechtsverkehr,* Remscheid, 1970, p. 28.

20. D. Mollat, *Introductio in Epistolas Sancti Pauli,* ed. 4, Romae, 1968, pp. 133–135.

21. Y. Congar, *Die Kasuistik des heiligen Paulus,* in *Verkündigung und Glaube,* Festschr. F.X. Arnold, Freiburg Br. Herder, 1958, pp. 16–41.

22. D. Mollat, *Introductio in epistolas S. Pauli,* pp. 162–163.

23. V. Furnish, *Theology and Ethics in Paul,* pp. 211–215.

The Changing Use
of the Bible
in Christian Ethics

James M. Gustafson

Part of this article originally appeared in *Religion,* edited by Paul Ramsey, 1965. Other excerpts are from Gustafson's book, *Christian Ethics and the Community,* 1971.

For Christian ethics, the Bible remains the charter document. But what it charters depends upon a number of other things that the Christian ethical thinker brings to it. For some it continues to be a book of morality; that is, its prescriptive statements and patterns of life have morally authoritative character that requires literal obedience. For many more, such a view is no longer possible, for historical-critical scholarship has indicated the relation of much that is said to the time and history in which it was written, and theological scholarship has questioned whether the morality of the Bible can be properly understood apart from such theological themes as eschatology, divine judgment, God's grace, Christian freedom, and human sin. Indeed, for a large part of Protestant ethics, the Bible is now less a book of morality than it is a book giving knowledge of God, his presence and his activity. Among Roman Catholics it has traditionally been relegated to dealing with questions of man's supernatural end, and questions of historical morality have been settled in terms of the natural law, often reinforced by biblical quotations. But this is also changing, for European books dealing with the "law of Christ" are making the biblical witness more central to the whole work of Roman Catholic ethics.

By examining what has happened to the use of the Bible in Christian ethics, we are forced to view other themes as well. Most particularly, we must examine different views of the importance of the work of God, Jesus Christ, and the Spirit that have profound effects upon the content and procedures of Christian ethics. Broader theological use of the Bible is particularly necessary where the Christian community desires to interpret theologically and ethically the importance of Christian faith for the extensive and complex issues of human morality in politics, economics, and other areas, and where the community accepts some responsibility for the temporal good of the whole society. A stricter *moral* use of scripture tends to lead to the development of an exemplary morality of a committed few who witness in their distinct patterns of life to a "higher" way. To use distinctions made by Ernst Troeltsch and Max Weber, where the community takes the high demands of biblical morality with literal seriousness, it tends to become sectarian (clearly defined over against the world) and sees its effect upon the world in terms of "exemplary" prophecy and conduct that might have indirect consequences for the temporal good. Where the community takes the Bible to refer primarily to more universal themes of God's governing and redeeming work, it tends to become "churchly" (blurring lines between the religious community and the world) and accepts broad social responsibility as an "emissary" people whose duty it is to make compromises and accept responsibility for cultural values.

There are no recent American writings of academic repute that assume in a simple way that the Bible provides the rules for the governing of the whole human community as if it were the rational norm and ideal of morality applicable to all regardless of their status in Christian faith. This kind of rationalistic moral idealism, characteristic of Tolstoy's use of the Christian teaching, forgets that the Bible is much more than a moral textbook; it is for writers of various persuasions a source for knowledge of God and a source for God's word of judgment and redemption to man. Thus, the moral teachings are seen within the wider framework of theological affirmations and of the Christian experience of sin and forgiveness through Jesus Christ. The Bible, to put it simply, has a different moral authority for Christians than it has for others. But the variations within this statement are in effect the story of Christian ethics throughout history.

Radical Reformation Groups

On the American scene there are Christian groups for whom a literal compliance with the gospel ethic—particularly its commands to love, to meekness, to service—is both an aspiration and a pattern of life. The historic peace churches in the Anabaptist and Quaker traditions, for example, have taken part of the moral teaching to require nonviolence, pacifism, and deeply sacrificial service as the proper expression of Christian life. But there are as yet no American academic treatises that give powerful theological defenses of the Anabaptist view, though in occasional writings such a person as John Howard Yoder promises to be a formidable and theologically informed interpreter and defender of this tradition. Among liberal Quakers, Rufus Jones and Douglas Steere have been more or less faithful to the tradition of a pacifist interpretation of both "inner light" and a Sermon on the Mount ethic. There is no expectation of great worldly success in such ethical teaching; these Christians expect to be a minority representation of faithfulness, and are prepared to suffer at the hands of a more expedient and prudential world.

Evangelical Conservative Protestants:
Revealed Morality

A larger segment of American Protestantism is represented by the conservative evangelical position, sometimes the fundamentalist one, in which the "propositional revelation" of the Bible has an authority in matters of both faith and conduct. The words of the Bible are quite literally the word of God, whether they tell us about God and his glory, about man and his rebellion, about the new life that conversion creates, or about the moral conduct that is required of the children of God. This tradition has begun to find new expressions in scholarly work in ethics. The major recent contributor is Carl F. H. Henry, whose *The Uneasy Conscience of Modern Fundamentalism* (1947) opened the way for discussions of social ethics among those groups that had formerly identified that interest with degenerate Christian liberalism. In a very large and ambitious work, *Christian Personal Ethics* [Eerdmans, 1957], Henry gives more specific expression to his view of biblical authority for ethics. It is framed by his larger conservative use of the Bible in matters of theology. His preference for the moral use of the Bible seems to combine elements of the Anabaptist tradition, which he honors in part because it does not make Christian ethics subjective and humanistic, and the Reformed tradition, which sought within the scripture a design and order for the lives of the members of the Christian church. The reality of Christian ethics comes from the "unique Divine inbreaking" that is recorded in the Bible. "The Christian ethic is a specially revealed morality—not merely religious ethics. It gains its reality in and through supernatural disclosure" (*Christian Personal Ethics,* p. 193). Since Christian ethics is a special and not a universal revelation, it is not accessible to all men; it is the ethics of the believing church. "The ethics of revealed religion therefore divides mankind into two radically opposed groups: the followers of the broad way and those of the narrow way" (p. 203). The divine will is clear: "What God has revealed in the inspired Scriptures defines the content of his will" (p. 264). The historic conviction is "that God has been pleased to reveal his will, and that he has done so in express commands, given to chosen men through the medium of human language, and available to us as the *Word* of God in written form" (p. 265). This will is particularized in the Old and New Testaments, though in a "progressive" way. "A later age is always called upon to 'fulfill' the continuing moral claim, although God may supersede certain positive laws in the newer era" (p. 269). Henry reminds his readers that they are not to take the moral teaching in isolation from the rest of biblical revelation; this is true of the details both of Old and New Testaments. Thus in studying the Sermon on the Mount, Jesus' larger teaching and the whole of the New Testament must be kept in view. But

> the Sermon remains an "ethical directory" for Christians. It contains the character and conduct which Jesus commends to his followers, the demand which the nature and will of God make upon men, the fundamental law of the Kingdom, and the ideal and perfect standard. It is the ultimate formula of ethics for which ideal human nature was fashioned by creation and is destined in eternity. Fallen nature is justified in Christ in conformity to it, and redeemed

nature approximates it by the power of the indwelling Spirit of God (pp. 325–26).

The seriousness with which the moral teachings of the Bible are taken by Henry can best be seen in contrast with Paul Lehmann's view of the Christian life. The way in which the authority of the Bible is understood by these men is, of course, radically different. Whereas Lehmann develops a biblical theology that describes the human maturity in faith in which man in his freedom is sensitive to the freedom of God, Henry is saying that God has declared himself on matters of morals as well as faith in highly particularized ways in the words of the Bible. Henry acknowledges that it is not always easy to move from moral propositions in the Bible to the particular situations in which man must act, but in contrast ot Lehmann, he has substantive, authoritative moral propositions from which to begin the process. The Bible is law as well as gospel.

Liberal Protestantism:
Revealed Morality in a Different Form

One of the characteristics of the ethics of liberal Christianity was its focus on the "spirit" of Jesus and on the authority of his teachings, as these are depicted in the gospel narratives. No intelligent theologians were so simple-minded as to assume that the teachings of Jesus could be immediately applied to the contemporary world, but they did seek the possibility of "translating" them into current needs. Macintosh is typical of this when he wrote, "What we may have to do . . . is to translate into the terms of our best twentieth-century empirical knowledge and world-view the principles of social action normatively present in the spirit and ideal of the Jesus of history and expressed by him, quite naturally, in terms of the concepts available in his day" (*Social Religion,* p. 5). Various aspects of the teachings and deeds of Jesus were used by various interpreters to serve as the basic framework for the fundamental pattern for moving from the authority of the "Jesus of history" to the contemporary world. Some used the notion of the kingdom of God; some took the command to love the neighbor. Macintosh chose the beatitudes to give the framework to his interpretation of the social content of the gospel. His use of the saying "Blessed are the poor, for theirs is the kingdom of God" not only illustrates his work, but also suggests the kinds of uses of the Bible that others made.

The kingdom of God is to be "the rule of God's will in human life, individually, and socially." Thus when Jesus spoke the saying,

> He must have meant that when, through the divine initiative and man's response, God's rule was established on earth and God's will was being done fully enough in a sufficient number of human lives for them to revolutionize social relations and make society a genuine brotherhood under the divine Fatherhood, poverty would soon be abolished (p. 42).

A related narrative is of Jesus' story of the workers in the vineyard (Matt. 20:1–16). From this narrative Macintosh draws the moral: "From everyone according to his ability; to every one according to his need." "A job for every one, and 'a living wage for every one willing to work.' " In summary, Macintosh is able by the alchemy of his religious thought and feeling to move from these accounts in the Bible to a definition of the social order that is coming through both God's work, and man's works.

> In the Kingdom the hungry will be fed, not by mere acts of charity, but by a system of justice under which they will be helped to help themselves. When the Kingdom is established, when God's will is being done, people will be brotherly enough to see to it that none hunger in vain, either for food or for social and economic justice (p. 45).

The use of the Bible typified by Macintosh had important effects upon the work of Christian ethics. It permitted a "translation" of biblical ideas into contemporary language in such a way that a program for "objective ethics"—that is, for the shaping of moral action in the world—could be authorized by the Bible. The kingdom of God could become a kind of cooperative democratic commonwealth, and thus provide the end toward which man's historical activity is to be directed. The beatitude "Blessed are the poor" could become the basis for proposing a genuinely "Christian communism" as both the ideal toward which men should move and the state of life that will exist in the kingdom.

But even before Macintosh wrote, the assumptions upon which this use of the Bible was made in ethics were undercut radically by biblical scholars. Much earlier, Albert Schweitzer had suggested that Jesus' ethic was an "interim" one, to be valid until the soon forthcoming kingdom would arrive. The form critics were questioning the historical authenticity of many of the sayings of Jesus, as well as narratives about him. And historically-minded men were raising questions about the easy translation of first-century language, with its own particular metaphors, into contemporary social life. If the words of the Bible were to be morally authoritative, the writer in Christian ethics had to find some other way to use them. In America as in Europe, he generally chose to depend upon a summary statement of them, such as in the command to love God and thy neighbor. Or biblical words became first of all a revelation of God, and the morality of the Bible more illustrative of a proper life in relation to God and man than a revealed morality. Certainly, what Carl F. H. Henry suggests as revealed morality is generally rejected or radically qualified, and most recent writers would never try to move from biblical statements to contemporary moral statements in the manner of D. C. Macintosh.

Love: The Summary of Biblical Ethics

The "law of love" became the major summary generalization of biblical morality. Reinhold Neibuhr, it will be recalled, suggested the centrality of love as the distinctive element in Christian ethics. Earlier for Niebuhr the source for this norm was primarily the transcendent morality introduced by the teachings of Jesus; later the crucifixion became the symbol of the highest form of love. In either case, the Bible presents to us an expectation that life is to be governed both inwardly and outwardly by love, both in the intentions of the moral man and in the formation of a state of affairs in the world. Niebuhr's long-time colleague John C. Bennett, whose writings and

work in ecclesiastical and ecumenical agencies are of central importance to the story of Christian ethics in recent decades, also fixes
upon love as the mark of Christian ethics. "The distinctive element
in Christian ethics is the primacy of love, the self-giving love that is
known fully to Christian faith in the Cross of Christ" (in A. Dudley
Ward, ed., *Goals of Economic Life,* 1953, p. 421). Thus a generalization is made on the basis of the Bible, a generalization that is moral
in its language, based upon both moral teachings and example in the
New Testament. This view of the Bible builds in a problem of translation, or at least transition, from the general moral propositions giv-
en in historically unachievable terms to the realities of the
time-bound, historically contingent world. The transition from Bible
to contemporary world is then made through the use of less uniquely
Christian "values" or terms, such as justice. These terms, and more
explicit imperative propositions derived from them, in turn regulate
the ends to be sought by moral man and the forms of action he will
use to seek those ends. The pure morality of love is always compromised in the movement from the Bible to the world. But there is a
sense in which the Bible still contains a revealed morality: it provides
distinctive moral norms or values that have authority for the Christian community. These now have a generalized form, rather than the
form of the particular propositions given in particular biblical texts.
Compromise is required when men who use the Bible in this way
wish Christian ethics to inform social and political moral responsibility, and not be merely the "narrow way" for an exemplary Christian
community. This use of the Bible is consistent with the preceding
generation of liberal theologians, who found in its morality the pattern for contemporary morality; the Bible continued to be in some
sense a book of moral teachings with a high level of authority.

The Bible:
Revealed Reality Rather Than Revealed Morality

Concurrently, however, a revolution in biblical theology was
taking place in Europe and, to a lesser extent, in America. The shift
might be overstated as one from ethics to faith, from religion to God,
from man to Jesus Christ. Under the impact of the crisis theologians,

and particularly Karl Barth, men were saying that the Bible is not the revelation of a morality, but the revelation of the living God; it does not cultivate a human cultural phenomenon called religion that has any significance in its own right, but it points to God and to God's call to men for faith in him; it is not centered upon what men are and ought to do, but upon Jesus Christ as the revelation of God, in the light of whom theological knowledge of men comes. This revolution in theology had much more far-reaching consequences for Christian ethics than did the reassessment of the moral potentialities of men, for it changed the prime point of reference for all thinking in ethics and all moral activity on the part of Christians. In the place of moral teachings, particularized or generalized, the new theology put God in his living, free activity. Thus Christian ethics had to think not about morality reduced to propositions, but about God and how life ought to be rightly related to his power and his presence. The Bible then finds a different use in the thinking of ethics, and its moral teachings are set in a different context. For Carl F. H. Henry both knowledge of God and moral knowledge are authoritatively given in "propositional revelation" in the words of the Bible. For Macintosh the Bible did not give propositional revelation, but its moral teachings expressed the spirit of the "Jesus of history" and thus in turn were a basic blueprint for morality. For Reinhold Niebuhr and John C. Bennett the Bible was not propositional revelation, but revealed God's self-sacrificial love, which in turn was conceptualized in images of commands and love. But for Karl Barth, the Bible first of all points toward the living God, known in Jesus Christ, and thus what is required of ethics is obedience to a Person, not a proposition, or, in the language of H. Richard Niebuhr, *response* to a Person, and not a rule.

H. Richard Niebuhr:
Response to a Revealing God

This change in the fundamental way of thinking, and thus in the use of the Bible, can be illustrated by some of the work of H. Richard Niebuhr. He found too much of Christian ethics trying to find "Christian answers" to problems of morality and culture, rather than being open and responsive to the work of the living Lord. In introducing his great work on *Christ and Culture* [Harper & Bros., 1951], Niebuhr says, "The belief which lies back of this effort . . . is the conviction that Christ as Living Lord is answering the question in the totality of history and life in a fashion which transcends the wisdom of all his interpreters yet employs their partial insights and their necessary conflicts" (p. 2). The crucial point is the stress on the notion that the *Living Lord is answering* in the totality of history and life. There are interpretations of what he is doing, but men are not finally to rely upon them, though they give partial insights. This means, it appears, that the Bible itself is of penultimate significance in the work of Christian ethics and that its importance is to enable men to understand and interpret what the "Living Lord" is saying and doing. It points beyond itself; its moral teachings point beyond themselves; the Christian community is to understand its morality in response to God rather than in response to statements about God. The Bible is more important for helping the Christian community to interpret the God whom it knows in its existential faith than it is for giving a revealed morality that is to be translated and applied in the contemporary world. This led Niebuhr to be critical of theologians who use such phrases as "the abolutism and perfectionism of Jesus' love ethic," including his distinguished brother. He retorts, "Jesus nowhere commands love for its own sake"; the virtue of Jesus' character and demand is not "love of love" but "love of God and the neighbor in God." "It was not love but God that filled his soul" (*Christ and Culture*, pp. 15–19). The Christian moral life, then, is not a response to moral imperatives, but to a Person, the living God.

The effect of this transposition in the function of the Bible can be seen in H. Richard Niebuhr's almost lyrical description of the meaning of love in Christian ethics. It is not a norm. Rather, love is an indicative before it is an imperative. "Faith in God's love toward man is perfected in man's love to God and neighbor."

> Through Jesus Christ we receive enough faith in God's love toward us to see at least the need for and the possibility of a responsive love on our part. We know enough of the possibility of love to God on our part to long for its perfection; we see enough of the reality of God's love toward us and

neighbor to hope for its full revelation and so for our full response."

Love is not a law, but "rejoicing over the existence of the beloved one"; it is "gratitude" for the existence of the beloved; it is "reverence" that "keeps its distance even as it draws near"; it is "loyalty," the "willingness to let the self be destroyed rather than that the other cease to be" [*The Purpose of the Church and Its Ministry,* Harper & Bros., 1956, pp. 33, 35]. Love is basically defined, then, in terms of attitudes and actions; it comes into being in the close interrelation of "God's love of the self and neighbor, of the neighbor's love of God and self, and of the self's love of God and neighbor." What the Bible makes known, then, is not a morality, but a *reality,* a living presence to whom man responds. For questions of morality, its authority is "educational," giving men knowledge of themselves and knowledge of God in the light of which they interpret their responsibilities and act; its authority is "corroborative," providing a court of validation that aids the Christian community in seeing its perversities and in verifying its true purposes.

Paul Lehmann:
Ethics of the Biblical Indicative

The alteration of the imperative mode in Christian ethics that is present in the writings of H. Richard Niebuhr is even stronger in the work of Paul Lehmann. In a widely acclaimed essay of 1953 ("The Foundation and Pattern of Christian Behavior," in *Christian Faith and Social Action,* ed. John A. Hutchison) that influenced the writing of Albert Rasmussen (*Christian Social Ethics,* 1956), Alexander Miller (*The Renewal of Man,* 1955), and others, Lehmann states that "an ethic, based upon the self-revelation of God in Jesus Christ, is more concerned about 'The Divine Indicative' than it is about the 'Divine Imperative.' The primary question is not 'What does God command?' The primary question is 'What does God do?' " (p. 100). Thus, the importance of the Bible for Christian ethics does not lie in its moral imperatives, but in its delineation of what God is doing to "make and keep life human." "Christian ethics . . . is oriented toward revelation and not toward morality"; and "Christian ethics aims, not at morality, but at maturity. The *mature* life is the fruit of Christian faith. Morality is a by-product of maturity" (*Ethics in a Christian Context,* 1963, pp. 45, 54). The importance of the Bible is what it tells about Jesus Christ. Thus in Lehmann's full-length treatise on Christian ethics there is no significant treatment of biblical morality, even as a guide to the mature life. Rather, the mature man discerns through his transformed motivation and his sensitive imagination what God is doing.

Joseph Sittler:
The Shape of the Engendering Deed

In a similar mode is the most significant contribution to Christian ethics in America made by a Lutheran theologian, Joseph Sittler's *The Structure of Christian Ethics* [Louisiana State University Press, 1958]. (Lutherans have only within the past decade begun to produce significant literature in Christian ethics: the work of George Forell, William Lazareth, and Franklin Sherman shows the emerging interest.) Sittler wishes to develop biblical ethics. But he does not do this from the distinctly moral statements in the Bible. Rather, there is a more important structure for understanding Christian morality that can be seen in the fact that God is not defined, but simply is what he does; that a vocabulary of relatedness rather than a vocabulary of substance abounds; that its logic is "the inner logic of the living, the organic." Biblical language is primarily descriptive and indicative. Jesus himself is to be seen in this way: the content of his importance is constituted "by a lived-out and heroically obedient God-relationship in the fire of which all things are what they are by virtue of the creator, all decisions are crucial in virtue of their witness to his primacy and glory, all events interpreted in terms of their transparency, recalcitrancy, or service to God's Kingly rule" (p. 12). The prime importance of the Bible for ethics is that it tells the story of "the shape of the engendering deed," that is, the record of what the living God has actually done in creation, redemption, and sanctification. The living God continues to engender man's involvement in what he is doing. Thus Christian ethics gives an account of the Christian life:

> A re-enactment from below on the part of man of the shape of the revelatory drama of God's holy will in Jesus Christ. . . . Suffering, death, burial, resurrection, a new life—these are actualities that plot out the arc of God's self-giving deed in Christ's descent and death and ascension; and precisely *this same shape of grace,* in its recapitulation within the life of the believer and the faithful community, is the nuclear matrix which grounds and unfolds as the Christian life (p. 36).

Christian ethics is the actualization of God's justification of man. It describes life according to a plotted arc; the arc, however, is not the morality given in the Bible, but rather the "shape of the engendering deed."

This indicative mode, with its particular use of the Bible, has not gone unchallenged in American Protestant ethics. It has been criticized in the extreme form for the absence of any procedures of rational reflection about what men are to do. Paul Ramsey, Robert Fitch, Alvin Pitcher, Clinton Gardner, and John C. Bennett have all written critiques on this issue. Indeed, it tends to become what has been called a "contextual"ethics, and against this has been pitted an "ethics of principles," which finds propositional moral imperatives, either directly from the Bible or mediated through the tradition, that are to provide the guidelines of conduct. This issue is reserved for exploration in the next section, "Procedures for Ethical Reflection."

The Bible in Roman Catholic Ethics

The use of the Bible has traditionally been the place where the difference between Roman Catholic and Protestant Christian ethics was clearest. Whereas most Protestants have turned to the Bible for the starting point of Christian ethics, whether personal or social, for most questions Roman Catholics have relied upon the natural law that is, in their interpretation, shared by all mankind. The recent American Catholics have shared in that tradition. There is a "science of ethics" independent from revelation. Indeed, the term *Christian ethics* has not been widely used among Roman Catholic writers. For most ethical questions, the distinctively Christian elements have not been of great importance. For example, one of the most widely read recent treatises on matters of American public ethics—*We Hold These Truths* (1960), by John Courtney Murray, S.J.—contains no references to biblical texts that Protestants traditionally grapple with on questions of the state, such as Romans 13:1–7. There is no effort to define what is going on in contemporary society in terms of "what God is doing." Rather, the theoretical foundations are in the Thomistic tradition of natural law. "The doctrine of natural law has no Roman Catholic presuppositions. Its only presupposition is threefold: that man is intelligent; that reality is intelligible; and that reality, grasped by intelligence, imposes on the will the obligation that it be obeyed in its demands for action or abstention" (p. 109). Most questions of ethics, and particularly public ethics, are dealt with on this natural-law foundation. The more distinctive "Christian" elements of religion deal with the theological virtues and with man's supernatural end, and these relate indirectly back upon the rational moral life. But even here the traditional pattern for interpretation is Thomistic, rather than in the first instance biblical. The morality of saints, with their imitations of Christ, has not been a general expectation for all Christians.

The major American treatise entitled *Christian Ethics* written by a Roman Catholic is remarkably free of biblical references. Dietrich von Hildebrand, in his 1953 publication, makes of Christian ethics a philosophical discipline that is distnct from moral theology.

> It is a pure philosophical exploration introducing no arguments which are not accessible through our *lumen naturale* (light of reason), whereas in moral theology faith is presupposed, and revealed truth which surpasses our reason is included in the argumentation. Christian ethics is a strict *philosophical* analysis, starting from the data accessible to our mind through experience [David McKay Co., p. 455].

All morality presupposes the existence of God, and the philosophical analysis of Christian morality obviously assumes that many human moral responses and virtues are possible only through Christian revelation. But the analysis does not begin with the datum of revelation in the Bible.

To look for the use of the Bible in Roman Catholic morality, then, one turns to *moral theology* and to the discussions of the Christian virtues. Moral theology presupposes divine revelation "and the proved conclusions of dogmatic theology." In moral theology texts long used in America, such as *Moral and Pastoral Theology,* by Henry Davis, S.J., there is a characteristic structure that brings no surprises. The Bible is used to substantiate the existence of a supernatural, ultimate end for man—namely, that he is to enjoy eternal beatitude in the vision of God. But the bulk of moral theology deals with the natural moral acts of man; here the Thomistic structure asserts itself vigorously as the dominant framework, and the Bible is quoted (so it appears to these Protestant eyes) to proof-text a point already established on principles independent of biblical discussion. Or the Bible is quoted as the divine revealed law that, like the natural law, participates in the eternal law in the mind of God. As particular instances of moral problems come into view, the procedures of casuistry are employed with great rational refinement, in contrast with what Sittler called the "organic language" of the scripture.

There are evidences of a changing pattern in Roman Catholic moral theology, however, that ought to be noted. Two currently widely read texts in moral theology—Bernard Häring's *The Law of Christ* [2 vols.; English trans., Paulist-Newman Press, 1961, 1963. Copyright © 1961 by The Newman Press] and Gérard Gilleman's *The Primacy of Charity in Moral Theology* (English trans., 1959)— and other writings appear to soften the distinction between the natural and the supernatural, and to place Christian love at the center of the whole interpretation of ethics. Indeed, the biblical text that gives these books of European origin their titles is from Romans: "For the law of the Spirit of the life in Christ Jesus has delivered me from the law of sin and of death." Whereas traditional Catholic ethics deals with the natural principles of morality first, and later comes to the higher law of love, Häring, Gilleman, and others begin with the more distinctively Christian and biblical principle of love and seek to keep it at the center of the whole enterprise of moral theology. A few quotations from Häring's Foreword demonstrate the new emphasis. "The principle, the norm, the center, and the goal of Christian Moral Theology is Christ. The law of the Christian is Christ Himself in Person. He alone is our Lord, our Saviour. In Him we have life and therefore also the law of our life." The emphasis here is on a *Christian* ethics, expressing the religious relationship with God in moral terms.

> In the love of and through the love of Christ for us He invites our love in return, which is a life truly formed in Christ. The Christian life is following Christ, but not through mere external copying, even though it be in love and obedience. Our life must above all be a life in Christ. Christian morality is life flowing from the victory of Christ, the hopeful anticipation of the Second Coming of the Saviour in the glorious manifestation of His final triumph on the great day of judgment (*The Law of Christ*, vol. I, p. vii).

Moral theology is reaffirming the biblical tradition, reaffirming those aspects of the Catholic tradition that set Christian ethics in the context of God's loving action and see the norm for every man to be a life sharing in union with Christ and in imitation of him. Häring affirms his purpose to be to expound the most central truths in the light of the inspired word of the Bible. Younger American clergy are quickly beginning to think in those new modes, and no doubt the Bible will find a different place in indigenous American moral theology as a result.

Discussion of the Christian virtues is a second place to see the use of the Bible. Traditionally, Catholics have tended to follow Thomas Aquinas in his distinction between the cardinal virtues and the theological virtues. The latter—faith, hope, and love—are gifts of grace given by participation in the sacramental life of the church. For them, obviously there is a distinctive Christian referent, derived through Catholic interpretation from the Bible. This two-level interpretation, however, is also being altered. A notable American book,

Dietrich von Hildebrand's *Transformation in Christ,* is one example of a more biblically centered (though obviously Catholic and not Protestant in exposition) interpretation of the Christian life. Perhaps the text that is central to this book is from 1 Peter 2: "That you may declare his virtues, who hath called you out of darkness into his marvelous light." It is a book that seeks to describe how, through baptism and communion, man is allowed to participate in the life of Christ. The shaping of the Christian life is not so much a matter of external heteronomous norms by which men are to be governed and ruled as it is one of finding the appropriate expression in life for what God has done for man in Jesus Christ. The "supernatural life" is not relegated to achievement by those set apart in the orders, nor is it in von Hildebrand's treatment something to be received in the life beyond death; it is both a reality and a task for the Christian believer (the author is himself a layman) in his present existence.

If a study of more recent Roman Catholic ethics leaves a correct impression, it is clear that the Bible is coming to play a far more significant role and have a more central location in Catholic literature. The traditional distinctions between the ethics of natural law and special Christian morality are being blurred. The biblical witness to God's own presence and action as being both matrix and context for Christian life is being stressed. And the central biblical conception of Christian love is becoming the norm under which all action is judged and directed. Yet no important writers have left the traditional philosophical language behind. What the impact of these mostly imported European writings will be on American Catholic ethics is still unclear, but if it continues to make its way on this continent, men like Father Murray who have reputations in Protestant America for being liberals are likely to appear to be highly traditionalistic.

European influences have been very important among both Catholics and Protestants in altering the place of the Bible in the study of Christian ethics. Between the World Wars American Protestant theologians followed the developments and debates of European theology and biblical scholarship with increasing care. The ecumenical movement, particularly the great 1938 Oxford Conference on Life and Work, provided the occasion for personal discussion and for the influence of Europeans on American ethics. The struggle of the confessing Christians in Germany against the Nazi state provided one of the most significant occasions in modern church history for reflections on the relation of biblical faith to moral concerns. Some of the writings of participants in the "theological revival" in Europe were translated into English. Anders Nygren's *Agape and Eros* was particularly influential in raising issues about the meaning of Christian love.

Since World War II, many important volumes of European theological ethics have become available in English and thus are widely read by students and teachers alike: H. Emil Brunner's *The Divine Imperative,* major volumes of Barth's *Church Dogmatics* that deal with ethics, the writings of Dietrich Bonhoeffer, Kierkegaard, Rudolf Bultmann, Helmut Thielicke, Gustaf Aulen, Gustaf Wingren, Jacques Ellul, and others. The points at issue between these writers are important, and the American reception of them has not lacked in discriminating sophistication. They all do, however, work from an understanding of the high theological authority of the Bible and thus, as conversation partners for American theological ethics, keep the Bible quite at the center of discussion.

Among Roman Catholics, biblical studies have had a new status in all spheres of theological research and discourse since World War II. This is bound to have effects not only on dogmatic theology, but also upon traditional Catholic distinctions between the general science of ethics, moral theology, ascetic theology, pastoral theology, and so forth. Very important also is the way in which the renewal of interest in biblical studies in both Catholicism and Protestantism has coincided with the expansion of the ecumenical discussion. It is clear that one of the directions that scholarship in Christian ethics will take in the next decades is cross-confessional critique and interpretation nourished in part by a common interest in the Bible as the charter document for the Christian movement in history.

The Place of Scripture
in Christian Ethics:
A Methodological Study

James M. Gustafson

Parts of this article originally appeared in *Interpretation* in 1970 and Gustafson's book, *Theology and Christian Ethics*, 1974.

The facets of the project indicated by this title are many and complex. Indeed, this chapter can only seek to provide some order, while doing some justice to the complexity. Certain markings can be fixed which will set both limits and direction for the present discussion; these ought to enable the reader to avoid some possible confusions.

First, the title indicates that this study does not concentrate primarily on what might properly be called "biblical ethics." Biblical ethics would be the study of the ethics in the scriptures. In itself this is a complex task for which few are well prepared; those who are specialists in ethics generally lack the intensive and proper training in biblical studies, and those who are specialists in biblical studies often lack sophistication in ethical thought. A comprehensive study of biblical ethics would, of course, render an effort to develop the place of scripture in Christian ethics easier, for one important question is the relation of biblical ethics to constructive Christian ethics. The problem here is parallel to the relation of the theology found in the Bible to constructive Christian theology.

A study of biblical ethics would include various concerns. One is the concrete moral teachings of the scriptures—what content they give to right conduct and to ends and purposes that are good. Biblical notions of justice, of peace, of the good life, of love, would be developed. Another concern would be the forms of moral discourse in scripture: moral commands, laws, the examples of persons, narratives of actions that are judged to be faithful or unfaithful to God's moral will, parables and allegories, paraenetic instructions, and others. Such a study could be done without reference to uses the findings would have for constructive purposes.

The study of biblical ethics requires focus on yet another concern, namely, the theology in the scriptures which both validates and provides content to the moral teachings. For the people of the Bible, morality was not separated from religion in the way that it has been both in theory and in practice in later developments; ethics was not separated from theology. God and his relations to men and the world were conceived in moral terms, as well as in other terms, and this makes theology an integral part of biblical ethics. Since there are theologies in scripture, this analytical task is in itself complex; its use as a basis for constructive Christian ethics is even more so.

In the present study we are alert to the problems raised by the absence of a full development of what are the biblical ethics, and this absence indicates where certain assumptions and warrants that are not fully justified can be found in our proceedings.

A second marking is that our primary attention is not a critical analysis of writings in Christian ethics in order to see how scriptures are used by various theologians and ethicists. Rather, the present modest constructive effort makes proposals that are subject to the critical scalpels of others. Two helpful articles have been published. Edward LeRoy Long has provided one framework for interpretation in his article "The Use of the Bible in Christian Ethics." David H. Kelsey's article "Appeals to Scripture in Theology" provides a pattern that is also suggestive for the study of Christian ethics.[1] Intensive critical analysis of the ways in which scripture is used in the literature of Christian ethics would yield the range of options from the past and provide a sturdier framework for positive proposals than that given in the present chapter. Some analysis of this sort is done here, but its function is subservient to other aims.

A third marking is more difficult to shape with precision. It calls attention to the fact that how an author uses scripture is determined to a considerable extent by how he defines the task of Christian ethics. Indeed, how one defines the field and methods of ethics, whether specifically Christian or more general, will make a difference in his uses of scripture. For example, if the study of ethics is focused on the structure of moral arguments about particular acts, the question of this article would be, "How is scripture used in particular moral arguments?" Kelsey's development of Toulmin's distinctions between data, warrant, and backing would be immediately applicable. If, however, one includes in ethics a concern for the formation of the moral agent, then scripture will be used in quite a different way.[2] Or, if one attends to a vision of the future good, or to the ontological structure of morality, his uses of scripture will be governed accordingly. While I would argue that the scope of Christian ethics is rather inclusive, many aspects will be left relatively unattended in the present chapter.[3]

In this chapter I intend to develop the significance and the limitations of the uses of scripture in Christian ethics. I shall also indicate some of the various points or levels in Christian ethical reflection where scripture is used. To keep at least a backdrop of concreteness in view, I shall draw attention to a complex event which has exercised the moral passions of the American people, namely, the invasion of Cambodia by American troops from South Vietnam in the last days of April 1970. Many articulate Christians have judged this to be morally wrong and have participated in various forms of action to express their indignation about it. Our major and long-range question is this: Why do Christians judge this to be morally wrong? How does scripture enter into their judgment? To keep the chapter manageable it is confined to moral judgments about actions and does not extend to the positive determination of what alternative courses of action are morally better, or what means and ends ought to be used. Before an attempt is made to answer directly this last question, however, it is necessary to isolate the points in the decision-making and action processes where moral assessments are pertinent. These are in the assessment of the meaning of the history in which the events take place, the motives and intentions of the decision-makers, the circumstances in which it is deemed proper to act, and the consequences of the action. It is also necessary to sort out some of the more general issues in the uses of scripture in ethics before we come to address the major question more directly. Finally, in addressing the question, it will be clear that other Christian ethicists might well wish to claim more or less than I do for the place of scripture, but it is hoped that at least the points at which the arguments can be made will be clear.

I
THE CAMBODIAN INVASION

Not all who believe the invasion of Cambodia to be a mistake would necessarily judge it to be morally wrong; even fewer would judge it to be wrong for "Christian ethical" reasons. The adjectives that would qualify the "wrong" suggest the various frameworks of interpretation that can be used in evaluating the action.

1. The argument is made that it is legally wrong. Persons who have defended the right of American military forces to be in Vietnam on legal grounds, in compliance with commitments, and at the invitation of a legally constituted government, draw a distinction between Vietnam and Cambodia precisely on those two points. There is a violation of the delicate fabric of international law when a power moves into the territory of another nation without invitation of its government and without treaty commitments that require it. The observation that the move is illegal could contribute to two different sorts of arguments about its immorality. First, it is immoral for a nation to violate international law. Second, it is not possible to universalize the principle used to justify the breaking of the law. To do so would seem to legitimate the invasion of any nation by any other nation in circumstances judged to be similar to those existing in Cambodia.

2. The argument is made that it is a military mistake. Here the appeal is not to a legal standard, but to previous military experience of a similar sort that has not led to the intended or desired consequences. To many persons the script used to justify this expansion of the war sound strikingly similar to those scripts used to justify previous escalations, and the evidence suggests that mutatis mutandis this will fail as well. The justification for the judgment are made largely on factual grounds: Under similar circumstances escalations have been justified, but have not led to peace. To dispute the argument, then, one would have to appeal to factual evidences which would in-

dicate that the circumstances are different at this time and place, and therefore the desired end is more likely to be achieved. There is a moral appeal in the argument in favor of the invasion, namely, that in the long run the action will save more lives, and particularly American lives. As in all moral arguments from potential consequences, so in this one it is difficult to adduce the compelling evidence. Perhaps if saving lives is the moral imperative, it would be better simply to withdraw; this is clearly the case if the concern is primarily of American lives. And even the latter concern is subject to critical scrutiny: Does it assume that American lives have greater worth—intrinsically or even instrumentally—than Indo-Chinese lives?

3. The argument is made that it is politically wrong. Military actions have to be seen in their political contexts and have always to be justified by the political purposes that they serve. The judgment about the political purposes involved in the Cambodian venture is made on two counts. First, it does not appear that this action is the correct means to achieve the desired political end, namely, peace in Southeast Asia. Second, even if it were the correct means, those who chose to engage in this action did not take fully into account the consequences for other political ends, such as the political responses of the Soviet Union, China, and Western European allies, and the announced intention of the administration to bring the American people back together again. Indeed, the political consequences, intended and unintended, appear to be much more complex than anything a brief paragraph suggests. The relations between a judgment that an action is politically wrong and that it is morally wrong are complex. One can seek a moral justification of the political ends themselves: For example, is there a persuasive if not definitive moral justification for the purpose of restraining the spread of Communism in Southeast Asia? This is itself a many-faceted question. Is Communism morally evil? Or are its presumed evil consequences sufficient to warrant the evils of protracted war to restrain it? Indeed, is revolution not morally right in much of the "third world" that has been dominated by Western political and economic interests? The question of the morality of means is asked. Are the means used proportionate to the end that is sought? If what is sought is the "well-being" of the people of the region, are there not better means than war to fulfill that end? Or

perhaps one does not expect such lofty moral ends from nation-states. Perhaps they are governed in their moral codes and actions by their own national interest. If that is the case, the question can still be raised as to whether the national interest of the United States is in any crucial way threatened by events in Southeast Asia.

4. An argument is made that it is economically wrong. This argument pertains to the whole military operation of which the Cambodian invasion is a part. Just as one moves quickly from what are politically correct objectives to some moral concerns, so also one moves from economic aspects. Here one confronts the arguments about the moral justifications for allocating priorities in the American economy and about the involvement of American business in the economies of the third world. Is the multibillion-dollar expenditure for the military involvement in Southeast Asia justifiable in the light of the many needs and purposes that would make for human well-being in the United States and in other parts of the world?

In each of these arguments there is an evaluative assessment of the circumstances in which action is occurring; there is no simple description of incontrovertible facts. In each there are different sorts of evaluation: Certain data are given higher valence in some arguments than they are in others; preferential evaluations of the significance of various causal factors are also involved. And, as we have shown, moral evaluations are either embedded in the other evaluations or are operating just behind the political, military, or other arguments.

II
WHERE THE ETHICAL ISSUES LIE

Before we can turn to the place of scripture in relation to the discussion of Cambodia, it is neceesary to sort out the ways in which moral evaluations themselves apply to any historical event.

One application is to *the structure and meaning of the historical process* or wider context in which particular events take place. This can be illustrated with reference to the differences that various views of history make in the interpretation of the course of particular events. A progressive view of history, such as was in vogue sixty years ago in many circles, might interpret the events in Southeast

Asia as part of the ongoing evolution of the human race, painfully breaking from the shackles of the past, but confidently moving toward a more nearly perfect future state of affairs. An alternative to this would be a Marxist view, adopted also by important Christians, that this struggle is part of a historical process of conflict between those who seek to retain their powers and exercise them in the repression of the weak and those who seek release from the bondage of oppression in their efforts to liberate themselves from colonial or other dominating powers. A third might be more radically eschatological; the future is drawing the present and the past toward itself in such a way that wars of the sort being fought are really revolutions of hope that a new day for mankind is dawning. In contrast to these three would be a view that sees the events as part of the ongoing struggle between the forces of disruption and disorder that always threaten the delicate fiber which restrains chaos and the forces that preserve the modicum of order that makes existence tolerable among men. Perspective on the more comprehensive meaning of historical events affects the evaluation of particular historical events; events are charged with different meanings from different perspectives; as a result of one's "view of history," certain features of events appear to be more salient and morally more significant than do other features. Biblical themes enter into the Christian's view of history and thus affect his judgments, as we shall subsequently see.

Moral evaluations are also applied to the *motives and intentions* of those whose access to power enables them to determine the direction of events more than most persons can. It we take the common philosophical distinction between motives as "backward-looking reasons" for action, and intentions as "forward-looking reasons" for action, we can see how moral evaluations enter into the assessment of each. To assess motives we can look at the commitment of the American nation to certain moral and social values, not only for its own people, but for others as well, which would provide justifying reasons for the action. These motives can be approached by asking on what grounds the United States is involved in Southeast Asia in the first place. Some lofty motives can be given in answer to this query: The nation is concerned with the preservation of freedom, with the rights of self-determination of peoples, with adherence to commitments made to other governments, with the credibility of the United States as a power that does not let its friends down in time of trouble. Such motives are subject to moral judgment in several respects. The consistency between national actions and the motives professed for them can be judged. One can also judge the moral worth of these motives in terms of whether those that appear to be dominant are worthy of their position, and whether other morally justifiable motives, such as social justice, are not left out. One can also judge whether the consequences of the actions that are justified by these motives do not create greater harm, suffering, and destruction than are worthy of the commitments which give them warrant. For example, while it is prima facie laudable to keep one's commitments, the question can be raised as to whether or not the destructive consequences of keeping those promises morally outweigh the obligation involved in them.

In a similar way, we can engage in a moral evaluation of America's intentions, its forward-looking reasons for being in Cambodia and, indeed, in Vietnam. Some of those that are professed reasons are incontrovertible in their most general form: We are seeking peace. (I paraphrase the comment of an undergraduate: "Killing for the sake of peace is like fornicating for the sake of virginity.") Other intentions of a political, moral sort are more arguable: We are seeking stability in the region. One can raise questions about the moral value of stability in relation to other moral values that are embedded in the political order, for example, justice—in terms of more nearly equitable distribution of rights, powers, economic resources.

Whenever motives and intentions are assessed, that difficult question arises as to whether the professed reasons are the real reasons for action. This points to the issue of the moral integrity of those persons who determine the exercise of powers—but further elaboration of this issue here is not possible.

Judging both the motives and the intentions of the nation involves also evaluating the *circumstances* in which these motives and intentions are acted out. The question is whether or not the actual situation warrants the actions based on the given reasons. In Southeast Asia this becomes the question of whether, for example, freedom is so threatened that it warrants the exercise of American military power to preserve it. It involves the question of whether the government to which the American commitments are made is a duly constituted, popularly elected one. In short, are the conditions that

America presumably seeks to rectify sufficiently threatening to the values it wishes to adhere to that there is warrant for the use being made of military, political, and ecomonic power?

The *consequences* of the extension of the war are also subject to moral evaluation. As critics of utilitarian and "consequentialist" ethics have long pointed out, it is not easy to judge consequences of actions in moral terms in an incontrovertible way. A moral judgment about a factual state of affairs is involved, and this requires a complex process. For example, most persons would agree that it is wrong to take human lives except under extreme conditions. Does the "benefit" gained by taking lives outweigh the cost of the moral value of the lives that are taken? If the balance of the consequences is not on the beneficial side, then it is judged morally wrong to take the lives. The consequences of massive military action are many and very complex. They extend through time; this makes it difficult to say precisely when one cuts off the calculation. Lives are not only physically destroyed, but human spirits are painfully warped; property is wasted, cultures are disrupted, repercussions in the realm of politics and economics are almost incalculable. In order to make a moral assessment of various consequences, clear notions of what constitutes the "good" and the "bad" have to be developed; and the factual aspects have to be judged in relation to these notions.

Even though these points are not exhaustive, they are perhaps the most salient in our experience. Our stated task is to interpret the place of scripture in Christian ethics. That can now be made more precise. 1) How is scripture used in the interpretation of the structure and meaning of the historical process of which the Cambodian events are a part? 2) How is scripture used in the assessments of the motives and the intentions of those persons who determine what forms of power are to be used in Southeast Asia and how these powers are to be used? 3) How is scripture used in the assessment of the consequences of the extension of the war?

III
WAYS OF USING SCRIPTURE

The existence of a variety of materials in scripture necessitates some general principles for clarifying a more coherent and simpler view of the message of scripture. The use of scripture in Christian ethics first involves the determination of the theological and ethical principles which will be used to bring coherence to the "meaning" of scripture's witness. In a previous publication I distinguished a view of scripture as the revelation of a morality that is authoritative for the judgments of Christians from a view of it as a revelation of theological principles that are used to interpret what "God is doing," and thus, in turn, can give clues to what man as a moral agent is to do in particular historical circumstances.[4] If scripture is the revelation of a morality, its application to the Cambodian invasion would require that one judge that event in accordance with moral laws, precepts, and commands given in scripture. If scripture is the revelation of the action of God, one applies it to the Cambodian invasion by interpreting that event in the light of an answer to the question, "What is God doing in our contemporary history, and particularly in Cambodia?" Here I would like to refine these types before proceeding to suggest a more constructive statement.

The most stringent use of scripture as revealed morality can be stated in the following way. Those actions of persons and groups which violate the moral law revealed in scripture are to be judged morally wrong. The idea of moral law becomes the principle for ethical interpretation. Two issues immediately emerge. One is the content of the moral law, and the other is the mode of its application. For Jewish religion these can be answered more simply than they can for Christians, although even in Judaism the answers are complex. The law would be the Torah, and *halachah* would provide the tradition for application. The parts of Torah that would be applicable, and the procedures for its application through Mishna, Talmud, the Codes, the Responsa, all involve judgments on the part of the learned rabbi who might come to a decision. But there would be clear biblical authority in the tradition for using biblical law, and the tradition provides a continuity of historical judgments and general procedures by which a new judgment might be made.

For Christian religion this use of scripture is even more difficult. What is the moral law that is revealed in the Bible? Torah would be an insufficient answer. There is also the "new law," and just what that is has to be determined. If the teachings of Jesus as recorded in the Gospels are the new law, then something like the method of *hala-*

chah might be appropriate; but on the whole the Christian theologians have not worked in this way. Further, if the new law is the "grace of the Holy Spirit written in the heart," as it has been judged to be by both the Catholic and Protestant traditions, it can no longer be limited in its references to the moral teachings of the scriptures interpreted to be law. It is "the life-giving law of the Spirit," to quote Romans 8:2 (NEB), a text that is persistently cited in the history of Christian ethical thought.

Christians have no codifications of the moral law of scripture and its interpretations comparable to the *Shulhan Arukh* and the Code of Maimonides; even the codifications of law in the canon law tradition of the Catholic Church appeal heavily to the natural law tradition developed in the West, rather than to scripture. Even Fundamentalists have highly selective ways of using biblical evidence. There are clearly ethical principles at work that govern their choices of texts to be applied to particular moral situations and that provide ways of explaining texts which prima facie would contravene the positions they would take.

Perhaps agreement on the primacy, if not the exclusiveness, of the "law of love" could be asserted about the Christian scriptures, recognizing their continuity with Jewish scriptures. "For the whole law can be summed up in a single commandement: 'Love your neighbor as yourself,'" writes Paul (Gal. 5:14, NEB), a claim also found in other parts of the scripture. If this were judged to be the material content of the new moral law, the modes of its application to situations like the Cambodian venture would vary markedly. For some persons it might have a pacifist application; one does not love himself by taking his own life; surely one does not love his neighbor by taking his. For others it becomes a high-level general principle which is applied to the complexities of a war through the mediation of the structure and the principles of just-war thinking.

A second use of scripture as revealed morality could be stated as follows: Those actions of persons and groups which fall short of *the moral ideals* given in scripture are to be judged morally wrong, or at least morally deficient. The notion of moral ideals becomes the principle of ethical interpretation. Three issues emerge here. The first is whether the language of moral ideals is itself warranted by scripture. Is the language of ideals as intrinsic to the scriptures as is the lan-

guage of law? How these questions would be answered depends to
some extent upon how one interprets "ideals." If a moral notion has
to refer to some timeless entity, a metaphysical value, in order to be
an ideal, it is safe to say that the language of ideals is more at home
in Greek ethics than in biblical ethics. If, however, it refers to a vision of the future in which "The wolf shall live with the sheep, and
the leopard lie down with the kid; the calf and the young lion shall
grow up together (Isa. 11:6, NEB)," the promised fulfillment might
well function as a vision of the ideal future. The New Testament idea
of the kingdom of God has functioned this way in Christian ethics
from time to time in Christian history, most prominently in the social gospel writers.

The theological doctrine that qualifies the use of the language of
ideals is eschatology. Whether an ethician uses the vision of an ideal
future is governed by his eschatological views. If he finds a warrant
for the language of ideals within those views, then *how* that vision is
used is also determined to a considerable degree by his eschatology.
The double problem of the use of scripture which we pointed out
previously confronts us again: One part of the problem is the significance of the eschatological context within the scriptures for understanding properly the biblical visions of ideal futures; the other is the
authority that the biblical eschatological context has for the use of
those visions in constructive Christian theological ethics.

The second issue that emerges in the use of the language of
ideals is that of their material content. The biblical imagery in Isaiah,
as well as elsewhere, suggests harmony between natural enemies, the
resolution of struggles in idyllic peace—a theme often portrayed in
Christian art. The social gospel writers did not hesitate to find consistent with the biblical vision of the coming kingdom of God almost
all values that were judged to promote human welfare: peace, love,
justice, harmony. They courageously developed these in terms of
ideals and goals for the society of their own time. Clearly, there is a
deep and broad gulf between the ideal of universal peace as part of
the biblical vision of the fulfillment and any war, including the Cambodian venture.

The third issue is the mode of application of a moral ideal to the
Cambodian or any other historical situation. If the basis for using an
ideal is that reality ought to be conformed to the ideal in all human

actions and states of affairs, a condemnatory verdict on the Cambodian venture is clear. If, however, the use of the ideal leads to the reckoning of *compromises* that men can live with, or *approximations* with which they can be satisfied, then a sliding scale of judgment has been introduced. The adoption of a more realistic view of the possibilities of political and moral achievement under the conditions of historical finitude and corruption leads to such applications. How much compromise with the ideal do the conditions of history, the particualr circumstances, require? What degree of approximation of the vision of the ideal future ought one to strive for under the political, social, and military conditions of our time? To give warrant for a judgment against the Cambodian venture one has to indicate, in this mode of thought, that the compromises are too great, that the present approximations are insufficient to merit moral approval of the policies of the government.

A third use of scripture as a revealed morality would be stated as follows: Those actions of persons and groups are to be judged morally wrong which are similar to actions that are judged to be wrong or against God's will under similar circumstances in scripture, or are discordant with actions judged to be right or in accord with God's will in scripture. Here the method is roughly one of analogy, and it has its share of difficulties. One is the problem of providing persuasive evidence that the circumstances of, for example, a political and military situation in our time are similar in any significant respects to the circumstances in biblical times. A second is the problem of determining which biblical events will be used for purposes of an analogical elucidation of the moral significance of present events. Some prior ethical commitment is likely to determine this choice. For example, one might choose the account of the "liberation" of the Hebrew people from bondage in Egypt as the biblical narrative most applicable to present history. This choice might be made on either one of two separate grounds or on a combination of them. First, it might be judged that the Vietnamese and Cambodian people are like the Hebrew people of old and that American power is like the power of Egypt. With more refined intervening steps provided, we might conclude that intervention in Cambodia is morally wrong just as repression of the Hebrews in Egypt was morally wrong. Second, we might judge that the crucial moral issue of our time, and of biblical times, is that of liberation from oppression and repression. A general moral and biblical theme, namely, liberation, is judged on theological and ethical grounds to be central to Christian ethics. On the basis of this judgment one could turn to scripture to find the historical events which reveal and elucidate this theme, and in turn use these events as analogies for events of the present time which seem to elucidate the same theme.

The primary question in the use of scripture for moral analogies is that of control. If present events are in control, then one first responds to these events and then on the basis of that response seeks biblical events that are similar to the present ones. The predisposition is to seek those events which will confirm one's present judgments. Thus, the choice of the exodus would be more congenial for a negative judgment on present repression of a small power by a great power than would some of the prophetic interpretations of the role of a great power in chastising a lesser power for its violation of God's ways for the nations. The biblical materials would be chosen on the basis of their affinity for a present moral judgment arrived at perhaps independently of biblical considerations. Biblical support could be found for the opinions one has formed on independent ethical bases.

If scripture is in control, then one is faced with the persistent question of which events are most nearly consistent with certain central tendencies of the biblical, theological, and moral witness. One would have to decide whether the Hebrew wars of conquest of Canaan were "truer" to the central themes of biblical morality than was the liberation accomplished by the exodus. (I have been told that the Calvinists in South Africa used the analogy of the chosen people's right to the land of Canaan to justify their expansion into the territory of the Africans in the nineteenth century). Some theological and ethical principle would have to be judged as normative for the whole of scriptural witness; this would in turn determine which events would be used as analogies normatively proper to current events, and thus as the basis for judging the moral rightness of present actions.

A fourth use of scripture is looser than the first three. It could be stated as follows: Scripture witnesses to a great variety of moral values, moral norms and principles through many different kinds of biblical literature: moral law, visions of the future, historical events, moral precepts, paraenetic instruction, parables, dialogues, wisdom sayings, allegories. They are not in a simple way reducible to a single theme; rather, they are directed to particular historical contexts. The Christian community judges the actions of persons and groups to be morally wrong, or at least deficient, on the basis of reflective discourse about present events *in the light* of appeals to this variety of material as well as to other principles and experiences. Scripture is one of the informing sources for moral judgments, but it is not sufficient in itself to make any particular judgment authoritative.

The obvious problem with this use is its looseness. The questions that were raised about what is in control are also pertinent here. It would be very easy to make a judgment on the basis of feelings or prevailing cultural values and then find *some support for it* in the variety of scripture's texts. The maintenance of any objective authority for the moral witness of the scriptures is difficult if one reconizes the variety of norms and values present there and also the historical character of the occasions in which these emerge. Thus, some efforts at generalization are necessary in order to bring some priorities of biblical morality into focus. The generalizations that are most nearly consistent with certain theological, ethical statements that appear to be more at the heart of the matter in the development of biblical religion would be used. Informed in a general way by biblical faith and morality, as well was by other relevant beliefs and moral commitments, one might judge the Cambodian venture to be wrong and proceed to cite biblical norms and values as corroborative evidence for one's judgment. We admittedly have less than absolute certitude that the judgment is biblically authorized, both because of the variety of material contents in the scriptures and because of the looseness of the way in which it is used. The necessity for appeals to the continuing tradition of Christian morality beyond the closing of the canon is taken for granted, and the fact that biblical morality is in many ways inapplicable, and in other ways wrong, is accepted.

Each of the ways in which the morality in the scripture is used can be given theological justification. Thus, no sharp line can be drawn between primarily moral and primarily theological uses of scripture in Christian ethics. But attention to some of the basically theological uses of scripture in Christian ethics, which subordinate its ethical content to its theological importance, helps us to see the range of opinion. I have argued elsewhere that the most significant alterations in Christian ethics in midtwentieth century took place not as a result of the reassessment of the liberal and optimistic interpretation of human nature, but as a result of the introduction into ethical thinking of the idea of a "God who acts," or a "God who speaks" in particular historical circumstances. Without further elaboration of that, it should be clear that biblical theology provided a framework for the interpretation of the historical events in which men and nations were involved; and out of this interpretation came certain assessments of the moral significance of events, certain clues about how they were to be judged, and what persons ought to do in them. The primary question became not "How ought we to judge this event?" nor even "What ought we to do in the event?" but "What is God doing in this event? What is he saying to us in this event?" Three articles published by H. Richard Niebuhr during World War II have titles which illustrate this: "War as the Judgment of God," "Is God in the War?" and "War as Crucifixion."[6]

The inspiration of a biblical understanding of an active God has to be specified by asking two sorts of questions. First, who is this God who acts? What do we know about him as "subject" or "person" or about his "nature" which will give a clue to the sorts of things he might be doing and saying? Second, what sorts of things has he said and has he done? What does he wish to accomplish by his acting? What do we know about his actions?

Insofar as scripture provides "data" for answering these questions, we are again faced with the task of formulating generalizations based upon a variety of materials.[7] Here we shall only indicate some of the themes that have been used in theological ethics. The theme of liberation currently finds wide usage with reference to the struggle both of black people in the United States and of colonial peoples of the world. "Jesus' work is essentially one of liberation," writes the articulate and influential James H. Cone, in his *Black Theology and Black Power.*[8] This becomes a warrant for both an evaluative description of the situation of black people in America and a normative direction for the activity in which Christians ought to be engaged. The themes of crucifixion and resurrection are used by another influential contemporary theologian, Richard Shaull, of Princeton. These terms provide a theologically warranted framework for interpreting the present course of events in a world of revolutions; the old orders must die in order for new life to be born, a life of hope and justice for all who are oppressed.[9] As does the liberation theme, so the crucifixion and resurrection theme provides a way of describing and evaluating the events of our times, and a normative thrust for the actions of Christians. They ought to be involved in the destruction of oppressive forms of life in order for new life to come into being. Jürgen Moltmann's highlighting of the theme of hope as central to biblical theology, Paul Lehmann's development of God's doing humanizing work, H. Richard Niebuhr's more complex view of God's creative, governing, judging, and redeeming work: each provides a theological ground upon which is constructed both an interpretation of the significance of events and a positive normative thrust with reference to what Christians ought to be doing. James Sellers, in his very suggestive *Theological Ethics,* takes the theme of promise and fulfillment to be central to the biblical witness. Traditional Lutheran theologians have used gospel and law, and orders of creation; Barth offers an interpretation of the God of grace who is yet the commander as a biblical theological foundation.

The use of biblical theological concepts to provide an evaluative description of historical events requires that further moves be made to determine how a particular event is to be judged and what ought to be done in those circumstances. These moves can be made in two ways or in a combination of them. One such move is from the built-in, normative content of the evaluative-descriptive terms to the basis both for moral judgment on the events and for prescriptions or guidelines for action in them. If, in Lehmann's ethics, one discerns what God is doing to make and keep human life human, whatever is not in accord with the human is judged to be wrong, and the prescriptions or guidelines for further action would be whatever is in accord with the human. The second move is a methodological one. In Lehmann's case, for example, the method for discerning both what is morally wrong and what one ought to do is akin in crucial respects to what philosophers designate as moral intuitionism; the judge and actor is sensitive to what God is doing, and in his theonomous conscience he perceives what is wrong and what he ought to do. In the case of others, however, the move from the evaluative-descriptive enterprise to the moral judgment and the prescription for action might involve a more elaborate and rational process of practical moral reasoning. The normative elements in the concepts used for the evaluative description are lifted out in statements of moral principles and values, and their application both to the judgment and to subsequent action is developed according to methods of rational moral argumentation.[10]

How the various biblical theologies of ethics use the morality or ethical teachings found in scripture is contingent upon methodological choices that can be given both theological and philosophical justification. For example, within Barth's theological ethics, it is the command of God, heard by the moral agent, that determines whether something is right or wrong. But this command is not a capricious one; it is likely to be in accord with the moral teachings of the decalogue and of Jesus. These moral teachings provide "prominent lines"; they are not unexceptionable rules or laws of conduct, nor are they moral ideals. They are coherent with the revelation of God in the scriptures; and thus, if one's judgment is not in accord with these prominent lines, it is doubtful whether one is really hearing God's command. More intensive analysis of this issue is not in order here.

IV

THE PLACE OF SCRIPTURE IN JUDGING
THE CAMBODIAN INVASION

In the light of the previous analyses, both of the points at which one makes moral judgments and of the ways in which scripture has been used to make them, brief constructive proposals can now proceed. Certain possibilities are ruled out, at least for simple application. For example, use of proof-text, either as the sole basis for making the judgment or in literalistic support of arguments made on other grounds, is not defensible. To cite the command "Thou shalt not kill" is not sufficient to defend the judgment that the invasion of Cambodia is morally wrong. Indeed, it is better to begin, not with the application of a particular text to a particular problem, but rather with a look at scripture's more pervasive significance.

First, in the largest dimensions, scripture has informed the moral ethos of Western culture, and particularly that of the Christian community. Even when the actual determinative moral ethos is not in accord with the more objectively normative elements of the wider ethos, the latter remains as a point of critical judgment on the former and on particular events. This affirmation involves not only a historical appeal, that scripture has informed the approvable moral values of our culture and religious community, but also a theologically normative appeal. The biblical witnesses testify to religious communities' developing understanding of what God's purposes for man and the world are; with a significant measure of confidence in the scriptures as a developing revelation of God's purposes, the Bible ought to inform the moral ethos of the culture and the church. The moral ethos of church and culture is always in a process of development or change in the light of new historical events and of unfolding awareness of the meaning of biblically informed morality for new issues. Indeed, the contributions of biblical tradition are not only unfolded, but often revised and judged wrong in the light of historical developments; for example, the inferior status of women, the acceptance of slavery, and the support of capital punishment. In this large dimension, then, one's appeal is not directly to scripture as a verbal basis for supporting a judgment that the Cambodian invasion is morally wrong, but rather to the moral values of the culture and the church which have been and ought to be informed by scripture.

Second, scripture provides data and concepts for understanding the human situation, both in terms of its limits and its possibilities. The biblically informed moral judge is not taken aback at the presence of moral evil in the world; he is not surprised that the technical and other achievements of a nation tempt it to pride, that its accumulation of many forms of power tempt it to arrogance, that its activities which are destructive of human well-being are rationalized by appeals to unexceptionable moral values and ends such as freedom and peace for men. Nor is he surprised by his own faulty moral judgments, past and present, for they are in part a result of his finitude: his limitations of time, place, knowledge, insight, sensitivity, and imagination all prohibit him from achieving that position of the "ideal observer" who can judge events as God himself could judge them. They are also a result of his sin: his bondage to nationalistic loyalties, his pride in the achievements of himself and his nation, his failure to consider the purposes of God, his longing to make secure what sustains his good life even at heavy cost to others, all keep him from hitting the moral mark.

Scripture also provides a vision of human possibilities. It gives clues to what God is enabling, as well as requiring, man to be and to do. It not only becomes a basis of confidence in the community of faith that the unknown future is in the care of a Being who is ultimately benevolently disposed toward his creation, but also provides a vision of what the human future ought to be and can be in the care of the God of love, of justice, of peace, of hope. Biblically informed vision sees in the longings for peace and justice that are found in protests against the Cambodian invasion and in the aspirations of oppressed people in the world, a thrust toward the future, not with the illusion that the kingdom is coming, but with the confident hope that present moral and social evils will no longer be tolerated. This scriptural faith disposes the Christian community toward moral seriousness, toward profound dissatisfaction with those events that are destructive of human life and value, toward aspirations for a future which is more fulfilling for all God's creation; and thus toward negative judgment on events which are not consistent with the possibilities that God is creating for man.

Third, and perhaps this is simply a specification of the second, scripture provides an account of the sorts of human actions and events which the morally and religiously serious communities of the past have seen to be in accord and out of accord with the purposes of God for man. Certain generalizations about God's prevailing aspirations and purposes for human life can be formulated on the basis of the scriptural witness. In the light of these generalizations present events can be judged to be more or less in or out of accord with those purposes. One need not appeal to strict analogies between events recorded and interpreted in scripture and events of the present, but rather one can appeal to theological affirmations that are informed and governed by the biblical witness. The purposes of God, as gleaned from the scriptures, provide not only a reason for being morally concerned about the Cambodian invasion but also the basis for moral values and principles in the light of which the events in Cambodia can be judged.

Fourth, the scriptures provide a variety of types of discourse which express the purposes of God as these were understood by the religious communities, and passages can be used as corroborating evidence (but not proof-texts) for the judgments made in the light of the more general theological and ethical principles that are used. Certain moral laws or precepts given in both Testaments can be used as concise specifications of the more general intent derived from scripture and can be brought to bear upon the judgment of particular events. One would not judge the Cambodian invasion to be morally wrong simply because it violates the love commandment; the love commandment is a specification of a moral precept consistent with the biblical understanding of God's will for men, and thus it has a theological backing which is also biblically based. Similarly, one might find that certain narratives of events in which writers understood the judgment of God to be present are applicable to the present historical occasion by way of a rough analogy. But the use of such narratives would be governed by their consistency with the generalizations about God's purposes that are gleaned from the whole of the scriptures. Other forms of discourse could function in a similar manner—parables, wisdom sayings. The appeal to these would not be on the basis of their absolute authority, but both as informing sources of judgment and as corroborations of judgments informed by a variety of appeals.

The procedures I am proposing are not *sola Scriptura* in character. In judging the Cambodian invasion to be morally wrong one is informed by and appeals to many other bases than scripture: to the accounts of what is happening; to an assessment of the motives, intentions, and consequences of what goes on there; to general ethical principles upon which most persons might agree without recourse to biblical backing for them. Indeed, the scriptures are not used as the exclusive source of backing, warrants, and data (to use Kelsey's patten of analysis) for the moral judgments of the Christian community on the Cambodian invasion. Ultimately for Christian ethics, a biblically informed theology provides the bases for the final test of the validity of particular judgments: For Christians these judgments ought to be consistent, consonant, coherent with the themes that are generalized to be most pervasive or primary to the biblical witness. But this is not to suggest that the judgments are solely derived from the scriptures; rather, there is a dialectic between more intuitive moral judgments and both scriptural and nonscriptural principles and values (recognizing that these latter two are not mutually exclusive); there is a dialectic between principles of judgment which have purely rational justification and which also appeal to the tradition expressed in scripture and developed in the Christian community.

This dialectical process is necessary for several reasons. First, there is a variety of theological and ethical themes in the scriptures themselves; and thus, while theological and ethical themes can be formulated to provide the dominant principles of interpretation for the whole of scripture, the variety itself must not be lost sight of. Biblical theology and ethics, for example, are not exclusively a theology and an ethic of love; thus love cannot become the single principle used to judge events and actions even within scripture.

Second, on theological grounds, themselves backed by scripture, it can be affirmed that the moral responsibility of men, and particularly of men who acknowledge God as lord, is to judge what God is enabling and requiring men to do under the natural, historical, and social conditions in which they live, not simply to apply biblical morality from an ancient time in a casuistic way. Thus, there is awareness of novelty both in the forms of moral evil that exist and in the opportunities for rectifying them. These aspects of novelty have to be taken into account in making a judgment. While the American invasion of Cambodia is not unlike many previous invasions in the history of the world, it is not the same as any other previous invasion in its character.

Third, the process of making a moral judgment about an event is undertaken with reference to principles and values that are widely shared with others outside the Christian community. These principles and values have their own status with practical, if not ultimate theoretical, independence from theological grounds and are properly appealed to in support of a judgment against the Cambodian invasion. The inferences drawn from these principles—the sorts of principles that a rough use of "natural law" has always acknowledged in the Christian tradition (and probably in scripture itself)—are usually consistent with those drawn from scripture. There might be, however, very special claims made upon those who seek to judge events within the framework of biblically informed Christian ethics: In the ethics of discipleship to Jesus Christ, for example, there is a weight of obligation to be willing to suffer and to die for the sake of the needs of the neighbor, or for the sake of the cause of witnessing to the requirements of peace, justice, and love in the world. There is a heavy pull toward the pacifist position, not only because of the primacy of love, but also because of many sayings, actions, and implications from varieties of literature in the New Testament.

In arriving at a moral judgment about the Cambodian invasion, scripture, informing one's particular analysis of that event, would be used at the various points, indicated earlier in the chapter, that moral judgments are made. A brief rehearsal of these points in relation to subsequent developments in the chapter will provide at least the outlines of a fuller account.

First, scripture informs the terms, concepts, or categories that one uses to give an account of the structure and meaning of the historical process of which the Cambodian invasion is a part. How this is done depends upon what theological principles are used (a) to provide generalizations about what the biblical meaning of human history is (or what those meanings are—to suggest pluralism in scripture), and (b) to decide which biblical accounts (precepts, narratives) are pertinent to the particular historical situation in which we now live. Choices made about the meaning of biblical theology are crucial for the interpretation of history. For example, if the theology is one of a struggle between God and the devil in history, and if God is judged to be on the side of Americans, and if the devil is identified with revolutionary forces in the world, then one gets a different account of the meaning of present history from what is derived if God is identified with the revolutionary forces in history, and the devil, or the powers of sin, are identified with American action. Or, if the crucial biblical theme is crucifixion and resurrection, and American action is identified with the powers of recalcitrance and oppression that are being crucified, a particular interpretation of the meaning of our present history is forthcoming.

Second, scripture informs the principles by which one judges the motives given for the justification of the American invasion. If, for example, one judges that the desire to protect American lives is morally insufficient to justify the extension of the war, various appeals that are briefly supported or derived might be cited. The special concern for American lives might be judged immoral because it violates a pressure toward the equal valuation of all human beings in the sight of their Creator and Redeemer, or it violates the principle of love of enemy (with the implication that one cannot easily justify killing persons who are the objects of one's love).

Third, scripture informs the principles and values used to judge the intentions and goals of the invasion in a process similar to the way it informs judgments of motives.

Fourth, scripture informs the principles used to assess the particular circumstances for which reasons are given as sufficient justification for the invasion. If the circumstances at the time of the invasion were judged to be a threat to the freedom of the Vietnamese and Cambodian people, an interesting and complex issue is opened. Part of the argument about it would be more or less factual—is their freedom really being more threatened by the presence of North Vietnamese and Viet Cong military forces than it is by the presence of American and South Vietnamese ones? But other issues which bear more directly on moral concerns are also raised. What sort of freedom are the Americans seeking to defend? What is the place of that sort of freedom in a scale of values that are pertinent to Southeast Asian culture as well as to a scale of values that might be more valid in the West? Should there be assessment not only of threats to freedom, but also of the destruction of life and property, of Cambodian village culture, and of self-determination? Or another line might be taken: Were the circumstances desperate enough to warrant the illegality and immorality of invasion? Scripture could not be used to provide texts which would "prove" that the invasion was wrong, but it could provide (to use Kelsey's terms) data, warrants, and backing for the principles and values that could counter the assessment of those circumstances that were used to justify the actions.

Finally, with reference to the judgment of consequences, one would ask whether the consequences are consistent with the understanding of the fulfillment of human life that a scripturally informed theology would support as being in accord with God's purposes for men. Scripture alone is clearly insufficient as a ground for assessing the consequences, for many historical developments have intervened since biblical times to enlarge the scope of the Christian community's understanding of what human life is meant to be, and particularly under the circumstances of the times in which we live. But one could give biblical data, warrants, and backing of the position that the consequences occurring are not in accord with those ends of man which scripture and the general moral values of mankind both support.

V

CONCLUSION

The suggested constructive procedure is more in accord with what I stated earlier to be a looser use of scripture than its use as moral law, moral ideals, or the source of moral analogies. Indeed, it can incorporate elements of each of these within it. It has the problems of the looser use; these ought to be fully acknowledged. The principal problem is to determine how decisive the authority of scripture is for one's moral judgment. Only the two extremes are absolutely precluded: It does not have the authority of verbal inspiration that the religiously conservative defenders of a "revealed morality" would give to it, nor is it totally without relevance to present moral judgments. Within the broad spectrum between the excluded extremes, a number of other judgments are crucial in determining both its authority and how it should be used. Some of these judgments are theological in character; they depend upon choices about what theological themes are central to scripture's understanding of God's work, God's purposes for man, and the human condition. Other judgments determine what moral principles and values are most consistent with the theological framework developed in relation to scripture. Still others are philosophical in character; how we use scripture is determined to some extent by our framework for interpreting the tasks of ethics as a discipline of thought. If it is focused on the assessment of consequences, scripture will be used differently from the way it will be used if its function is to provide unexceptionable rules of conduct. Another question of the authority of scripture can be approached by asking whether there is a "method of ethics" in the scripture, and if there is, whether the Christian ethician in the present is bound to its use. The answer I have suggested to the first is that there are several methods of ethics in the Bible; how they will be used is determined by what methods are judged to be consistent with one's theological principles as well as by judgments made on philosophical grounds.

The outcome of this essay on the question of authority of scripture can thus be stated succinctly, but indefinitely. Scripture *alone* is never the final court of appeal for Christian ethics. Its understanding of God and his purposes, of man's condition and needs, of precepts, events, human relationships, however, do provide the basic *orientation* toward particular judgments. Within that orientation many complex procedures and appeals are exercised, and there is room for a great deal of argumentation. The most decisive justification for this looser use of scripture can be stated as follows: The vocation of the Christian community is to discern what God is enabling and requiring man to be and to do in particular natural, historical, and social circumstances. Its moral judgments are made in the light of that fundamental ought, or demand. Thus, scripture deeply informs these judgments in ways I have outlined, but it does not by itself determine what they ought to be. That determination is done by persons and communities as finite moral agents responsible to God.

Notes

1. Edward LeRoy Long, "The Use of the Bible in Christian Ethics," *Interpretation,* XIX (1965), 149–62; David H. Kelsey, "Appeals to Scripture in Theology," *Journal of Religion,* XLVIII (1968), 1–21. For a study of Rauschenbusch's use of scripture see James M. Gustafson, "From Scripture to Social Policy and Social Action," *Andover-Newton Quarterly,* IX (1969), 160–69.

2. I have developed a proposal on this point in chap. 7.

3. For elaboration of this see *Christ and the Moral Life* (New York: Harper & Row, 1968), chap. 1, and "Theology and Ethics," *Christian Ethics and the Community* (Philadelphia: Pilgrim Press, 1971), pp. 83–100.

4. "Christian Ethics in America," *Christian Ethics and the Community,* pp. 23–82.

5. See the arguments in support of capital punishment developed by J.

J. Vellenga in "Christianity and the Death Penalty," *The Death Penalty in America,* ed. Hugo A. Bedau (Garden City: Doubleday Anchor Books, 1964), pp. 123–30. With reference of Matt. 5:21f, Vellenga writes: "It is evident that Jesus was not condemning the established law of capital punishment, but was actually saying that hate deserved capital punishment (p. 126)." "If one accepts the authority of Scripture, then the issue of capital punishment must be decided on what Scripture actually teaches and not on the popular, naturalistic ideas of sociology and penology that prevail today (p. 129)."

6. The three appeared in the *Christian Century,* LIX (1942), 630–33; 953–55; and LX (1943), 513–15.

7. For a critical analysis of the work that has been called biblical theology see Brevard Childs, *Biblical Theology in Crisis* (Philadelphia: Westminster Press, 1970).

8. James H. Cone, *Black Theology and Black Power* (New York: Seabury Press, 1968), p. 35.

9. See, for example, Shaull's article, "Christian Theology and Social Revolution (I)," *The Perkins School of Theology Journal.* XXI (1967–68), 5–12.

10. I have developed these issues in "Two Approaches to Theological Ethics," *Christian Ethics and the Community,* pp. 127–38.

The Role and Function
of the Scriptures
in Moral Theology

Charles E. Curran

This article originally appeared in *Proceedings of the Catholic Theological Society of America* in 1971.

The function of the Scriptures in moral theology has been a perennial question for the science of moral theology. Today the question assumes even greater importance and urgency in the light of two tendencies in contemporary theology which may even represent contradictory trends. On the one hand, the biblical renewal has made a great contribution to the development of moral theology in the last decade. The contemporary moral theologian has rejected the moral manuals of the past for many reasons, but the failure to find a basic orientation and grounding in the Scriptures frequently is mentioned as a most important lack in the older textbooks.

On the other hand, there has been another trend which has expanded the concept of revelation to cover much more than just the word of God in the Scriptures. An increasing emphasis, at some times in an exaggerated way, has been given to this world and the wisdom which persons in this world can acquire from one another and from their worldly existence. Theologians have recently been asking what if anything is distinctive about Christian ethics which has its primary source in the Scriptures. In the midst of a plurality of sources of ethical wisdom what are the role and function of the Scriptures?

This paper will discuss the question from three different aspects: the advantages that have accrued to Catholic moral theology in the last decades because of a greater emphasis on the Scriptures; the inherent limitations of the use of the Scriptures in moral theology; two fundamental methodological questions governing the use of the Scriptures in moral theology

I
CONTRIBUTIONS OF BIBLICAL THEOLOGY

Vatican Council II attests that a greater stress is given to the role of the Scriptures in moral theology than has been given in the past. It would be wrong to ascribe the beginning of such a movement to Vatican II, for the Council merely made its own and officially sanctioned a movement which had already begun in the Church. The Dogmatic Constitution on Divine Revelation emphasized that Sacred Scripture is the soul of all theology.[1] The Decree on Priestly Formation reiterated these words and specified that the scientific exposition of moral theology should be more thoroughly nourished by scriptural teaching.[2]

The history of moral reflection in the Catholic tradition from certain Fathers of the Church such as Clement of Alexandria and Augustine down to the present reveals an insistence on the fact that Sacred Scripture is not the only source of ethical wisdom and knowledge for the Christian. There is a human wisdom in which all men share and participate because of their common humanity. This gnoseological recognition of a source of ethical wisdom and knowledge (human reason) outside the Scriptures corresponds to the more ontological understanding of the relation of the human to the divine, or of what was later called the relationship between the natural and the supernatural. The theological understanding of love in the Catholic tradition well illustrates this approach. Catholic theology has understood the revealed *agape* of the Bible in terms of continuity with, and a perfection of, human love. Likewise the knowledge and understanding of human love also contribute to our understanding of Christian love.[3]

The use of the Scriptures in moral theology has varied at different historical periods, and in the period from Trent to Vatican II the role of the Scriptures in moral theology was very limited.[4] Recent historical studies show that in this period moral theology became separated from dogmatic and spiritual theology and acquired the narrow goal of training priests as judges in the sacrament of penance, with an accompanying minimalistic and legalistic approach concerned primarily with sinfulness of particular acts. At best the Scriptures were employed in a proof text fashion to corroborate arguments that were based on other reasons. In the seventeenth and eighteenth centuries there was a call for a more scriptural approach to moral theology, but the attempts along this line failed because they were entwined in the polemic of the rigorists and probabiliorists against the laxists and probabilists. A more biblically oriented approach to the whole of moral theology first appeared in the Tübingen school and is best exemplified in the manual of Bernard Häring which, despite its necessarily transitional character, stands as the greatest contribution to the renewal of moral theology since the sixteenth century.[5]

Perhaps the major contribution of the biblical renewal in moral theology has been the insistence that Christian morality is a religious ethic. Rudolph Schnackenburg in his influential book *The Moral Teaching of the New Testament* insists on seeing the moral teaching of Jesus as part of the entire God-man relationship. The ethical teaching of Jesus must always be seen in the light of the good news. The manuals of moral theology by wrenching Christian ethics away from its relationship with the full Christian mystery of the saving act of God in Christ very often fostered a Pelagian mentality. The biblical renewal together with the ecumenical dialogue with Protestants has rightly emphasized the primacy of the saving intervention of God and thus avoided the one-sided approach of the past, which pictured man as saving himself by his own effort and actions.[6]

The Model of Relationality and Responsibility

The insistence on a religious ethic in the context of the entire God-man relationship has helped alter the basic structure or model of moral theology itself. The Christian is viewed as one who responds to the activity and the call of God. The theological emphasis on the Word only accentuates the dialogical structure of the Christian life.

The Christian moral life is man's response to the saving word and work of God in Jesus Christ. The important biblical concept of covenant reinforces the primacy of response and of the dialogical structure of the Christian life.[7]

Ethicists in general and Christian ethicists in particular have discussed three general types of ethical models which depend on the basic understanding of the structure of the moral life: teleological, deontological, and responsibility ethics. Teleological ethics conceives the ethical model primarily in terms of the end or goal. Actions are then good or bad insofar as they help or hinder this movement to attain the end. Deontological ethics sees ethics primarily in terms of duties, obligations, or imperatives. The model of responsibility understands man as freely responding in the midst of the multiple relationships in which he finds himself.[8]

In commenting on the use of the Bible in Christian ethics Edward LeRoy Long, Jr. employs such a threefold typology.[9] The Bible has been used in a prescriptive sense as the revelation of God's will. In a more fundamentalistic approach, some see the Bible as a book containing the revealed will of God. Others such as Calvin and Dodd also accept this basic model but employ it in a more nuanced way. Dodd, for example, speaks of precepts that give a quality or direction to our actions. The second model sees the Scriptures as supplying principles or ideals which the Christian tries to attain in his daily life. Such an approach obviously corresponds to the teleological approach. Long sees the third model of responsibility and relationality in the ethics proposed on the basis of the Scriptures by Joseph Sittler and Paul Lehmann.

One could interpret the very perceptive study by James M. Gustafson on ethics and the Bible in much the same way.[10] Gustafson sees the Bible as being used by the Christian ethicist in two different ways—either as revealed morality or as revealed reality. Conservative, evangelical Protestants exemplify the revealed morality approach, for they see in the Scriptures the revealed will of God for man. Such a model obviously employs deontological language and imagery. Liberal Protestants adopted a variation of the revealed morality approach by taking biblical notions such as the kingdom of God and making them the ideal or the goal for the social life of man. Reinhold Niebuhr and John C. Bennett followed somewhat the same path by making love the ideal or the goal towards which the Christian strives. Notice the teleological model in such ethics.

Gustafson points out that a revolution has occurred in biblical theology especially under the influence of Karl Barth so that the bible is not the revelation of a morality but the revelation of the living God and his activity. "In the place of moral teachings particularized or generalized, the new theology put God in his living, free activity. Thus Christian ethics had to think not about morality reduced to propositions, but about God and how life ought to be rightly related to his power and his presence."[11]

Gustafson then shows how such an understanding of the Scriptures leads to the relationality and responsibility motif as the primary model for the understanding of Christian ethics. Man constantly responds in his freedom to the concrete action of God working in this world.[12] I believe that the biblical renewal for the reasons mentioned earlier has brought about the same emphasis on the model of relationality and responsibility in Catholic moral theology without necessarily accepting all the presuppositions of a Barthian theology of the Word.[13]

The Scriptural renewal not only emphasized the primacy of the relationality motif but also argued against the primary insistence on either the teleological or deontological models in Christian ethics. There is no doubt that in popular Catholic life and thought the deontological model was primary. The moral life of the Christian was seen in terms of law and the will of God. The biblical renewal with its emphasis on covenant and the love of God runs somewhat counter to the supremacy of the deontological model.[14]

Even more importantly, in Catholic theology the biblical renewal pointed out the secondary role of law in the life of the Christian. The ten commandments were now viewed not as laws in themselves, but within the context of the covenant as expressions of personal commitment and relationship with God.[15] The renewal of biblical theology showed the subordinate and relative position of law not only in the Old Testament but also in the New Testament. The ethical teaching of Jesus was seen primarily in terms of conversion, *agape,* or the following of Christ and not primarily in terms of law.[16] Scripture scholars exercised considerable influence by showing the true nature of the law of the Spirit in Paul, which is not primarily a written or propositional law, but the love of the Spirit poured into our hearts.[17]

The Thomistic understanding of the moral life employed the teleological model—God as the last end of man. The biblical witness, however, does not picture God primarily as the ultimate end but as the person who invites man to share in the fullness of his life and love through the Paschal Mystery.[18] In Protestant liberal theology there had been the tendency to adopt some scriptural ideal such as the kingdom of God as the goal for the social life of Christians. Catholic theology was never tempted to accept some biblical concept as the goal or ideal of social life, since Catholic social ethics was based almost exclusively on the natural law concept of the common good as the controlling idea in social ethics.

There are also reasons inherent in contemporary biblical scholarship itself which argue against using deontological or teleological models for the development of biblical moral theology or Christian moral theology. Biblical scholars acknowledge the cultural and historical limitations imposed on the written word of the Scriptures. Thus parts of the Scriptures cannot be wrenched from their original context and applied in different historical and cultural situations without the possible danger of some distortion. What might be a valid and true norm in biblical times might not be adequate today. Thus one cannot without further refinement take biblical norms and automatically see them as always obliging in different contexts of our historical lives. The same reasoning also argues against finding goals and ideals in the Scripture which can then be proposed without any modification for our contemporary circumstances.

The breakthrough book in Catholic moral theology, Bernard Häring's *The Law of Christ,* well exemplifies the dialogical understanding of man the moral responder in the context of the covenant relationship. The title of Häring's book, however, illustrates the transitional character of the work, for the primary model of law, even though understood in terms of the law of Christ, bespeaks a primacy of deontological categories. In contemporary Catholic moral theology the responsibility and relationality motif has emerged as most fundamental.[19] There are important philosophical reasons also supporting such a choice, but the original impetus in the historical development came from the Scriptural renewal. In my understanding of Christian ethics the primary model should be that of responsibility and relationality, but there remains a need for some teleological and deontological considerations even though they are of secondary importance.

Other Biblical Contributions

A third important contribution of the Scriptural renewal in moral theology has been the realization that all Christians are called to perfection. An older theology reserved the gospel call to perfection to those who received the vocation to follow the evangelical counsels, whereas the majority of Christians merely lived in the world and obeyed the commandments and precepts (primarily of a natural law character) required of all. The biblical teaching did not inspire such a neat distinction between precept and counsel, but rather called for the total response of the Christian to the gift of God in Christ Jesus.[20] This important attitude changed the purpose and format of Catholic moral theology which could no longer be content with the partial goal of training judges for the sacrament of penance to distinguish between mortal and venial sin and between sin or no sin. Moral theology now considers the life of Christians who are called to be perfect even as the heavenly Father is perfect.

The realization that all Christians are called to such perfection in their change of heart and moral response led to a fourth contribution of biblical morality to moral theology. Growth, development, and creativity became important ideas for contemporary moral theology. The Christian life no longer could be viewed in terms of passive conformity to minimalistic laws obliging all. A closer study of Old Testament ethics forced Catholic moral theology to be more open to the realities of growth and development in the moral life. A few years ago Catholic commentators reflected on the problems proposed for moral theology in the light of the ethical teaching of the Old Testament which in many ways exemplified the reality of growth and development.[21] In theoretical areas such as the understanding of conscience or man's response to the call of God there was a development in the understanding which gradually placed more emphasis on the interiority of the personal response. God calls his people through conscience or the innermost part of the person and not through extrinsic means or persons such as angels.[22]

In practical moral matters the Old Testament created questions for moral theology precisely because some of the values and norms proposed by moral theology today were not accepted in the Old Testament. To explain the Old Testament attitudes to questions of marriage and sexuality it was necessary to accept some concept of growth and development. Logically moral theology would also see the need to apply the same attitude toward growth and development to some contemporary situations.[23]

The emphasis on growth and development in the light of the call to perfection called for a greater appreciation of the active virtues and the creative aspects of the Christian's response to God. The model of responsibility without denying the place of goals and norms also gives priority to the more active and creative aspects of the Christian life.

A fifth important contribution of the biblical renewal in moral theology was the importance given to historicity. Biblical studies indicated the importance of salvation history, which gave a more central role to eschatology. Many differences in moral theology can often be traced to different understandings of eschatology which so profoundly color our understanding of man and his life in this world.

The centrality of history in biblical thinking was in contrast with the lesser importance attributed to history in the manuals of Catholic moral theology. From a philosophical perspective it was only natural that theories giving more importance to the historical aspects of existence should come into prominence in Catholic thought. The biblical renewal exercised another influence in the area of historicity. Biblical scholars used the tools of historical research in examining the Scriptures because of the historical and cultural limitations inherent in the Scriptures and other historical documents. The need to understand and interpret the Scriptures in their historical context easily led to a study of the moral teachings of the Catholic Church in the light of their historical contexts. The way thus opened up for a constant reinterpretation and reevaluation of past teaching in the light of changing historical circumstances.

A sixth important contribution of the biblical influence on moral theology concerns the stress on interiority and the total person with a corresponding lesser emphasis on the individual, external act itself. The Scriptures view man primarily in terms of his faith relationship to God and neighbor, with individual acts seen as expressing the basic attitude of the person and his relationships. Contemporary theologians elaborated on the biblical theme of conversion as the fundamental response to the call of God. Conversion as the basic change of heart interiorizes the moral response of the total person but at the same time has a social and a cosmic dimension.

The reasons contributing to the primacy of the relationality and responsibility motif also give greater importance to interiority in the Christian life. The teaching on the law of the Spirit as the primary law of Christian morality insists on the moral life embracing the heart of the person, with the external act seen as an expression of this fundamental orientation of the person. The biblical theology of sin put great emphasis on interiority, the change of heart, and the breaking of man's multiple relationships with God, neighbor, and the world.[24] Theologians on the basis of the Scriptural data and in the light of other philosophical data developed the theory of the fundamental option as a better understanding of the reality of sin in the life of the Christian.[25]

The biblical contribution to moral theology in the last few years has not only affected the important aspects mentioned thus far, but has also had some influence on the approach to particular moral questions. One illustration is the teaching on private property and the goods of creation. Studies of both the Old Testament and the New Testament have underlined the communal dimension of property.[26] The goods of creation exist primarily for all mankind. Old Testament legislation such as the Jubilee Year indicates a way to safeguard the communal aspect of the goods of creation. The prohibition against usury or interest on a loan was based on the fact that an Israelite should not take advantage of a brother's need to make money from him. Again these biblical attitudes together with other considerations, such as the influence of increasing socialization brought about renewed emphasis in Catholic theology on questions of property and the goods of creation.

The influence of the Scriptural renewal in moral theology has been enormous. Many significant changes which have occurred in moral theology in the last two decades owe much to the fact that the

Scriptures were taken as the soul of theology and the starting point for systematic reflection on the Chrisian life. Obviously other factors such as philosophical considerations and signs of the times also played an important part in the renewal of moral theology, but the starting point of the renewal was the return to the Scriptures. However, moral theology has also become aware of the inherent limitations of the Scriptures in moral theology.

II

LIMITATIONS IN THE USE OF THE SCRIPTURES IN
MORAL THEOLOGY

The most succinct summary of the limitations of the Scriptures in moral theology is the statement that biblical ethics is not the same as Christian ethics. This point is readily acknowledged today by both Catholic and Protestant ethicians. The biblical renewal has emphasized the historical and cultural limitations of the Scriptures so that one cannot just apply the Scriptures in a somewhat timeless manner to problems existing in different historical circumstances. In addition the Scriptures were not really confronted with many of the moral problems we face today. Even among biblical theologians there are those who admit that the Scriptures teach little or no social morality.[27] There has been in theology an embarrassment about the attitude towards slavery and woman in certain parts of the Scriptures, especially in Paul. Also the teaching of the Scriptures is often colored by eschatological considerations which make it difficult to apply them directly to any contemporary situation. The hermeneutic problem arises precisely because biblical morality and Christian morality are not the same.

From this basic understanding of the limitation of biblical ethics in the discipline of Christian ethics one should be cautioned about possible dangers in the use of the Scriptures in moral theology. A perennial danger is the use of the Scriptures as a proof text. An isolated Scriptural text is used to prove an assertion for the present time without realizing the vast difference which might exist between the biblical and the contemporary contexts. Likewise there is the constant danger that the individual biblical text may be taken out of its own proper biblical context. Sacred Scripture cannot be legitimately employed in a proof text manner.

Too often the manuals of moral theology did employ such a use of the Scriptures. The conclusion was arrived at on other grounds, and then one text from the Scriptures was given as a proof of the assertion. Even today there continue to exist in both Catholic and Protestant theology some glaring examples of a proof text approach to the Scriptures in moral theology.

Bo Reicke translates the first Epistle of Peter, 2:18 as: "You workers, be submissive to your masters with all respect, not only to the good and reasonable ones, but even to the difficult ones."[28] Reicke in his commentary defends his choice of workers rather than slaves so that the passage will have meaning for contemporary Christian workers. The meaning of the passage according to Reicke is clear. "Regardless of provocation Christian workers should not rebel or fail in respect towards their employers."[29] Christ is the model of every suffering worker. "He did not stoop as many oppressed people on earth to reviling and threatening, vs. 23, but committed his case to the righteous Judge. No striving after personal liberty or antisocial behavior or opposition to the existing order can be allowed to impair the Christian workers' imitation of Christ."[30] He later comments that Christianity will bring about a social revolution but through spiritual means.[31] However, I do not think that one can use the Scripture in this way to argue against the possibility of a legitimate strike by Christian workers.

Eschatological Influence

Another vexing aspect of the hermeneutic problem concerns the eschatological coloring of the teaching of Jesus especially the Sermon on the Mount. In opposition to the liberal Protestant theology which saw the Sermon on the Mount as a blueprint for bringing about the presence of the kingdom of God in this world, Schweitzer and others maintained that such an intention was far removed from Jesus who was just proposing an interim ethic for the short time before the coming of the end of the world.[32] There has been much theological discussion about the ethical teaching of the Sermon on the Mount, but in one way or another eschatological considerations must enter into the picture.[33] Thus one cannot simply transpose the ethical teaching of the Scriptures to the contemporary scene without some attention to eschatological considerations.

The biblical teaching on marriage and celibacy calls for some such interpretation, for eschatological considerations apparently downplayed the importance which marriage should have.[34] One major problem in Catholic life and moral theology at the present time, the question of divorce and the pastoral care of divorced people, raises the crucial question of the teaching on the indissolubility of marriage in the New Testament. In my view such a teaching can be interpreted in the light of eschatology so that the absoluteness of Catholic practice and teaching should be somewhat relaxed.

Catholic teaching upholds the indissolubility of *ratum et consummatum* marriages and frequently invokes Scriptural references including Mt. 19:9, as well as Mt. 5:32. However, some problems arise even within the Catholic tradition, for only *ratum et consummatum* marriages are declared absolutely indissoluble while other marriages can be dissolved. There is no explicit warrant within the Scriptural tradition for this. Paul in his letter to the Corinthians allows some exceptions in the case of the indissolubility of marriage despite the absoluteness of the saying of Jesus. In fact, even the famous exception clauses in Matthew, (except for the case of πορνεία), have always proved somewhat difficult to interpret in the light of the present teaching of the Catholic Church.[35]

Many different interpretations have been proposed for the exception clauses in Matthew. The more traditional solution among Catholic exegetes interpreted Matthew to allow separation but not remarriage. A more modern interpretation indicates that the exception clauses refer to a marriage which is not valid from the very beginning. One cannot debate here the merits of the various solutions which have been proposed, but I would conclude that even in the New Testament times of Paul and the redactor of Matthew some exceptions were apparently made in the absolute teaching proposed by Jesus. Likewise the teaching of Matthew on divorce is also found in the context of the Sermon on the Mount where eschatological considerations are of considerable importance. I propose that the indissolubility of marriage is proposed as an ideal, but that in the world between the two comings of Jesus it is not always possible to achieve the fullness of that ideal.[36] Another important factor concerns the practical problems involved in coming up with pastoral solutions to the question of divorces so that one can maintain the ideal, protect innocent persons, and still realize that in this world it is not always possible to live up to the fullness of the ideal.

Problems of Systematization and Selection

In general the limitations of the use of biblical ethics in Christian ethics arise from the differences between the two. However, problems exist even within the context of biblical ethics itself which also serve as a limitation and possible danger in the use of biblical ethics in Christian ethics. Two different possible approaches to biblical ethics are illustrated by the two most widely acknowledged contributions by Catholic authors to biblical ethics. Rudolf Schnackenburg adopts an historical or chronological approach to the moral message of the New Testament by considering the moral teaching in the Synoptics, in the early Church in general, in John, in Paul, and in the other New Testament writers.[37] Ceslaus Spicq in his well documented, two volume study arranges the moral teaching of the New Testament around ten major themes each of which includes some subsidiary themes.[38]

Spicq himself is well aware of the difficulty of presenting any synthetic or systematic understanding of biblical morality.[39] Within the Scriptures different books treat the same matter with different emphasis (e.g., the concept of love). Likewise any attempt at systematization or synthesis involves an interpretation of the biblical teaching. The fact remains that there is great divergence even within the biblical message itself which makes it most difficult to arrive at a satisfying synthesis of biblical teaching or biblical morality. In a somewhat larger context Roland Murphy argues that the notion of "the unity of the Bible" should be interred precisely because of the diversity existing within the Scriptures. "In every case the rubric of unity turns out to be incomplete, whether it be covenant, *Heilsgeschichte,* or promise-fulfillment. Every such category, while it has a value in itself, is simply too limited to deal with the variety offered by the biblical material."[40] I would argue that even in the area of biblical morality such a unity or perfect synthesis remains impossible of achievement. There exists even within the Scriptures a plurality of understandings of the moral life. Thus even within the Scriptures themselves there remains an inherent limitation in developing a systematic biblical morality.

A more noticeable limitation arises from the fact that the Scriptures themselves even in moral matters are in need of interpretation. Whether implicitly or explicitly the theologian will bring his own presuppositions to his interpretations of biblical morality. The danger is that we often forget the existence of such interpretations and presuppositions and uncritically acclaim the biblical approach of a particular author.

Spicq, for example, in summarizing his massive two volume work obviously shows his own theological presuppositions. Spicq insists that the Christian life does not primarily consist of obedience to rules but is a living out of the life of the new creature in Christ Jesus. The moral life follows from an ontology of the new creature. Spicq obviously interprets the biblical message in the light of the Catholic teaching on the transformation of the individual by God's redeeming grace. The Christian now has a regenerated nature which becomes the source of his life and actions.[41] Roger Mehl on the basis of his theological presuppositions takes issue with Spicq's interpretation. God's gift is his presence, but his presence never becomes a nature or a structure. Such an ontology or substantialist philosophy according to Mehl can never truly present the biblical understanding of the God-man relationship.[42]

Two different interpretations of Paul's understanding of the Christian life also illustrate the different theological presuppositions of the two authors. George Montague's study of Pauline morality exhibits on its cover jacket the basic presupposition of his thesis. The full title is: *Maturing in Christ: Saint Paul's Program for Christian Growth.*[43] The cover jacket then cites one Pauline text: "If anyone is in Christ, he is a *new creature.*" Montague's thesis maintains that a basic transformation into the new creature takes place in the life of the Christian.[44] Victor Paul Furnish in his study of Pauline ethics denies the two fundamental presuppositions of Montague. First, Furnish refuses to accept the concept of a mystical union of the

Christian with Christ. The being of the believer is not merged with the being of Christ. "The categories used to describe the believer's association with Christ are all *relational* not *mystical* categories."[45] Logically, Furnish also denies at the end of his book any possibility of progress in the life of the Christian according to Paul. Paul's preaching insists that the "fullness of life is not attained but given, and that Christian obedience is not an expression of man's effort gradually to realize his own innate possibilities, but an ever repeated response to the ever newly repeated summons of God."[46] Montague's basic thesis is thus denied by Furnish although Montague would not positively explain his thesis in the same terms in which Furnish denied the possibility of progress in the life of the Christian.

Another example of differing interpretations of biblical teaching is illustrated in James Sellers' choice of the concept of promise and fulfillment as the basic stance in Christian ethics. "The Judaeo-Christian faith then affirms a distinctive understanding of what is happening to man; he is moving from promise to fulfillment."[47] Paul Ramsey also argues from the Judaeo-Christian tradition and from the concept of covenant, but he emphatically denies Sellers' emphasis on fulfillment. Precisely on the basis of eschatology and of covenant fidelity Ramsey rules out the primacy of fulfillment in any understanding of the Christian moral life. Ramsey consistently opposes a teleological approach to Christian ethics precisely because of the fact that fulfillment or the attainment of the goal is not always possible for the Christian.[48]

A related danger in the use of the Scriptures in moral theology involves the selective use of the Scriptures in keeping with one's own presuppositions. The Social Gospel approach to Christian ethics, for example, concentrated on the teaching of the prophets in the Old Testament and the teaching of Jesus in the New Testament, since these two sources are most consonant with the theological presuppositions of the Social Gospel approach. Walter Rauschenbusch in his *Christianity and the Social Crisis* well illustrates such an approach.[49]

The first of Rauschenbusch's seven chapters considers the teaching of the prophets, while the second chapter deals with the teaching of Jesus. In the third chapter he treats the more difficult problem of the social impetus of early Christianity. Rauschenbusch realizes there is not much social teaching in Paul, whom he describes as a radical in theology but a social conservative. But Paul was not as apathetic towards social conditions as is generally presumed. In this context he praises the social concerns of the Epistle of James, which had been rejected in the strict Lutheran tradition.[50] Rauschenbusch's attempts to prove the social implications in the teaching of the early Church are often exaggerated and unacceptable. "The Christian Church was of immense social value to these people. It took the place in their life which life insurance, sick benefits, accident insurance, friendly societies, and some features of trade-unions take today."[51] There are other exaggerated claims made to support his basic contention.[52] Thus one can see the dangers of selectivity in the choice of the Scriptural texts which are used and the twisting of other parts of the Scriptures to fit in with the presuppositions.

Obviously those who make Christ the center of the moral life of the Christian tend to be quite selective in their use of Scripture and place importance on those texts which support their positions while passing over much of the biblical materials (especially the Old Testament) in silence. Bonhoeffer understands the foundation of the Christian life in terms of formation, or better, conformation with the unique form of him who was made man, was crucified, and rose again. Man does not achieve this formation by dint of his own efforts, but Christ shapes man in conformity with himself.[53] The Scripture employed by Bonhoeffer includes many important Christological texts in the New Testament—Gal 4:19; 2 Cor 3:18; Phil 3:10; Rom 8:29, 12:2, Phil 1:21; Col 3:3.[54] Again the critical ethician realizes the selectivity involved in such a use of Scripture. Obviously some selectivity must be employed, but the critical ethician needs to probe the implicit presuppositions behind the selection of certain aspects of the Scriptures.

Another somewhat related danger arises from the selection of one biblical theme as primary and as coloring one's whole approach to Christian ethics. Reference has already been made to Sellers' choice of promise and fulfillment as the most basic aspect in Christian ethics. Again, it will always be necessary to choose some basic starting point in Christian ethics; but some themes which have been chosen do not seem to be that basic or central. Thus such a selection tends to distort the Christian ethics built around it. Today some theologians are developing a theology of liberation based also on biblical categories.[55] Difficulties arise, however, when this becomes the primary and even the exclusive emphasis in moral theology, for other important considerations go unheeded. In the field of social ethics, order and security are other aspects of the question even though some theologians may have overemphasized these aspects in the past. Especially in the light of the fads which have existed in theology in the past few years there remains constant danger of taking one aspect of the biblical message and making it so central and exclusive that the full biblical message is not properly understood.

III
Two Methodological Questions

There are two important foundational questions concerning the use of the Scriptures in moral theology which relate to the question of methodology. The first question concerns the precise way in which Christian ethicians have employed or should employ the Scriptures. The second question centers on the exact relationship between the content of the ethical teaching of the Scriptures and the content of non-biblical ethical teaching.

In examining the different ways in which moral theology employs the Scriptures, I believe that the fundamental difference stems from one's basic understanding of the relationship between Christian ethics and other forms of ethics especially philosophical ethics. Is Christian ethics just a certain type or species, if you will, of ethics in general? Does the methodological approach to Christian ethics depend on considerations common to all forms of ethical discourse? Or is the methodological approach to Christian ethics different from all other ethical methodologies precisely because of the distinctive aspect of Christian ethics? If the methodology of Christian ethics differs from the methodology of other forms of ethics because of the distinctive nature of Christian ethics, the ultimate reason must be found in the relationship of Christian ethics to revelation, grace and the Scriptures.

A Fundamental but Limited Question

Note the limited yet very fundamental aspects of the question being pursued. The answer to this question will not solve all the methodological questions about the use of the Scriptures in moral theology, but it will indicate the first steps that should be taken in constructing such a methodology. At least logically there are two different methodological approaches which could be taken in response to our question. The one approach derives its content from the Scriptures, revelation, and the other sources of ethical wisdom for the Christian. In this approach one could use the Scriptures to argue for a particular methodological approach (e.g. a responsibility model rather than a deontological model), but the methodological structure would be common to all possible forms of ethics. The second approach would be a methodology which is peculiar to Christian ethics because of the distinctive character of Christian ethics which must bear some relationship to its Scriptural basis.

With these two possibilities in mind one could set out to examine the different generic approaches which have been employed by moral theology or Christian ethics in the past to determine if there have been two such generic approaches to the methodology of Christian ethics. Such a thorough review is impossible here, but one can use the research of others in this area. James M. Gustafson has analyzed two different approaches in Christian theological ethics.[56] Gustafson briefly describes the one approach as the more intuitional and the other as the more rational approach. Gustafson cites Paul Lehmann as an example of the intuitional approach, for Lehmann maintains that Christian ethics responds to the question of what God is doing in the world to make and keep human life more human. Lehmann generally does not spell out criteria for discerning this humanizing activity of God, but he often appeals to intuition. The second approach is more rational in its methodology and allows for more ethical argument in discussing what should be done.

One could argue that the difference between the two generic approaches comes from different philosophical understandings of ethics. The one would follow an intuitional, philosophical method and the other a more rational, philosophical method. However, I propose that the ultimate reason for the two different methodological approaches mentioned by Gustafson does not come from two different philosophical approaches as such. Rather the difference lies in an approach which employs a rational methodology which could be common to any and all forms of ethics, and in an approach which sees Christian ethics as so distinctive that it even has a methodology which is distinctive from all other ethical methodologies.

Those who employ the approach Gustafson describes as intuitional are in general those Christian ethicians who see Christian ethics as essentially distinct from other forms of ethics and thus posit a distinctive methodology for Christian ethics. This distinctive methodology bears some relationship to the revealed character of Christian ethics. Gustafson cites Lehmann as an example of the intuitional approach, but Lehmann willingly admits there is neither identity nor an intrinsic relationship between Christian ethics and philosophical ethics. Rather there is an ultimate chasm and even opposition between Christian ethics and philosophical ethics. "The radical incompatibility between Christian and philosophical ethics is the irreconcilability of their respective views of human self-determination."[57] Lehmann adopts the Barthian position by asserting that for philosophical ethics man makes ethics, but for Christian ethics, God makes ethics, for God initiates and establishes the humanity of man. Lehmann then cites Barth again to prove his fundamental assertion that the grace of God protests against every humanly established ethic as such. The specifically and formatively ethical factor cannot be given rational generalization.[58]

Lehmann thus indicates that a Barthian approach to theology accepts a distinctive methodology for Christian ethics which differs from every other ethical methodology. The Bible tells us of the actions of the living God, and it is with the actions of the living God that Christian ethics must begin and not with any philosophical understanding of man. Barth in no way accepts a fundamentalistic approach to the Scriptures. The Word and concrete command of God are not the same as the written word of the Scriptures. The role of the Scriptures in moral theology is secondary, but through analogy man may arrive at his decision in the light of the Scriptures. Barth's Christian social ethics with its emphasis on analogy has been challenged precisely because of its seeming lack of rational structure.

There are few criteria given to indicate how the analogy occurs, and many of the analogies which Barth draws seem to be quite arbitrary. Barth cannot accept rational criteria for establishing any movement by analogy from the Word of God to concrete ethical problems.[59]

Barth and Lehmann both illustrate the first approach which views Christian ethics as an altogether distinctive type of ethics precisely because of the theology of revelation, the Word and Scriptures. The distinctive aspects of Christian ethics stems from their theology of the Word and the concrete command of God. Since such an approach rejects a biblical fundamentalism, the written word of God does not have the primary place in their ethic; but somehow or other, as the record of the acts of the living God, it does bear on the concrete situation here and now. Although Lehmann and Sittler in the United States seem to adopt such a generic approach, there can be no doubt that such an approach with its Barthian roots is much stronger in continental, European Protestant thought.[60]

A. Dumas raises the precise problem of how Christian social ethics goes from Sacred Scripture to contemporary problems.[61] Dumas points out the difficulties in the approach of liberalism which tried to reduce the gospel message to the essential core which would be true in all circumstances. On the other hand the Orthodox approach tries merely to repeat perhaps in different language the revealed word of the Scriptures. Both approaches are wrong because in trying to assure a universalism to the word of God they fail to come to grips with the existentialism and singularity of the biblical message. Dumas proposes a hermeneutic of explicitation in which the contemporary Christian and the Christian ethicist see the Bible not as an archetype but as a parable which is normative for the present circumstances. However, there exists little or nothing in terms of rational criteria or even debatable criteria for discerning how precisely the Bible functions as a parable for normatively directing Christian ethics today.

The editors of *Christianisme Social* describe the function of Christian ethics not as applying principles derived from other historical and cultural circumstances to questions of the present times, but rather as interpreting for our times a Word which had been a living word in a different setting. The editors of this journal try to find a direct relationship between the concrete biblical word and the precise social situation of the present.[62] Again, little or nothing is said about the criteria for developing this hermeneutic, and no criteria which can be rationally debated or discussed are proposed. In somewhat the same vein, F. Florentin speaks of a certain discernment which contemporary man receives from the Scriptures, but the process of how this discernment takes place is not developed.[63]

I personally cannot accept this generic approach to the methodology of Christian ethics, which sees it as distinctive from all other ethical methodology. Although the proponents of this generic approach do not make the written word of the Scriptures normative in itself without further interpretation, their use of the Scriptures in terms of analogy, parables, etc. does not seem to furnish an adequate methodology for Christian ethics in general and for the use of the Scriptures in Christian ethics in particular.

In general I would opt for a methodology in Christian ethics which is common to the ethical enterprise and is not distinctive. The methodology of Christian ethics exists in continuity with ethical methodology in general. This position is in keeping with the Catholic theological tradition and is also accepted by many contemporary Protestant ethicians. Obviously this is a very generic approach and there can be many different methodological approaches within this generic option. This paper is considering just the most fundamental and basic of the questions confronting methodology in Christian ethics. Christian ethicians adopting such a generic approach that sees Christian ethics in continuity with the general ethical enterprise will generally admit the Scriptures are not the sole source of ethical wisdom for the Christian, but that Christian ethics also derives wisdom and knowledge from other human sources. This generic approach will thus rely on human wisdom and reason as well as on the Scriptures, a factor that will greatly influence the role and function of the Scriptures in moral theology.

Once one has opted for a methodology common to all ethical theory, there remains almost an infinite variety of such theories which one can choose. One must try to establish on the grounds of ethical thinking and Christian understanding what is the best type of theory to employ. Obviously this paper cannot consider all the different possibilities. The consideration will be limited to one brief observation and then a sketch of a possible development of the methodology to be employed in Christian ethics and the way in which it would use the Scriptures.[64]

The brief observation concerns the danger of oversimplification. Some methodological approaches to Christian ethics appear to be erroneous precisely because they fail to consider all the elements that should enter into the ethical consideration. Perhaps no mention is made of the decision process itself, or the attitudes and dispositions of the subject, or the values and goals in the Christian life. In general an ethical approach must try to be as comprehensive as possible by considering all the elements that go into ethical considerations, even though some will obviously have priority and be of greater importance. The Scriptures as well as human wisdom can be of help in all these areas.

Perhaps the most fundamental question in ethics is that of stance, horizon, or posture. The horizon or ultimate way in which the Christian looks at reality is in my judgment in the light of the Christian mysteries of creation, sin, incarnation, redemption, and resurrection destiny. Obviously, such a posture includes its own presuppositions. The stance is not defined in terms of any one value, disposition, or goal, precisely because any one such value, ideal, or goal with its specific content does not seem apt to serve as a basic stance. The basic stance proposed here is more formal in the sense that it indicates the structure of the Christian experience. This tries to give a formal intelligibility rather than a content intelligibility. Such a choice obviously indicates a distinct emphasis on the subject pole of human experience.

The second most fundamental ethical question concerns the general model for understanding the Christian moral life. Earlier, mention was made of the three general approaches of ethics to this question, and the model of relationality and responsibility was chosen in the light of the biblical understanding of man.

There are at least four other important considerations which should be present in ethics: 1) values, goals, or ideals; 2) dispositions and attitudes of the subject, or virtues, if you prefer; 3) norms; 4) the process of moral judgments and decisions. Obviously the question of moral judgments and decisions will always be the most decisive consideration, but these other aspects cannot be neglected.

In the more general questions of stance and model, the Scriptural input will be more important, but it will not be the only aspect of the question. There are ethical presuppositions in my own decision to see the stance, not in terms of content, but as a way of structuring the manner in which the Christian intends reality and the world in which he lives. On the other more specific ethical considerations, with the emphasis on the judging and decision making process, the role and function of the Scriptures will be less. The precise way in which the Scriptures can contribute in all these areas is both partial and limited in view of the hermeneutic question itself. This has only been a brief sketch of a possible development of methodology in Christian ethics, once one answers the basic question by seeing the methodology of Christian ethics in terms of ethical theory in general and not as something distinctive to Christian ethics. Obviously, within this generic approach there remain many possible options. In all these the input of the Scriptures will be limited because of the historical and cultural limitations of the word of God as found in the Scriptures, and will be interpreted in the light of the ethical methodology chosen.

A Content Question with Methodological Overtones

In the midst of the ethical and religious pluralism in which we live there arises not only the question of the ethical methodology employed by moral theology and its use of the Scriptures, but also the question of the content or the substance of biblical ethics and moral theology in comparison with other religious and philosophical ethics. The generally accepted approach of the past affirms a great difference between the revealed morality of the Bible and the non-revealed morality of other ethics. Today there appears to be a tendency, with which I concur, to disagree with the older approach.[65] This question obviously has important methodological implications for Christian ethics.

In the past, the question of the relationship between Christian ethics and other ethics was phrased in terms of the existence of a source of ethical wisdom and knowledge which the Christian shares with all mankind in addition to the revealed wisdom of the Scriptures. An affirmative response to the question led to the further question of the exact relationship between the revelational and the nonrevelational sources of ethical wisdom and knowledge for the Christian. Precisely under the impact of the consciousness of religious and ethical pluralism, as well as the apparent lack of ethical superiority in Christian ethics and in the Scripture, the question now takes on a different aspect: is there any great difference in content between Christian ethics, with revelation and the Scriptures as the reason for its possible distinctive character, and other human ethics?

One way to approach the problem is to institute a comparison between biblical ethics and non-revealed ethics. Some significant work has been going on in this area and is illustrated by the question of the decalogue in the Old Testament. Christians generally have the image that God revealed his law to the people of the Old Testament even if they are sophisticated enough to realize there was no historical apparition or revelation to Moses amid thunder and lightning. The developing research in this area is most interesting, for the trend shows an ever growing awareness of the lack of distinctiveness between the biblical law of the Old Testament and the non-revealed law of the contemporaries of Israel.

Albrecht Alt in 1934 distinguished two types of law in Israel, the apodictic and the casuistic and acknowledged that the casuistic law was common to all people in the Near East, but the apodictic law was unique and peculiar to Israel. Such a position bolstered the notion of the distinctive and unique qualities of the revealed morality.[66] More contemporary scholarship, however, disputes the conclusion proposed by Alt and realizes that apodictic law was also common to other peoples in the Near East. Even the general covenant form is not something unique, but exists also in the Hittite Suzerainty treaties.[67]

In this context the question has been raised about the origin of the decalogue as we know it today. Obviously there is a connection between the form of the decalogue and its use in worship, so that some commentators have concluded that the form of the decalogue as we have it today probably arose within the context of the cult. However, Gerstenberger and others claim that the apodictic law of the decalogue had its origin not in the treaty or in the cult but in the clan.[68] Again notice in these theories a tendency away from a distinctiveness concerning the circumstances of the decalogue.

J. J. Stamm appears to accept the conclusion that the content of the revealed morality of the Old Testament "came about in a much more secular way than is often supposed."[69] Gerstenberger maintains that one cannot conclude that Israel's law is better or more moral than that of her neighbors, or that it is unique because it is revealed. Israel's law when brought into the context of the covenant comes to express fully what was already inherent in it: the necessity of the framework of relationship which breaks through that which is merely moral.[70] Thus the Old Testament gives the new context of the covenant with Yahweh for a law which was not unique, and even this general covenant context is somehow or other inherent in the law.

Carroll Stuhlmueller in the light of recent biblical studies (primarily relating to the Old Testament but also including some studies about the New Testatment) specifically asks the question about the relationship between revealed morality and the so-called natural law. Stuhlmueller concludes that the origins of the revelation of Israel will be recognized not as a lightning bolt from above but as God's living presence with all men of good will.[71] "Biblically, the world at large contributes what men of faith can then identify as the presence of God speaking His will for human well-being."[72] At this juncture I would only add the cautionary note that human experience also reflects the limitations and sinfulness of men so that not everything that appears in human experience is necessarily good and to be accepted uncritically.

One could continue such a comparative study down through all the Scriptures including the teachings of the prophets, the wisdom literature, Jesus, Paul, John, and the early Christian community as compared with their contemporaries and others. This area provides a fertile field for possible future development and research. Interestingly, recent studies tend to be very modest in claiming any superiority for the biblical morality. Seán Freyne in a recent study of biblical morality in both the Old and the New Testaments admits that the content of biblical morality is similar to the content of non-revealed morality.[73] The contribution of the prophets to the moral teaching of Israel does not derive from any special revelation of content from God, but the prophets merely refined the traditional morality.[74] Freyne comments that what is striking in the teachings of Jesus is his agreement with and acceptance of the better insights and formulations of the late Jewish moral thinking. As far as the content of the moral life is concerned, Jesus inherited and refined rather than innovated.[75]

Freyne does, however, admit a purifying influence of faith on the insights of secular morality.[76] Freyne staunchly argues for a different motivation and context for biblical ethics, but "the actual content of their morality will thus be often similar to that of their surrounding neighbors, at least in the more lofty formulations of these."[77] The difference he sometimes mentions in content between biblical and non-biblical morality is that of refinement and purification. Perhaps this coheres with the caveat expressed earlier that human experience will also always contain the limitations and sinfulness which mark our human existence, but the loftiest aspects of human experience will often correspond with the best of the biblical ethic.[78]

One can also examine the questions of the relationship between biblical, or Christian, and non-revealed morality in a more systematic and theological approach. Is there a distinctively Christian ethic? A growing number of studies indicate that on the level of ethical conclusions and proximate values, norms, and dispositions, there is nothing distinctive about the Christian ethic. John Macquarrie maintains that the distinctively Christian criterion coincides with the criterion which is already guiding, at least implicitly, the moral aspiration of all men—the idea of an authentic or full humanity. Macquarrie finds the distinctiveness of Christian ethics not in the ultimate goals or fundamental principles but in the special context within which the moral life is considered.[79] Interestingly, Macquarrie links Christian and non-Christian ethics not on the basis of redemption but of creation.[80]

I have denied the existence of a distinctively Christian ethic with regard to ethical conclusions and proximate dispositions, goals, and attitudes; but the reason for the identity was not creation but redemption. It seems to me that Josef Fuchs takes much the same approach. Fuchs first distinguishes between the level of the transcendental or intentionality and the level of the categorical. On the level of the categorical Christ did not really add anything new. The distinctively Christian appears on the level of the transcendental and intentionality. Near the end of the article Fuchs also admits that the humanist operates not only on the level of the categorical but also on the level of the intentional, the transcendental, and the unthematic.[81]

If one were to interpret Fuchs in the light of Rahner, which is acceptable in the light of Fuchs' own writings, the difference on the level of the transcendental or unthematic could possibly be only the difference between the explicit and the implicit, and not necessarily a difference of greater and lesser. In accord with Fuchs' article one could also conclude that the specifically Christian aspect does not add anything to the "proximate dispositions, goals, and attitudes of Christians." Yet these dispositions, goals, attitudes, and values would be considered in an explicitly Christian context, but non-Christians too can and do cherish "self-sacrificing love, freedom, hope, concern for the neighbor in need, or even the realization that one finds his life only in losing it."[82]

In the above paragraphs I am trying to clarify and further a dialogue begun by Richard A. McCormick, S.J.[83] McCormick argues that the gospel should bring about distinctive attitudes and intentions. He then appeals to both Fuchs and Gustafson as supporting or being close to his position. McCormick finds support in Fuchs because Fuchs refers to "transcendental norms (e.g. the following of Christ, leading a sacramental life, the life of faith, etc.)."[84]

Perhaps the following of Christ can illustrate the question. I am interpreting Fuchs as agreeing with my conclusion: "The explicitly Christian consciouness does affect the judgment of the Christian and the way in which he makes his ethical judgments, but non-Christians can and do arrive at the same ethical conclusions and also embrace and treasure even the loftiest of proximate motives, virtues and goals which Christians in the past have wrongly claimed only for themselves."[85] Certainly the Christian explicitly reflects on the imitation of Christ, but the proximate attitudes, values, and goals that come from this are the same attitudes that other people can arrive at in other ways. My earlier article spelled out some of these attitudes as self-sacrificing love, freedom, hope, concern for the neighbor in need, or even the realization that one finds his life only in losing it.

Another way of trying to express the same reality was to say that Christians and non-Christians "can and do share the same general ethical attitudes, dispositions and goals."[86] "General" in this case refers to such a concept as self-sacrificing love which the Christian could share with other men in general, but he sees it in terms of explicit reference to Jesus Christ, which thus modifies the general concept not necessarily by adding to its content but by explicitly referring to Jesus Christ. In this way the following of Christ motif leads the Christian to the same conclusions and proximate attitudes that others can arrive at on other grounds and through other conceptualizations. Obviously I am not saying that all non-Christians do arrive at these dispositions, but they can come to them. Likewise all Christians do not live up to such lofty ideals.

Gustafson has not directly asked the question as posed here, but he appears to assume that there is a greater difference between Christian and non-Christian ethics than the solution proposed here. Gustafson does stress the "differences that faith in Jesus Christ *often does make, can make,* and *ought to make* in the moral lives of members of the Christian community."[87] The question must eventually go back to the theological discussion of the relationship between the Christian and the non-Christian. Since in my opinion this difference can at times be only the difference between explicit and implicit, then one can maintain the conclusion proposed above.

The Pastoral Constitution on the Church in the Modern World proposes a methodology of viewing reality in terms of the gospel and human experience. Accepting this formulation, I would conclude that the gospel does not add a power or knowledge which *somehow or other* is not available in the consciousness of man called by God with regard to ethical conclusions and proximate dispositions, goals, and attitudes. The gospel does make explicit, and explicitly Christian, what can be implicit in the consciousness of all men who are called by God. Precisely because the link between the Christian and the non-Christian is not based on creation only, but also on redemption, then the redemptive power and knowledge that the Christian has in the gospel are also available somehow or other to all men. The difference in the specific area of ethics mentioned above is between explicit and implicit, and not between more or less.

Human experience thus can have implicitly what is explicitly found in the gospel and also cherish the same proximate ethical ideals, dispositions, and decisions; but human experience also reflects the limitations and sinfulness of man (as the Scriptures do also). This realization will also have important repercussions on the way in which moral theology uses the Scriptures. I still see the important role of the Scriptures in terms of explicitly allowing us to reflect on who the Christian is and what his attitudes, dispositions, goals, values, norms, and decisions are. However, in no sense can the Scriptures be used as a book of revealed morality precisely because of the hermeneutic problem. The Scriptures do furnish us with information about the self-understanding of the people who lived in convenant relationshp with God and how this helped shape their lives and actions. The Christian and the Christian ethicist today must continue to reflect on this experience as recalled in the Scriptures, but they must also reflect on the experience of other men as they try to determine how they should live and respond to Jesus Christ in our times.

This section has not attempted to develop a complete methodology for the use of the Scriptures in moral theology, but rather has considered perhaps the two most fundamental questions involved in constructing such a methodology. The methodology of Christian ethics is not distinctive but is based on ethical methodology in general as viewed in the light of the gospel message and human experience. Secondly, the ethical wisdom and knowledge portrayed in the Scriptural experience remains quite similar to the ethical experience of all mankind. The primary difference is the explicitly Christian character of the gospel which will not affect the proximate ethical dispositions, attitudes, and goals as well as concrete conclusions, but will color the explicit self-understanding of the Christian and the decision process he employs.

Notes

1. Dogmatic Constitution on Divine Revelation, n. 24. English references to Council documents are taken from: *The Documents of Vatican II,* ed. Walter M. Abbott, S.J.; trans. ed. Joseph Gallagher (New York: Guild Press, 1966).
2. Decree on Priestly Formation, n. 16.

3. Contrast the different approaches to *agape* in the Protestant and Catholic traditions in the following: Andres Nygren, *Agape and Eros* (New York: Harper Torchbook, 1969); M. C. D'Arcy, S.J., *The Mind and Heart of Love* (New York: Meridian Books, 1956). For further comment on these discussions about the meaning of love within the Roman Catholic tradition, see Jules Toner, *The Experience of Love* (Washington/Cleveland: Corpus Books, 1968); Giovanni Volta, "Per un'indagine razionale sull'amore," in Carlo Colombo, *et al., Matrimonio e Verginità* (Milan: La Scuola Cattolica, 1963), pp. 9–49.

4. For an adequate historical summary and for further bibliographical references, see Edouard Hamel, S.J., "L'Usage de l'Écriture Sainte en théologie morale," *Gregorianum,* XLVII (1966), 56–63; J. Etienne, "Théologie Morale et renouveau biblique," *Ephemerides Theologicae Lovanienses,* XL (1964), 232–241.

5. Bernard Häring, C.SS.R., *The Law of Christ,* (3 vols.; Westminster, Md.: Newman Press, 1961, 1963, 1966).

6. Rudolf Schnackenburg, *The Moral Teaching of the New Testament* (New York: Herder and Herder, 1965), pp. 13–53. The original German edition of his very influential work appeared in 1954.

7. J. L'Hour, *La morale de l'alliance* (Paris: Gabalda, 1966).

8. For a description of these three different types of ethical models and arguments in favor of the responsibility model, see H. Richard Niebuhr, *The Responsible Self* (New York: Harper and Row, 1963).

9. Edward LeRoy Long, Jr., "The Use of the Bible in Christian Ethics," *Interpretation,* XIX (1965), 149–162.

10. James M. Gustafson, "Christian Ethics," in *Religion,* ed. by Paul Ramsey (Englewood Cliffs: Prentice-Hall, 1965), pp. 309–316.

11. *Ibid.,* p. 316.

12. *Ibid.,* pp. 316–320.

13. It is precisely the anti-philosophical stance and the theological actualism in Barthian thought that I cannot accept.

14. Albert Gelin, *The Key Concepts of the Old Testament* (New York: Sheed and Ward, 1955). In this and the following paragraphs references will be made to works which seem to have been influential within the Roman Catholic world. There are obviously other studies which are of equal and even more importance that were done within the Protestant community.

15. Philippe Delhaye, *Le Decalogue et sa place dans la morale chrétienne* (Bruxelles: La Pensée Catholique, 1963); Matthew J. O'Connell, "Commandment in the Old Testament," *Theological Studies,* XXI (1960), 351–403.

16. Examples of these different approaches in Catholic theology with

considerable emphasis on the biblical themes include: Bernard Häring, "Conversion," in P. Delhaye *et al., Pastoral Treatment of Sin* (New York: Desclée, 1968), pp. 87–176; Ceslaus Spicq, O.P., *Agape in the New Testament,* (3 vols.; St. Louis: B. Herder, 1963, 1965, 1966); Fritz Tillmann, *The Master Calls* (Baltimore: Helicon, 1960). Again note the European origin of these influential works in Roman Catholic theology even in the United States.

17. Perhaps the most influential article in this area was: Stanislas Lyonnet, S.J., "Liberté du chrétien et loi de l'Ésprit selon saint Paul," *Christus,* I (1954) 6–27. This article has been translated into numerous languages and has appeared in many different places. See also Philippe Delhaye, "Liberté chrétienne et obligation morale," *Ephemerides Theologicae Lovanienses,* XL (1964), 347–361; Florence Michels, O.L.V.M., *Paul and the Law of Love* (Milwaukee: Bruce, 1967).

18. In this context E. Hamel seems to present a position that has not fully integrated moral theology into a newer perspective derived from the biblical approach. He wants to maintain the existing tracts in moral theology; e.g., *de fine ultimo,* but give them a biblical perspective. Hamel, *Gregorianum,* XLVII (1966), 76.

19. Albert R. Jonsen, *Responsibility in Modern Religious Ethics* (Washington/Cleveland: Corpus Books, 1968).

20. For an illustration of the approach of biblical theology in this area, see Ignace de la Potterie, S.J., and Stanislas Lyonnet, S.J., *La Vie selon L'Ésprit* (Paris: Éditions de Cerf, 1965). For a theological development based on the scriptural evidence, see John Gerken, *Toward a Theology of the Layman* (New York: Herder and Herder, 1963).

21. Philippe Delhaye, "Le récours à l'ancien testament dans l'étude de la théologie morale," *Ephemerides Theologicae Lovanienses,* XXXI (1955), 637–657.

22. Antonio Hortelano, *Morale Responsabile* (Assisi: Cittadella editrice, n.d.), pp. 19–27.

23. The importance of growth in the moral life was emphasized by Louis Monden, S.J., *Sin, Liberty and Law* (New York: Sheed and Ward, 1965), pp. 87–144.

24. *Théologie de Péché,* ed. by Philippe Delhaye (Tournai: Desclée et Cie, 1960).

25. For a recent and representative article with pertinent bibliography, see John W. Glazer, S.J., "Transition between Grace and Sin," *Theological Studies,* XXIX (1968), 260–274.

26. P. Christophe, *L'usage chrétien du droit de propriété dans l'Écriture*

et la tradition patristique (Paris: Lethielleux, 1964); P. Grelot, "La pauvrété dans l'Écriture Sainte," *Christus* XIII (1961), 306–330.

27. "Jesus no more intended to change the social system than he did the political order. He never assumed a definite attitude on economic and social problems" (Schnackenburg, p. 122).

28. Bo Reicke, *The Anchor Bible: The Epistles of James, Peter and Jude* (Garden City, New York: Doubleday, 1964), p. 97.

29. *Ibid.*, p. 98.

30. *Ibid.*, p. 99.

31. *Ibid.*, p. 100.

32. Albert Schweitzer, *The Quest of the Historical Jesus* (New York: Macmillan, 1948). The famous second edition of this volume was first published in Germany in 1913.

33. For a summary and evaluation of approaches to the eschatological aspect of Jesus' teaching with arguments against realized eschatology, see Richard H. Hiers, *Jesus and Ethics* (Philadelphia: Westminster Press, 1968).

34. Gerken, pp. 37–54.

35. For recent bibliography on the question, see William W. Bassett, "Divorce and Remarriage: The Catholic Search for a Pastoral Reconciliation," *American Ecclesiastical Review*, CLXII (1970), 100–105; Richard A. McCormick, S.J., "Notes on Moral Theology," *Theological Studies*, XXXII (1971), 107–122.

36. Among exegetes who accept such an approach are: Bruce Vawter, C.M. "The Biblical Theology of Divorce," *Proceedings of the Catholic Theological Society of America*, XXII (1967), 223–243; Wilfrid Harrington, "Jesus' Attitude Towards Divorce," *Irish Theological Quarterly*, XXXVII (1970), 199–209.

37. Schnackenburg, *The Moral Teaching of the New Testament*.

38. Ceslaus Spicq, O.P., *Théologie Morale du Nouveau Testament*. (2 vols.; Paris: Galbada, 1965). For a discussion of the different approaches to biblical morality itself, see Franco Festorazzi, "Il problema del metodo nella teologia biblica," *La Scuola Cattolica*, XCI (1963), 253–276.

39. Spicq, *op. cit.*, I, 9–16.

40. Roland E. Murphy, O.Carm., "Christian Understanding of the Old Testament," *Theology Digest*, XVIII (1970), 327.

41. Spicq, *op. cit.* II, 756–761.

42. Roger Mehl, *Catholic Ethics and Protestant Ethics* (Philadelphia: Westminster Press, 1971), p. 112.

43. George T. Montague, S.M., *Maturing in Christ: Saint Paul's Program for Christian Growth* (Milwaukee: Bruce, 1964).

44. *Ibid.,* especially pp. 101–110.

45. Victor Paul Furnish, *Theology and Ethics in Paul* (Nashville: Abingdon, 1968), p. 176.

46. *Ibid.,* pp. 239–240.

47. James Sellers, *Theological Ethics* (New York: Macmillan, 1968), p. 63.

48. Paul Ramsey, *Deeds and Rules in Christian Ethics* (New York: Charles Scribner's Sons, 1967), pp. 178–192.

49. Walter Rauschenbusch, *Christianity and the Social Crisis,* ed. by Robert D. Cross (New York: Harper and Row, Torchbook, 1964), pp. 93–142.

50. *Ibid.,* pp. 98–99.

51. *Ibid.,* p. 132.

52. Rauschenbusch's summary of the attitude of the primitive Church is exaggerated (pp. 139–142). The Spirit of Christianity stirred women to break down restraints, caused some people to quit work, awakened in slaves a longing for freedom, disturbed the patriotism and loyalty of citizens. "All of its theories involved a bold condemnation of existing society. . . . Christianity was conscious of a far-reaching and thorough political and social mission" (p. 140).

53. Dietrich Bonhoeffer, *Ethics* (New York: Macmillan, 1962), pp. 17–23.

54. These Scripture texts are cited by Bonhoeffer, pp. 17–19.

55. E.g. Gustavo Gutiérrez, M., "Notes for a Theology of Liberation," *Theological Studies,* XXXI (1970), 243–261.

56. James M. Gustafson, "Two Approaches to Theological Ethics," *Union Seminary Quarterly Review,* XXIII (1968), 337–348.

57. Paul L. Lehmann, *Ethics in a Christian Context* (New York: Harper and Row, 1963), p. 274.

58. *Ibid.,* pp. 268–284.

59. Karl Barth, *Community, State and Church,* introduction by Will Herberg, (Garden City: Doubleday Anchor Books, 1960), pp. 171–186. For an analysis and critique of Barth's use of analogy, see Herberg's introductory essay, "The Social Philosophy of Karl Barth," pp. 31–38.

60. Joseph Sittler, *The Structure of Christian Ethics* (Baton Rouge: Louisiana State University Press, 1958).

61. A. Dumas, "De l'archétype à la parabole," *Le Supplément,* XCII (1970), 28–46.

62. "Au lecteur," *Christianisme Social,* LXXIV (1966), 281–283.

63. Françoise Florentin, "L'ethique sociale et l'étude biblique," *Christianisme Social,* LXXIV (1966), 297–302.

64. For a very similar approach which also strives to be more comprehensive than most approaches, see James M. Gustafson, "The Place of Scripture in Christian Ethics: A Methodological Study," *Interpretation,* XXIV (1970), 430–455. Gustafson exemplifies his methodological use of the Scripture in Christian ethics by considering one particular problem. For a study of the methodological use of the Scriptures by Rauschenbusch, see James M. Gustafson, "From Scripture to Social Policy and Social Action," *Andover-Newton Quarterly,* IX (1969), 160–169.

65. Charles E. Curran, "Is There a Distinctively Christian Social Ethic?" in *Metropolis: Christian Presence and Responsibility,* ed. by Philip D. Morris (Notre Dame, Ind.: Fides Publishers, 1970), pp. 92–120. A French translation appeared in *Le Supplément,* XCVI (1971), 39–58. A brief summary of the conclusion appears on p. 114: "The explicitly Christian consciousness does affect the judgment of the Christian and the way in which he makes his ethical judgments, but non-Christians can and do arrive at the same ethical conclusions and also embrace and treasure even the loftiest of proximate motives, virtues, and goals which Christians in the past have wrongly claimed only for themselves."

66. Albrecht Alt, "The Origins of Israelite Law," *Essays on Old Testament History and Religion* (Garden City: Doubleday Anchor Books, 1958). In this section I am heavily dependent on the following summaries of recent biblical interpretations: Alexa Suelzer, S.P., *The Pentateuch* (New York: Herder and Herder, 1964). This book gives a fine history of the development of thinking on the Pentateuch especially in Roman Catholic thought, but it is now too dated to include the results of more recent scholarly investigations. Johann Jakob Stamm with Maurice Edward Andrew, *The Ten Commandments in Recent Research,* Studies in Biblical Theology, Second Series, n. 2 (Naperville, Ill.: Alec R. Allenson, 1967); Edward Nielsen, *The Ten Commandments in New Perspective,* Studies in Biblical Theology, Second Series, n. 7 (Naperville, Ill.: Alec R. Allenson, 1968); Carroll Stuhlmueller, "The Natural Law Question the Bible Never Asked," *Cross Currents,* XIX (1969), 55–67.

67. *Ibid.,* pp. 60–61.

68. Stamm and Andrew, *op. cit.,* pp. 66–68.

69. *Ibid.,* pp. 73–74.

70. *Ibid.,* pp. 74–75. Note that these authors here report and generally accept the conclusions of Gerstenberger. They do express the wish that Gerstenberger had repeated near the end his earlier emphasis on the distinctive context of the covenant and the Sinai revelation.

71. Stuhlmueller, *art. cit.,* 63.

72. *Ibid.,* p. 59.

212 / *Charles E. Curran*

73. Seán Freyne, "The Bible and Christian Morality," in *Morals, Law and Authority,* ed. by J. P. Mackey (Dayton: Pflaum Press, 1969), p. 7.

74. *Ibid.,* p. 10.

75. *Ibid.,* p. 19.

76. *Ibid.,* p. 25.

77. *Ibid.,* p. 34.

78. I would tend to disagree with Freyne's comment (pp. 34–35) that the added element in biblical morality is the assurance that what they are doing is God's will for them.

79. John Macquarrie, *Three Issues in Ethics* (New York: Harper and Row, 1970), pp. 87–91.

80. *Ibid.,* p. 88.

81. Josef Fuchs, S.J., "Gibt es eine spezifisch christliche Moral?" *Stimmen der Zeit,* CLXXXV (1970), 99–112.

82. I am here interpreting Fuchs as being in accord with my conclusions, *Metropolis: Christian Presence and Responsibility,* p. 114.

83. McCormick, *Theological Studies,* XXXII (1971), 71–78. I am guilty of complicating the discussion by not correcting an earlier version of my manuscript which I had sent to Father McCormick. The final version differs somewhat from that which McCormick used, since I tried to clarify my thought as a result of helpful discussions with McCormick and others at the symposium where the paper was originally given.

84. *Ibid.,* p. 77.

85. *Metropolis: Christian Presence and Responsibility,* p. 114.

86. *Ibid.*

87. James M. Gustafson, *Christ and the Moral Life* (New York: Harper and Row, 1968), p. 240.

The Use of Scripture in Ethics

Allen Verhey

This article originally appeared in *Religious Studies Review 4* in 1978.

The Bible has always been important in the moral traditions of Judaism and Christianity. Throughout their histories and across their divisions the Jewish and Christian communities have affirmed that scripture is an authority for moral discernment and judgment. And the ethicists of those communities, at least those who consider their work part of the common life of the believing community, have acknowledged that scripture is also an authority for ethics.

To say scripture is an authority is not yet to say what moves are authorized in an argument "from the Bible to the modern world."[1] To distinguish between "authority" and "authorization" is the first step toward methodological clarity (Kelsey, 1968; Verhey, 1975). The question of *whether* (and, within the believing communities, the agreement that) scripture is a source and canon for moral discernment and judgment must be distinguished from the questions of *what* this source provides or *how* this canon functions as a norm. In spite of the agreement that scripture is an authority, there are wide disagreements about the authorization for moving from scripture to moral claims.

Recently there has been an increasing interest in "bridging the gap" between biblical studies and ethics (Birch and Rasmussen, 1976, 43) and an increasing awareness of the problems in building such a bridge. Consequently, some recent literature self-consciously addresses the methodological problems of moving from scripture to moral claims, while practical moral literature continues to use scripture in various ways as a source and canon. I shall examine the methodological issue by attending to this recent literature, both Jewish and Christian. The intention is not to "solve the problem" but rather to identify some critical methodological questions, some resources for relating scripture and ethics,[2] and, occasionally, a developing consensus.

An initial survey of the critical literature will identify some of the principal methodological questions. These will provide the framework for a survey of recent recommendations, whether explicit or implicit, for the use of scripture. The methodological and practical consequences of answers to these questions will thus come into view, along with a variety of recommendations and resources. Finally, the essay will attempt to draw some conclusions for the making and judging of recommendations for the use of scripture.

I

The critical literature describes a variety of ways in which scripture has been used in theological ethics and/or describes the reasons for this diversity. The following survey will attend first to the recognition of the diversity and then to the reasons for it.

Methodological self-consciousness has been served by some useful descriptive work which shows the diversity and gives some order to it. That the patterns for providing order differ is itself instructive, suggesting different methodological issues.

James M. Gustafson (1970) provides a pattern based on the mode of ethics in which scripture is taken as an authority.[3] Gustafson begins by making a basic distinction between a "moral use" and the "theological use." Advocates of the moral use take scripture to be the source of a morality that is authoritative for discernment and judgment. The advocates of the theological use take scripture to be the source of the knowledge of God which shapes and informs our response to God. Within the "moral use" Gustafson distinguishes a moral-law model, a moral-ideal model, an analogical model, and a "great variety" model. (This fourth model is Gustafon's own recommendation. It refuses to reduce the great variety of forms of moral instruction in scripture to a single form or the great variety of moral themes in scripture to a single theme.) Within each of these models and within the "theological use" the options multiply as writers answer the questions of what material content the Bible provides and how it is to be applied. It is at this point that Gustafson's essay is methodologically very informative. His focus on the mode of ethics reveals rather than hides other significant methodological questions, including the nature of scripture, the message of scripture, and the relation of biblical materials to other sources of moral insight.

Others have undertaken the descriptive task with a focus on these other questions. Wolfgang Schweitzer describes and orders the diversity in terms of different answers to questions about "the whole message of scripture" and "the connection of the Word of God and the human words in the Bible" (1951, 137–38). He presents six options: (1) ecclesiastical authority takes precedence over the use of scripture in ethics; (2) fundamentalism's identification of the word of God and the human words of scripture; (3) liberalism's selection from among the human words of those to be regarded as the word of God; (4) the identification of the word of God with the religious significance of the history reported and interpreted in human words; (5) the identification of the word of God with the kerygma which evokes the self-understanding expressed in human (and "mythological") words; and (6) the identification of the word of God with Christ, who is witnessed to by all the human words.

Zvi E. Kurzweil (1973) describes the variety in the use of scripture in Jewish ethics from a similar perspective. He demonstrates how the differing judgments of S. R. Hirsch, Franz Rosenzweig, and Martin Buber concerning the relation of scripture and revelation affect their use of scripture in discernment and judgment. Kurzweil does not claim that this typology is exhaustive, but he does relate the positions of Hirsch, Rosenzweig, and Buber to Orthodox, Conservative, and Liberal Judaism. (For a similar typology of the use of scripture within Judaism, see Arthur Gilbert, 1968).

David Kelsey's recent study of the uses of scripture in theology (1975) also begins by providing some order for the diversity of uses. He discerns a pattern in the ways in which scripture is "construed": as content (whether propositional or conceptual), as narrative (whether of acts of God or of a history of which Christ is the agent) or as images (whether expressive of a self-understanding, a world-

process, or the self-world relation). Kelsey's work is an important resource not only because this description of diverse uses among
theologians can be transferred to ethicists but also because he is concerned with the reasons for the diversity. Kelsey shows that a decision about how to construe the text is dependent upon a decision
about the "wholeness" of scripture and that decisions about the
"wholeness" of scripture cannot be defended by exegetical arguments alone (contra the challenge of Scroggs to the authority of
scripture; Scroggs, 1970). These decisions are, rather, of a piece with
an imaginative proposal concerning the mode of God's presence in,
through, and over against the church. That proposal, the "discrimen" which determines how scripture is construed and used, is of a
piece with the way in which one comes to participate in the life of the
church. Kelsey insists that there are intimate relations between the
concepts of "scripture" and "church," and between one's authorizations (for moving from scripture to theological claims) and one's
concrete participation in and understanding of the church. Some
years before Kelsey, Gustafson (1961, especially chs. 4–6) had called
attention to the relation of the Bible and the church. Subsequently,
Birch and Rasmussen (1976) and Everding and Wilbanks (1975)
have devoted chapters to the role of the church. (See also Yoder,
1974.) Indeed the importance of the believing community as the context for the authority and appropriation of biblical materials seems to
be part of a developing consensus. Jewish voices have expressed a
similar appreciation of the importance of the community (e.g., Jacobs, 1964; Siegel, 1966).

Other writers have been concerned with the reasons for the diverse uses of scripture and have identified methodologically important questions. C. Freeman Sleeper (1968a, 1969) insists on the
critical importance of the questions of "sources" (the nature of these
writings), "perspective" (the question appropriate to them), and
"communication" (what one understands—and communicates—
when one understands them). Charles E. Curran (1972), after emphasizing both the contributions of biblical studies to Roman Catholic moral theology and the limitations in the use of biblical materials,
draws attention to the methodological importance of the question of
the relation of biblical materials to nonbiblical sources (also James
Barr, 1969).

My own work (1975) is also concerned less with describing the diversity of uses than with the reasons for it. I attempt to describe the morphology of self-conscious recommendations. I draw on Henry D. Aiken's analysis of the levels of moral discourse (1962)[4] and Toulmin's categories of nonformal logic (1968)[5] to analyze Walter Rauschenbusch's use of scripture.[6] After identifying the warrants Rauschenbusch uses to move from biblical data to moral claims, I examine his arguments in which those warrants are themselves the claims. In such arguments the relevance of certain sets of data—specifically, judgments about the message of scripture, the nature of scripture, and the question appropriate to scripture—is not questioned. These judgments themselves, of course, can be questioned and become the claims of still other arguments. Rauschenbusch also argues for his warrants on the basis of other sets of data, notably, the agreement of claims thus licensed with natural moral certainties; in such arguments he also has to argue for the relevance of these data. The methodological importance of the question of the relation of the Bible to other sources of moral wisdom thus comes into view. The warrants which license inferences from scripture to moral claims are acknowledged to be subject to the criteria of consistency and nonidiosyncracy, as well. "Nonidiosyncracy" establishes the methodological relevance of tradition and the community. Finally, in examining the arguments defending judgments about the message of scripture, the nature of scripture, and the question appropriate to scripture, I show that Rauschenbusch's experience of the authority of scripture in his own moral life is vitally important to these judgments and, therefore, to the warrants for moving from scripture to moral claims. That the morphology of Rauschenbusch's recommendation for the use of scripture is not unique I seek to show by an analysis of the quite different recommendation of Carl F. H. Henry.

This survey of studies that describe and explain the diversity in the use of scripture suggests that we may profitably analyze recent recommendations with respect to their answers to the following questions. (1) What are these writings? (2) What question is appropriate to them? (3) What does one understand when one understands them? (4) What is the relation of biblical materials to other sources of moral wisdom? Other questions, of course, are also relevant. The questions of consistency and nonidiosyncracy provide formal criteria for any recommendation. The question of the mode of ethics has a bearing on the selection of questions to be asked of scripture and on the defense of their appropriateness. Theological affirmations may provide backing for a particular view of the relevance of other sources or data for claims about the nature of scripture; thus theological questions may be relevant to the use of scripture through their bearing on the four critical questions identified. Other questions are relevant, then, but self-conscious reflection about authorizations for particular uses of scripture will surely have to attend to these four questions.

II

2.1 What Are These Writings?

The most obvious example of the relevance of answers to this question is simply the use of different canons. Judaism, Protestantism, and Roman Catholicism do not identify scripture in precisely the same way; appeals to scripture are clearly limited to data recognized and accepted as canonical.

The question and responses to it are, of course, much more complex than that. David Kelsey (1975) has insisted that doctrines about scripture are second-order in character, that whereas the "authority of scripture" is simply given with the concept of "church," doctrines about scripture are invoked to explain a use established on other grounds. Even if doctrines about scripture are "second-order," however, they still establish expectations for the way scripture will function.

Thus, one of the important debates within the Jewish community about the use of scripture concerns the eighth principle of Maimonides. *Torah min hashamayim* ("The Torah is from heaven"). For Orthodox thinkers like Immanuel Jacobovitz this principle is as close to the essence of Judaism as the postulate of monotheism. Orthodoxy's insistence on this principle identifies the words of Torah with the words of God and, consequently, receives as normative any law or rule found in Torah, recognizing "the equal sanctity of all parts of the Torah and its laws" (Jacobovitz, 1966, 110). Other Jewish thinkers quite candidly reject that principle and select some words or concepts or images as authoritative (e.g., Talmon, 1972). Without suggesting that the issue is settled, there does seem to be a developing consensus around what Louis Jacobs calls the "middle way" (1964). The "middle way" attempts to affirm Maimonides' eighth principle while also recognizing the human origin of the words of Torah. The result is usually an emphasis on the law coupled with an emphasis on the dynamic growth of *mitzvot* through interpretation and application within the community (Fox, 1975; Siegel, 1966).

Within the Christian community a similar debate can be found. On the one hand fundamentalists like Harold Lindsell insist that the words of the Bible are simply identical with the words of God (1976). Lindsell's rigid view of inerrancy insists that laws or rules found in scripture must be received as normative (1973). Of course there are other inference-licenses *implicity* at work which effectively deny the "equal sanctity" of all the laws found in the Bible, but Lindsell does not attend to them.[7] On the other extreme is the recent work of Jack Sanders (1975; cf. Verhey, 1976), whose recommendation for the continuing use of scripture quite candidly demands a selection of those concepts which "modern man" can accept. Between these extremes there seems to be a developing consensus, identified by Birch and Rasmussen as the "important two-part consensus" that "Christian ethic is not synonymous with biblical ethics" and that "for Christian ethics the Bible is somehow normative" (1976, 45–46, 143–54; see also Curran, 1972; Schweitzer, 1951; Gustafson 1970). This consensus rejects both the identification of the human words with the word of God that is sometimes found among the heirs of fundamentalism, and the separation and division of the human words from the divine word that is sometimes found among the heirs of liberalism. It acknowledges the union of the divine word and the human words in scripture without identifying, confusing, separating, or dividing them.

This "Chalcedonian" consensus does not resolve the methodological problems, but neither is it without methodological and practical consequences. It is methodologically important as a limiting suggestion. A great variety of recommendations could be made within recognition of the "Chalcedonian" union of the human words and the divine word in scripture—but some specific recommendations are ruled out.

2.2 What Question is Appropriate?

The methodological importance of this question was clearly demonstrated by Rudolf Bultmann. Bultmann, of course, recommends *what* question should be put to the text as well as showing *that* some question is always put to the text. However one judges Bultmann's recommendation about what question to ask, we all are indebted to him for so clearly showing that some question is unavoidably asked.

Any self-conscious recommendation for the use of scripture in ethics will have to judge both the *level* of moral discourse at which appropriate inquiry is made and the *type* of question which may appropriately be asked. And on analysis must deal with both, attending first to the level, then to the type, and finally to the relevance of views of man as moral agent to these judgments.

With respect to the level of moral discourse at which inquiry is made, Aiken's categories are helpful in describing the diversity of practice.[8] Jacobovitz (1959) and Blidstein (1975) look for answers on the moral level, where the question is, What ought I to do? Jacobovitz (1962) even defends the primacy of the "letter" over the "spirit" of the law: "The practical regulations governing Jewish conduct define theology, our philosophy, our ethics, and our attitude vis-à-vis any intrinsically abstract subject or problem." Solomon Freehof's responsa use the legal materials more loosely "our guidance but not our governance" (1960, 22). Sometimes his use seems quite subjective, without any conscious methodology, but in at least one article (1970) Freehof makes clear his distillation of certain principles from law and custom: these in turn are used to defend challenge, or reform moral rules, including those found in scripture. Here the focus is on the ethical level, where the question is, How shall I decide what moral rules are right? For Freehof and similar thinkers, of course, the moral rules defended or criticized are themselves biblical or halakhic, but their continuing authority depends on their consistency with the ethical principles distilled from scripture. Other Jewish thinkers use scriptural data to claim neither moral rules nor ethical principles, but to develop a perspective which justifies and shapes the moral quest itself. These thinkers judge that the appropriate level at which to inquire of scripture is the *post-ethical level,* where the question is, Why be moral? Thus Hans Jonas uses scripture to develop a perspective on man and nature which he contrasts with what he takes to be the contemporary perspective (1970). Martin Buber's radical insistence that the post-ethical level is the appropriate one for inquiry of scripture leads to a refusal to use scripture as a source of laws or principles (1948).

Christian ethicists also differ regarding the level at which it is appropriate to inquire of scripture. The biblicism of Lindsell allows inquiry at the moral level, but other thinkers who distinguish the tasks of biblical ethics and Christian ethics also defend the legitimacy of inquiry at the moral level. Brevard Childs, for example, describes a reflective process for seeking biblical warrants at the decision-making level (1970), and Richard Mouw (1972) seems to claim the appropriateness of inquiry at the moral level in his defense of an ethic of obedience to divine commands against the charges of being infantile, despotic, irrational, or stultifying. James Sellers, on the other hand, is quite candid in insisting that inquiry at the moral level is inappropriate. "Scripture we take to be *constitutive* for major dogmatic or theological themes, *criteriological* for ethical reflection, but *invalid* for morality as such" (Sellers, 1966, 101; also Houlden, 1973, 115–25). Those moralists (and there are many) who appeal to scripture to defend love as the basic ethical principle agree on the appropriateness of inquiries at the ethical level (e.g., Fitch, 1970; Ramsey, 1970; Van Ouwerkerk, 1965); decisions about the mode of applying this principle may affect the use of scripture at other levels. (Furnish, 1972, provides a summary of work on love which merits the attention of Christian ethicists.) But love is not the only biblical response to inquiries at this level (e.g., Reumann and Lazareth, 1967).

Other Christian ethicists assume or argue that the appropriate level at which to inquire of scripture is the post-ethical level. H. R. Niebuhr, for example, in a passage that has regrettably been ignored, says that Jesus gives us no new ethics, neither principles nor rules, but rather reveals the lawgiver to whom we are responsible. This revelation, without providing rules or principles, makes the law more

stringent, extends and intensifies it, forces a revolutionary transvalu-
ation of it, and converts it from a coercive imperative to a free response (Niebuhr, 1941, 156–75; on Niebuhr, see Gustafson, 1963).
Rudolf Bultmann insists that the only appropriate question is that of
self-understanding, and that the biblical answer is radical obedience
apart from rules or principles or ideals, even those found in scripture
(e.g., 1958; on Bultmann, see Oden, 1964; Schrey, 1966; Hiers, 1968;
Sleeper, 1968a; Stackhouse, 1968). Examples could be multiplied
both of those who *recommend* that inquiries be made at this level
(Curran, 1972; Kraemer, 1965; Sleeper, 1968a; Everding and Wilbanks, 1975; Bouwman, 1969) and those who actually *use* scripture
primarily or exclusively at this level (Cone, 1969; Sleeper, 1969;
Moltmann, 1965; Lehmann, 1963; Barth and Fletcher, 1964).

There is diversity also with respect to the *type* of question which
is judged appropriate. This diversity reflects some enduring disputes
in ethics, one of which concerns whether considerations of duty or of
goal are more basic. Wolfhart Pannenberg (1969), Reumann and Lazareth (1967), and William Baird (1964) agree that inquiries are appropriate at the ethical level but not at the moral level. Yet, their
questions differ. Pannenberg asks, "How shall we decide what is
good?," and moves from the eschatological teachings of Jesus to a
statement of the kingdom of God as a social ideal. The resemblance
of the question and answer to the American Social Gospel is not un-
noticed; Pannenberg only insists on distinguishing his own eschatology and ethics from the "superficial optimism" of liberalism (1969,
115). Reumann and Lazareth (1967) ask, "How shall we decide what
is right?," and discover the biblical reply of righteousness and justice.
Baird (1964) asks for precedents, and then, abstracting certain principles, both teleological and deontological, from Paul's response to
the urban culture of Corinth, takes them to be authoritative for the
churches' response to analogous problems in contemporary cities
(see also Rahtjen, 1966).

Another enduring dispute reflected in differing judgments about
the appropriate type of question is the distinction and relation between individual and political morality. Roger Mehl (1966) thinks
social and political questions are inappropriate to the New Testament and suggests that they can be addressed only by a set of analogical inferences from Jesus' personal and apolitical kingdom ethic. But

John Yoder (1972) and Jürgen Moltmann (1968) disagree. Yoder inquires of the New Testament for a "particular social-political-ethical option" (1972, 23); Moltmann insists that the appropraite question—the "question of theodicy, the question of suffering in expectation of God's just world"—today takes a political and social form (1968, 100). (It may be observed that, although Yoder and Motlmann agree that the political question is appropriate, they ask it at different *levels* of moral discourse.)

These judgments about the level at which inquiry is appropriate and about the type of question asked are related to judgments about the nature of scripture, the authority of other sources, the message of scripture, and man as a moral agent. The relevance of judgments about man as a moral agent deserves attention. To use H. Richard Niebuhr's categories (1963), "man-the-citizen" who accepts the authority of scripture will think it appropriate to ask for laws or "constitutional" principles, "man-the-artisan" will judge the appropriate question to be about ideals and ends, and "man-the-answerer" will ask for a perspective on the things that are happening to him and for images to discern the action of God in those things (cf. Long, 1965). But the relevance of judgments about man extends beyond Niebuhr's synecdoches. Sleeper argues against Bultmann (Sleeper, 1968a) and Funk (Sleeper, 1968b) and for his own recommendation at least partly on the basis of the inadequacy of the existentialist view of the self. The perspective from which questions get asked, he argues, must be more appreciative both of the interaction of self and society (contra Bultmann) and of the importance of "act" as well as "speech" to our self-knowledge (contra Funk). Stackhouse (1968) tellingly contrasts Rauschenbusch's and Bultmann's use of scripture with respect to their different understandings of how man's historicity influences decision making. Theological anthropology is no less relevant. Mouw's defense of the use of scripture at the moral level argues that "sin has affected human capacity for moral deliberation to the degree that we are desperately in need of divine guidance" (1972, 40). Jacques Ellul (1969) also appeals to the category of sin, but for Ellul morality is itself part of the fallen order, part of the pride of man who thinks himself wise and refuses to rest in God's free decision. Thus, to ask scripture for rules or principles or ideals or analogies—i.e., for a morality—is to ask an inappropriate and sinful question. Because of Ellul's dialectical position, however, the "impossible" Christian ethic is nevertheless "necessary," and his methodological point is waived in practice. It serves only as a caution against the moral pride in biblicism and as a safeguard for the free decision of God in particular circumstances. In practice, the commands and narratives of scripture are used to mark "the continuity of the revelation" within which decisions must find their place.[9]

Without arguing for a particular view of man as a moral agent, certain limiting suggestions may be based on a respect for the reason-giving capacity of the moral agent. That reason-giving capacity does not necessarily demand that biblical moral rules or commands be omitted, but it does require that they be connected with more general biblical principles and perspectives. Reason-giving capacity does not necessarily imply that a sensitive conscience may not "intuit" God's action in the world, but it does imply that the conscience be made sensitive not only by some nonmoral images of God, but also by the kinds of reasons and principles which stand behind biblical moral claims. It may also be observed that Neibuhr's synecdoches are just that, that the "whole" very likely involves all three parts, and that the "answerer" usually responds in terms of what is "good" or "right."

2.3 What Does One Understand When One Understands These Writings?

The question of the wholeness or message of scripture is not a new one, nor are recent recommendations the first to emphasize its methodological significance. St. Augustine insisted that any movement from scripture to moral claims is licensed if and only if it is consistent with the double love commandment, which he identified as the message of scripture.

The World Council's attempt to find a biblical foundation for social criticism and construction depended on the judgment that "the primary message of the Bible concerns God's gracious and redemptive activity for the saving of sinful man that he might create in Jesus Christ a people for himself" (Richardson and Schweitzer, 1951, 240). This "activity" has its "center and goal" in Jesus Christ.

Hendrik Kraemer's contribution to the World Council's attempt to develop "a purely biblical social ethic" insists that "Christ is the center of the biblical message in its entirety" (1965, 30). Then, of course, christological judgments become relevant methodologically. Kraemer understands Christ as "the entering of the eternal, living God ino time" (ibid.), and that bears on the methodological issue in the consequent "tension of the transhistorical and historical character of the biblical message" (31). The transhistorical character prohibits system-making or casuistry based on scripture, but the historical character enables us to find behind and in the narratives and concrete regulations a direction or perspective which will take a different embodiment in our own historical situation. A similar emphasis on the transhistorical Christ can be found in Jacques Ellul for whom the New Testament narratives present a Jesus Christ who transcends moral distinctions, who is deliverer and yet commander (1971, 1972; on Ellul, see Eller, 1972). Amos Wilder's critique of Kraemer (1966) concerns both the way Kraemer has identified the message of scripture and his mode of applying that message. The two are not unrelated. Wilder prefers a "trinitarian" rendering of the message of scripture; partly on that basis he rejects Kraemer's mode of applying the kerygma which tended to abstraction, to isolation from the actualities of life then and now, and to the exclusion of a legitimate casuistry.

Gustavo Gutierrez (1973) understands "liberation" to be the meaning of the scriptures. The critical christological judgment here is that Christ is the complete savior, the total liberator. The generalization that liberation is the message of scripture underlies a hermeneutic which takes the exodus experience as paradigmatic, both for God's intentions and for man's participation in his own liberation. Other moves from scripture to moral claims are licensed if and only if they are consistent with the central theme of liberation. There are many others besides Gutierrez who take scripture as a narrative focused on the exodus and Jesus Christ. For all of these scripture provides a history of complete salvation oriented toward the future in which a contemporary praxis of liberation can participate. Some of these are other third-world theologians (Assmann, 1974); some are black (Cone, 1969, 1970); some are women (Ruether, 1972); and some are white males from developed countries (Verkuyl, 1970).

Within black theology J. Deotis Roberts (1971) insists that Cone has not understood the whole message of scripture, which involves reconciliation as well as liberation, and partly on that basis disagrees with Cone's mode of applying "liberation" in his unreserved endorsement of "black power."

John Yoder concludes his fascinating book by insisting that "a social style characterized by the creation of a new community and the rejection of violence of any kind is a theme of New Testament proclamation, from beginning to end, from right to left" (1972, 250). This provides the warrant for his moves from scripture to moral claims throughout the book. The christological judgment here focuses on the historical Jesus as teacher and pattern; this Jesus is what one understands when one understands the New Testament. Movements in argument can be tested by their consistency with that understanding. Richard Mouw, in a book designed partly to foster Reformed-Anabaptist dialogue (1976), summarizes the biblical message in terms of creation, fall, redemption, and the future age, and draws on this summary in his own use of scripture and as a criterion by which to test other uses of scripture. It is in terms of this more trinitarian summary that Mouw expresses his appreciative reservations about Yoder's work (with its focus on Jesus as teacher and pattern) and faults William Stringfellow's identification of government with Babylon (1973) for being inattentive to the themes of creation, preservation, and redemption as they bear on politics. Mouw differs from Yoder on the message of scripture but resembles him in the place given scripture in applying those understandings at the ethical and the moral levels of discourse. Mouw is close to H. R. Niebuhr's judgments about the message of scripture; the two differ greatly, however, in their use of scripture at the ethical and moral levels, a difference rooting in differing judgments about scripture, man as a moral agent, and the relevance of other sources of moral wisdom.

The examples could be multiplied. James Sellers (1966) is self-conscious about the methodological importance of his proposal that the "wholeness" of scripture is its portrayal of the divine promise for man and its fulfillment; the emphasis falls on Christ as the pattern for human wholeness. Colin Morris' use of scripture (1969) depends on his judgment that one understands "revolution" when one understands the scripture; his christological focus is on the "historical Jesus" discovered by S. G. F. Brandon. In contrast, James Douglass (1968) insists that nonviolence inheres in the biblical message of "revolution."

Some authors have challenged either the possibility or the necessity of judgment about the wholeness of scripture. For some conservative Protestants such a judgment represents an attempt to escape the authority of all scripture. Carl F. H. Henry, for example, insists that the scriptures' moral propositions themselves form "a unitary whole" (1957, 346). Analysis of Henry's movement from scripture to claims, however, demonstrates the crucial importance of Henry's judgment that forensic atonement is the message of scripture (see Verhey, 1975). Brevard Childs (1970) describes "the crisis in biblical theology" as at least in part due to a breakdown in the movement's consensus about the message of scripture. He refuses to recommend any new understanding of the whole to fill the vacuum and, instead, sees the whole of scripture as a control on the use of any part. Attention to the whole canon will serve as a check on the rationalizing use of scripture and will help one discern "the continuity of the one covenant God's directing and leading his people according to his will" (1970, 136). Childs' is an important corrective; he uses it brilliantly in a chapter on sexuality, but an implicit judgment about what one understands when one understands the canon is operative and should be made explicit (see Verhey, 1973).

James Gustafson (1970, 1971) suggests that scripture witnesses to a great variety of values, norms, principles, and perspectives in different kinds of literature, and that this variety is not reducible to a single theme. He acknowledges, however, that "some efforts at generalization are necessary in order to bring some priorities of biblical morality into focus" (1970, 444). Birch and Rasmussen (1976) develop these insights of Childs and Gustafson in the context of their helpful analyses of the modes of ethics, the church as communal context, and the relevance of nonbiblical sources. Again it may be asked whether some judgment about the wholeness of scripture is not necessary, particularly since they state that a moral decision that violates the biblically-based identity of the church "is suspect even though it might be claiming biblical support" (194). If that is going to serve as anything more than a purely formal principle, and if the church's sense of identity is going to remain open to criticism and reform by the word of God, then it is essential to risk a proposal about what one understands when one understands the scripture.

Jewish thinkers seldom write about the message of scripture. Leo Baeck's insistence that the message of scripture is its "ethical monotheism" (1948) seems to have little continuing influence. There are a few echoes (e.g., Swyhart, 1975) of M. M. Kaplan's suggestion (e.g., 1966) that the scripture is really about the convenant as the concept of Jewish community which stands as a prototype for the world community. Martin Buber's existential reading of the literature as a report and elicitation of an encounter with the Eternal Thou (1948) seems to have been more influential among Christian than among Jewish ethicists, but some continuing influence can be seen (Cohen, 1973; Fackenheim, 1968, is influenced by Buber but allows a much larger place for the law). Eric Gutkind (1952) judges the message of scripture to be resistance to the inequities of the status quo inspired by a vision of the messianic social hope. Representatives of Reform Judaism sometimes still identify the message of scripture with some prophetic summary like Micah 6:8 (Himmelfarb, 1966, 4). Many Jewish writers, however, simply insist that what one understands when one understands the scripture is the Torah, the laws of Moses. Even within orthodox Judaism, however, that judgment can be variously nuanced, with important methodological effects. Norman Lamm, for example, agrees that what one understands when one understands the scripture is Torah, but he quite rightly insists that "Torah" is more than "nomos," that it "includes the full spectrum of spiritual edification: theological and ethical, mystical and rhapsodic" (1966, 125). While this judgment neither relativizes nor limits the use of scripture to provide moral laws interpreted and applied by rabbis, it does license and emphasize a much broader and more "haggadic" use of scripture concerned with disposition and perspective alongside an "halakhic" use (Lamm, 1971).

Without venturing a proposal for construing the wholeness of scripture, certain limiting recommendations for methodological proposals may be offered in light of this survey. First, judgments about the wholeness of scripture are methodologically necessary; moral discourse would be served by candor about these judgments. Second, these judgments rest not so much on an exegetical demonstration as they do on the experience of the authority of scripture in the context of one's own moral struggles, on the one hand, and the believing community and its moral tradition, on the other. Third, judgments about the message may not be substituted for the writings themselves. They may be fashioned and exercised only while reverently listening to the canonical text within the believing community.

2.4 What Is the Relevance of Other Sources?

Judgments about the nature of scripture, the question appropriate to scripture, and the message of scripture are acknowledged as relevant to arguments that certain warrants for moving from scriptural data to moral claims ought to be adopted. But there is no such shared acknowledgment of the relevance of other souces. Some writers issue a theological veto of natural morality, thus rendering other sources irrelevant to the recommendation and use of authorizations for moving from scripture to moral claims. At the other extreme some insist on the autonomy of morality and posit consistency with other sources of moral wisdom as the basic authorization for appeals to scripture. Between these extremes of a theological veto and a wholly autonomous morality there are many who call for some form of dialogue between scripture and other sources.

The theological veto of natural morality and of philosophical ethics was typical of neo-orthodoxy. H. D. Lewis (1951), for example, severely criticizes this feature of Brunner's ethic. In its neo-orthodox form it influenced World Council discussions; Visser't Hooft called for an "ethic of inspiration," based on the Bible alone, and among those who responded to the call was H. Kraemer (1965). From the first, there was opposition to this position, first by William Temple and later by others (Alan Richardson 1951, is noteworthy). At Louvain (WCC, 1971) this rejection seems finally to have been overridden. Jacques Ellul (1969) is probably the most important contemporary representative of this neo-orthodox veto of natural morality and moral philosophy. Some of these thinkers are content with a biblically-informed perspective or a biblically-sensitized conscience that can intuit the work and will of God from within the *koinonia*

(Lehmann, 1963); others accord a much larger place to scripture in discerning concretely the will of God; none, however, would appeal to moral philosophy or natural morality to test their authorizations or to help apply a biblical perspective. Neo-orthodoxy was not the first to take this position, of course. It was typical of the Anabaptist tradition, of which Yoder (1972, 19–22) is representative, and of orthodox Judaism, of which Jacobovitz is an example (1966). Here the rejection results in a refusal to acknowledge possible challenge to a biblical moral rule (whether located in the sayings of Jesus or the Torah) from moral philosophy or natural morality.

The other extreme, the insistence on the autonomy of morality and the use of scripture only insofar as it is consistent with other sources is seldom proposed seriously by Christian or Jewish moralists. Jack T. Sanders (1975), however, suggests that his work relieves us of the "temptation" to look to the Bible if we wish to develop coherent ethical positions. "We are freed from bondage to that position, and we are able to propose that tradition and precedent must not be allowed to stand in the way of what is humane and right" (130). This position surrenders control of decisions to other sources than those which are intimately related to the religious community's moral identity. The surrender of identity along with control is the charge Harold Fisch (1975) levels against Ernst Simon. Simon (1975) had said that the neighbor whom the Jew is to love (Lev. 19:18) is exegetically and historically limited to the fellow-Jew, but that that interpretation violates "moral sense" and is to be discarded for an extra-halakhic ethical norm of universal neighbor-love. Fisch counters that Jews must stick with Torah so that Jewish moral tradition and identity are not surrendered to "ethical humanism."

Between these extremes may be placed a whole spectrum of positions recommending some form of dialogue between scripture and natural morality. Among Jewish writers Eugene B. Korn (1975) comes close to affirming a wholly autonomous morality, and struggles with the implications. He argues for the autonomy of the moral law, for the independence of moral statements from their source in Torah or even in God. "One cannot claim moral justification by citing a Biblical verse or halakhic exegesis" (210). The ritual laws, however, different in kind from moral laws, are binding on the Jews precisely because they are found in Torah. The position Korn seems to adopt here, one which would add biblical duty (ritual) to an independent natural morality, quickly shades off into a stance that places biblical ethics and natural morality in paradoxical tension when Korn insists that the halakhic Jew must submit simultaneously to two authorities when deciding what to do (208). Such a simultaneous submission to the Torah and autonomous morality will allow neither the theological veto's suspension of the ethical nor a wholly autonomous dismissal of halakhah. Agreement between these sources cannot be demonstrated, but is an assumption made in faith.

The simultaneous submission to two authorities, Torah and natural moral wisdom, has been suggested by a number of other Jewish writers. Some of these have emphasized that within traditional halakhic interpretation of Torah the rabbis used other sources as well (Gilat, 1973; Fox, 1975; Borowitz, 1964, 1970; Petuchowski, 1970). Others have emphasized the mutual influence of the Bible and other sources on contemporary Jews (Bergmann, 1970). This dialogue between scripture and other sources is open to differing interpretations and emphases: scripture and the other sources may coexist in paradoxical tension, one may supplement the other, scripture may transform natural morality, or other sources may prompt changes in halakhic exegesis. Recommendations for dialogue are consistently unclear about whether the Bible or natural morality has "the last word." The suggestion of Borowitz (1970), however, is methodologically clearer than most: the Torah has been and is to be applied in terms of criteria that allow and demand use of other sources, namely, the criteria of practical feasibility, economic viability, ethical significance, and spiritual meaningfulness.

Christian writers, too, have recommended some form of dialogue. Among them, too, different interpretations and emphases are found, along with a fairly consistent refusal to be precise about which has the last word. Nevertheless, a consensus may be developing that (at least at the level of perspective) scripture has the last word and that this biblical perspective limits, corroborates, and transforms appeals to natural morality on other levels of moral discourse. That at least seems to be the methodological recommendation of the Roman Catholics Charles Curran (1972) and Bernard

Häring (1966), and of the Protestants Birch and Rasmussen (1976), James Sellers (1966), and James Gustafson (1970). That Curran clearly puts more stress on natural morality than, for example, Sellers does demonstrates that even within this consensus work remains to be done; the consensus on dialogue and on some general guidelines for how it is to be conducted is, nevertheless, both clear and important.

Judgments about the relevance of natural morality to the use of scripture may be seen in the context of the more general question about the relation of Christian ethics to moral philosophy or natural morality and the still more general question of the relation of Christ and culture. Perhaps the course of wisdom is to be content with H. Richard Niebuhr's appreciation of the appropriateness of each of the types of relation between Christ and culture in different contexts. Nevertheless, we may propose some more limiting methodological proposals that are sympathetic to the developing consensus. The rejection of natural morality as wholly an effect of sin does injustice to God the creator and preserver, and to the persons he creates and preserves. Accordingly, the use of scripture may not ignore natural morality or philosophical ethics; dialogue is essential. The revelation holds us to, rather than suspends, our reality as moral beings. Nevertheless, that revelation is a redemptive revelation, a transforming revelation, which makes total claims and insists on the last word.

III

This survey of resources for relating scripture to ethics does not prescribe the "correct" way to move from scripture to moral claims, if there is such. But it does suggest certain conclusions about making and judging such claims. The authority of scripture is a necessary affirmation for ethicists who construe their work as part of the life of the believing community. Acknowledging the authority of scripture commits the ethicist to self-conscious reflection and candor about the authorizations for moving from scripture to moral claims. Reflection about these authorizations will attend to the questions I have identified, and to the theological, anthropological, and ethical data relevant to answering them. No recommendation may violate either the

"Chalcedonian" unity of the divine word and the human words or the moral agent's capacity to hear and give reasons. Recommendations will involve judgments about the wholeness of scripture, but those judgments may be fashioned and exercised only while reverently listening to the whole canon within the believing community. Recommendations must neither reject natural morality nor allow it the "last word." These limiting proposals, along with the tests of consistency and nonidiosyncracy, still leave room for a variety of recommendations. That variety need not be rued. It may indeed be celebrated, for it may keep us from both pride and sloth concerning our recommendations and keep us attentive to the whole scripture and to the community in our concern with and for the world.

Notes

*The author expresses his appreciation to the Mellon foundation for supporting his research on this topic in the summer of 1976.
  1. The World Council of Churches study reports published under that title (WCC, 1949) are a part of the recent history of our question. The attempt to formulate an adequate basis for social criticism and construction had led to a debate between the advocates of some kind of natural law ethic and the advocates of "an ethic of inspiration." The "ethic of inspiration" apparently triumphed, for in 1946–49 study conferences were convened with the convictions that the Bible gave them unity and that the Bible's unity would give them a foundation for social thought and action. Within these conferences new debates emerged. Karl Barth's emphasis on gospel and Anders Nygren's advocacy of law was only one such debate. The participants did succeed in hammering out some final theses about the authority of scripture (Richardson and Schweitzer, 1951, 240–44), but the conclusion observes the variety of modes of applying scripture and explains that "interpreters diverge because of differing doctrinal and ecclesiastical traditions, differing ethical, political, and sociological situations, differing temperaments and gifts" (243).
  The consensus that had been reached began to dissolve with the decline of the Biblical Theology Movement (see Childs, 1970), and in 1967 the meeting of the Faith and Order Commission at Bristol called for the initiation of

a new study of biblical authority more attentive to and appreciative of the diversity of the biblical materials, more realistic about our distance in time from the biblical situation, and more sensitive to other "authorities" (James Barr, 1969). A new report was adopted in 1971 (WCC, 1971).

2. Recent works in biblical ethics are, of course, an important resource for relating scripture and ethics. But such works will interest us only when they move beyond describing the content or form of moral exhortation within scripture to recommending a particular use of those findings. *Religious Studies Review* will provide a bibliographical essay by Leander Keck on early Christian ethics.

3. Edward Leroy Long, Jr. (1965, 1967), also describes and orders the diversity in terms of the mode of ethics.

4. Aiken (1962) distinguishes four levels of moral discourse; the emotive, moral, ethical, and post-ethical levels. (1) At the "emotive" level we simply express without reflection our emotive responses to certain actions or states of affairs. (2) At the "moral" level we become reflective about what we ought to do, appealing to data about the situation and to relevant moral rules. (3) When—as is sometimes necessary—these moral rules are challenged, then we move to the critical assessment of the rules themselves. This takes place at the "ethical" level, where more general ethical principles are used to test whether the moral rule still makes a legitimate claim on us or not. (4) Finally, at the "post-ethical" level one tries to justify the basic ethical principle(s) when there is no more general ethical principle to which to appeal. (Here Aiken's prescriptivism states "decision is king," but one need not be a prescriptivist to notice the difference in level of discourse.) Aiken's levels are also referred to by Birch and Rasmussen (1976).

5. Toulmin's categories of nonformal logic (1968) are claim, datum, warrant, qualifier, condition of rebuttal, and backing. Toulmin's categories are used very advantageously by Kelsey (1967, 1968, 1975).

6. Rauschenbusch provided a basis for reflection about the use of scripture for others as well (Gustafson, 1969; Max Stackhouse, 1968).

7. I have sought to show (1975) what other warrants and conditions of rebuttal for the movement in argument from scripture to moral claim are operative in Carl F. H. Henry's more perceptive and sophisticated work from a similar perspective (Henry, 1957).

8. See note 4 above.

9. This move is quite similar to Karl Barth's (1961) where, after having insisted on the theological character of revelation, he uses scripture to provide "formed references," which while not quite "moral law" are quite close to it in practice.

Bibliography

AIKEN, HENRY DAVID
1962 "The Levels of Moral Discourse." In his *Reason and Conduct,* 65–87. Knopf.
ASSMANN, HUGO
1976 *Theology for a Nomad Church.* Corpus.
BAECK, LEO
1948 *The Essence of Judaism.* Schocken.
BAIRD, WILLIAM R.
1964 *The Corinthian Church: A Biblical Approach to Urban Culture.* Abingdon.
BARR, JAMES
1969 "The Authority of the Bible: A Study Outline." *Ecumenical Review* 21/2, 135–51.
BARR, O. SYDNEY
1969 *The Christian New Morality: A Biblical Study of Situation Ethics.* Oxford.
BARTH, KARL
1961 ET *Church Dogmatics.* Volume 3/4. T. & T. Clark.
BARTH, MARCUS and VERNE FLETCHER
1964 *Acquittal by Resurrection.* Holt, Rinehart, & Winston.
BERGMANN, SAMUEL HUGO
1970 "Expansion and Contraction in Jewish Ethics." In his *The Quality of Faith: Essays on Judaism and Morality.* Jerusalem: Youth and Hechalutz Department, World Zionist Organization.
BIRCH, BRUCE C., and LARRY RASMUSSEN
1976 *Bible and Ethics in the Christian Life.* Augsburg.
BLIDSTEIN, GERALD
1975 *Honor Thy Father and Mother.* KTAV.
BOROWITZ, EUGENE
1964 "Subjectivity and the Halachic Process." *Judaism* 13/2. 211–19.
1970 "Authentic Judaism and the Halachah." *Judaism* 19/1. 66–67.
BOUWMAN, GIJS
1969 "Can we Base our Spiritual Life Today on the Bible?" In Christian Duquoc (ed.), *Spirituality and Secularization,* 23–35. Concilium, 49. Paulist.
BUBER, MARTIN
1948 ET "The Man of Today and the Jewish Bible." In his *Israel and the World,* 89–102. Shocken.

BULTMANN, RUDOLF
1958 ET *Jesus and the Word.* Scribner's.

CHILDS, BREVARD
1970 *Biblical Theology in Crisis.* Westminster.

COHEN, ARTHUR A.
1973 "Revelation and Law." In Robert Gordis and Ruth Waxman (eds.), *Faith and Reason: Essays in Judaism,* 273–79. KTAV.

CONE, JAMES H.
1969 *Black Theology and Black Power.* Seabury.
1970 *A Black Theology of Liberation.* Lippincott.

CURRAN, CHARLES E.
1972 "Dialogue with the Scriptures: The Role and Function of Scriptures in Moral Theology." In his *Catholic Moral Theology in Dialogue,* 24–64. Fides.

DOUGLASS, JAMES W.
1968 *The Non-Violent Cross: A Theology of Revolution and Peace.* Macmillan.

ELLER, VERNARD
1972 "How Jacques Ellul Reads the Bible." *Christian Century,* November 29, 1972, 1212–15.

ELLUL, JACQUES
1969 ET *To Will and to Do.* Pilgrim Press.
1971 ET *The Judgment of Jonah.* Eerdmans.
1972 ET *The Politics of God and the Politics of Man.* Eerdmans.

EVERDING, H. EDWARD, and DANA W. WILBANKS
1975 *Decision-Making and the Bible.* Judson.

FACKENHEIM, EMIL
1968 *Quest for Past and Future: Essays in Jewish Theology.* Indiana University Press.

FISCH, HAROLD
1975 "A Response to Ernst Simon." In Marvin Fox (ed.), *Modern Jewish Ethics: Theory and Practice,* 57–61. Ohio State University Press.

FITCH, ROBERT E.
1970 *Of Love and of Suffering.* Westminster.

FOX, MARVIN
1975 "Judaism, Secularism and Textual Interpretation." In Marvin Fox (ed.), *Modern Jewish Ethics: Theory and Practice,* 3–26. Ohio State University Press.

FREEHOF, SOLOMON
1960 *Reform Responsa.* Hebrew Union College Press.

1970 "Death and Burial in the Jewish Tradition." In Daniel Jeremy Silver (ed.), *Judaism and Ethics,* 199–212. KTAV.

FURNISH, VICTOR PAUL

1972 *The Love Commandment in the New Testament.* Abingdon.

GILBERT, ARTHUR

1968 "Jewish Attitudes Toward the Bible." In P. Benoit et al. (eds.), *How Does the Christian Confront the Old Testatment?,* 147–51. Concilium, 30. Paulist Press.

GHAT, YITZCHAK D.

1973 "The Halakah and its Relationship to Social Reality." *Tradition* 13/4, 68–87.

GUSTAFSON, JAMES M.

1961 *Treasure in Earthen Vessels: The Church as a Human Community.* Harper & Brothers.

1963 Introduction to H. Richard Niebuhr, *The Responsible Self.* Harper & Row.

1969 "From Scripture to Social Policy and Social Action." *Andover Newton Quarterly 9/3,* 160–69.

1970 "The Place of Scripture in Christian Ethics: A Methodological Study." *Interpretation* 24/4, 430–55. Reprinted in his *Theology and Christian Ethics.* Pilgrim Press, 1974.

1971 "The Relation of the Gospels to the Moral Life." In Donald Miller and D. Y. Hadidian (eds.), *Jesus and Man's Hope 2,* 103–17. Pittsburgh Theological Seminary. Reprinted in his *Theology and Christian Ethics.* Pilgrim Press, 1974.

GUTIERREZ, GUSTAVO

1973 ET *A Theology of Liberation.* Orbis.

GUTKIND, ERIC

1952 *Choose Life: The Biblical Call to Revolt.* Henry Schuman.

HÄRING, BERNARD

1966 *Toward a Christian Moral Theology.* University of Notre Dame Press.

HENRY, CARL F. H.

1957 *Christian Personal Ethics.* Eerdmans.

HIERS, RICHARD H.

1968 *Jesus and Ethics: Four Interpretations.* Westminster.

HIMMELFARB, MILTON

1966 "Introduction." In *The Condition of Jewish Belief,* 1–6. Complied by the editors of *Commentary* magazine. Macmillan.

HOULDEN, J. L.

1973 *Ethics and the New Testament.* Penguin Books.

JACOBS, LOUIS
1964 *Principles of the Jewish Faith: An Analytical Study.* Basic Books.
JACOBOVITZ, IMMANUEL
1959 *Jewish Medical Ethics.* Bloch.
1962 "Review of Recent Halakhic Periodical Literature." *Tradition* 4/2, 257–70.
1966 Response in *The Condition of Jewish Belief,* 109–16. Compiled by the editors of *Commentary* magazine. Macmillan.
JONAS, HANS
1970 "Contemporary Problems in Ethics from a Jewish Perspective," In Daniel Jeremy Silver (ed.), *Judaism and Ethics,* 29–48. KTAV.
KAPLAN, MORDECAI M.
1966 Response in *The Condition of Jewish Belief,* 117–22. Compiled by the editors of *Commentary* magazine. Macmillan.
KAYE, BRUCE
1976 *Using the Bible in Ethics.* Grove Books.
KELSEY, DAVID
1967 *The Fabric of Paul Tillich's Theology.* Yale.
1968 "Appeals to Scripture in Theology." *Journal of Religion* 48/1, 1–21.
1975 *Uses of Scripture in Recent Theology.* Fortress.
KORN, EUGENE B.
1975 "Ethics and Jewish Law." *Judaism* 24/2, 201–14.
KRAEMER, HENDRIK
1965 *The Bible and Social Ethics.* Fortress.
KURZWEIL, ZVI E.
1973 "Three Views on Revelation and Law." In Robert Gordis and Ruth B. Waxman (eds.), *Faith and Reason: Essays in Judaism,* 186–96. KTAV.
LAMM, NORMAN
1966 Response in *The Condition of Jewish Belief,* 123–31. Compiled by the editors of *Commentary* magazine, Macmillan.
1971 *Faith and Doubt: Studies in Traditional Jewish Thought.* KTAV
LEHMANN, PAUL
1963 *Ethics in a Christian Context.* Harper & Row.
LEWIS, H. D.
1951 *Morals and Revelation.* George Allen & Unwin.
LINDSELL, HAROLD
1973 *The World, the Flesh, and the Devil.* Canon.
1976 *The Battle for the Bible.* Zondervan.

LONG, EDWARD LEROY, JR.
1965 "The Use of Scripture in Ethics." *Interpretation* 19/2, 149–62.
1976 *A Survey of Christian Ethics.* Oxford University Press.
MEHL, ROGER
1966 "The Basis of Christian Social Ethics." In John Bennett (ed.), *Christian Social Ethics in a Changing World,* 44–58. Association Press.
MIRANDA, JOSE PARFIRIO
1974 *Marx and the Bible.* Orbis.
MOLTMANN, JÜRGEN
1965 *Theology of Hope,* Harper & Row.
1968 "Toward a Political Hermeneutic of the Gospel." In his *Religion, Revolution and the Future,* 83–107. Scribner's.
MORRIS, COLIN
1969 *Unyoung, Uncolored, Unpoor.* Abingdon.
MOUW, RICHARD
1972 "Commands for Grown-ups." *Worldview* 15/7, 38–42.
1976 *Politics and the Biblical Drama.* Eerdmans.
NIEBUHR, H. RICHARD
1941 *The Meaning of Revelation.* Macmillan.
1963 *The Responsible Self: An Essay in Christian Moral Philosophy.* Harper & Row.
ODEN, THOMAS C.
1964 *Radical Obedience: The Ethics of Rudolf Bultmann.* Westminster.
PANNENBERG, WOLFHART
1969 ET *Theology and the Kingdom of God.* Westminster.
PETUCHOWSKI, JAKOB
1970 "Plural Models within the Halakah." *Judaism* 19/1, 77–89.
RAMSEY, PAUL
1970 "The Biblical Norm of Righteousness." *Interpretation* 24/4, 419–29.
RAHTJEN, BRUCE D.
1966 *Scripture and Social Action.* Abingdon.
REUMANN, JOHN, and WILLIAM LAZARATH
1967 *Righteousness and Society: Ecumenical Dialogue in a Revolutionary Age.* Fortress.
RICHARDSON, ALAN
1951 "An Anglican Contribution." In Alan Richardson and Wolfgang Schweitzer (eds.), *Biblical Authority for Today,* 112–26. London:SCM Press.

RICHARDSON, ALAN, and WOLFGANG SCHWEITZER (EDS.)
   1951 *Biblical Authority for Today*. London: SCM Press.
ROBERTS, J. DEOTIS
   1971 *Liberation and Reconciliation: A Black Theology*. Westminster.
RUETHER, ROSEMARY
   1972 *Liberation Theology*. Paulist.
SANDERS, JACK T.
   1975 *Ethics in the New Testament*. Fortress.
SCHREY, HEINZ-HORST
   1966 "The Consequences of Bultmann's Theology for Ethics." In
   Charles W. Kegley (ed.), *The Theology of Rudolf Bultmann*. 183–201.
   Harper & Row.
SCHWEITZER, WOLFGANG
   1951 "A Survey of the World Position." In Alan Richardson and Wolfgang Schweitzer (eds.), *Biblical Authority for Today* 129–54. London:
   SCM Press.
SCROGGS, ROBIN
   1970 "Tradition, Freedom, and the Abyss." *Chicago Theological Seminary Register* 60/4 (May 1970). Reprinted in Martin E. Marty and
   Dean G. Peerman (eds.), *New Theology No. 8,* 84–101. Macmillan,
   1971.
SELLERS, JAMES
   1966 *Theological Ethics.* Macmillan.
SIEGEL, SEYMOUR
   1966 Response in *The Condition of Jewish Belief,* 223–28. Compiled by
   the editors of *Commentary* magazine. Macmillan.
SIMON, ERNST
   1975 "The Neighbor (Re'a) Whom We Shall Love." In Marvin Fox
   (ed.), *Modern Jewish Ethics: Theory and Practice,* 29–56. Ohio State
   University Press.
SLEEPER, C. FREEMAN
   1968a "Ethics as a Context for Biblical Interpretation. *Interpretation*
   22/4, 443–60.
   1968b "Language and Ethics in Biblical Interpretation, *Journal of Religion* 48/3, 288–310.
   1969 *Black Power and Christian Responsibility*. Abingdon.
STACKHOUSE, MAX L.
   1968 "Editor's Introduction." In Walter Rauschenbusch, *The Righteousness of the Kingdom*. Abingdon.
STRINGFELLOW, WILLIAM
   1973 *An Ethic for Christians and Other Aliens in a Strange Land.* Word.

SWYHART, BARBARA ANN
  1975 "Reconstructionism: Hokhma as an Ethical Principle. *Judaism*
  24/4, 436–46.
TALMON, SHEMARYAHU
  1972 "The Bible in Contemporary Israeli Humanism." *Judaism* 21/1,
  79–83.
TOULMIN, STEPHEN
  1968 *The Uses of Argument.* Cambridge.
VAN OUWERKERK, COENRAAD A. J.
  1965 "Gospel Morality and Human Compromise." In Franz Böckle
  and C. A. J. van Ouwerkerk (eds.), *Moral Problems and Christian Per-
  sonalism,* 7–21. Concilium, 5. Paulist.
VERHEY, ALLEN
  1973 Review of Brevard Childs, *Biblical Theology in Crisis.* In *Reflection* 70/2, 14–15.
  1975 "The Use of Scripture in Moral Discourse: A Case Study of Walter Rauschenbusch." Ph.D. dissertation, Yale University.
  1976 Review of Jack T. Sanders, *Ethics in the New Testatment* (1975).
  In *Reformed Review* 29/3, 186–89.
VERKUYL, J.
  1970 *The Message of Liberation in Our Age.* Eerdmans.
WILDER, AMOS
  1966 *Kerygma, Eschatology, and Social Ethics.* Fortress.
WORLD COUNCIL OF CHURCHES
  1949 *From the Bible to the Modern World.* Geneva: World Council of
  Churches.
  1971 "The Authority of the Bible." In *Faith and Order: Louvain, 1971.*
  Faith and Order Paper No. 59. Geneva: World Council of Churches.
  Also in *Ecumenical Review* 23/4 (1971), 419–37.
YODER, J. HOWARD
  1972 *The Politics of Jesus.* Eerdmans.
  1974 "The Biblical Mandate." In Ronald J. Sider (ed.), *The Chicago
  Declaration,* 88–116, Creation House.

The Moral Authority of Scripture:
The Politics and Ethics
of Remembering

Stanley Hauerwas

This article originally appeared in Hauerwas' book, *A Community of Character: Toward a Constructive Christian Social Ethic,* 1981.

I
A PROPOSAL FOR UNDERSTANDING
THE MORAL AUTHORITY OF SCRIPTURE

The canon does not contain its own self-justification but rather directs our attention to the tradition which it mediates. For to say the least which has to be said, without the tradition there is no shared memory and therefore no community. Our study of the canon has led to the conclusion that no one interpretation of the tradition can be accorded final and definitive status. The presence of prophecy as an essential part of the canon means that it will always be possible and necessary to remold the tradition as a source of life-giving power.[1]

Joseph Blenkinsopp's claim about the canon and its relation to prophecy and a community sufficient to sustain prophecy is crucial for understanding how scripture does and/or should function ethically. We currently have difficulty in appreciating the moral role of scrupture because we have forgotten that the authority of scripture is a political claim characteristic of a very particular kind of polity. By "political" I do not mean, as many who identify with liberation theology, that scripture should be used as an ideology for justifying the demands of the oppressed. The authority of scripture derives its intelligibility from the existence of a community that knows its life depends on faithful remembering of God's care of his creation through the calling of Israel and the life of Jesus.

To construe the authority of scripture in this way, moreover, is most nearly faithful to the nature of biblical literature as well as the best insights we have learned from the historical study of the Bible. The formation of texts as well as the canon required the courage of a community to constantly remember and reinterpret its past. Such remembering and reinterpretation is a political task, for without a tradition there can be no community. That we no longer consider remembering as an ethical or political task manifests our questionable assumption that ethics primarily concerns decisions whereas politics brokers power.

When we so limit ethics and politics, the scripture, particularly in its narrative mode, cannot but appear as a "problem." For the narrative requires a corresponding community who are capable of remembering and for whom active reinterpreting remains the key to continuing a distinctive way of life. But when one begins to look at an ethic sufficient for guiding the wider society, the narrative aspects of scripture have to be ignored. Such an ethic, though often claimed to be biblically "inspired" or "informed," must be freed from the narratives of scripture if it is to be the basis for judging or making common cause with those who do not share those narratives in their own history. So what is presented as the "biblical ethic" has been made over into a universal ethic that does not depend on memory for its significance but turns on "reason" or "nature."

As a result, we could easily forget that a biblical ethic requires the existence of a community capable of remembering in the present, no less than it did in the past. Where such a community does not exist the most sophisticated scholarly and hermeneutical skills cannot make scripture morally relevant. What John Yoder describes as the free church understanding of the significance of community is necessary for any appreciation of the moral significance of scripture. He points out that the

> bridge between the words of Jesus or of the apostolic writings and the present is not a strictly conceptual operation,

which could be carried out by a single scholar in an office, needing only an adequate dictionary and an adequate description of the available action options. The promise of the presence of Christ to actualize a definition of his will in a given future circumstance was given not to professional exegetes but to the community which would be gathered in his name (Mt. 18:19) with the specific purpose of "binding and loosing" (Mt. 18:18). Classical Protestantism tended to deny the place of this conversational process, in favor of its insistence on the perspicuity and objectivity of the words of Scripture. Catholicism before that has provoked that extreme Protestant answer by making of this hermeneutical mandate a blank check which the holders of ecclesiastical office could use with relative independence. The free church alternative to both recognizes the inadequacies of the text of Scripture standing alone uninterpreted and appropriates the promise of the guidance of the spirit throughout the ages, but locates the fulfillment of that promise in the assembly of those who gather around Scripture in the face of a given real moral challenge. Any description of the substance of ethical decision-making criteria is incomplete if this aspect of its communitarian and contemporary form is omitted.[2]

Failure to appreciate how the biblical narratives have and continue to form a polity is part of the reason that the ethical significance of scripture currently seems so problematic. Indeed, many of the articles written on the relation of scripture and ethics focus on ways scripture should not be used for ethical matters. Yet if my proposal is correct, that very way of putting the issue—i.e., how should scripture be used ethically—is already a distortion. For to put it that way assumes that we must first clarify the meaning of the text—in the sense that we understand its historical or sociological background—and only then can we ask its moral significance. David Kelsey has reminded us, however, that claims about the authority of scripture are in themselves moral claims about the function of scripture for the common life of the church. The scripture's authority for

that life consists in its being used so that it helps to nurture and reform the community's self-identity as well as the personal character
of its members.[3]

To reinstate the moral and political context required for the interpretation of scripture, moreover, demands that we challenge what
Kelsey has characterized as the "standard picture" of the relation between scripture and theology. The "standard picture," supported by
a variety of theological agendas, assumes that if scripture is to be
meaningful it must be translated into a more general theological medium.[4] Such "translation" is often deemed necessary because of the
texts' obscurity, cultural limits, and variety, but also because there
seems to be no community in which the scripture functions authoritatively. As a result we forget that the narratives of scripture were
not meant to describe our world—and thus in need of translation to
adequately describe the "modern world"—but to change the world,
including the one in which we now live. In the classic words of Erich
Auerbach, scripture is not meant

> merely to make us forget our own reality for a few hours, it
> seeks to overcome our reality: we are to fit our own life into
> its world, feel ourselves to be elements in its structure of
> universal history. . . . Everything else that happens in the
> world can only be conceived as an element in this sequence;
> into it everything that is known about the world . . . must
> be fitted as an ingredient of the divine plan.[5]

I would only add that scripture creates more than a world; it
shapes a community which is the bearer of that world. Without that
community, claims about the moral authority of scripture—or rather
the very idea of scripture itself—make no sense. Furthermore, I shall
argue that claims about the authority of scripture make sense only in
that the world and the community it creates are in fact true to the
character of God. In order to develop this proposal, the concepts of
"moral authority" and "scripture" must be analyzed to show how
each gains its intelligibility only in relation to a particular kind of
community. Before doing so, however, it should prove useful to examine how many current problems associated with the moral use of

scripture are, in part, the result of attempts to ignore or avoid the necessity of a community in which it is intelligible for scripture to function authoritatively.

II
THE SCRIPTURE AS A MORAL PROBLEM

James Gustafson has observed that "in spite of the great interest in ethics in the past thirty years, and in spite of the extensive growth of biblical studies, there is a paucity of material that relates the two areas of study in a scholarly way. Writers in ethics necessarily make their forays into the Bible without the technical exegetical and historical acumen and skills to be secure in the way they use biblical materials. But few biblical scholars have provided studies from which writers in ethics can draw."[6] Likewise, Brevard Childs suggests that "there is no outstanding modern work written in English that even attempts to deal adequately with Biblical material as it relates to ethics."[7]

No doubt the problem of specialization is a real one, but our current inability to use the scriptures ethically involves more fundamental conceptual and methodological issues. For, as we shall see, appeal to scripture is not equivalent to appeal to the text in itself, and it is the latter, rightly or wrongly, which is the subject of most current scholarly effort.[8] I am not suggesting that critical analysis of the development of the biblical text is theologically questionable, but that often it is simply unclear what theological significance such work should have. However, for Christian ethics the Bible is not just a collection of texts but scripture that makes normative claims on a community.

The confusion surrounding the relation of text to scripture has not resulted in ethicists (and theologians) paying too little attention to current scholarly work concerning the Bible; rather their attention is far too uncritical. It has been observed that there is finally no substitute for knowing the text, and it is often unfortunately true that theologians and ethicists alike know the current theories about the development of the text better than the text itself.[9] As a result, claims about an ethic being biblically informed too frequently turn out to mean that the ethic is in accordance with some scholar's reconstruction of "biblical theology," e.g., the centrality of covenant or love in the Bible.[10] And ironically, as James Barr has shown, the very notion of "biblical theology" distorts the variety of biblical material by failing to take the text seriously.[11]

The conceptual issues raised by the ethical use of scripture involve not only how we should understand scripture, but also how ethics should be understood. We often have a far too restricted understanding of the "ethical." For example, Childs asks "How does the Bible aid the Christian in the making of concrete ethical decisions," without considering whether "ethics" is or should be primarily about "decisions"?[12] Consequently, attempts to explicate the "ethics" of scripture have tended to concentrate on those aspects— Decalogue, the Sermon on the Mount, Wisdom books, the command to love—that fit our intuitive assumptions about what an "ethic" should look like. But this manner of locating the "biblical ethic" not only confuses the questions of the ethics in the scripture with the ethical use of scripture, but has the unfortunate effect of separating and abstracting the ethics from the religious (and narrative) contexts that make them intelligible.

Gustafson has often observed that how authors use scripture is determined as much by how they define the task of Christian ethics as how they understand the nature and status of scripture.[13] Birch and Rasmussen have also suggested that once the moral life is understood as not only involving decisions but also how actions mold the character of individuals and of a community, the narratives of scripture are as important as the commandments; the Psalms afford the most explicit moral teachings.[14] But pictures die harder even than habits and many persist in thinking that a biblical ethic must be one that tells us "what to do in circumstances X or Y." When ethics is equivalent to advice, issues of interpretation or community need not arise.

In fairness it should be said that the persistence of the idea that the Bible is some sort of "revealed morality"[15] has been deeply ingrained in our culture by the church itself. Moreover it is an idea shared by conservative and liberal alike as they appeal to different parts of scripture in support of ethical positions that they have ironically come to hold on grounds prior to looking to scripture. Thus claims about the moral significance of scripture are used to reinforce decisions about ethics derived from nonscriptural sources.

Though they may appear to be radically different, those who would have us obey everything in the scripture that looks like moral advice—e.g., that women should keep quiet in church (1 Cor. 14:34–36)—and those who would have us act according to the more general admonitions—e.g., that we should be loving (1 Cor. 13)—share many common assumptions. Both look to scripture as containing a revealed morality that must or should provide guidance. And each, often in quite different ways, has a stake in maintaining that the "biblical ethic" be distinctive or unique when compared with other ethics.[16]

The assumption that to be ethically significant the Bible must contain some kind of "revealed morality" not only creates a nest of unfruitful problems but finally betrays the character of the biblical literature. The very idea that the Bible is revealed (or inspired) is a claim that creates more trouble than it is worth. As Barr has pointed out, "the term *revelation* is not in the Bible a common general term for the source of man's knowledge of God, and some of the main cases found are eschatological, i.e., they look forward to a revealing of something *in the future*. Perhaps this suggests another way of thinking. The main relation of revelation to the Bible is not that of an antecedent revelation, which generates the Bible as its response, but that of a revelation which *follows upon* the existent tradition, or, once it has reached the fixed and written stage, the existent scripture. The scripture provides the frames of reference within which new events have meaning and make sense."[17]

The problem of revelation aside, however, the view that the Bible contains a revealed morality that can be applied directly by the individual agent, perhaps with some help from the biblical critic, flounders when considering the status of individual commands. For some moral aspects of scripture—such as the *Haustafeln* (household codes: Col. 3:18–4:1, Eph. 5:21–6:9; 1Pet. 2:13–3:7)—strike many today as not only morally irrelevant but morally perverse. The common strategy for dealing with such statements is to dismiss them as the product of the limitations of the early church's culture, which had not yet been sufficiently subjected to the searching transformation of the Gospel. But that strategy suffers from being too powerful, for why should the *Haustafeln* be singled out as culturally relative and texts more appealing to modern ears such as "there is neither Jew nor Greek, there is neither slave nor free, there is neither male nor female; for you are all one in Christ Jesus" (Gal. 3:28) be exempted?

Besides moral positions that simply strike us as wrong, scripture also contains commands that many feel are too "idealistic" to be workable. The admonition not to resist "one who is evil" (Matt. 5:39) may work at an interpersonal level, but most Christians assume that it makes no sense as a social policy. Attempts to "explain" such statements as "ideals," or as "law that provides consciousness of sin," or as requiring eschatological interpretation result in a feeling that we really do not need to treat them with moral seriousness after all.[18]

Thus attempts to formulate a "biblical ethic" result in the somewhat embarrassing recognition that the "morality" that is said to be "biblical" is quite selective and even arbitrary. Various strategies are used to justify our selectivity, such as appealing to "central" biblical themes or images, like love. No doubt love has a central place in the Bible and the Christian life, but when it becomes the primary locus of the biblical ethic it turns into an abstraction that cannot be biblically justified. Indeed when biblical ethics is so construed one wonders why appeals need be made to scripture at all, since one treats it as a source of general principles or images that once in hand need no longer acknowledge their origins. In fact, once we construe Christian ethics in such a way, we find it necessary to stress the "uniqueness" of the "biblical concept of love covenant," or some other equally impressive sounding notion.

Finally the attempt to capture the ethical significance of scripture by a summary image or concept makes it difficult to be faithful to our growing awareness that the ethics in the scripture are bound in an intimate way with the life of Christ; nor can they be dissociated from the life of the community that arose around his life.[19] The more we try to mine scripture for a workable ethic, the more we are drawn to separate such an ethic from the understanding of salvation that makes such an ethic intelligible in the first place.[20] Insisting that the biblical ethic is first an indicative before being an imperative[21] will hardly suffice to provide an account of the complex nature of the moral life manifest in the early Christian community, nor can that distinction inform us how we are to live and think in a manner appropriate to Christian convictions regarding God and his relation to our existence.

In an attempt to avoid separating the ethics of scripture from the theological context that makes them intelligible, the suggestion has been made that scripture is not so much a revealed morality as a revealed reality. Thus for H. R. Niebuhr the Bible is not morally important in that it gives us knowledge of itself, "but because it gives us knowledge of God acting on men, and of ourselves before God."[22] What the Bible makes known, then, "is not a morality, but a reality, a living presence to whom man responds."[23] The Bible does not so much provide a morality as it is the source of images and analogies that help us understand and interpret the nature of our existence.[24]

This suggestion that scripture is revealed reality has the virtue of being more appropriate to the nature of scripture than does the idea of "revealed morality." But it too lacks appreciation for the political nature of the very concepts of authority and scripture associated with the idea of "revealed morality." As a result, scripture is mined for concepts and images, which are claimed to be biblically warranted but have the effect of legitimating the loss of any continuing engagement of a community with the biblical narratives. Emphasis on the Bible as the revelation of God can give the impression that scripture can be known and used apart from a community that has been formed and sustained by the reality that gives substance both to the scripture and to that community. No image of God, no matter how rich, can substitute for the "life-giving power" which Blenkinsopp suggests arises from a community's capacity to sustain the prophetic activity of remembering and reinterpreting the traditions of Yahweh.

III
THE MORAL AUTHORITY OF SCRIPTURE

Thus, the very definition of the problem of the relation of scripture and ethics, as well as the suggestions designed to deal with that problem, often suffer from a failure to appreciate how claims for the

authority of scripture are political. Indeed, the overtly political assertion that scripture has authority is seldom analyzed. Rather it is accepted as a statement of fact, when it is by no means clear what it
means to say that scripture or anything else has authority. Therefore
it is necessary to provide an account of authority that may illumine
how scripture is or should be used in the life of the church.

Although my analysis of authority will be distinct from an explicit discussion of scripture, the very meaning of scripture entails
authoritative judgment. As David Kelsey has reminded us, to say
"these texts are Christian scripture" is but a way of saying "these
texts are authoritative for the life of the Christian church." So claims
about the authority of scripture are analytic, since the scriptural
texts' "authority for theology is logically grounded in and dependent
on their authority for the life of the church generally. But since, concretely speaking, the life of church taken as some sort of organic
whole *is* 'tradition', that means that the texts' authority for theology
is dependent on their being authority for 'tradition.' "[25] Therefore, to
call certain texts "scripture" means in part that the church relies
upon them in a normatively decisive manner.

This situation is not peculiar to the Christian community, for
the very meaning of authority is community dependent. Though authority is often confused with power or coercion, it draws its life
from community in a quite different manner. Like power, authority
is directive; unlike power, however, it takes its rationale not from the
deficiencies of community but from the intrinsic demands of a common life.[26] The meaning of authority must be grounded in a community's self-understanding, which is embodied in its habits, customs,
laws, and traditions; for this embodiment constitutes the community's pledge to provide the means for an individual more nearly to approach the truth.

The language of community is open to a great deal of misunder-
standing, given its association with small, tightly knit groups. Yet the
fact that a community requires authority indicates that it is a mistake
to think of community in personal rather than institutional terms. A
community is a group of persons who share a history and whose
common set of interpretations about that history provide the basis
for common actions. These interpretations may be quite diverse and
controversial even within the community, but are sufficient to pro-

vide the individual members with the sense that they are more alike than unlike.

The diversity of accounts and interpretations of a community's experiences is exactly the basis of authority. For authority is that power of a community that allows for reasoned interpretations of the community's past and future goals. Authority, therefore, is not contrary to reason but essential to it. Authority is the means by which the wisdom of the past is critically appropriated by being tested by current realities as well as by challenging the too often self-imposed limits of the present. A person or institution may be the way authority is exercised, but their authority derives only from their ability to justify their decision in terms of the shared traditions of the community.

Thus, there is an essential connection between authority, tradition, and change. Reasoning from tradition is the primary form and method of authority. As James Mackey has pointed out, tradition "is a dimension of life itself. It is the whole way of life of a people as it is transmitted from generation to generation. So tradition shares with life the characteristics of being something which we do (if that is the correct word) and may do very well indeed, and may do for a very long time, before we bother to provide ourselves with a general theory about what it is that we are doing."[27]

Traditions by their nature require change, since there can be no tradition without interpretation. And interpretation is the constant adjustment that is required if the current community is to stay in continuity with tradition. As Mackey suggests, "Change and continuity are two facets of the same process, the process we call tradition. So much so that continuity can only be maintained by continual development, and development or change is only such (and not simply replacement) because of continuity. Tradition means continuity and change, both together and both equally."[28]

This is even more true when the tradition of a community is based on witnessing to non-repeatable events. For such events must be fitted within a narrative that is an interpretation. But that interpretation must remain open to a new narrative display not only in relation to the future, but also whenever we come to a new understanding of our past. That is why, as Barr reminds us, it is so often the case that interpretation of the scripture does not mean the discovery of new meaning (as if there was no previous meaning there), but the reappropriation of the tradition with a greater depth of understanding.[29] Interpretation does not mean or require departure from the tradition, though justified discontinuity is not illegitimate, but rather that the scripture is capable of unanticipated relevancy through reinterpretation.[30]

It is particularly useful to note how fundamentally political is this understanding of the relation of tradition and authority. Although revolutions may occur without tradition,[31] politics depends on tradition, for politics is nothing else but a community's internal conversation with itself concerning the various possibilities of understanding and extending its life. In fact, the very discussion necessary to maintain the tradition can be considered an end in itself, since it provides the means for the community to discover the goods it holds in common. Without the authority of the tradition to guide such a discussion there would be no possibility of the community drawing nearer to the truth about itself or the world.

Yves Simon illustrates this feature by his refusal to justify authority from what he called a deficiency theory of community. The deficiency theory holds that authority is necessary to secure the unified action of a community because not everything is normal, because wills are weak or perverse and intellects ignorant or blinded.[32] In contrast Simon argued that authority is required, not because we are deficient, but because as the number of deficiencies in a society or individuals decreases, the number of available choices increases. Therefore, according to Simon, "The function of authority with which we are concerned, i.c., that of procuring united action when the means to the common good are several, does not disappear but grows as deficiencies are made up; it originates not in the defects of men and societies but in the nature of society. It is an essential function."[33]

Authority is required, not because there is any one perception of the common good that controls all others, but because there are many ways of seeking such a good. The necessity of authority grows from the fact that morality unavoidably involves judgments that by their nature are particular and contingent—that is, they could be otherwise. Tradition is but the history of a community's sharing of such judgments as they have been tested through generations. Authority is not, therefore, an external force that commands against our will; rather it proceeds from a common life made possible by tradition. Authority is not only compatible with freedom, but requires it, since the continued existence and excellence of the community is possible only by forming and perfecting new members. Yet freedom is not an end in itself, but the necessary condition for a community to come to a more truthful understanding of itself and the world.

Particularly important in this respect is Simon's contention that true authority must always call a community to what it has not yet become. He does not deny that authority must be grounded in community, or that whatever is identified as the common good must be built on what the community is, but he sees that authority must always continue to act as a witness to the truth if it is to be legitimate. Authority, therefore, functions at those points where the tradition of a community engages in the discussion necessary to subject its politics to the search of and judgment by the truth.

The fact that truth is known only by the conversation initiated by the tradition and carried out through political means signals something essential about the character of truth. For if truth could be known without struggle, there would be no need for the kind of politics I am suggesting is integral to its discovery. Truth in this sense is like a "knowing how"—a skill that can only be passed from master to apprentice. Tradition and authority are crucial to such a process, as they must guide us to what others have found to be true, even though in the process we may well find that in order to be faithful to the tradition we must criticize our current guides. The place of tradition and authority in this sense is no less required for the development of intellectual disciplines, including science, than the more practical aspects of our existence.

In summary I have suggested that authority requires community, but it is equally true that community must have authority. For authority is that reflection initiated by a community's traditions through which a common goal can be pursued.[34] Authority is, therefore, the means through which a community is able to journey from where it is to where it ought to be. It is set on its way by the language and practices of the tradition, but while on its way it must often subtly reform those practices and language in accordance with its new perception of truth.

By regarding scripture as an authority Christians mean to indicate that they find there the traditions through which their community most nearly comes to knowing and being faithful to the truth. Scripture is not meant to be a problem solver. It rather describes the process whereby the community we call the church is initiated by certain texts into what Barr has called the "vivid and lively pattern of argument and controversy" characteristic of biblical traditions.[35]

The Scripture is not an authority because it sets a standard of orthodoxy—indeed the very categories of orthodoxy and heresy are anachronistic when applied to scripture—but because the traditions of scripture provide the means for our community to find new life.[36] Blenkinsopp reminds us:

> That those responsible for the editing of the biblical material did not on the whole expunge views in conflict with their own, but rather allowed them to exist side by side in a state of unresolved tension or unstable equilibrium, is clearly a fact of significance for the understanding of Judaism—and, *mutatis mutandis,* of Christianity also. It suggests that one may appeal to a fixed tradition with absolute seriousness and still affirm its "infinite interpretability" (Scholem). Given the formative influence of different interpretations of the tradition on the shape and self-understanding of the community at different times, it also suggests that the community must be prepared to accept creative tension as a permanent feature of its life.[37]

Therefore when Christians claim scripture as authority for their community they are not claiming that the Bible is without error; or that the genres of the Bible are unique; or that the Bible contains a unique understanding of man, history, or even God as opposed to Greek or some other culture; or that the Bible manifests a unique *Weltanschauung* or contains an implicit metaphysics that still remains largely misunderstood; or that the Bible contains images without which we cannot achieve an adequate self-understanding; and so on. Rather to claim the Bible as authority is the testimony of the church that this book provides the resources necessary for the church to be a community sufficiently truthful so that our conversation with one another and God can continue across generations.

IV
SCRIPTURE AS MORAL AUTHORITY

This analysis of the authority of scripture lacks concreteness, however, since it leaves what scripture means quite unanalyzed. One can agree formally that scripture has or should have such authority for Christians, but still ask what it is about scripture that compels such authority. Even before that, however, one must ask what is meant by *scripture,* for I have already noted that scripture cannot simply be identified with the collection of texts we find in the Bible.

David Kelsey's analysis of the way theologians use scripture demonstrates that theologians "do not appeal to some objective text-in-itself but rather to a text construed *as* a certain kind of whole having a certain kind of logical force. To call each different way of construing the text 'scripture' is to use 'scripture' in importantly different ways. In short, the suggestion that scripture might serve as a final court of appeals for theological disputes is misleading because there is no one, normative concept of 'scripture.' Instead, there seems to be a family of related but importantly different concepts of 'scripture.' "[38]

As a means for exploring the different concepts of scripture Kelsey suggests that in each case we must ask what aspect of scripture is taken to be authoritative. His book consists in an analysis of three ways that theologians have located the authoritative aspect of biblical writing, namely: (1) the Bible as containing doctrinal or conceptual content; (2) the Bible as the source of mythic, symbolic, or imagistic expression of a saving event; (3) the Bible as the recital of a narrative. One of the interesting results of Kelsey's analysis is that those who look at the Bible as a source of doctrine and those who criticize this approach as failing to appreciate the Bible as a record of God's action in history equally fail to appreciate the narrative mode of much of the material in scripture. Ironically, as Kelsey shows, the emphasis on "God acting in history" is structurally similar to the construal of scripture in terms of concepts such as covenant, promise, and so on.[39]

There is no need for me to repeat here the work that Kelsey has already done so well. But one aspect of his analysis is critical for the development of my proposal. Kelsey notes the difference between scripture's uses in the common life of the church and its uses in theology.[40] A theologian's "working canon" and the "Christian canon" are not identical, for the theologian is obliged to decide what it is *in* scripture that is authoritative. And such a decision often results in an appeal to certain patterns characteristically exhibited by whatever aspect of scripture the theologian takes to be authoritative.[41]

So a theologian's claim that the scriptures have authority for the church will involve ascribing some sort of wholeness to the text or set of texts.[42] But because various kinds of wholeness can be ascribed to the texts, there can be no one concept of scripture. The theologian's attempt to propose how scripture should be understood and used in the church derives from an act of imagination that Kelsey, borrowing from Robert Johnson, calls a *discrimen*—that is, "a configuration of criteria that are in some way organically related to one another as reciprocal coefficients."[43]

Therefore, according to Kelsey, the relationship between the church, scripture, and theology turns out to be formally similar to the notorious "hermeneutical circle." For "the concrete ways in which biblical texts are used as scripture in the church's common life help shape a theologian's imaginative construal of the way that use is conjoined with God's presence among the faithful. The determinate patterns in scripture suggest a range of images from which he may select or construct a root metaphor for that *discrimen*. The particularities of the concrete use of scripture unique to the common life of the church as he experiences it will shape which image strikes him as most apt. Then, secondly, it is that imaginative characterization of the central reality of Christianity, 'what it is finally all about,' that *is* decisive for the way the theologian actually construes and uses biblical texts as scripture in the course of doing theology."[44]

Kelsey's analysis is particularly illuminating for exposing the influence the church has on how we construe scripture. Theologians, to be sure, make suggestions about how scritpure can or should be understood, but such suggestions must be fueled by the common life of the church in both its liturgical and moral forms. So a theologian may construe and use scripture in ways determined by a "logically prior imaginative judgment," but that is not all that needs to be said. For such judgment, as Kelsey suggests, must be schooled by a community whose life has been shaped by the narratives of the scripture. How we use scripture is finally an affair of the imagination, but it is nonetheless a political activity, since our imagination depends on our ability to remember and interpret our traditions as they are mediated through the moral reality of our community.

For all its perspicacity, however, Kelsey's analysis fails to do justice to the ways in which scripture morally shapes a community. The idea of a *discrimen* suggests a far too singular and unifying image, whereas the actual use of scripture in the church, in liturgy, preaching, and in morality, is not so easily characterized. In fact I would maintain that many of the difficulties attendant upon locating the authoritative aspect of scripture in doctrine, concepts, or saving event(s) revolve around the attempt to provide a far too coherent account of scripture. Put differently, one reason the church has had to be content with the notion of a canon rather than some more intellectually satisfying summary of the content of scripture is that only through the means of a canon can the church adequately manifest the kind of tension with which it must live. The canon marks off as scripture those texts that are necessary for the life of the church without trying to resolve their obvious diversity and/or even disagreements.

Still, it may be asked, why these texts? My answer is simply: these texts have been accepted as scripture because they and they alone satisfy what Reynolds Price has called our craving for a perfect story which we feel to be true. Put briefly, that story is: "History is the will of a just God who knows us."[45] Therefore the status of the Bible as scripture "separated both from other written works and from the continuous accretion of oral tradition, represents a fundamental decision to assign a special status to the material it contans and to reconize it as the classic model for the understanding of God."[46] We continue to honor that decision made by the ancient church, however, because it is a decision that "makes sense" in relation to the basic nature of Christian faith. Faith is Christian because it relates itself to classically-expressed models. This is much the same as what people mean when they say, rather vaguely and ambiguously, that 'Christianity is a historical religion.' Christian faith is not whatever a modern Christian may happen to believe, on any grounds at all, but faith related to Jesus and to the God of Israel. The centrality of the Bible is the recognition of the classic sources for the expression of Jesus and of God."[47]

The scripture functions as an authority for Christians precisely because by trying to live, think, and feel faithful to its withness they find they are more nearly able to live faithful to the truth. For the scripture forms a society and sets an agenda for its life that requires nothing less than trusting its existence to the God found through the stories of Israel and Jesus. The moral use of scripture, therefore, lies precisely in its power to help us remember the stories of God for the continual guidance of our community and individual lives. To be a community which lives by remembering is a genuine achievement, as too often we assume that we can insure our existence only by freeing ourselves from the past.

V
The Morality of Remembering; The Scripture as Narrative

Obviously I am convinced that the most appropriate image—or as Kelsey insists, *discrimen*—for characterizing scripture, for the use of the church as well as morally, is that of a narrative or a story. James Barr rightly points out that the dealings of God with man in the Bible are indeed describable as a cumulative process, 'in which later elements do build upon what was said and done at an earlier time. As I have argued, the literature is meant to be read as a story with a beginning and a progression. All 'acts of God' and incidents of the story make sense because a framework of meaning has already been created by previous acts, remembered in the tradition; they are 'further acts of one already known, of one with whom the fathers have already been in contact and have passed on the tradition of this contact.' "[48] It is certainly true, as Barr recognizes, that scripture contains much material that is not narrative in character. But such material, insofar as it is scripture, gains its intelligibility by being a product of and contribution to a community that lives through remembering. The narrative of scripture not only "renders a character"[49] but renders a community capable of ordering its existence appropriate to such stories. Jews and Christians believe this narrative does nothing less than render the character of God and in so doing renders us to be the kind of people appropriate to that character. To say that character is bound up with our ability to remember witnesses to the fact that our understanding of God is not inferred from the stories but is the stories.[50]

One of the virtues of calling attention to the narrative nature of scripture is the way it releases us from making unsupportable claims about the unity of scripture or the centrality of the "biblical view of X or Y." Rather, the scripture must be seen as one long, "loosely structured non-fiction novel" that has subplots that at some points appear minor but later turn out to be central.[51] What is crucial, however, is that the scripture does not try to suppress those subplots or characters that may challenge, or at least qualify, the main story line, for without them the story itself would be less than truthful.[52]

Through scripture we see that at crucial periods in the life of Israel and the church, questions about how to remember the stories were not just questions about "fact" or accuracy, but about what kind of community we must be to be faithful to Yahweh and his purposes for us. So the question of the status of the Davidic kingship of Israel now in Exile could not be avoided as Israel sought to survive as a community without being a "nation."[53] The issue is not just one of interpretation but of what kind of people can remember the past and yet know how to go on in a changed world.

Moreover one does not need to be a New Testament scholar to recognize that questions in the early church about how to tell the life of Jesus were also issues about the kind of community needed to live in keeping with the significance of that life. How the story should be told was basically a moral issue, since it was also a question about what kind of people we ought to be. The unity of the Gospels is not dependent, therefore, on whether they can be made to agree on the details of Jesus' life or even whether various theologies are compatible; rather, the unity of Gospels is based on the unquestioned assumption that the unity of these people required the telling of the story of this man who claimed to be nothing less than the Messiah of Israel.[54]

The fact that we now have a canon and recognize its authority in the church does not mean that we can be any less concerned about that kind of community we must be to remember rightly through the biblical narrative. Our selectivity and arbitrariness in using scripture ultimately result from our attempt to be something less than a people capable of carrying God's story in the world. For who "wants to hear about brave deeds when he is ashamed of his own, and who likes an open, honest tale from someone he's deceiving."[55] The canon is not an accomplishment but a task, since it challenges us to be the kind of people capable of recalling the stories of our fathers and mothers, on which our existence continues to depend.

The temptation, now that we have the canon, is either to objectify scripture in a manner that kills its life, or to be willing in principle to accept the validity of any interpretation by way of acknowledging the scripture's variety. Both responses fail to meet the moral challenge of being a people who derive their identity from a book. The continued existence of Israel is alone enough to make us recognize that the question of what kind of community we must be to be faithful to God is not an issue settled by the mere fact we possess a canon. I have tried to show how the very nature of the biblical literature requires us to be as able to remember as those who produced the literature.

The question of the moral significance of scripture, therefore, turns out to be a question about what kind of community the church must be to be able to make the narratives of scripture central for its life. I have already argued that such a community must be capable of sustaining the authority of scripture through use in its liturgy and governance. But first and foremost the community must know that it has a history and tradition which separate it from the world. Such separation is required by the very fact that the world knows not the God we find in the scripture.[56]

The virtues of patience, courage, hope, and charity must reign if the community is to sustain its existence. For without patience the church may be tempted to apocalyptic fantasy; without courage the church would fail to hold fast to the traditions from which it draws its life; without hope the church risks losing sight of its tasks; and

262 / Stanley Hauerwas

without charity the church would not manifest the kind of life made possible by God. Each of these virtues, and there are others equally important, draws its meaning and form from the biblical narrative, and each is necessary if we are to continue to remember and to live faithful to that narrative.

As I have suggested, Christians continue to honor the decision of their ancestors to fashion a canon because they believe the scripture reflects the very nature of God and his will for their lives. Put more concretely, scripture has authority for Christians because they have learned as a forgiven people they must also be able to forgive.[57] But to be a people capable of accepting forgiveness separates them from the world: The world, under the illusion that power and violence rule history, assumes that it has no need to be forgiven. Part of the meaning of the "world," therefore, is it is that which assumes it needs no scripture, since it lives not by memory made possible by forgiveness, but by power.

Being a community of the forgiven is directly connected with being a community sustained by the narratives we find in scripture, as those narratives do nothing less than manifest the God whose very nature is to forgive. To be capable of remembering we must be able to forgive, for without forgiveness we can only forget or repress those histories that prove to be destructive or at least unfruitful. But Christians and Jews are commanded not to forget, since the very character of their community depends on their accepting God's forgiveness and thus learning how to remember, even if what they must remember is their sin and unrighteousness.[58] By attending closely to the example of those who have given us our scripture, we learn how to be a people morally capable of forgiveness and thus worthy of continuing to carry the story of God we find authorized by scripture.

VI
THE MORAL USE OF "BIBLICAL MORALITY"

Some may well wonder whether this account of the moral authority of scripture has really helped us advance beyond the problems concerning the use of "biblical morality" described in section two. It may be objected that all I have done is redescribe as "moral" aspects of scripture and the process of its development which we already knew.[59] I may be right that remembering is a moral activity that requires a particular kind of community, especially if the stories we find in the scripture are to be remembered, but that still does not help us to know what to do with the more straightforwardly "moral" aspects of scripture—i.e., the Decalogue or the Sermon on the Mount. Nor does it help us understand what we are to do with those aspects of scripture that now seem irrelevant or, even worse, morally perverse.

For example, the complexity of the analysis offered here tends to obscure the straightforward command "Thou shalt not commit adultery," (Ex. 20:14) or the equally significant, "Do not resist one who is evil" (Matt. 5:39). In spite of all that one must say about the need to understand such passages in context, I am impressed by those who live as if such commands should directly govern their affairs. None of us should lose the suspicion that our sophistication concerning the cultural and theological qualifications about "biblical morality" often hides a profound unwillingness to have our lives guided by it.

Yet I contend that the position developed here does help us better comprehend the more straightforwardly moral portions of scripture. It keeps us from turning commands found there into isolated rules or principles that are assumed to have special status because they are in the Bible. Rather it proposes that Christians (and we hope others) take them to heart (and mind) because they have been found to be crucial to a people formed by the story of God. Such commands stand as reminders of the kind of people we must be if we are to be capable of remembering for ourselves and the world the story of God's dealing with us.

To take the prohibition of adultery, it does not claim to be intelligible in itself, but draws its force from the meaning and significance of marriage in the Jewish and Christian communities. Marriage in those communities derives from profound hope in and commitment to the future, witnessed by the willingness and duty to bring new life into the world. Moreover for those traditions family and marriage have special significance as they are also an expression of the relation these people have with their God. The prohibition against adultery does not therefore derive from a set of premises concerned directly with the legitimacy of sexual expression, though without doubt it has often been so interpreted, but from the profoundest commitment of the community concerning the form of sexual life necessary to sustain their understanding of marriage and family.

Nor does the prohibition against resisting evil derive from an assumption about violence as inherently evil, but rather from the community's understanding of how God rules his creation. For how can a people who believe God is Lord of their existence show forth that conviction if they act as if the meaning of their existence, and perhaps even history itself, must be insured by the use of force? The nonviolence of the church derives from the character of the story of God that makes us what we are—namely a community capable of witnessing to others the kind of life made possible when trust rather than fear rules our relation with one another.

I do not assume that all the moral advice and admonitions found in scripture have the same significance or should positively be appropriated. Each must be evaluated separately and critically. Of course, before we decide that certain aspects of scripture are no longer relevant—e.g., the *Haustafeln*—we must make sure we understand them through an exegesis as accurate as we can muster. And we must remember that a set of historical-critical skills will not guarantee an accurate reading. Our analysis will also depend on the questions we learn to put to the text from participating in a community which acknowledges their formative role.

The command for wives to be subject to their husbands, for example, comes only after the admonition that everyone in the church must be subject to the other out of "reverence for Christ" (Eph. 5:21). It does not say that wives should be subject to husbands as an end in itself, but rather as "to the Lord." So the manner of being "subject" cannot be read off the face of the text nor can it be made clear by exegesis alone. In fact, exegesis itself points us to recall the ways in which we as members of the church have learned to be subject to one another as faithful disciples of Christ. That direction should effectively restrain a contemporary reader from trying to understand "subordinate" from a perspective that assumes all moral relations which are not "autonomous" are morally suspect.

There is no doubt that the *Haustafeln* are in danger of great distortion and harm if they are lifted out of their theological and community context and turned into great admonitions meant to apply to any community. But that is just what their existence in scripture should prohibit. One need not agree with Yoder's argument that the *Haustafeln* were necessary because the freedom established by this new community created the possibility of insubordination in order to appreciate how the *Haustafeln* are but reminders of the radical nature of the new community that has been called into existence— namely, one where service to the other is freed from concern with status and envy.[60]

Finally, there can be no ethical use of scripture unless we are a community capable of following the admonition to put "away falsehood, let every one speak the truth with his neighbor, for we are members of one another. Be angry but do not sin; do not let the sun go down on your anger, and give no opportunity to the devil. Let the thief no longer steal, but rather let him labor, doing honest work with his hands, so that he may be able to give to those in need. Let no evil talk come out of your mouths, but such as is good for edifying, as fits the occasion, that it may impart grace to those that hear. And do not grieve the Holy Spirit of God, in whom you were sealed for the day of redemption. Let all bitterness and wrath and anger and clamor and slander be put away from you, with all malice, and be kind to one another, tenderhearted, forgiving one another, as God in Christ forgave you" (Eph. 4:25–32).

Notes

1. Joseph Blenkinsopp, *Prophecy and Canon* (Notre Dame, Ind.: University of Notre Dame Press, 1977), p. 152.

2. John Howard Yoder, "Radical Reformation Ethics in Ecumenical Perspective," *Journal of Ecumenical Studies,* Fall 1978, p. 657. I think it is no accident that the best recent book that utilizes scripture for ethics is Yoder's *The Politics of Jesus* (Grand Rapids, Mich.: Eerdmans, 1972). Yoder was able to see the New Testament with fresh eyes because he came from a separated community with the physical and intellectual space and time to appreciate the radical demands in scripture.

3. David Kelsey, *The Uses of Scripture in Recent Theology* (Philadelphia: Fortress Press, 1975), pp. 208–209.

4. Ibid., pp. 185–192. Kelsey oberves, "the translation picture wrongly assumes that 'meaning' has only one meaning. By suggesting that theological proposals express the same 'meaning' as the biblical texts that authorize them, it obliges one to assume that the texts do have some sort of meaning. What the translation picture obscures, however, is that 'meaning' may be used here in two different senses. That is, it obscures the possible conceptual discontinuity between text and proposal," p. 190. See also James Barr, *The Bible in the Modern World* (New York: Harper and Row, 1973), p. 141.

5. Erich Auerbach, *Mimesis* (Princeton, N.J.: Princeton University Press, 1968), p. 48. This is, of course, the quote as well as the theme which dominates Hans Frei's *The Eclipse of Biblical Narrative* (New Haven, Conn.: Yale University Press, 1974), p. 3. That Frei's analysis is crucial for the argument of this essay is obvious. Frei, even more than Barth, has helped me see that the problem is not in our scriptures but in ourselves.

6. James Gustafson, "Christian Ethics" in *Religion,* ed. Paul Ramsey (Englewood Cliffs, N.J.: Prentice-Hall, 1965), p. 337. See also Gustafson, *Christian Ethics and the Community* (Philadelphia: Pilgrim Press, 1971) for an excellent overview of recent attempts to use the scripture ethically. For Gustafson's own more constructive proposals, see his *Theology and Christian Ethics* (Philadelphia: Pilgrim Press, 1974), pp. 121–159. Bruce Birch and Larry Rasmussen provide an equally helpful account in their *Bible and Ethics in the Christian Life* (Minneapolis: Augsburg, 1976), pp. 45–78.

7. Brevard Childs, *Biblical Theology in Crisis* (Philadelphia: Westminster Press, 1970), p. 124.

8. This is, of course, the problem that Childs is struggling with in his *Introduction to the Old Testament as Scripture* (Philadelphia: Fortress, 1979). I think he is right to suggest that the crucial issue resides in how we understand the significance and function of the canon, but I think that Childs fails to adequately indicate the interdependence of canon and community. Therefore his sense of the status of the text appears too unmediated. However, he rightly suggests that "the fixing of a canon of scripture implies that the witness to Israel's experience with God lies not in recovering such historical processes, but is testified in the effect on the biblical text itself. Scripture bears witness to God's activity in history on Israel's behalf, but history per se is not a medium of revelation which is commensurate with a canon," p. 76. For a very helpful analysis of the differences between the Bible as scripture and as text, see Kelsey, pp. 198–201.

9. It is important not only that theologians know the text; it is

equally important how and where they learn the text. It is my hunch that part of the reason for the misuse of the scripture in matters dealing with morality is that the text was isolated from a liturgical context. There is certainly nothing intrinsically wrong with individuals reading and studying scripture, but such reading must be guided by the use of the scripture through the liturgies of the church. For the shape of the liturgy over a whole year prevents any one part of scripture from being given undue emphasis in relation to the narrative line of scripture. The liturgy, in every performance and over a whole year, rightly contextualizes individual passages when we cannot read the whole. As Aidan Kavanagh has recently observed, "the liturgy is scripture's home rather than its stepchild, and the Hebrew and Christian bibles were the church's first liturgical books." *The Shape of Baptism: The Rite of Christian Initiation* (New York: Pueblo Publishing Co., 1978), p. xiii.

10. Even more damaging in this respect than the subsequent ethical concentration of a limited range of "biblical concepts" is the underwriting of destructive prejudices of the scripture scholars. For example, Joseph Blenkinsopp has documented the often implicit anti-Semitism involved in portrayals of the history of Israel, so that the second temple period was invariably interpreted as a time of "decline." See his "The Period of the Second Commonwealth in the Theology of the Old Testament," forthcoming from Paulist Press, New York. E. P. Sanders has exposed the equally distorting interpretation of Paul by Protestants who tended to read back into Paul's relation to Judaism the issues of the relation of Protestantism to Catholicism. See his *Paul and Palestinian Judaism* (Philadelphia: Fortress Press, 1977).

11. See, for example, James Barr's criticism of "biblical theology" in his *The Bible in the Modern World,* pp. 135–136. Kelsey's critique of the "biblical concept" approach to scripture is equally devastating. *The Uses of Scripture in Recent Theology,* pp. 25–29.

12. Childs, *Biblical Theology in Crisis,* p. 130. For a particularly egregious example of the failure to appreciate the significance of the question of how "ethics" should be understood as well as the claim that the New Testament ethic must be judged by its adequacy for negotiating the "modern world," see Jack Sanders, *Ethics in the New Testament* (Philadelphia: Fortress Press, 1975). For a critique of Sanders, see my "A Failure in Communication: Ethics and the Early Church," *Interpretation,* 32/2 (April 1978), pp. 196–200.

13. Gustafson, *Theology and Christian Ethics,* pp. 122–123.

14. Birch and Rasmussen, p. 185. Birch and Rasmussen's book has the virtue of being the most methodologically aware of how different concep-

tions of ethics will determine not only what and how one identifies descriptively the "ethics in the scripture," but also the continuing status of that ethic for use today.

15. Gustafson has drawn and analyzed the distinction between "revealed morality" and "revealed reality" in *Theology and Christian Ethics,* pp. 129–138 and in *Christian Ethics and the Community,* pp. 48–51. He notes that the Bible as revealed morality can be understood in terms of law, ideals, analogies, and as a pattern of interpretation.

16. For example, Paul Ramsey maintains that the conception of justice in the Bible is radically different from all others because it consists in the principle: "To each according to the measure of his real need, not because of anything human reason can discern inherent in the needy, but because his need alone is the measure of God's righteousness toward him." *Basic Christian Ethics* (New York: Scribner's 1950), pp. 13–14. Ramsey is a classical example of an ethicist exploiting the assumption that biblical theology is primarily a matter of locating the central "biblical" concepts. Thus Ramsey stresses the centrality of love and covenant on the assumption that by doing so his ethic is thereby "biblical."

17. Barr, *The Bible in the Modern World,* p. 122.

18. For what remains a very useful discussion of these issues, see John Knox, *The Ethics of Jesus in the Teaching of the Church* (Nashville: Abingdon Press, 1961). As noted this issue involves the still controversial question of eschatology and ethics in the New Testament. In that respect it is still worth anyone's time to read Amos Wilder, *Eschatology and Ethics in the Teaching of Jesus* (New York: Harper and Row, 1939) and Hans Windisch, *The Meaning of the Sermon on the Mount* (Philadelphia: Westminster Press, 1949).

19. Victor Paul Furnish in his *Theology and Ethics in Paul* (Nashville: Abingdon, 1968) and *The Love Command in the New Testament* (Nashville: Abingdon, 1972) has emphasized both these themes with great effect.

20. See, for example, Robert Tannehill's *Dying and Rising with Christ* (Berlin: Verlag Alfred Topelmann, 1967), pp. 80–83, for substantiation of this point.

21. Furnish resorts to this means of expression simply because he has no other conceptual or moral means to articulate the way Paul's ethics is but an extension of his theology. For an effective critique of Furnish's method in this respect, see Gil Meilander, "Does Gift Imply Task?: Some Ethical Reflections" (unpublished paper read to Ethics Section of the AAR, 1979).

22. James Gustafson, "Introduction to H.R. Niebuhr's *The Responsible Self* (New York: Harper and Row, 1963), p. 23. For an extensive analysis of

H. R. Niebuhr's use of scripture, see Ben Jordan, "The Use of Scripture in the Ethics of H. R. Niebuhr" (diss., Emory University, 1974).

23. Gustafson, *Christian Ethics and the Community,* pp. 50–51.

24. See, for example, Gustafson's attempt to illuminate the Cambodian invasion through the use of scriptural analogies in *Theology and Christian Ethics,* pp. 138–145.

25. Kelsey, p. 97.

26. Those familiar with the work of Yves Simon will recognize how dependent this account of authority is on his work. In particular, see his *Philosophy of Democratic Government* (Chicago: University of Chicago Press, 1951), pp. 1–71, 144–194. See also Clarke Cochran's very helpful "Authority and Community: The Contributions of Carl Friedrich, Yves Simon, and Michael Polanyi," *American Political Science Review,* 71/2 (June 1977), pp. 546–558.

27. J. P. Mackey, *Tradition and Change in the Church* (Dayton, Ohio: Pflaum Press, 1968), p. x. Ironically Catholic theologians at Tübingen were among the first to realize the importance of this for understanding the significance of scripture. It is a tragedy that they were silenced before they were appreciated. See James Burtchaell's *Catholic Theories of Biblical Inspiration Since 1810* (Cambridge: Cambridge University Press, 1969).

28. Mackey, pp. 42–43. Those familiar with Kuhn's analysis of the development and change in science will see that many of the issues discussed and debated about his account are relevant here. Indeed I suspect a very interesting comparison could be drawn between the breakdown and reinterpretation of traditions in the Bible and those in science. That Kuhn's work might be relevant to such analysis should not be surprising, for I suspect that Kuhn's interpretation of science gains its inspiration from politics. For an attempt to develop this suggestion, see Richard Vernon, "Politics as Metaphor: Cardinal Newman and Professor Kuhn," *The Review of Politics,* 41/4 (October 1979), pp. 513–535.

29. James Barr, *Old and New Interpretation* (New York: Harper and Row, 1966), p. 190. However Barr goes on to remind us that "this positive evaluation of the 'tradition,' i.e., of the body of previous decisions and interpretations, of customs and accepted methods, nevertheless should not conceal from us the fact that this tradition can constitute the chief agency for the damaging and distorting of the meaning of the Bible." He notes, however, that this cannot be corrected by the possession of "pure" theological presuppositions, but rather the "primary ethical problem in interpretation will very often, perhaps always, lie *within* the Church," p. 191. That is why the church must always remember that the Bible belongs to the world and not

the church only. "When the Church addresses the world on the basis of the Bible, it invites people to look for themselves and see if these things are not so. The possibility that people may do this looking for themselves carries with it a consequence on the more scholarly level: non-Christian interpretation of the Bible is a possibility, indeed it is more, it is a reality," p. 191.

30. "What is needed is more awareness of how religious texts live by reinterpretation. The very mechanics of creative interpretation in the religious realm requires that we understand the Bible, not as a philosophical text expressing certain ideas, but as scripture, inspired and authoritative and consequently capable of assuming new meanings. This understanding leads to the puzzling insight that in the living religious traditions continuity is affirmed and achieved by discontinuity. Authority is affirmed and relevance asserted by reinterpretation." Krister Stendahl, "Biblical Studies in the University," in *The Study of Religion in Colleges and Universities,* ed. P. Ramsey and J. Wilson (Princeton, N.J.: Princeton University Press, 1970), pp. 30–31.

31. See, for example, Jon Gunnemann's extremely interesting interpretation of revolutions in terms of Kuhn's understanding of a paradigm shift in his *The Moral Meaning of Revolution* (New Haven, Conn.: Yale University Press, 1979).

32. Simon, pp. 29–30.

33. Ibid., p. 33. In his *A General Theory of Authority* (Notre Dame: University of Notre Dame Press, rpt. 1980), Simon points out that the "need for authority and the problem of the need for a distinct governing personnel have often been confused: it is already clear that they are distinct and that the argumentation which establishes the need for authority, even in a society made of ideally enlightened and well-intentioned persons, leaves open the question of whether some communities may be provided with all the authority they need without there being among them any distinct group of governing persons," p. 49. So to claim scripture as authority does not preclude the necessity of distinct officers and others in the church exercising authority. But again as Simon reminds us, "when an issue is one of action, not of truth, the person in authority has the character of a leader; but when the issue is one of truth, not of action, the person in authority has the character of a witness. Indeed, a witness may also be a leader and, in the capacity of leader, exercise command. But in the mere witness, and universally in the witness as such, authority does not involve, in any sense or degree, the power to give orders and to demand obedience. We would say that an event, for some time considered doubtful, finally has been established by the authority of sound and numerous witnesses. We would go so far as to say that yielding to their testimony is a duty and a matter of honesty. The authority of the mere witness is nothing else than truthfulness as expressed by signs which make it

recognizable in varying degrees of assurance," p. 84. In this respect the authority of scripture is surely that of a witness which, however, tests the authority of any who would lead in the church. For the development of this idea of authority in relation to the papacy, see my and Robert Wilken's "Protestants and the Pope," *Commonweal,* 107/3 (February 15, 1980), pp. 80–85.

34. Cochran observes that the modern attack "on tradition as such, however, is fundamentally an attack on history. It is at bottom an attempt to escape history and the necessarily historical (and therefore limited) existence of man. Tradition is what makes historical existence bearable by giving some meaning and perspective to the distance between the given and the demanded. Political theorists can do little, perhaps, directly to respond to the practical crisis of authority. Yet ideas have consequences, and the practical crisis of authority has roots in the undernourished soil of our theoretical understanding of authority, tradition, knowledge, and community," p. 557. The church, however, not only has the opportunity to enrich "ideas" but to provide the positive experience of tradition and community.

35. Barr, *The Bible in the Modern World,* p. 147.

36. Of course it is true, as Barr observes, that tradition comes before scripture, as well as following after it. *Bible in The Modern World,* p. 127. However as Kelsey has observed the concepts of "tradition" and "scripture" are not on a logical par. " 'Tradition' is used to name, not something the church uses, but something the church *is,* insofar as her reality lies in a set of events and practices that can be construed as a single activity. 'Scripture' is used to name, not something the church is, but something she must *use,* according to some concepts of 'church,' to preserve her self-identity," p. 96.

37. Blenkinsopp, *Prophecy and Canon,* p. 94. For a fascinating study of the problem of authority in Paul, see John Schutz, *Paul and the Anatomy of Apostolic Authority* (Cambridge: Cambridge University Press, 1975). Schutz's primary thesis is that "Jesus' death brings life to the Christian, but not without Jesus' life. So Paul's death is also Paul's life, his weakness, his power; and this weakness or suffering alone can stand for the union of the two, just as the cross stands for Christ's death and new life. The work of Christ is the work of God and cannot be taken from God's hand. But the appropriation puts Paul into the life of the communities alongside of the gospel, itself power and weakness. This is how the authority of the apostle is to be understood. In Paul's whole apostolic life one sees the manifestations of God's same act which one sees in the gospel itself," p. 246.

38. Kelsey, pp. 14–15. Elsewhere Kelsey suggests "To call a text or set of texts 'scripture' is not only to say that their use in certain ways in the church's life is essential to the preservation of her identity, and therefore to

say that they are 'authoritative' over that life, it is also to ascribe some sort of wholeness to the text or set of texts. However, there is an irreducible variety of kinds of wholeness that may be ascribed to the texts. Thus 'scripture' turns out to be, not one concept, but a set of different concepts that bear one another some family resemblances. All uses of 'scripture' are dialectically related to uses of the concept of 'church' and entail ascribing authoritativeness and wholeness to the texts called 'scripture'; this much all uses of 'scripture' share. But in the actual practice of appealing to scripture in the course of doing theology, there turns out to be an irreducible logical diversity of ways the texts are concretely construed as 'whole,' " pp. 100–101. Later I will suggest that the kind of "wholeness" that is most appropriate to the scripture is that of a story.

39. Kelsey, pp. 37ff.

40. Ibid., p. 94.

41. Ibid., p. 101.

42. It is important to note that ascriptions of "wholeness" to the canon are not identical with claims about the "unity" of the canon. Kelsey, p. 106. See also Barr's very useful discussion of the problem of the "unity" of scripture, *The Bible in the Modern World,* pp. 98ff.

43. Kelsey, p. 160.

44. Ibid., p. 205.

45. Reynolds Price, *A Palpable God: Thirty Stories Translated from the Bible: With an Essay on the Origins and Life of Narrative* (New York: Atheneum, 1978), p. 14. Of course as Price himself would emphasize such a story is indeed complex—so complex it requires the many narrative lines of scripture for us to understand what the existence of such a God entails.

46. Barr, *The Bible in the Modern World,* pp. 117–118.

47. Ibid., p. 118. For an extremely interesting account of the concept of a "classic" and its importance for Christian theology, see David Tracy, "Theological Classics in Contemporary Theology," *Theology Digest,* 25/4 (Winter 1977), pp. 347–355.

48. Barr, *The Bible in the Modern World,* p. 147. See also, Barr, *Old and New in Interpretation,* pp. 21ff and his "Story and History in Biblical Theology," *Journal of Religion,* 56/1 (January 1976), pp. 1–17. In the latter Barr suggests that the narrative form of the Old Testament better merits the title of story rather than history, though much of it illumines as well as recounts history. I cannot here try to deal with what Frei calls the "history-like" quality of the biblical narrative and the questions thereby raised about the "accuracy" of scripture. However I think Frei is exactly right to challenge the assumption that the "real" meaning of the text resides in how accurately or inaccurately the writers report occurrences. For an extremely

fruitful discussion of these issues, see Julian Hartt's chapter "Story as the Art of Historical Truth," in his *Theological Method and Imagination* (New York: Seabury Press, 1977), and James Coughenour, "Karl Barth and the Gospel Story: A Lesson in Reading the Biblical Narrative," *Andover Newton Quarterly*, 20 (1979), pp. 97–110.

49. Kelsey interprets Barth in this manner, p. 39ff.

50. Kelsey, p. 45.

51. Ibid., p. 48.

52. From this perspective the most important question about how to tell the story in the scripture still involves how to understand the connections between the two testaments. And it is important to note that this is not just a matter of studying the text but, as I have argued, continues to be a political issue of the nature of the Christian community as well as Judaism. As Blenkinsopp has suggested, "In view of the break between Christianity and Judaism towards the end of the Second Commonwealth—profoundly tragic in its consequences as it has been—the two faiths must necessarily address a critique to each other, and such a critique will necessarily inform any attempt to give a theological account of the classical texts to which both bodies appeal. Is it inconceivable that such mutual testing be carried out in dialogue and co-operation? And, from the Christian side, what would an Old Testament theology look like which at least envisioned such a situation by taking Judaism with absolute theological seriousness?" "The Period of the Second Commonwealth in the Theology of the Old Testament," p. 29. In his *Discerning the Way* (New York: Seabury, 1980), Paul Van Buren rightly argues that the relationship between the Hebrew scriptures and the Apostolic Writings is "unavoidably a question of the relationship between the Jewish people and the Gentile church," p. 139. I am in deep sympathy with Van Buren's attempt to take seriously the fact that the God Christians worship is Israel's God.

53. Blenkinsopp, *Prophecy and Canon*, pp. 78–79.

54. Charles Talbert has suggested that though the early Christians agreed that God was present in Jesus for our salvation, they differed about how that presence was manifest in Jesus. As a result the Gospel was preached and written down in different ways—some concentrated on the miracles, some morality, some knowledge of the future. But what is important is that the "canonical gospels appear to be attempts to avoid the reductionism of seeing the presence of God in Jesus in only one way and attempts to set forth a comprehensive and balanced understanding of both the divine presence and the discipleship it evokes." "The Gospel and the Gospels," *Interpretation*, 33/4 (October 1979), pp. 351–362. As Talbert has shown elsewhere, what was crucial about the Gospels is not their genre, but the kind of

discipleship they assumed appropriate to the character of Jesus. See his *What is a Gospel: The Genre of the Canonical Gospels* (Philadelphia: Fortress Press, 1977).

55. This is a statement by Fiver from Richard Adams' *Watership Down* (New York: Avon Books, 1972), p. 124.

56. Blenkinsopp suggests that "the prophetic canon found a place alongside Torah as a compromise or way of maintaining a balance between law and prophecy, institution and charisma, the claims of the past and those of the future. Such an inclusive canon, which contained within itself both the seeds of tension and the means of overcoming it, corresponds to something important in the makeup of Judasim and Christianity. Both faiths can test the truth of the proposition that a theocratic institution which excludes prophecy and the millenarian hope leaves itself open to assimilation, while prophecy left to itself tends of its nature toward disunity and sectarianism. It is the fate of prophecy to be always necessary and never sufficient." *Prophecy and Canon,* p. 116. However, as I have tried to suggest, without a prophetic community there is no chance that the moral force of the scripture story can be intelligible.

57. On the political presuppositions of forgiveness, see Hadden Willmer, "The Politics of Forgiveness," *The Furrow,* April 1979, and my "Forgiveness and Political Community," *Worldview,* 23/1–2 (January–February 1980), pp. 15–16.

58. In his otherwise admirable *The First Followers of Jesus* (London: SCM Press, 1977), Gerd Theissen suggests "in the New Testament for the first time the revolutionary—and healthy—insight that to take any human ethical requirement seriously will demonstrate its inadequacy, that ethics without forgiveness is a perversion, and that there is more to morality than morality, if it is to remain human. This recognition certainly points far beyond the particular historical context in which it came into being. But at one time it was a contribution towards overcoming a deeprooted crisis in Judaism. The identity of Judasim could not be achieved by rival intensifications of the demands of the Torah, each of which sought to outbid the others; the only answer was the recognition of divine grace. In the last resort, solidarity between men could not be achieved by an intensification of norms; this could only heighten latent and open aggressiveness. What was needed was a new relationship to all norms: putting trust and freedom from anxiety before demands of any kind," p. 107. Not only does this accept a far too restricted sense of "morality," but more damaging is the assumption that forgiveness was absent prior to the coming of Jesus and the church. I have tried to suggest that the ability of Israel to reinterpret her traditions presumed a profound experience and understanding of forgiveness. Theissen's argument in

this respect still betrays the Protestant reading of Paul that has recently been challenged by E. P. Sanders in his *Paul and Palestinian Judaism.* Sanders rather decisively shows that for Paul the problem with Judaism was not the law, but that it is not Christianity—that is, a new community based on the work and person of Jesus, p. 552.

59. If this is the case, it is but another indication that ethics at best is only bad poetry— that is, it seeks to help us see what we see every day but fail to see rightly. Put differently, ethics is an attempt to help us feel the oddness of everyday. If ethicists had talent, they might be poets, but in the absence of talent, they try to make their clanking conceptual and discursive chains do the work of art.

60. Yoder, *The Politics of Jesus,* p. 178.

Scripture and Christian Ethics

James F. Childress

This article originally appeared in *Interpretation* in 1980.

The use of Scripture for deliberation and justification in making moral judgments is a crucial and neglected function of the Bible in Christian ethics.

Scripture can, does, and should shape the Christian moral life in many ways. Several recent interpretations of how Scripture functions have overemphasized some features of the moral life—vision and perspectives, images and metaphors, stories, loyalties, and character. What these interpretations underestimate or distort is the role of Scripture in Christian moral deliberation and justification. For the most part, these interpretations emphasize *influence* rather than *reflection*. Reflection on the moral requirements of Scripture, or warranted by Scripture, is, to be sure, one mode of influence; but it tends to receive short shrift. Other features of the moral life receive primary and sometimes exclusive attention.[1]

I
RESPONSIBILITY: DELIBERATION AND JUSTIFICATION

Some of these interpretations take "responsibility" as the image or mode of the moral life.[2] Unfortunately, responsibility is frequently construed to exclude or lessen the importance of deliberation and justification in the moral life. An adequate interpretation of responsibility, however, would emphasize deliberation and justification alongside features of the moral life that are currently highlighted.

276

Responsibility has received extensive and intensive scrutiny in the last twenty years. In the theological context, the work of H. Richard Niebuhr has been especially prominent and seminal, despite many ambiguities and gaps that remained at his premature death. Niebuhr's attempt to develop the idea of responsibility as a third way of approaching ethics—beyond both deontology and teleology—fails for reasons that need not concern us here. What is more important for our purposes is his interpretation of responsibility. In contrast to deontology's views of a man as a citizen or obeyer of laws, and teleology's view of man as a maker, from the standpoint of responsibility man is an answerer, engaged in dialogue, and responding to actions upon him. There are four elements in responsibility. First, we *respond* to actions. Second, we make our responses in terms of our *interpretations* of those actions. Third, we are *accountable* or answerable in that we direct our actions "in anticipation of answers to our answers." Fourth, we make our answers in the context of *social solidarity,* a continuing community of agents.[3]

In practically all definitions of responsibility, Niebuhr's third feature is prominent, but it often finds clearer expression than he provided, partly because of his fear of legalism. As H.L.A. Hart has suggested, the original sense of "answer" that is involved in "responsibility" is not answering questions, though this is not unimportant, but rather "answering or rebutting accusations or charges, which if established, carried liability to punishment or blame or other adverse treatment."[4] It may be necessary to take the risk of legalism in order to offer an adequate interpretation of responsibility, for we and others have to answer for our actions in relation to certain standards and consequences. Such answering occurs in a social setting in which we answer to our consciences, as socially formed, and to others who demand that we indicate why our actions should not be considered as wrong, unjustified, and blameworthy. The setting may take various forms, such as legal and moral, and the relevant principles and rules, justifications and excuses, and sanctions may vary from context to context. Our interest is primarily in the moral setting, which, as I shall argue later, may be illuminated by comparison with law.

The importance of moral justification, of answering or rebutting charges, is frequently overlooked or denied by philosophers and theologians who otherwise find the idea of responsibility attractive. I have already suggested that the fear of legalism may have influenced Niebuhr's thought in this regard. Legalism, however, covers a multitude of issues. In addition to concerns about reducing discretion and freedom in the moral life, there are theological objections to legalism. For example, to protect God's freedom, Karl Barth replaced moral justification by an inner certainty of God's command, while Walter Künneth repudiated moral justification to emphasize the centrality of religious justification—a person does not achieve righteousness but is declared righteous by God.[5] Non-theological reasons include the contention that to concentrate on moral justification is to draw too heavily on legal analogies which distort the moral life. The most appropriate analogies, according to this argument, are aesthetic rather than legal. Some interpreters are interested in how moral conduct is shaped by various influences, including metaphors and stories, that are not reducible to the moral principles and rules that may be explicitly invoked in justification. Furthermore, so the argument might go, the reasons invoked in public moral justification may simply be rationalizations for conduct that is based on other grounds such as self-interest or even subconscious forces.

Such objections fail to dislodge justification in the moral life or in ethical analysis. On theological grounds, it is possible to argue that there is greater continuity (although not identity) between moral justification and religious justification than some theological critics of moral justification have recognized. Within a Catholic framework, that continuity might be expressed in the language of religious justification completing but not destroying moral justification. Even if this continuity thesis is not adequate, it is possible to affirm the importance of moral justification without implying that it either limits God's freedom or obviates the need for God's justification. Regarding the non-theological objections, no doubt excessive reliance on legal analogies in thinking about responsibility distorts the moral life and ethics; but excessive reliance on aesthetic analogies, or an interpretation of the moral life exclusively in aesthetic language, also distorts the moral life by neglecting features that are both prominent and important. Among these features is moral justification, the appeal to moral principles, rules, and values to defeat charges of moral liability.[6] Such appeals, of course, involve images, metaphors, and stories; and any adequate account of moral justification must incorporate them too.

The distinction between *justification* of an obligation and *recognition* of an obligation may suggest, in part, how images, metaphors, and stories are important along with principles and rules.[7] Obligations (and correlative rights) are established and justified by appeals to principles and rules. For example, the obligation to get a patient's informed consent before an operation is justified or constituted by the principle of respect for persons. Whether the physician recognizes this obligation will depend, of course, on various factors in his or her background: training, images. Within a Christian framework, an obligation to render assistance to others, even at inconvenience and risk to oneself, is justified or constituted by the principle of love of neighbor. But the parable of the Good Samaritan, for instance, may enable us to *recognize* that obligation.

A parallel debate in jurisprudence may be suggestive. Legal realists such as Jerome Frank contended that the law, or legal principles and rules, function as *stimuli,* as influences, for judges rather and as *reasons.*[8] That is, they are factors that can help explain decisions along with what the judge had for breakfast, his or her background, and the like. They enable us to predict behavior and also to influence behavior.[9] Legal realism neglected the function of principles and rules in the justification of judgments and decisions. It tended to think about appeals to principles and rules as mere rationalization for behavior "influenced" or "caused" by other factors. It neglected the internal aspect of law, concentrating instead on the external aspect. It failed to see the judges' and others' experience of legal principles and rules as binding. And they offer reasons in terms of these principles and rules; they do not merely react to stimuli.

Even those who are persuaded by arguments for the importance of moral justification may wonder whether "justification" is the most appropriate term in part because it has the ring of *ex post facto* reasoning and suggests that the agent takes a moral stance and then tries to show that the reasons for it are stronger than the reasons against it. Such friendly critics might propose the language of moral argument or discourse in order to emphasize that the debate is open

and that it may occur before as well as after the act has been per-
formed. While these points are well taken, the term "justification"
does not exclude them if we keep in mind the context of justification:
answering or responding to charges that a particular course of action
is wrong and blameworthy. H. Richard Niebuhr's understanding of
accountability in terms of dialogue obscures the legal-like features of
justification in the moral context. Whether in debate with oneself or
with others, there is an adversarial relation in that reasons are pitted
against each other to determine which course of action is morally
justified.

Deliberation involves the considerations that are also invoked in
justification. As John Dewey noted, deliberation is "an imaginative
rehearsal of various courses of action."[10] It includes the prospective
justification of those actions in the light of moral rules and principles. Since the same considerations are involved in both deliberation
and justification, I shall sometimes use "justification" to cover both
processes.

II
RELATIONS BETWEEN SCRIPTURE AND ETHICS

Neither Scripture nor ethics is monolithic. Scripture includes
many different sorts of materials that are relevant to morality and to
ethics, and they function in many different ways in relation to the
moral life (e.g., in worship). In addition, as I have emphasized, we
need to avoid simplistic anlayses of morality and ethics which reduce
their complexity and richness. In this section I shall use the model of
morality and ethics that I sketched in the preceding section to suggest a way to incorporate biblical ethics into Christian ethics for deliberation and justifcation.

First, it is important to distinguish between the *authority* of
Scripture and the *authorizations* that Scripture gives for moral judgments, rules.[11] Even Christian theologians who recognize Scripture
as an authority may dispute whether it has authority in particular areas (e.g., politics) and whether it authorizes some judgments (e.g.,
that abortion is morally wrong). While acknowledgement of the authority of Scripture in part defines the Christian ethicist, in contrast

to some other ethicist, there is vast room for dispute about what Scripture authorizes and justifies.

Second, I shall concentrate on *authorizations* in accord with the deliberation-justification model. This emphasis in no way denies the importance of other influences of Scripture on morality and on ethics (e.g., perspectives, images, and character). And what Kelsey observes about Christian theology may also apply to Christian ethics: "Perhaps scholarly study of Scripture bears on theology more through its impact on the theologian's religious life than by any direct relation to theological argument."[12] Authorizations themselves may vary, as Kelsey's appropriation of Stephen Toulmin's categories indicates.[13] My discussion of authorizations or justifications (terms that I shall use interchangeably) will not be comprehensive; it will only indicate a few important ways to construe the relevance of Scripture to ethics.

Third, I do not claim that Scripture is the exclusive authority for Christian ethics; nor do I indicate exactly how this authority relates to other authorities. Recent proposals of a dialogical relation between Scripture and other authorities point in the right direction, though they do not adequately analyze this relation (e.g., whether Scripture is a, or the, primary authority and particularly whether it is the final court of appeal). Allen Verhey holds that Scripture is the final word for the "perspective" on morality, and that this "biblical perspective limits, corroborates, and transforms appeals to natural morality on other levels of moral discourse" such as principles and rules.[14] But the question remains how principles and rules in or authorized by Scripture relate to the biblical perspective and to principles and rules of natural morality.

Fourth, it is a commonplace that we should not confuse biblical ethics with the use of the Bible in ethics. That distinction is sound, but it is sometimes drawn so as to establish a use of the Bible that pays practically no attention to biblical ethics. For example, some ethicists hold that the Bible discloses a reality, a person, God, to whom we respond rather than a morality that we should apply to our lives, thereby indicating a way around biblical ethics.[15] A defender of a revealed reality, rather than a revealed morality, may hold that God as creator, redeemer, and preserver is disclosed in Scripture. We are to be responsible to this God who is acting upon us. Thus, the first question of morality is not What ought I (we) to do? but What is going on? which means What is God doing? The agent interprets what is going on in light of images, metaphors, in Scripture and elsewhere in order to be responsible and to make a fitting response.[16]

This model of responsibility, I have already argued, fails to see the role of reason-giving, deliberation, and justification. Verhey contends that respect for the moral agent's capacity to give reasons suggests some limits and directions in the use of biblical rules, principles, and perspectives:

> That reason-giving capacity does not necessarily demand that biblical moral rules or commands be omitted, but it does require that they be connected with more general biblical principles and perspectives. Reason-giving capacity does not necessarily imply that a sensitive conscience may not 'intuit' God's action in the world, but it does imply that the conscience be made sensitive not only by some nonmoral images of God, but also by the kinds of reasons and principles which stand behind biblical moral claims.[17]

Not only is there a reason-giving capacity; there is also a reason-giving necessity imposed by our responsibility to God, to self, and to others, including the Christian community.

My own religious community is the Society of Friends (Quakers), and it might be supposed that I would deemphasize deliberation and justification in order to emphasize response to the leadings of the Spirit, answering that of God in every person. Although Quakers have emphasized the disclosure of God in Scripture and, especially, in experience, their view of the moral life is complex. George Fox, for example, gave various reasons for the rightness and wrongness of particular modes of conduct; and these reasons cannot be reduced to intuition whether humanistic (conscience) or theological (Spirit). For example, he appealed to the following norms: unity of mankind, natural affections, the primitive order, humanity, and ordering all to the glory of God. These broad categories of relationships were established originally, and the Spirit commands their restitution and preservation. Fox also appealed to the historical Christ, for the Light or the Spirit Within and the historical Christ do not command different actions: "Christ saith, swear not at all, the light will say the same to thee, in thee: Christ saith, he that lusteth after a woman committeth adultery with her in his heart; this light will tell thee the same, bringing thy works to it, and loving it . . ." In short, if Fox accepted theological intuitionism, it was modified by tests of the Spirit such as consistency with itself, and these tests included appeals to Scripture. Fox wrote, "God is a God of order." Or, as Friends affirmed their pacifism in the seventeenth-century conflicts in England, they contended that the Spirit is not "changeable" so as to command one thing yesterday and another today or tomorrow. If an action is according to that of God in others, it should also be according to Scripture. Friends thus used Scripture as a revealed morality as well as a revealed reality though they did not believe that revelation had ceased with Scripture.[18]

In the finest analysis of Scripture and ethics that I know, Gustafson distinguishes four ways of using Scripture as revealed morality: law, ideals, analogies, and "great variety" (the last encompassing various "moral values, moral norms and principles through many different kinds of biblical literature").[19] Numerous questions arise about all these uses of Scripture. For law and ideals, key questions are determination of content and application. For analogies and "great variety," the issue of control is also very important. It is important to recognize and affirm this variety of uses of Scripture as revealed morality. To reduce Scripture's moral requirements to any single category is to distort both morality and Scripture.

Scripture itself appears to warrant construal of its moral requirements in several different ways. For example, the Ten Commandments can be construed as law; peace and justice can be construed as ideals. In addition, analogical reasoning is wonderfully depicted in the exchange between the prophet Nathan and King David after the latter's affair with Bathsheba and his arrangement of her husband's death. Nathan confronted David with a story about a man who owned many sheep but killed his neighbor's only lamb in order to have a feast. David was outraged and indicated that the culprit should be killed. Nathan replied: "Thou art the man" (II Sam. 11 and 12). This sort of analogical reasoning is also required by the so-called Golden Rule in its various forms (see Matt. 7:12), since one point of this rule, also present in various other societies and traditions, is the principle of universalizability: treat similar cases in a similar way.[20] The biblical materials appear in many different forms (e.g., parables and wisdom sayings) and a significant theological judgment is involved in construing these moral statements as law, as ideals, or as sources of analogical reasoning.

I propose that we think about some of Scripture's moral statements in terms of principles and rules, especially in terms of principles that establish presumptions and burdens of proof for the moral life. This perspective perhaps encompasses some elements of Gustafson's "great variety," but it also operates with a broader understanding of law (in its contemporary usage). Here again the legal analogy is appropriate and helpful. As Dworkin has argued against some positivist theories of law, law cannot be reduced merely to rules; it includes principles as well.[21] Principles and rules have a different logic in law and morality. Principles are more general and fundamental than moral rules and offer grounds for rules. For example, the moral rule, "it is wrong to lie," may be grounded in the moral principle of respect for persons. If we construe the Fifth (or Sixth) Commandment as "Thou shalt not commit murder," it might be viewed as a moral rule that applies in an all or nothing fashion. If, however, we construe this commandment as "Thou shalt not kill," it might be viewed as a moral principle that indicates a direction or presumption.

The language of presumptions may also be useful. Various devices of legal argumentation have been transferred to extralegal argumentation for many centuries.[22] They may also illuminate moral deliberation and justification as I have conceived them in the first section of this essay. Moral presumptions establish a *prima facie* case for a course of action. For example, there is a moral presumption that killing is unjustified; an act of killing has a *prima facie* case against it. This presumption is based on many different parts of Scripture including, for example, the commandment to love one's neighbors as oneself. We could concentrate on the strength of the presumption or on the weight of the burden of proof to be borne by anyone who would hold that killing is morally justified in particular circumstances.

A moral presumption is always relevant, but it may not always be decisive. Perhaps some presumptions are conclusive, but most are rebuttable. Within moral discourse, one major task is determining whether any moral presumptions are conclusive. For too long Christian ethics has tried to avoid absolutes. There may well be some (e.g., do not commit murder, do not commit rape, and do not act cruelly). Legitimate opposition to conceiving the moral life wholly or even mainly in terms of absolutes should not blind us to specific modes of conduct that may appropriately be conceived as absolutes. Such absolutes, or conclusive presumptions, may be few and may not take us very far in the moral life, but they should not be ignored. Determining which, if any, presumptions are absolute and which are rebuttable is a difficult substantive moral and theological task. Part of this task is not only determining the *strength* of presumptions, but also determining their *meaning*. For example, if "lying" is defined as intentionally withholding the truth from or deceiving someone who has a right to the truth, it is possible to hold that the moral presumption against lying is conclusive. If, however, "lying" is defined as an intentional discrepancy between thought and speech, it is difficult to hold that the moral presumption against lying is conclusive. It would be a defensible presumption. Similar points could be made about the distinction between murder and killing within just-war theory.

Of course, caution should be exercised in developing analogies between moral and legal argumentation. Use of legal and legal-like terms such as presumption and burden of proof in the moral sphere should not blind us to important differences. For example, morality does not have the procedures that prevail in law, and moral terms can rarely be as precise as legal terms. Nevertheless, the analogies between law and morality can remind us of features of moral deliberation and justification that may be overlooked under the impact of aesthetic and other metaphors.

Frequently the Bible is viewed as a *resource for problem-solving.*[23] While this viewpoint is not inappropriate, we should not forget that the Bible is also a *source of moral problems.* Moral dilemmas do not simply exist as problems that we try to resolve by appeals to Scripture. Without Scripture, without some of the moral principles, rules and presumptions that it contains and warrants, Christians would not face some moral dilemmas. At least, these dilemmas would be defined differently. One role of the Christian ethicist is to bring to light principles and rules in and warranted by Scripture that may engender dilemmas. The ethicist is compelled by Scripture to be a "trouble-maker" as well as a "trouble-shooter."[24] Thus, the ethicist has a responsibility within the Christian community to direct attention to principles and rules that *constitute* obligations that may otherwise be overlooked or neglected. In addition, he or she should direct attention to biblical stories, images, metaphors that may enable us to *recognize* obligations. As an authority for Christians, Scripture demands that we face some moral issues that we might otherwise avoid. To ignore or downplay the place of Scripture, including the principles and rules it contains and warrants, in Christian moral deliberation and justification is to distort its authority.

Notes

1. For example, while recognizing being *and* doing. Bruce B. Birch and Larry L. Rasmussen write: "Our contention is that the most effective and crucial impact of the Bible in Christian ethics is that of shaping the moral identity of the Christian and of the church" (*Bible and Christian Ethics* [Minneapolis, Augsburg Publishing House, 1976] p. 104). See esp. the writings of Stanley Hauerwas, *Character and the Christian Life* (San Antonio, Trinity University Press, 1975): *Vision and Virtue* (Notre Dame, Fides Publishers, 1974): and *Truthfulness and Tragedy* (Notre Dame, University of Notre Dame Press, 1977). Attention to deliberation-justification as well as to other features of the moral life can be seen in James M. Gustafson, "The Place of Scripture in Christian Ethics: A Methodological Study," *Interp,* 24:430–55. (October 1970) and "The Relation of the Gospels to the Moral Life," in *Theology and Christian Ethics* (Philadelphia, United Church Press, A Pilgrim Press Book, 1974) which also contains the first essay.

2. See, for example, H. Richard Niebhur, *The Responsible Self: An Essay in Christian Moral Philosophy* (New York: Harper and Row, Publishers, 1963), especially Appendix A. This theme also appears in H. Edward Everding and Dana M. Wilbanks, *Decisoion-Making and the Bible* (Valley Forge, Judson Press, 1975) and Charles Curran, "Dialogue with the Scriptures: The Role and Function of the Scriptures in Moral Theology," in *Catholic Moral Theology in Dialogue* (Notre Dame, Fides Publishers, 1972). Edward LeRoy Long has a helpful analysis of response and relationality in "The Use of the

Bible in Christian Ethics: A Look at Basic Options," *Interp,* 19:149–62 (April 1965).

3. Niebuhr, *The Responsible Self,* p. 65. For an excellent interpretation of responsibility in theological literature, see Albert R. Jonsen, *Responsibility in Modern Relgous Ethics* (Washington, Corpus Books, 1968).

4. *Punishment and Responsibility: Essays in the Philosophy of Law* (Oxford, Clarendon Press, 1968), p. 265.

5. See my discussion in *Civil Disobedience and Political Obligation: A Study in Christian Social Ethics* (New Haven, Yale University Press, 1971), pp. 165–67.

6. For a discussion of levels or tiers of moral justification, see Tom L. Beauchamp and James F. Childress, *Principles of Biomedical Ethics* (New York: Oxford University Press, 1969), chap. 1.

7. For the distinction between constitution of obligation and recognition of obligation, see George Schrader, "Autonomy, Heteronomy, and Moral Imperatives," *J Ph* 60:65–77 (1963).

8. See Jerome Frank, *Law and the Modern Mind* (Garden City, N.Y., Doubleday and Company, Inc.: Anchor Books, 1963) and Ronald Dworkin's brief discussion of legal realism in his *Taking Rights Seriously* (Cambridge, Harvard University Press, 1978), pp. 3–4.

9. For example, Niebuhr wrote: "when I view my life from the standpoint of its existence in responsibility I am not so much aware of *law in the form of demand* as of the action of other beings upon me in *anticipated and predictable ways.* In my responsive relations with others I am dealing not with laws but with men, though with men who are not atoms but members of a system of interactions. If law is present here it is present more in analogy to natural law in the modern or perhaps nineteenth-century sense than to *obligatory, political law" (The Responsible Self,* p. 78 [emphasis added]). See also his analogy of the motorcar driver, pp. 108f.

10. *Theory of the Moral Life* (New York: Holt, Rinehart and Winston, 1960), p. 135.

11. See David Kelsey, "Appeals to Scripture in Theology," *JR* 48:1–21 (1968) and Allen Verhey, "The Use of Scripture in Ethics," *Rel St Rev* 4:28–29 (January 1978). Kelsey writes, " . . . to call a set of writings 'scripture' is to say that they ought to be used in certain normative and rulish ways in the common life of the church" (*The Uses of Scripture in Recent Theology* [Philadelphia, Fortress Press, 1975], p. 164). This is a very valuable study for ethics as weli as for theology.

12. "Appeals to Scripture in Theology," p. 21.

13. *Ibid.* See also Kelsey, *The Uses of Scripture.*

14. "The Use of Scripture in Ethics," p. 35.

15. This helpful distinction between revealed morality and revealed reality is drawn by Gustafson in "The Place of Scripture in Christian Ethics" p. 439, and in "Christian Ethics," in Paul Ramsey, ed., *Religion* (Englewood Cliffs, Prentice-Hall, 1965), pp. 309–25.

16. Niebuhr, *The Responsible Self.*

17. "The Use of Scripture in Ethics," p. 32.

18. See my " 'Answering That of God in Every Man': An Interpretation of George Fox's Ethics." *Quaker Religious Thought,* 15:2–41 (Spring, 1974), esp. pp. 10–11 where these points are made with documentation.

19. "The Place of Scripture in Christian Ethics" p. 444. Although Gustafson appears to favor "revealed reality" rather than "revealed morality" his study suggests that the former requires the latter, at least in the form of "great variety."

20. See Marcus G. Singer, "The Golden Rule," *Philosophy,* 38:293–314, No. 146 (October 1963).

21. See *Taking Rights Seriously.*

22. As Nicholas Rescher writes, "Transposition of various devices of legal argumentation to debate in rhetoric was already clear with the ancients (e.g., in Aristotle's *Topics* and *Rhetoric,* and in Cicero's *De inventione*). But it was not until 1828 that Richard Whately took a crucial further step in his *Elements of Rhetoric.* Though part of the law of evidence since antiquity, and though tacitly present throughout as a governing factor in disputing practice, the ideas of *burden of proof* and of *presumptions* were first introduced explicitly into the theoretical analysis of *extralegal* argumentation in Whately's treatment of rhetoric" (*Dialectics: A Controversy-Oriented Approach to the Theory of Knowledge* [Albany, State University of New York Press, 1977]). As the subtitle indicates, Rescher concentrates on epistemology rather than on ethics. J. Philip Wogaman is one Christian ethicist who has used the language of presumptions to indicate the structure of Christian moral judgment-making. See *A Christian Method of Moral Judgment* (Philadelphia, The Westminster Press, 1976).

23. See Birch and Rasmussen, *Bible and Christian Ethics,* esp. chap. 6.

24. See Ralph Potter, "The Logic of Moral Argument," in Paul Deats, Jr., ed., *Toward a Discipline of Social Ethics* (Boston, Boston University Press, 1972), pp. 93–114, esp. 105–6

Scripture, Liturgy, Character, and Morality

Richard A. McCormick, S.J.

This article originally appeared in *Theological Studies* in 1981.

Moral theology concerns itself with both character formation and decision-making. Perhaps attention has fallen somewhat one-sidedly on the latter to the neglect of the former.[1] Here a brief roundup will have to suffice to point up recent efforts to redress this imbalance.

Jeremy Miller, O.P., uses the book of Bruce Birch and Larry Rasmussen[2] to underline the importance of the Church (as community) for Christian ethics.[3] The Church influences character in three ways: as shaper of moral identity, bearer of moral tradition, community of moral deliberation. For instance, where moral identity is concerned, it is clear that the Church's actions (liturgy, preaching) function as socializing factors. More attention to character formation would tie liturgy more closely with moral theology.

Miller suggests—rightly, I believe—that Vatican II's notion of the Church as People of God would provide a Christian anthropology that would put appropriate emphasis on "the inner discerning power the Christian can claim in living out the demands of discipleship." This would mean also that a more prominent place is required for principles of dissent. Furthermore, an emphasis on the theology of grace would mean a tighter union of morality and spirituality.

The directional emphasis suggested by Miller seems certainly justified. We might say that we have been putting a heavy emphasis on the pair right-wrong, to the neglect of those considerations (virtue, formation, character) involved in the pair good-bad. When appropriate adjustment is made, we will be much more concerned with factors influencing character, especially liturgy and the sources of Christian spirituality. A concrete but not insignificant gesture-of-resolve in this direction might be adoption of the usage "moral-spiritual life."

Enda McDonagh notes the emerging sense of the need to integrate the liturgical life of the Church, personal prayer, and "Christian living in the world (formally treated in moral theology)."[4] His study explores, therefore, the relationship between liturgy and morality.

He notes and develops several links. The first is that of "mystical" experience (the experience of God). In liturgy—which is community remembering—we recall in celebration the life, death, and resurrection of Jesus Christ in such a way that we appropriate more deeply our own present identity. In doing so, we enjoy the present experience of God. "In Christian liturgy history is the way to mystery, the human activity of celebration the way to mystical experience." Thus in liturgy we have celebration, remembering, identity, and mystical experience.[5]

These same four elements occur in the moral life. In moral activity we celebrate others, achieve fuller self-identification and self-transcendence. Finally, "moral response to a human other has the potential of encounter with the divine other." Both liturgy and moral action involve us, through temporalities, in opening to the experience of God as Father of Jesus Christ (McDonagh's so-called "mystical" element).

Second, McDonagh states that by remembering and retelling the story and events of Jesus Christ, the liturgy enters into the essential moral education of Christians. The biblical narratives and their liturgical commentary are intended to reveal the basic meaning and direction of Christian living as discipleship. In his development of this point, McDonagh scores a widespread rationalism in moral theology, as if the "mystical" encounter promoted by liturgy and discernible in moral activity has "no bearing on the analysis and resolution of concrete problems." Rather, the recall of God's relationship with humankind and its realization in Jesus *illuminates in endless ways* the moral dilemmas one faces from fidelity to a marriage partner to sharing the goods of the earth."[6] Here I wish

McDonagh would have been more specific. Concretely, what form does such illumination take? Does it simply reconfirm what is in principle knowable by human insight? Or does it provide a broader, more satisfying context for analyzing concrete problems? Or does it result in substantially different judgments? These are not insignificant questions; they are constantly put to me by my colleagues in moral philosophy. An answer is not satisfactory until it deals analytically with a concrete moral problem, and in terms other than the merely parenetic. I shall return to this below.

McDonagh ends his stimulating essay by attending to a third linkage between liturgy and morality, that of liturgy as source of structure and direction for the communities in which we lead our moral lives. Here he very helpfully outlines how liturgy acts as a corrective for dualistic attitudes toward the body and pleasure, toward the earth and our care of it, toward individualistic or collectivistic tendencies, toward triumphalistic assessments of our moral achievements. McDonagh began his study by expressing the hope that he could "carry a little further" the task of relating liturgy and morality. He has done far more than that.

An entire issue of the *Journal of Religious Ethics* is devoted to liturgy and ethics. Just a few items will be lifted out here. Paul Ramsey and D. E. Saliers addressed the relationship of liturgy and ethics at the January 1979 meeting of the Society of Christian Ethics.[7] Ramsey insists that the engendering event gives shape to the engendered liturgical response ("a formed reference to divine events"). But this is true as well for Christian morality and Christian faith. Thus Ramsey refers to the *lex orandi, lex credendi, lex bene operandi* as having the same ordering principle. Between these three responses (*orare, credere, operari*) there is both parity (no one deserves a priority over the other) and reciprocity. In Christian ethics, e.g., the notion of agape must be continually nourished by liturgy and the entire biblical narrative; otherwise it loses its meaning and collapses into a pale philosophical concept.

Ramsey then applies in illuminating fashion the relation of liturgy and morality to two practical instances: second marriages and abortion. In the Eastern Orthodox tradition, theology and ethics are contained, subsumed, and conveyed by the liturgy. The liturgy for a second marriage (after a failed first) is straightforwardly penitential in character and is a way of making a theological statement about marriage.

Next Ramsey turns to abortion. He shows, amply and correctly, the shape of biblical thought on abortion. "And it is the shape of Christian liturgies so far as the Bible has not been excluded from them." Anyone who believes that the Bible says nothing definitive to the abortion question Ramsey believes has not listened to biblical evidence or has responded: "Speak, Lord, and thy servant will think it over." Ramsey urges: "Far more than any argument, it was surely the power of the Nativity Stories and their place in ritual and celebration and song that tempered the conscience of the West to its audacious effort to wipe out the practice of abortion and infanticide."[8] So Ramsey is arguing that liturgy affects morality not merely by transforming the moral agent and his/her perspectives and character in a general way (which it does), but also by presenting substantial concrete moral content. This is vintage Ramsey—which means that it is an entertaining, enlightening, and provocative piece.

In rather marked contrast to Ramsey, Donald E. Saliers argues that the relations between liturgy and ethics are most adequately formulated by specifying how certain affections and virtues are formed and expressed in liturgy. By this he does not mean an instrumentalist understanding of worship, where liturgy is viewed as a means to moral exhortation or motivation. Rather, good liturgy, as a rehearsal of narratives, is the imaginal framework of encounter with God in Christ and a continual reembedding of persons into the perspectives of God's actions toward us and the world. As such, it molds our vision and moral character.

Yale's Margaret Farley, in a thoughtful response to these studies, grants that Ramsey and Saliers have made important points.[9] But they do not "raise the most critical issues confronting us today in the worshipping life of the Church." Many Christians experience liturgy as deadening, impoverishing, and burdensome. Farley identifies three causes of this. First, liturgical structures too often incorporate the divisions of class, race, and sex that violate our deepest Christian convictions about the Church as *koinonia*. Second, there is a disparity between word and reality in worship. *Diakonia* (service) after the example of Jesus is shaped by the model of servant; yet the reality too often is a pattern of power and domination. Furthermore, there are drastically different views of what *diakonia* must mean in our contemporary world. Until these differences and tensions are resolved, they will continue to impact deleteriously on the worshiping community.

Finally, there is the contemporary experience of the death of symbols. Since these are utterly essential to liturgy, it is no wonder that liturgy fails to be for so many a meaningful rehearsal of divine realities.

William Everett notes that Ramsey and Saliers have focused on different aspects of the Word central to faithful life (Saliers on a greater personal openness to God's Word and character formation, Ramsey on the right orders set forth in Scripture).[10] But neither copes successfully with the realities of social pluralism. Social pluralism refers to the fact that any worshiping person is a member of associations, institutions, communities whose interests may compete with, complement, or ignore one another.

In Saliers' approach, Everett sees an accommodation to social pluralism that is, if I understand him correctly, excessively individualistic, even a kind of escapism. Ramsey is much readier, through his emphasis on right structures, to challenge easy social pluralism, but Everett finds the approach a form of emerging sectarianism (the distinction between holy community and profane society). He feels that the impetus toward right social order and right character has to be reworked in our time to lead to critical engagement of social and cultural pluralism.

Everett proposes the notion of "public" as the vehicle of this reworking. "The public is a pattern of ways for acting about important matters." Liturgy disposes us to become "public beings." "Not only do we rehearse the stories of past action, we project new scenarios to test the judgments of the public realm." The article is stimulating, but even after several readings, the notion of publicity remains obscure to me.

The volume of the *Journal of Religious Ethics* ends with a brief but thoughtful essay by Philip Rossi, S.J.[11] Rossi's thesis is that the character of our moral agency as Christians has its most fundamental formative ground in Christian public worship. This is so because it is in liturgy that we are exposed to the narratives that shape our lives. Rossi contrasts the contours of this shaping (God as the Lord of life) with those dominant in our culture (the agent as solitary, morally autonomous individual).

It seems that Rossi's presentation is what we might call the "ideal." That is, the character of our moral agency ought to be fundamentally formed by exposure to biblical narratives in liturgy. But whether that is actually achieved by contemporary liturgy is another question, as Farley has pointed out so clearly.

Since it is liturgy, especially through remembering and rehearsal of narrative accounts, that shapes our moral consciousness and character, it is important that the relation of the biblical narratives to moral life be accurately understood. Two recent studies have focused on this question.

Stanley Hauerwas examines the moral authority of Scripture.[12] He sees it ultimately as one about the kind of community the Church must be in order to make the narratives of Scripture central to its life. The Church's life depends on faithful remembering of God's care for creation through the vocation of Israel and Jesus. Scripture is the vehicle of that remembering. Its dominant mode is narrative. Thus the Bible is not a logical unit or finished whole; indeed, some of its prescriptions strike us as irrelevant, even perverse. Only within the narrative context can we place the explicitly moral sections of Scripture (exhortations, commandments).

Hauerwas argues that those who see Scripture as by and large irrelevant to ethics have mistakenly seen ethics as primarily a matter of decisions. It is not. It also concerns the character of individuals and of a community, "what kind of community we must be to be faithful to Yahweh and his purposes for us." Once we see this, we see that the narratives of Scripture are as important as the commandments.

James Childress believes that interpretations such as that of Hauerwas overemphasize some features of the moral life (vision and perspectives, images and metaphors, stories, loyalty and character) to the detriment of the role of Scripture in moral justification.[13] These interpretations highlight influence rather than reflection. Actually, Childress argues that aesthetic interpretations (images, metaphors, stories) aid us to recognize obligations, but justification of them comes through appeal to principles and rules. Childress concludes his brief essay by insisting that there is a variety of uses of

Scripture as revealed morality. "To reduce Scripture's moral requirements to any single category is to distort both morality and Scripture." Clearly, Childress feels that the restriction of Scripture to
formative narrative is such a reduction.[14]

The literature on liturgy and ethics is relatively young and
sparse, but it is extremely interesting. Here I want to raise one problem that was hinted at by Childress. It is clear that moral theology
has a great deal to do with character and community formation, and
that the biblical stories through liturgy play an essential role here. It
is also clear that moral theology has a great deal to do with moral
deliberation and justification. But what is the relationship of these
two? How do the biblical narratives as formative relate to justification in moral discourse? It is clear, of course, that good people will
generally make right decisions, as Aristotle noted. But that is not
sufficient as an answer, for moral theology seeks a more systematic
and reflexive understanding.

There are any number of possible answers to this question, no
one of which is adequate or exclusive of others. The problem I am
raising here is indicated in two distinctive emerging tendencies in recent literature. On the one hand, those who emphasize vision and
character (and the biblical narratives that impact on them) do not
often engage in moral justification with regard to concrete moral
problems. When they do, the moral "justification" (so it seems to
some observers) is either not a true justification or not an original
one (sc., it is knowable by other than biblical sources). Thus Childress has referred to this form of writing as an overemphasis.

On the other hand, those who are concerned with concrete moral problems and a disciplined analysis of their solution say little
about vision and character and the biblical-liturgical materials that
nourish and shape them. In other words, they act like moral philosophers. There is ample witness to this in the literature on bioethics, as
James Gustafson has repeatedly pointed out.[15] Unless these two
trends are brought together, what goes for moral theology will increasingly become either sectarian exhortation or unbiblical rationalism.

An interesting article by Stanley Hauerwas on abortion will illustrate the concern I am outlining.[16] Hauerwas argues that Christian
opposition to abortion has failed because we have accepted a "liber-

al" culture's presupposition that our convictions must be expressed in terms acceptable to a pluralist society. In doing so, we have not exhibited our deepest convictions, convictions which alone make the rejection of abortion intelligible. Specifically, Hauerwas argues that we have tried to present abortion independently of the kind of people we would like to become. Thus the arguments pro and con abortion are fragments torn from the context that gave them intelligibility.

Hauerwas sees the roots of this dilemma in the presupposition on which our liberal society is founded: how to prevent people from interfering with one another. The government is restricted to this and is expected to be neutral on the very subjects that matter most. Thus liberalism seeks an account of morality divorced from the kind of persons we are or want to be. That falsifies the way moral injunctions function. Taken together, moral injunctions describe a way of life.

As Christians, we have failed because we have tried to argue abstractly. We should rather have presented abortion as an affront to our basic convictions about what makes life meaningful, to our way of life. To do this, we must tell stories that show the correlation between the prohibition of abortion and the story of God and His people. "It is only when we have done this that we will have the basis for suggesting why the fetus should be regarded as but another of God's children."

More positively, Hauerwas urges that the Christian prohibition of abortion rests on our conviction that life is not ours to take. Life is God's creature, under the lordship of Jesus. Furthermore, for Christians, as people determined to live within history, children are seen as duty and gift. It is in displaying themes such as these that we will best serve our society on the abortion question.

Two things in this extremely interesting study could easily be overlooked and need explicit reference. First, Hauerwas notes that "the broad theological claims I am developing cannot determine concrete cases." This means that such themes cannot function as criteria for rightfulness or wrongfulness in individual instances. Second, of the desire for new life that is part of the Christian form of life, Hauerwas says: "Such a desire is obviously not peculiar to Christians." Of the love of those we did not choose, he says that "the existence of such a love of those we did not choose is not unique or limited to Christians." Moreover, he concludes that "Christians should certainly wish to encourage those 'natural' sentiments that would provide a basis for having and protecting children."

What have we here? We have (1) an attitude not specific or peculiar to Christians (2) which does not decide rightfulness or wrongfulness in individual cases.

I want to raise several points. First, here is an attitude which does not determine in individual cases the morally right or wrong. What, then, does it do? Must we not say that it nourishes sentiments or dispositions preparatory to individual decisions? That is broadly known as parenesis, at least in so far as it relates to individual decisions. Or, in Childress' language, it is a perspective which helps to *recognize* an obligation, but not to *justify* it or its violation.

Second, if it is not specific to Christians, then are not the Christian warrants for it confirmatory rather than originating? I have suggested elsewhere (on abortion) that "these evaluations can be and have been shared by others than Christians of course. But Christians have particular warrants for resisting any cultural callousing of them."[17] The point I am raising here is epistemological. It is not whether *de facto* and historically Christians have rejected abortion because of their story and the community they wanted to be. One can make a strong case for that, as Ramsey has. The question is rather whether this rejection of abortion is in principle unavailable to human insight and reasoning (sc., without the story or revelation).[18] If it is, then the only way to know that abortion (and many other things) is to be rejected is to be part of the story. That is inherently isolationist. Whatever it is, it is certainly not Catholic tradition or the story of the Catholic community. Its story is precisely that many of these moral demands are epistemologically separable from its story, though confirmed by it. "Particular warrants" of the Christian for rejecting abortion do not raise the issue of how one originally knows God's will within a storied community.

Third, if Christian convictions on abortion (and similar concrete moral questions) are indeed in principle available to human insight (sharable by others than Christians), is it not more productive in a pluralistic society to urge one's convictions in the public forum in terms of what is sharable in that forum?[19] That is what many popes and Catholic bishops throughout the world have done. Or negatively, are Christians not argued right out of the current controversy by presenting their convictions in terms of particular and often unsharable warrants? If we argue our conviction in terms of a unique community story, others need only assert that their story is not ours. The conversation stops at that point. Hauerwas is aware of this difficulty (indeed, he raises it), but, in my judgment, he does not adequately answer it.

Hauerwas has pursued these general themes in another stimulating study.[20] In speaking of the Christian commitment to peace, he states that it is not based on "the inherent value of life but on the conviction that the refusal to resort to war cannot be consistent with the Kingdom we have only begun to experience through the work of Christ and his continuing power in the church." He says much the same thing about slavery, sc., that we reject it not because it violates inherent human dignity but because "we have found that we cannot worship together at the table of the Lord if one claims an ownership over others that only God has the right to claim."

Two reflections. The first concerns the nature of moral argument. Appeals to "the type of people or community we want to be" (who acknowledge Jesus as Lord and Lord of life) are certainly true. They are also certainly not moral arguments in the sense of justifications for the moral rightness or wrongness of any individual action. To think that they are is to confuse Christian parenesis with justification.

Concretely, Hauerwas asserts that Christians reject slavery not because it violates human dignity but because "we have found that we cannot worship together at the table of the Lord if one claims an ownership over others. . . ." One might respond: if that is the *only* reason why Christians reject slavery, perhaps it clarifies why they did not do so for nineteen centuries. Discomfort at the Eucharistic meal helps to *recognize* wrongdoing, to use Childress' language. It is not the only or primary validation (justification) of it as wrong.

In another context Hauerwas notes: "When asked why we do or do not engage in a particular form of activity, we often find that it makes perfectly good sense to say 'Christians just do or do not do that kind of thing.' And we think that we have given a moral reason. But it is moral because it appeals to 'what we are,' to what kind of people we think we should be."[21] I am suggesting here that "moral reason," as Hauerwas uses the term, does not pertain to the genre of moral argument understood as justification.[22]

My second reflection follows immediately from the first. Hauerwas states that, e.g., Christians reject slavery not because it violates inherent human dignity but because we cannot worship together with those who engage in it. Here he contrasts and separates what ought not be separated. Christian warrants are continuous with and interpenetrate human warrants, at least in the Catholic tradition. In this sense Christian warrants are confirmatory. The Christian story does not replace the notion of "inherent human dignity"; it supports and deepens it.

What it seems (and I emphasize "seems") Hauerwas is actually doing is denying the relevance, perhaps even the existence, for the Christian, of what has been badly called for centuries the natural moral law. I suspect he does this because he conceives of it as a set of principles (and their warrants) developed through discursive reasoning. (He would be aided and abetted in this distortion by certain Catholic formulations such as that of the then [1940] Holy Office that "direct sterilization is against the law of nature.")

But this is not what the natural moral law in its earliest and most genuine sense means. It refers to *naturaliter nota,* those things known immediately and connaturally.[23] The existence of such knowledge is admitted, so many exegetes argue, in Romans, where the fault of nonbelievers is said to be precisely suppressing such knowledge. Elsewhere Schüller has argued that unless we know (moral consciousness) what faithfulness means, we will have no idea of what faithfulness to Christ could possibly mean and thereby commit the entire moral life to blind obedience, indeed to incoherence.[24] If Hauerwas exalts Christian warrants so much that he denies the existence of such knowledge (cf. his not because of "the inherent dignity of our humanity," "inherent value of life"), I believe it must be said that he has diminished the very Christian story to which he appeals; for part of that story is that basic moral knowledge and correlative justifications are not exclusive to this community. To overlook this is to annex the Christian story to a single reading of it.

There is a great deal in Hauerwas' recent writing that is powerful and compelling. For instance, he is right on target in attacking the assumptions of the modern liberal state which lead it to neutrality where our deepest values are concerned. However, overemphasis (in Childress' words) on those Christian perspectives that attack these assumptions can force on them a burden in moral discourse that they cannot always bear, and in doing so can lead to a sectarianism that could easily be counterproductive.[25]

Notes

1. For an interesting article calling attention to the one-sidedness of either of these contrasts, cf. Thomas R. Ulshafer, S.S., "Jacques Maritain as a 'Mixed Deontological Ethicist of Agency,' " *Modern Schoolman* 57 (1980) 199–211.

2. *Bible and Ethics in Christian Life* (Minneapolis: Augsburg, 1976).

3. Jeremy Miller, O.P., "Ethics within an Ecclesial Context," *Angelicum* 57 (1980) 32–44.

4. Enda McDonagh, "Liturgy: Expression or Source for Christian Ethics?" in Stanley Hauerwas, ed., *Remembering and Reforming: Toward a Constructive Christian Moral Theology* (Univ. of Notre Dame, forthcoming).

5. For a study on how this happens in terms of models of consciousness, cf. Donald E. Miller, "Worship and Moral Reflection: A Phenomenological Analysis," *Anglican Theological Review* 62 (1980) 307–20.

6. Emphasis added.

7. Paul Ramsey, "Liturgy and Ethics," *Journal of Religious Ethics* 7 (1979) 139–71; D. E. Saliers, "Liturgy and Ethics: Some New Beginnings," ibid. 173–89.

8. Ramsey, "Liturgy and Ethics" 162.

9. Margaret A. Farley, "Beyond the Formal Principle: A Reply to Ramsey and Saliers," *Journal of Religious Ethics* 7 (1979) 191–202.

10. William Everett, "Liturgy and Ethics: A Response to Saliers and Ramsey," ibid. 203 f.

11. Philip J. Rossi, S.J., "Narrative, Worship and Ethics: Empowering Images for the Shape of Christian Moral Life," ibid. 239–248.

12. Stanley Hauerwas, "The Moral Authority of Scripture: The Politics and Ethics of Remembering," forthcoming as in n. 43 above.

13. James Childress, "Scripture and Christian Ethics," *Interpretation* 34 (1980) 371–80.

14. The rest of the issue of *JRE* contains interesting articles on concrete aspects of biblical ethics by Gene Outka, John Howard Yoder, David Little, and Charles M. Swezey.

15. Most recently in "A Theocentric Interpretation of Life," *Christian Century* 97 (1980) 754–60.

16. Stanley Hauerwas, "Abortion: Why the Arguments Fail," *Hospital Progress* 61, no. 1 (1980) 38–49.

17. Richard A. McCormick, S.J., "Abortion: A Changing Morality and Policy?" *Catholic Mind* 77, no. 1336 (Oct. 1979) 42–59, at 51.

18. This point has been made recently by P. Gaudette, "Jesus et la decision des chrétiens," *Science et esprit* 32 (1980) 153–59, at 158.

19. In contrast to Hauerwas, Walter Kern, S.J., states that Catholic social teaching can make an important contribution to the discussion of fundamental values. However, this is only possible if "it argues on a broadly human basis, that is, not a specifically Christian one" ("Zur Grundwertediskussion," *Stimmen der Zeit* 198 [1980] 579–84, at 580). This does not mean abandoning specifically Christian convictions (e.g., on the indissolubility of marriage). It is simply a recommendation about how one discusses these in the public arena. Christian convictions ought to be presented in the public forum; but this does not mean that they have to be, or should be, presented as Christian.

20. Stanley Hauerwas, "The Church in a Divided World: The Interpretative Power of the Christian Story," *Journal of Religious Ethics* 8 (1980) 55–82.

21. Hauerwas, "Abortion" 42.

22. Hauerwas writes: "Our theological convictions and corresponding community *are* a social ethic, for they provide the necessary context for us to understand the world in which we live. The church serves the world first by providing categories of interpretation that offer the means for us to understand ourselves truthfully . . ." ("The Church in a Divided World" 75). We all would agree to that. "Contexts" and "categories of interpretation" are not in themselves, however, adequate justifications of rightfulness and wrongfulness of individual actions, necessary as they truly are. In this sense they are not a social ethic if by that term we mean to exhaust all that is requisite to moral justification. To think that such "moral reasons" are moral justifications is to ask them to bear a burden they cannot bear. It is not a moral justification to say "Christians do not do these things." It is simply an assertion that reminds one to go back to his/her tradition and find out why. When pressed, I believe Hauerwas would admit this; for he refers to "theological convictions that *shape* our reasoning." They do not replace it. This point is made well by Martin Honecker, "Vernunft, Gewissen, Glaube,"

Zeitschrift für Theologie und Kirche 77 (1980) 325–44. Honecker refers to theological contributions as those which "broaden our horizons and open our insights" (344). In a statement (Oct. 22) explaining his now famous "lust" statement, John Paul II referred to Christ's words as "the basis for a new Christian ethos which is marked by a transformation of people's attitudes." An "ethos" and "transformation of attitudes" are necessary but not sufficient conditions for moral discourse.

23. Cf. the recently republished essay of Jacques Maritain, "De la connaissance par connaturalité," *Nova et vetera* 55 (1980) 181–87, esp. 185–86. Also interesting in this regard is V. Ferrari, O.P., "Il primo principio morale," *Angelicum* 57 (1980) 45–53.

24. Bruno Schüller, S.J., "Wieweit kann die Moraltheologie das Naturrecht entbehren?" *Lebendiges Zeugnis,* March 1965, 41–65.

25. Some of the points raised here have been urged from a different perspective by J. Wesley Robbins, "Narrative, Morality and Religion," *Journal of Religious Ethics* 8 (1980) 161–76.

The Biblical Hermeneutics of Juan Luis Segundo

Alfred T. Hennelly

This article originally appeared in *Theologies in Conflict: The Challenge of Juan Luis Segundo,* 1979.

An intense debate on method has erupted in the past decade, encompassing both the northern and southern hemispheres of the world. Recent works by such authors as Bernard Lonergan, David Tracy, and Gregory Baum have had considerable influence in the North Atlantic nations.[1]

Like his colleagues, Segundo considers the question of method to be of the utmost importance, stressing that "the one thing that can maintain the liberating character of a theology is not its content but its method" and that "in this lies the best hope of theology for the future."[2] Consequently, the key issue of methodology will be discussed in this chapter. Some articles of Segundo will first be considered, followed by the fullest elaboration of his method in *The Liberation of Theology.*

I
A DYNAMIC LEARNING PROCESS

An illuminating example of Segundo's approach may be found in an early article on the Second Vatican Council entitled "Toward a Dynamic Exegesis."[3] There he expresses the view that the most important difference between "conciliar" and "postconciliar" theologians lies in the fact that the former employ a "static exegesis that only examines the solutions presented by the Council" while the latter operate with "a dynamic exegesis that examines the directions pointed to by the Council."[4] For it is clear to him that Vatican II, which combines clearly divergent theological conceptions, posed quite a number of problems that it left unresolved and that must continue to be confronted by the whole church.

In the article Segundo employs a dynamic exegesis with regard to the texts of *Gaudium et Spes* concerning two basic questions. The first of these asks whether the church is to be considered a perfect society, complete in itself, or rather whether an "interdependence of dialogue" defines its essential relationship to the world.[5] A second area of interrogation is concerned with the relation of human history and of human progress toward the arrival of the kingdom of God, a question that evoked different responses in different parts of *Gaudium et Spes.*[6] Our concern here lies in his emphasis that the approach to Christian sources must be a dynamic and not a static one.

Another article, published at approximately the same time, shows that this applies not only to conciliar documents but also and more importantly to the normative texts of Christianity, that is, to the Bible itself.[7] In the article Segundo offers an ecumenical critique of a work written by a group of Protestant authors. His major objection is to its approach to Scripture and specifically to a schematizing tendency in this regard. It is defined as "a tendency to compare, in a very simple and direct way, events of the world of today with ideas or images taken from the Bible."[8] The obvious difficulty with this is that thousands of years of enormous changes and ever-increasing complexity have elapsed since biblical times and that the schematic approach does not take this into account. One of the examples adduced is the contribution of José Míguez Bonino, which correlates in detail the similarities existing between the Judaizers in St. Paul's time and inhabitants of the western Christian world of today. Such an approach, Segundo believes, is incapable of illuminating new situations" in a world radically different from the biblical one."[9]

A more recent article returns to the same problem in connection with a Catholic book on the Bible, which was written in close collaboration with Paraguayan peasants.[10] Segundo's objection to this book is based on his fundamental hermeneutical principle that the Bible must be understood as a process of education; in the book, however, "the Bible loses its true nature as a process in order to become a message."[11] The literalism of the book's applications, he feels, leads inevitably to a conservative, and not to a creative or liberating, theology, again because the applications "represent a teaching, and not a learning how to learn."[12] The author notes that in this article he is merely pointing out the major features of the problem; for the promised nuances and refinements we must turn to *The Liberation of Theology*.

II
THE HERMENEUTIC CIRCLE

This book comprises a revised version of a series of lectures delivered by Segundo while he was a visiting professor at Harvard Divinity School in 1974. In it he is forthright in stating categorically the critical differences that distinguish a liberating theology from what he calls "academic" or "classical" theology, that is, theology as it is practiced in the centers of learning of the western world. Before considering those differences, it is essential to grasp his fundamental methodology, which is referred to as "the hermeneutic circle."[13]

The same term has been applied in the past to the exegetical approach of Rudolf Bultmann, but Segundo believes that his method corresponds better to the strict sense of the circle. On its most fundamental level, the method involves "the continuous change in our interpretation of the Bible, in function of the continuous changes in our present reality, both individual and social."[14] In order for present reality to change, one must be to some extent dissatisfied with it, and thus raise questions concerning it that are "so rich, general, and basic that they oblige us to change our usual conceptions concerning life, death, knowledge, society, politics, and the world in general."[15] And once these new and more profound questions are posed to the scriptural texts, it is essential that our interpretation of the texts change also, for otherwise the new questions would either receive no answer or answers that are conservative and useless.

This preliminary description of the method is further clarified by the delineation of four steps that are essential to its proper exercise:

First, our manner of experiencing reality, which leads to ideological suspicion; *second,* the application of ideological suspicion to the whole ideological superstructure in general and to theology in particular; *third,* a new manner of experiencing theological reality, which leads us to exegetical suspicion, that is, to the suspicion that current biblical interpretation does not take into account important data; and *fourth,* our new hermeneutic, that is, the new way of interpreting the source of our faith, which is Scripture, with the new elements at our disposal.[16]

The concept of "suspicion" used here is derived from Paul Ricoeur; it is based on Segundo's hypothesis that ideologies connected with current social conditions are unconsciously ruling our present theological ideas and pastoral practice.

It is also important to note that the first stage of the circle always involves the experience of a definite problem, and an act of will or commitment on the part of the knower to find a solution to the problem. Segundo concludes from this that "a hermeneutic circle always supposes a profound human commitment, that is, a consciously accepted partiality, based certainly not on theological criteria but on human ones."[17]

At this point, it is obvious that the hermeneutic circle is in need of considerable clarification, so that its procedures may be understood more precisely. To accomplish this, Segundo considers in some detail the works of four writers—Harvey Cox, Karl Marx, Max Weber, and James Cone; his objective is to determine whether they have succeeded in completing the four steps of the circle and, if not, to point out precisely at what point they have failed. In discussing these authors, I will merely select some key areas that appear to shed light on the understanding of the hermeneutic circle.

III
THE CIRCLE IN PRACTICE

The first example considered is the well-known best-seller of Harvey Cox, *The Secular City.*[18] In this work Cox is describing his own experience of the new realities of secularization and urbanization as well as the new approach to solving problems on a purely *pragmatic* level that these phenomena entail. He explicity rejects the approach of Paul Tillich, who held that every person asks *ultimate* existential questions, and that Christian revelation provides an answer to these. Rather Cox appears to commit himself to the new pragmatic approach.

This brings us to the third step in the hermeneutic circle, where it would be logical to address new questions to Scripture from the perspective of pragmatic humanity. However, although such an interrogation could be fruitful in the opinion of Segundo, Cox does not take this approach. Rather his direction can be perceived in his analysis of The Girl or Miss America: "The Protestant objection to the cult of The Girl must be based on the realization that The Girl is an idol. . . . The values she represents as ultimate satisfactions—mechanical comfort, sexual success, unencumbered leisure—have no *ultimacy.*"[19]

It is patent from this argument that Cox's method, when all is said and done, is identical with Tillich's. At the same time, although apparently his failure is at the third point in the circle, deeper reflection shows that he did not even complete the first stage; that is, he never *really* accepted or committed himself to pragmatic humanity's values right from the outset. Since the partiality mentioned earlier is lacking, therefore, Cox has interrupted the hermeneutic circle at its very first point.

The second author treated, Karl Marx, can certainly not be faulted for such a lack of partiality, since his efforts were clearly directed over many years to a struggle with and on behalf of the proletariat. And in an attempt to explain why the masses of the proletariat did not achieve victory in the struggle, Marx advanced to the second point of the circle by elaborating his ideology of historical materialism. Segundo summarizes the essence of this theory in one sentence taken from *The Communist Manifesto:* "The ruling ideas of each age have always been the ideas of the ruling class."[20]

A key factor in any revolutionary process, moreover, must be the recognition of such an ideological superstructure by the revolutionary classes and its transformation on behalf of the revolution. But Marx did not apply ideological suspicion to the whole superstructure, not only because his social analysis was weak and superficial when applied to industrial societies but even more because he totally rejected any possible liberating function for religion. Thus Marx presents an example of failure at the second point of the hermeneutic circle.

The classic of Max Weber, *The Protestant Ethic and the Spirit of Capitalism,*[21] is next introduced as an example of failure to attain the third stage in the circle, that is, the suspicion of current biblical interpretation. Weber describes himself as an amateur theologian, but Segundo believes he was a brilliant one: "Amateur theologian that he was, Weber expounds dogmas correctly and interrelates them intelligently; moreover, he had an excellent grasp of the differences between the thought of Calvin and that of the two principal theologies of his time, the Lutheran and the Catholic."[22]

Although Weber has been termed the "Anti-Marx," Segundo believes that he actually complements and carries forward the work of Marx, for he attempts to uncover the religious ideologies of Calvinism that corresponded to the mode of production in the early stages of capitalism. As Weber himself expressed it, "We only wish to ascertain whether and to what extent religious forces have taken part in the qualitative formation and quantitative expansion of that spirit in the world."[23] An important contribution that he made, according to Segundo, was his utilization of psychology to ascertain the correspondence between certain religious values and their economic counterparts.

Although he moved a step beyond Marx, then, it must finally be acknowledged that Weber terminated the hermeneutic circle at its third point. For if one asks whether as a result of his work he saw the need for a new and more profound evaluation of Calvinism or whether he was motivated to undertake a more probing reinterpretation of Scripture, the answer is obviously no. To use Weber's own words, "we are concerned, not with *evaluation,* but with the historical significance of the dogma."[24] Occasional exceptions to his detached stance occur, as when he notes that in Calvin's doctrine "the Father in heaven of the New Testament, so human and understanding, who rejoices over the repentance of a sinner as a woman does over the lost piece of silver she has found, *has disappeared.* His place has been taken by a transcendental being beyond the limits of human understand-

ing."[25] However, in general, the desire for scientific objectivity
constitutes an insuperable obstacle to a further development of the
circle at its third point.

The last book considered, James Cone's *A Black Theology of
Liberation,*[26] is adjudged to be the only one that successfully com-
pletes all four stages of the hermeneutic circle, although Segundo admits that its language is at times shocking and demagogic. In the first
stage there can be no doubt that Cone is partial, that is, totally committed to the black community and its struggle for freedom. An important observation in this respect by Segundo is that "every
hermeneutic involves conscious or unconscious partisanship. It
adopts a partisan position even when it claims and believes that it is
neutral."[27]

When he reaches the second point of the circle, Cone manages
to achieve a high level of suspicion with regard to the whole American superstructure, including the dominant theology. This appears
clearly in his charge concerning American white theology:

> It has been basically a theology of the white oppressor,
> *sanctioning through religion* the genocide of Indians and the
> slavery of black people. From the very beginning to the
> present, white theological thought in the United States has
> been "patriotic," either by defining the theological task *in-
> dependently of black suffering* (the liberal northern ap-
> proach) or by defining Christianity as compatible with
> racism (the conservative southern approach). In both cases,
> *theology has become a servant of the state,* which has only
> meant death to black people.[28]

The central ideological weapon that Cone uncovers is white theology's pretense of "colorblindness," a ploy which manages to disguise
the basic cause of oppression.

Cone moves to the third point of the circle, the suspicion of theology, by noting that, when the question of black liberation is
broached to white theologians, they invariably, "quibble on this issue
and move from one point to another, always pointing to the dangers
of *extremism on both sides.* In reality, they cannot make a decision,
because others have really made it for them."[29] After noting that

"the sources and norm [of theology] are presuppositions that determine *which questions are to be asked,* as well as what answers are given," Cone goes on to emphasize that "the manner of working of black theologians has to be such as to destroy the corruptive influence of white thought by building theology on the sources and norm that are *appropriate to the black community.*"[30] In summary, he believes that black theology must be founded on a double norm, "the liberation of black people and the revelation of Jesus Christ."

Finally, Cone arrives at the last point of the circle, that is, a new interpretation of Scripture based on the richer and more profound questions that have been raised. His hermeneutic is summarized as follows:

> If we read the New Testament correctly, the resurrection of Jesus means that the Lord is also present today in the midst of societies, bringing about his liberation of the oppressed. He is not confined to the first century, and thus our talk of him in the past assumes importance only insofar as it leads us to an *encounter* with him today. As a black theologian, I want to know what God's revelation means here and now as the black community participates in the struggle for liberation.[31]

Segundo believes that Cone's interpretation is in accord with the biblical documents, where it is clear that there are divergences in God's message according to the different historical circumstances of his people. He also agrees with Cone in his departure from a false and alienating universalism and in his assertion that orthopraxis is more important than orthodoxy, that is, "the truth is only truth when it is the basis for truly human attitudes."[32]

Segundo voices some disagreements with Cone in the last point of the circle, for example, on the reasons why the biblical possibility of a vocation for redemptive suffering is excluded for black people. But these are incidental; his fundamental assertion is that Cone's book provides an excellent example of the methodology of the hermeneutic circle.

The author is also aware that his painstaking analysis of the circle may at times have appeared tedious and abstract. Thus he goes on to present several examples of the method that are more practical in import and that have perhaps already been utilized by the average intelligent Christian on his or her own initiative. Segundo observes that the "common sense" of such people should not be deprecated, for it can often make a significant contribution to necessary ideological criticism within the church.

IV
CONTEMPORARY USE OF THE CIRCLE

The first example is related to sacramental practice. From the entire preceding discussion, it should have become obvious that "a liberating theology is of necessity a historical theology, based on questions that arise from the present," and that "only a Christian community with a keen historical sensibility can provide the basis for such a liberating theology."[34] However, the sacraments, and especially the Eucharist, stress exactly the opposite approach, and their emphasis on the same cycle of feasts, the same actions and texts, etc., fosters an ahistorical atmosphere. Considering that the main contact of most Catholics with their religion is through the Mass, the fact is that it "constitutes the polar opposite of a religion based on historical sensibility. With the exception of minor details, the Sunday Mass remains the same before and after a general disaster, an international crisis, or a profound revolution."[35]

Continuing his hermeneutic circle, the author is led to ideological suspicion of the emphases that are dominant in contemporary sacramental theology. The suspicion is expressed with characteristic bluntness: "Is it by chance that this conception and practice of the sacraments is perfectly adapted to the interests of the dominant classes and is one of the most powerful ideological factors in maintaining the status quo?"[36] This leads to the fourth point of the circle, that is, a new hermeneutic of the Christian sources, especially passages such as Hebrews 10:9–14. And the conclusion derived from the reinterpretation is that "religious efficacy is ruled out for any and every ritual, cult, or assembly, to the extent that such a ceremony supposes that the grace of God was not given once and for all, but that it must be won over and over again by means of religious rites."[37]

Yet another example of the application of the circle has to do with the question of *unity* within the church. The preservation of unity is often viewed as a supreme value which must take precedence over any historical divisions that may actually exist among the members on basic issues. By thus making unity an absolute, however, the church is forced into the position of holding "that the issues of suffering, violence, hunger, and death are less critical than religious formulas or rites."[38] Moreover, the unity achieved takes place only on the level of language; for, if "one person conceives of a God who permits dehumanization, while another rejects such a God and believes only in a God who struggles unceasingly against such things," then the obvious conclusion is that they do not really believe in the same God nor share the same faith.[39]

Once again, the circle leads back to Scripture and a fresh look at texts that are often used to bolster the emphasis on unity at any price (such as 2 Cor. 5:18ff. and Col. 1:20), since they are concerned with "reconciliation." And it soon becomes apparent that the eschatological reconciliation mentioned in these citations is meant to be brought about by the real liberation of human beings and not by any "pious blindness" to real oppression or to the real remedies of oppression. Consequently, it would seem essential to be able to distinguish those who are suffering oppression and those who are causing it; moreover, this seems to have been perfectly clear to the writers of the New Testament, for "when did Christ reconcile himself with the Pharisees, or when did Paul reconcile himself with the Judaizers?"[40] In short, the circle is concluded with the realization that true reconciliation and unity can be achieved only in and through a real struggle for justice.

A last example of the circle involves a return to the understanding of God mentioned in the previous one. But it is not so much a question of the *concept* of God that is involved, which is the manner in which classical theology might formulate the question, but rather: "*What kind of God* lies behind the attitudes in the first two examples?" Here Segundo advances his belief that the understanding of God that evolved in the Christian West moved the question to a level that was far too simplistic. For use of the word "God" as the one certain sacred name may have solved the question of polytheism on a linguistic level, but it should be obvious that "using the same name does not guarantee that one is talking about the same person, especially when the descriptions contain contradictory traits."[41]

This serious problem was taken up by Vatican II in a well-known text that suggested the responsibility of believers for the phenomenon of atheism: "To the extent that [believers] neglect their own training in the faith, or teach erroneous doctrine, or are deficient in their religious, moral, or social life, they must be said to conceal rather than reveal the authentic face of God and religion."[42] However, the logical conclusions of this statement have not always been drawn with the same rigor that Segundo employs in his analysis. For the deficient attitudes and practices mentioned in the text must be based on a false understanding of God, that is, to put it bluntly, faith in a nonexistent God; otherwise, how could it make sense for believers to hide something that they clearly possess?

Segundo also believes that it is far too simplistic to place the blame for the immutable, impassible, self-sufficient image of God that developed in the West on the influence of Greek philosophy on Christian thought. This, when all is said and done, has not achieved much impact on popular thinking, but remains the province of comparatively few specialists. Rather ideological suspicion leads him to conclude that more generalized social and historical factors fostered such a development. For humanity's perennial tendency is to project its own real or imagined victory onto God; but "in the societies in which we live, economic and social competition is a condition of survival and eventually of victory."[43] Since my personal victory will inevitably entail diminution or suffering for others, I must cultivate the qualities of impassibility and self-sufficiency, and it is precisely those attributes that tend to be projected onto God. Thus two very different gods arose, of which "one was the authentic God of revelation, the other was an inauthentic and nonexistent god, which gave rise to atheism and was conveniently attributed to the influence of Greek philosophy."

Once again Segundo stresses that the worship of a nonexistent god is pure and simple idolatry; moreover, idolatry can not be exorcised by formal statements of orthodoxy, since "one can recite all the creeds in the history of Christian theology and still believe in an idol."[44] He concludes the circle by a fresh hermeneutic of scriptural texts such as Matthew 16:1–4. Here and in other places in the New Testament, Jesus accuses the most monotheistic people in the world at that time of idolatry, for they insisted on signs from heaven while refusing to acknowledge God's real liberative actions taking place before their very eyes.

V

CHALLENGE TO CLASSICAL THEOLOGY

Clearly the application of the hermeneutic circle extends much further than the above examples. Its use can be traced throughout the other chapters of *The Liberation of Theology* and, indeed, is discernible in all of Segundo's published works. For the present it would seem helpful to attempt to synthesize the differences that Segundo sees between this method and the usual ones adopted by classical or academic theology. In his introduction to *The Liberation of Theology,* he observes that liberation theology has evoked a certain academic contempt in the world centers of theological scholarship. As a reaction to this, his book involves a conscious effort to move to the attack and to confront the reigning methodologies in the world centers of theology, challenging them to justify their own procedures. It should be stressed, however, that this is intended to open up a dialogue, for it is meant "not as a nationalistic or provincial challenge but one that is properly and constructively theological."[45]

The basic difference between the two methodologies, then, is stated bluntly at the outset. For academic theology readily acknowledges that, in order to understand the biblical texts, it must employ many sciences that shed light on *the past,* such as history, cultural anthropology, ancient languages, form criticism, and so forth. However, at this point a curious anomaly becomes apparent: this theology declares itself independent of those sciences that seek to interpret *the present,* adducing as a rationale its need to preserve the autonomy of theology. In this vein, a theologian as progressive as Edward Schillebeeckx is quoted to the effect that theology can never be ideological, to which Segundo replies: "He appears to believe naively that the word of God is applied to human realities in a laboratory immune to all the ideological tendencies and struggles of the present."[46] By contrast, a liberating theology is obliged continuously to juxtapose the disciplines that are concerned with the past *as well as* those that interpret the present in order to understand the word of God as a real message addressed to us *here and now.* Such a conception, he believes, would "free academic theology from its atavism and chilly ivory tower, and remove its very foundation: the belief that it is a simple, eternal, and impartial interpretation or authorized translation of the word of God."[47]

At the conclusion of his book, Segundo returns to the same point with great vigor. He charges that academic theology, when it evades the problems of the present, is merely taking the easy way out. On the other hand, liberation theology "does not allow the theologian to set aside lightly—as academic theology often does—the great problems of today of history, biology, evolution, social change, and many others, on the pretext that they belong to other fields and disciplines."[48]

Another key methodological difference that is stressed repeatedly through the book concerns the question of the *partiality* of the theologian. It has already been noted that such partiality is considered essential for the proper use of the hermeneutic circle, both in its first point—a commitment to change reality, and its third point—a commitment to change theology. The liberation theologian accepts this need for commitment explicitly and consciously. On the other hand, "academic theology can ignore its unconscious partiality, but the very fact that it poses as impartial is a sign of a conservative partiality in its very point of departure. . . . The most academic theology is intimately, though perhaps unconsciously, linked with the psychological, social, or political status quo."[49] Thus an adamant denial of the myth of theological neutrality must be considered a basic foundation stone in Segundo's or any other theology of liberation.

A very important corollary of this view is that partiality must also apply to the usually taboo area of politics, since "every theology is political, even one that does not speak or think in political terms." Again, what is sought is a conscious and explicit recognition of this unavoidable reality. Segundo's judgment on the refusal to do so is severe: "When academic theology accuses liberation theology of being political and of engaging in politics, thus pretending to ignore its own relation with the political status quo, what it is really looking for is a scapegoat for its own guilt complex."[50]

Also, the so-called political theology of Europe is considered to be fundamentally divergent from a liberation approach. For it makes the attempt to derive political options from theological sources and concepts, "whereas the theology of Jesus derives theology from openness of heart to the most pressing problems of human beings, going so far as to suggest that one cannot recognize Christ or eventually know God, except from the perspective of a commitment to the oppressed."[51] In Segundo's view the approach of seeking theological signs from heaven is clearly the method of Pharisaical theology, and yet it is so widespread that "it is difficult to find a theologian, even a highly intelligent one as Rahner undoubtedly is, who does not turn the real order of things and problems upside down."[52]

Notes

1. Bernard Lonergan, *Method in Theology* (New York: Herder and Herder, 1972); David Tracy, *Blessed Rage for Order: The New Pluralism in Theology* (New York: Seabury Press, 1975); and Gregory Baum, *Religion and Alienation: A Theological Reading of Sociology* (New York: Paulist Press, 1975).

2. Juan Luis Segundo, *Liberación de la teologia* (Buenos Aires: Carlos Lohlé, 1975), p. 192. All references and my translations are from the original Spanish edition. An English translation, which appeared after this chapter was written, is entitled *The Liberation of Theology* (Maryknoll, N.Y.: Orbis Books, 1976). Cf. Alfred T. Hennelly, "The Challenge of Juan Luis Segundo," *Theological Studies* (March 1977):125–35.

3. "Hacia una exegesis dinámica," *Vispera* (October 1967):77–84.

4. Ibid., p. 78.

5. Ibid., pp. 78–80.

6. Ibid., pp. 80–83.

7. "América hoy," *Vispera* (August 1967):53–57. The book referred to

is *América hoy: Acción de Dios y responsabilidad del hombre* (Montevideo: II Consulta Latinoamericana de Iglesia y Sociedad [ISAL], 1966).

8. Segundo, "América hoy," p. 56.

9. Ibid., pp. 56–57.

10. "Teologia: Mensaje y proceso," *Perspectivas de Diálogo* (December 1974):259–70. The book under consideration here is identified only as *Vivir como hermanos* and is by José Luis Caravias.

11. Segundo, "Teologia," p. 265.

12. Ibid., p. 269.

13. A very interesting parallel to Segundo's approach may be found in the article of Frederick Herzog, "Liberation Hermeneutic as Ideology Critique?" *Interpretation* (October 1974):387–403. Although Herzog is in dialogue with North American and European theologians in this work, many of his conclusions are strikingly similar to Segundo's.

14. Segundo, *Liberación*, p. 12. Cf. the remarks of Wolfhart Pannenberg: "The insight that it is no longer possible for a present-day interpreter naively to identify himself with the primitive Christian texts—unless by means of a self-deception—makes it possible for the first time to seek the continuity of the Christian tradition in the *way* in which, from its inception, ever *new* forms of its interpretation were released" (*Basic Questions in Theology*, vol. 1 [Philadelphia: Fortress Press, 1970], p. 145.)

15. Segundo, *Liberación*, p. 13. The concept of "ideological suspicion" is also emphasized by Jürgen Moltmann as, for example, when he observes that "political hermeneutics sets out to recognize the social and political influences on theological institutions and languages in order to bring their liberating content into the political dimension and to make them relevant towards really freeing men trapped in certain vicious circles" (*The Crucified God: The Cross of Christ as the Foundation and Critcism of Christian Theology* [New York: Harper and Row, 1974], p. 318).

16. Segundo, *Liberación*, pp. 13–14.

17. Ibid., p. 18. Philip J. Scharper has stressed this partiality in a general article on liberation theology, where he notes that "these theologians of liberation have attempted to read the Scriptures through the prisms of the poor. That, in itself, represents a radical departure in theologico-scriptural methods. We are perhaps unaware of the fact that most of the theologians—Protestant and Catholic—who have had such a heavy influence on American theologians and American theology have tended to be, almost by definition, members of the upper middle class, indeed forming something of a social and intellectual elite" ("The Theology of Liberation: Some Reflections," *Catholic Mind* [April 1976]:45).

18. Harvey Cox, *The Secular City: Secularization and Urbanization in Theological Perspective* (New York: Macmillan, 1965). The discussion of Cox covers pp. 14–18 of *Liberación.*

19. Segundo, *Liberación,* p. 16; Cox, *Secular City,* p. 197.

20. Segundo, *Liberación,* p. 20. The quotation of Marx is from "Manifiesto del Partido Comunista," in Marx-Engels, *Obras escogidas en dos tomos,* vol. 1 (Moscow: Progreso, 1971), p. 37. The treatment of Marx occupies pp. 19–25 of *Liberación.*

21. Max Weber, *The Protestant Ethic and the Spirit of Capitalism* (New York: Charles Scribner's Sons, 1958).

22. Segundo, *Liberación,* p. 28.

23. Ibid; Weber, *Protestant Ethic,* p. 91. On this text, Segundo observes that "at least in theory, it is difficult to find a more genuine expression of the thought of Marx with regard to ideological analysis in relation to historical materialism."

24. Segundo, *Liberación,* p. 31; Weber, *Protestant Ethic,* p. 101.

25. Segundo, *Liberación,* pp. 32–33; Weber, *Protestant Ethic,* p. 103. In an indirect way, Segundo himself does not hesitate to pass judgment on Weber, for he asks pointedly: "One might well wonder whether it is not even more inhuman to understand this network of implications without passing any judgment, than it was to have created it in the belief that it was in basic harmony with the sources of revelation" (*Liberación,* p. 32). His treatment of Weber covers pp. 26–34.

26. The references here will be to the Spanish translation of Cone's book, *Teología negra de la liberación* (Buenos Aires: Carlos Lohlé, 1973).

27. Segundo, *Liberación,* p. 34.

28. Ibid., pp. 37–38; Cone, *Teología negra,* p. 18.

29. Segundo, *Liberación,* p. 39; Cone, *Teología negra,* p. 87.

30. Segundo, *Liberación,* pp. 39–40; Cone, *Teología negra,* pp. 38–39.

31. Segundo, *Liberación,* pp. 42–43; Cone, *Teología negra,* p. 46. Segundo adds that this is an essential hermeneutical principle, for "the value of this orientation in achieving a richer interpretation of Scripture consists in the rediscovery of the pedagogical principle that guides the whole process of revelation: God himself appears to be different according to the different situations of his people." Segundo devotes pp. 34–45 to the analysis of Cone's book.

32. Segundo, *Liberación,* p. 44. He adds that " 'doing the truth' is the revealed formula for this priority of orthopraxis over orthodoxy when it is a question of truth and of salvation."

33. The following examples were first presented in the paper, "Las élites latinoamericanas: Problemática humana y cristiana ante el cambio so-

cial," in *Fe cristiana y cambio social en América Latina: Encuentro de El Escorial,* 1972 (Salamanca: Sígueme, 1973), pp. 203–12.

34. Segundo, *Liberación,* p. 48.

35. Ibid., p. 49.

36. Ibid., pp. 49–50. Another articulation of this question, which is central to all areas of Segundo's theology, follows immediately afterwards: "Would it be too offensive to acknowledge that sacramental *theology* has been more influenced by unconscious social pressures than by the gospel itself?"

37. Ibid., p. 50.

38. Ibid, p. 51.

39. Ibid. His conclusion is that "therefore a common faith does not exist in the church: the only thing shared in common is the formula used to declare the faith. And, since the formula doesn't identify anything, are we not justified in speaking of a formula that is *empty* vis-à-vis the decisive options of history?"

40. Ibid., p. 53.

41. Ibid., pp. 53–54. Segundo believes that Karl Barth would have agreed with him on this crucial theological issue; however, he goes on to note that "Barth was always more sensitive to the danger of ideology stemming from philosophy than to the danger of ideologies that are intimately bound up with sociopolitical struggle."

42. *Gaudium et Spes,* no. 19, in Joseph Gremillion. *The Gospel of Peace and Justice: Catholic Social Teaching Since Pope John* (Maryknoll, N.Y.: Orbis Books, 1976), p. 258.

43. Segundo, *Liberación,* p. 56. A related development is discussed with great acumen by William Coates in *God in Public: Political Theology Beyond Niebuhr* (Grand Rapids, Mich.: Wm. B. Eerdmans Publishing Company, 1974). A good summary of his thought is the following: "Freudianism and existentialism are essentially individualistic and subjective creeds which exalt the person or the self over history, without at the same time offering a challenge to the shape of history. Both movements are now in a state of exhaustion precisely because they built on the weakest aspect of bourgeois ideology: the self in its ahistorical capacities. When, therefore, a large number of Christian thinkers linked up with these two schools of thought in the hope of providing a contemporary vehicle of interpretation for the Gospel, they succeeded only in arriving at the same dead-end at the same time" (p. 110).

44. Segundo, *Liberación,* p. 56. A further discussion on this important question of the image of God will be initiated in chapter eight in connection with Christian spirituality. More recently, Segundo has again utilized the circle to uncover the ideology behind the campaign for "human rights" con-

320 / Alfred T. Hennelly

ducted by the United States government. As a result of systematic economic oppression, he insists, "the tragedy of the situation is that those who shape and control the defense of human rights are (despite undeniable good will in individual cases) the very same ones who make such rights impossible on three quarters of the planet" ("Derechos humanos, evangelización e ideología," *Christus* [November 1978]:34).

45. Ibid., pp. 9–10.

46. Ibid., pp. 11–12. Dorothee Soelle has pointed out a similar focus on the past with regard to the theological method of form criticism: "In actual practice the sociological aspects of the method are almost always confined to antiquity—to the first-century church—and are rarely applied to the modern situation" (*Political Theology* [Philadelphia: Fortress Press, 1974], p. xiii).

47. Segundo, *Liberación*, p. 25.

48. Ibid., p. 266.

49. Ibid., p. 18. In his *Theory and Practice* (Boston: Beacon Press, 1973), Jürgen Habermas insists that "no theory and no enlightenment can relieve us of the risks of taking a partisan position and of the unintended consequences involved in this" (p. 36). He also explains the task of critical sociology as asking "what lies behind the consensus, presented as a fact, that supports the dominant tradition of the time, and does so with a view to the relations of power surreptitiously incorporated in the symbolic structures of the systems of speech and action" (pp. 11–12).

50. Segundo, *Liberación*, p. 88.

51. Ibid., p. 95.

52. Ibid., p. 90. Segundo has also stressed the importance of the hermeneutic circle for all theological education in "Perspectivas para una teología latinoamericana," *Perspectiva Teológica* 9 (January–June 1977):9–25.

A Critical Appraisal
of Segundo's Biblical Hermeneutics

Anthony J. Tambasco

This article originally appeared in Tambasco's book, *Juan Luis Segundo and First World Ethics: The Bible for Ethics,* 1981.

When one begins a critique of a liberation theologian, one already feels on the defensive. This study is in the academic realm. It seeks to establish principles rather than practice. It is done in the context of first world theology, by an author who lives in the context of the capitalist economic system. Let me begin, therefore, by stating that the study was undertaken because of the merits which I perceived Segundo to have, even for first world theology and ethics. His thinking is sophisticated and cannot be described as simplistic or myopic. It bears out the warning that Robert McAfee Brown gives against oversimplified or pseudo-issue critiques of liberation theology.[1]

At the same time, the method of this theology is newly elaborated and can only grow in sophistication through dialogue and critique. As much as is possible in this chapter I will try to take the position of the liberation theology of Segundo and will try to identify in some way with the perspective of commitment to the poor in Latin America. By the same token, I assume that concern for the poor does not necessitate my accepting all the methods and conclusions of Segundo. It is only by dialogue and critique that his own theology avoids becoming an inbred, sterile and factious reflection. It is that same dialogue and critique that will make Segundo speak even more clearly to the first world as well as to the third.

It must be noted, at the same time, that our study is not concerned with an overall view of Segundo or of liberation theology.[2] It seeks to penetrate his specific methodology for biblical hermeneutics and its relationship to Christian ethics.

I
Marxist Social Analysis and Revelation

We have stated that our evaluation does not embrace all of Segundo's liberation theology. In that case it will not be a detailed study of the content of Marxism. However, our critique will begin with some observations on the use of Marxist social analysis and the adequacy of social analysis in general as the starting point for biblical hermeneutics.

Time and again in our presentation of Segundo we have come against the same basic question regarding his methodology. If social analysis is always the starting point, then where is the revelation? Does not the use of sociology in Segundo's fashion dictate that revelation is a human determination rather than a divine initiative? Our answer is that this is not necessarily so, although Segundo may be guilty of excess in his use of sociology in such an *exclusive* way.

Segundo seems to be building on the theory of revelation propounded by theologians such as Karl Rahner and others who claim that God reveals only through the human and that good theology is ultimately good anthropology. Rahner writes:

> As soon as man is understood as the being who is absolutely transcendent in respect to God, 'anthropocentricity' and 'theocentricity' in theology are not opposites but strictly one and the same thing, seen from two sides. Neither of the two aspects can be comprehended at all without the other. Thus, although anthropocentricity in theology is not the opposite of the strictest theocentricity, it *is* opposed to the idea that in theology man is one particular theme among others.[3]

As Rahner unfolds his explanation of this principle, he links the objective knowledge of God to the subjective possibilities and limits of the knowing human person. "Whenever one is confronted with an object of dogma, one inquires as to the conditions necessary for it to be known by the theological subject, ascertaining that the *a priori* conditions for knowledge of the object are satisfied, and showing that they imply and express something about the object, the mode, method, and limits of knowing it."[4] According to Rahner, it is not a question of humanity dictating the revelation, but it is a question of God revealing himself in and only through human existence. Moreover, if this reality is not to leave humanity on the level of an abstract, unhistorical transcendent being, then the same process must unfold in history as humanity struggles to bring its *a priori,* prereflexive knowledge to the status of *a posteriori,* reflexive knowledge in history.

What Rahner expresses in rather complicated philosophical language Segundo describes in simpler terminology: "The passages [of the New Testament] which allow theologians to discourse on what God is *in himself,* independent of our life and history, can be counted on one's fingers; and it is even doubtful whether they can be separated from a context wherein God consistently reveals himself in dialogue with human existence."[5] The particular merit of Segundo is to make explicit that socio-economic and political influences affect how humanity sees itself and, therefore, how it conceives the revelation of God. "Thus it does not take too much imagination to realize that the infinite, inaccessible God-as-nature, the creator of an order prior or indifferent to the existence of each individual, is at the same time the projection and justification of our desire and our effort to rigidly structure other people within our societal life."[6]

What Segundo says about starting his hermeneutic circle from social analysis, then, may not necessarily remove divine initiative from revelation. Nevertheless, once we move from the level of *a priori,* pre-reflexive knowledge to that of *a posteriori* and self-conscious knowledge of God there is the need for criteria to safeguard that the insights derived are truly objective and not just projections of human subjective needs. Segundo himself demonstrates the concern for objective truth: "We cannot go along with the idea [of Marx and Freud] that reason is totally dominated by practical interests. Nor can we agree that the idea of God is merely the projection of some more or less hidden intention of the individual or society. But their suspicion helps us to realize that while the idea of God can be liberative, it may also be the source of much hypocrisy."[7]

We are back again to our question of objectivity. While Segundo does say often enough that he seeks objectivity in the Bible, he does not seem to ever center in on the exact criteria for theological, exegetical or ethical truth. It remains a shortcoming of his hermeneutic circle. Nevertheless, he does make some cryptic statements that we can enlarge on, and which may perhaps give us some criteria for objectivity. At the same time, they will require that we qualify the hermeneutic circle.

Early in his presentation of the hermeneutic circle Segundo writes: "A hermeneutic circle in theology always presupposes a profound human commitment, a *partiality* that is consciously accepted—not on the basis of theological criteria, of course, but *on the basis of human* criteria."[8] He never spells out what these human criteria are, but we can attempt that in our critique. The human criteria are the totality of other ideologies[p] which give insight into human existence, which provide context and balance to socio-political analysis, and which relativize it and prevent its becoming an ideology.*

To phrase this in more classical theological terms, revelation comes through the human historical situation. We cannot escape this reality in searching for objectivity, but we can use it to approach objectivity. Every human situation, because it is historically conditioned must be relative and, therefore, in danger of becoming subjectively distorted as the full vehicle of divine revelation. What prevents this distortion is the balance of other historically conditioned insights. We can never attain absolute objectivity, but we can approach it with greater assurance by the totality of human experience as vehicle of revelation.

Use of this criterion requires more than anything else an evaluation of the ideology[p] to see if it genuinely describes human reality and is thus a fitting vehicle for revelation. It also demands that we place a particular ideology[p] into the context of other ideologies[p] in

---

*Ideology[n] is ideology in the negative sense meaning the total view of life supporting the dominant group in society. Ideology[p] is ideology in the positive sense meaning the system of goals and means that serves as the necessary backdrop for any human option or line of action.

order to see it in proper perspective and to come closer to the authentic revelation. We will do this with Segundo's own ideological perspectives, especially with his Marxist social analysis. There seem to be some weaknesses in his approach that can be pointed out by a testing of the ideology.

Another criterion that we may find helpful is built on what Segundo has said previously about Christ as part of a learning process. It may be that application of the text of Scripture is a second-step procedure based on deutero-learning, but Christ still performs some normative function as part of proto-learning. One is not free to bypass the first steps or to construct an ideology^p just out of human experience. Previous human experience—albeit couched in an inevitable ideology^p—has already captured an insight into divine revelation which must be normative in some way for future generations.

What we are saying ultimately is that if Christ is to function in any fashion as norm, as part of proto-learning, then there must be a true dialectic between text of Scripture and human experience or ideology^p. Christ does not negate human experience, but he does relativize any particular human experience. The danger with identifying theology with anthropology is that one can shift too easily to the side of immanence in revelation and lose the transcendence. The genuine Christian path is a delicate balance and a dialectic between immanence and transcendence.

> If and as long as these historical mediations are really mediations of the presence and acceptance of the mystery of God, and while retaining their relative nature yet prove themselves even in this way as unavoidable for the historical being of man in this aeon before the direct vision of God is reached, history and transcendence will never be subject in Christianity to an ideology of immanence, i.e., to the idolisation of intramundane powers, or to an ideology of transmanence and transcendence, i.e., to the idolisation in empty, formal abstractions of man's transcendentality by grace.[9]

Segundo himself has said that faith relativizes every ideology^p, but one wonders if in practice he acknowledges this. If one begins always with social analysis and ideology[p], then one does not have a dialectic. In almost all that we have exposed of Segundo's circle we have reiterated over and over that social analysis is the foundation, the beginning, the challenge and the precondition to exegesis and theology. It may be a good thing overstated, for theology and the Bible must also be the foundation, the beginning, the challenge of social analysis from a Christian perspective. There must be a dialectic. Segundo seems not to accept this.

On the other hand, it is quite conceivable that Segundo recognizes the dialectic and is simply presenting one side of the picture because of his commitment to the poor. After all, it is not simply an academic question. He says explicitly in one place, "We have seen that the notion of God stemming from revelation and our interpersonal relations in societal life condition each other mutually."[10] He explicitly states that the divine revelation must be something which transcends the human and would, then, seemingly be in dialectic with the human: "If there is no divine intervention in history, not only is the biblical account mythological, but the interpretation of it is merely human."[11] My guess, therefore, is that Segundo himself, if pressed, would admit that the hermeneutic circle is a valid methodology for partial insight into the biblical text, so long as a dialectic can be maintained whereby Scripture challenges the preceding stages and relativizes the insights of social analysis and ideology[p].

With this background on the nature of revelation, its dialectic with social analysis, and the criteria for determining its objectivity, we can undertake more specific critique of Segundo's hermeneutic circle. Granted the validity of using social analysis as a vehicle of revelation, our first question is over the adequacy of Marxist social analysis as this vehicle. Of course, as we mentioned previously, our question is not concerned with an evaluation of Marxism as such, but rather with Marxism as interpreted by Segundo.

To begin with, Segundo does bring to Roman Catholic theology a less fearful approach to Marxism, an approach which allows the possibility of dialogue. Vatican II gave some initiative in that direction by vaguely dialoguing with modern atheism through its document on *The Church in the Modern World*. However, the general attitude has been one of misgivings about Marxism and the denial of any possibility of dialogue. Some of the staunchest critics of liberation theology reflect this viewpoint within Roman Catholicism, for their chief argument is that Marxism is necessarily linked to atheism and is therefore inimical to any theological use.[12] Segundo is more optimistic and thus opens the door to an area of thought that has influenced an entire sphere of the globe and that must be reckoned with in the modern world.

Our author is able to take this approach, which seems valid in our analysis, for several reasons. The first reason is summed up well by Robert McAfee Brown: "If Aquinas could create a medieval theology by responding to a non-Christian (Aristotle), there is no reason why theologians today could not create a contemporary Christian theology by responding to another non-Christian (Marx)."[13] In addition, the use of Marxism becomes even more of a possibility when we consider that there are many versions of Marxism, all of which owe something to Marx and none of which merely repeat him. Segundo himself observes,

> Those who identify themselves with Marx and his thinking have a thousand different ways of conceiving and interpreting "Marxist" thought. Aside from that fact, the point is that the great thinkers of history do not replace each other; rather, they complement and enrich each other. . . . After Marx, our way of conceiving and posing the problems of society will never be the same again. Whether everything Marx said is accepted or not, and in whatever way one may conceive his "essential" thinking, there can be no doubt that present-day social thought will be "Marxist" to some extent: that is, profoundly indebted to Marx.[14]

With such broad possibilities of interpreting Marx there are no *a priori* difficulties of using him for theology, and we have seen adequately enough the points that Segundo has derived from his version of Marx. It may be a question of overusing Marx or emphasizing him excessively that needs to be challenged, rather than the use of Marx as such. We will treat that question in the next section.

If we are maintaining a dialectic between biblical text and the social analysis then we must also ask if there are any aspects of Segundo's use of Marx that would be inimical to use by theology. Does theology challenge anything that must be rejected in Marxism? In this regard Segundo again gives indication that he recognizes a genuine dialectic between text and human experience, for he addresses what appear to him to be problems in Marx that would make it impossible to use him for theology and exegesis.

Segundo addresses himself to the accusations that Marxism is necessarily atheistic or that it is necessarily linked to materialistic determinism.[15] He refutes both charges as not being essential to Marx and so, enables Marx to be useful for insights into the Bible. As Segundo presents Marxist social analysis, therefore, it can be an adequate vehicle for revelation and it can serve well as the first steps of the hermeneutic circle offering insights that affect how we read the Bible. We must address now, however, the question of overstatement and the question of objectivity through the testing of ideology[p] in the light of other ideologies[p].

II
THE TESTING OF IDEOLOGY

Our reservations with Segundo's hermeneutic circle throughout this study have centered on the problem of verifiability. His observations are well taken about the impossibility of arriving at absolute truths as the content of faith, and about all faith having to work itself out in particular ideologies. The problem is in controlling the ideology so that it does not evolve from ideology[p], an efficacious means of faith, into ideology[n], an all-consuming system.

We have already noted how Segundo's methodology calls for Marxist and other social analysis as the starting point for theology and exegesis. We also have other explicit examples of how he assumes that his Marxist sociology is accurate and an always valid starting point for theology. He says, for example, that eschatology requires an opening toward the future, and then draws on definitions of the political left which define it as the conquest of that which is unrealized, as the openness toward utopia. With this definition of the left, our author can then make the claim: "For that very reason the sensibility of the left is an intrinsic feature of an authentic theology."[16] It seems on the one hand that this definition of the left is too broad to verify that Marxism must underlie theological analysis, for there can be many versions of the political left. On the other hand, the definition is too narrow in saying that only the left is open toward the future. Right-wing politics can have the sense that the future must embrace past traditions. It can be open to the future in another way. In other words, Segundo's assumptions are not totally verified, and not always valid. Once again, this critique does not eliminate his methodology, but it does qualify it. There is a problem of verifiability.

On the same occasion Segundo made a claim similar to the one above: "[Liberation theology] is theology seen not from one of the various possible standpoints, but from the one standpoint indicated by Christian sources as the authentic, privileged one for the understanding of divine revelation in Jesus Christ."[17] If faith must work itself out in relative ideologies, then how can there be one privileged standpoint? This seems to deny the hermeneutic circle itself. It points to the need for verification of the first steps, and not the simple assumption that they are an accurate view of life.

Finally, on this same point, we can question the statement of Segundo: "Evangelizing, then, presupposes . . . that we ourselves find and communicate the essential of the good news."[18] We can ask ourselves how it is possible to get to the essential without any ideology? Put another way, why should we assume that Segundo's perspective from commitment to the poor, a perspective of Marxism, is the essential message of Christianity? It is the problem of objectivity or verifiability.

As we try to verify the ideological positions of Segundo, we can make some observations that qualify his social analysis and thereby modify the presuppositions that we would bring to the hermeneutic circle. We can notice, for instance, that the problem of massification is a real danger within socialism as well as within capitalism. Segundo himself observes how Lenin needed to posit the existence of the masses even within the socialist state, but he seems to accept that as an integral part of political and social analysis. He is negative about massification only when it is seen as oppressive capitalism massifying the poor in order to enslave them in their oppression. It seems to me that massification is a negative element in any situation, although it may not be totally inescapable in this world. Even within socialism, therefore, there is the danger of depersonalizing individuals for the sake of the collectivity. It is a danger which trades one form of massification for another.

We find an invaluable insight in the notion of massification. However, the verifying of that view leads us to root it in a pluralistic social analysis. It seems not the insight of Marxist sociology alone, and is not overcome by Marxist sociology alone.[19] It does not necessarily lead us to an anti-capitalistic reading of the Bible, although it may lead us to a political reading of the Bible which opposes massification of humanity.

These qualifications that we bring to Marxist social analysis also lead us to ask if there is not still some hope for a theory of development. While Marxism may have some insights into the way capitalism leads the underdeveloped countries more and more deeply into poverty, it may not have the full truth in saying that socialism is the only way out. For one thing, the initial process of socialism simply perpetuates a discrimination between classes, for it merely reverses the dominating and the dominated. "The people" can be as unjust as the rich property owners whose possessions they take over. As Pierre Bigo observes:

Why have a revolution if it simply means denying to some what has been for all too long kept from others: the right to be judged according to a norm of justice not defined simply on the basis of class interests?

Every human being, every group attains equity only through a hard struggle against all that masks and alters justice in the human heart.[20]

It seems, moreover, that even when Marxism attempts to remedy the problems of poverty and massification, it achieves success only by also incorporating capitalist techniques. As Bigo observes, "Marx himself accepts the creativity of capital in at least one instance. His thesis on qualified work, a multiple of simple work, is well known. . . . And if qualified work has a right to a higher revenue, is it not as one sort of capital?"[21]

In similar fashion, the socialist reality is inclined more and more to recognize the creativity in humanity's tendency to save and to invest. This leads to compensating efforts which promote these tendencies, and ultimately says that absolute equality is counterproductive. In the same way, initiative and real interest in work comes from a genuine participation in the fruit of that work. A total collectivity dampens initiative. For this reason we find socialist nations reorganizing enterprises to give relative autonomy to each unit, with workers sharing in the decision-making. It becomes a modified type of property ownership. Once again, Segundo may have a valuable insight into the problems of the poor and may bring valuable presuppositions to this theology and exegesis, but the first steps of his hermeneutic circle need verifiability and cannot simply be assumed as accurate views of life. When verification is attempted, his views need modification, although they do not seem to have to be rejected outright.

Even granting the need to posit a plurality of political analyses behind the phenomenon of massification, another question arises as to the extent to which masses and minorities should be used as sufficient categories of society. It is one thing to divide humanity into masses and minorities, oppressor and oppressed, on a theoretical level. It is another to form these categories in the concrete. Segundo may thus be guilty of not extending the categories enough, while in other ways overusing the categories.

We have just seen that Segundo may be too restricted in using masses and minorities because he relies too much on Marxist social analysis, at least derivatively through Lenin. We can now add that he may be too restricted in keeping only to the economic realm in any social analysis. There are other forms of alienation besides the economic, whether the latter be from capitalism or socialism. Consideration must be given to sex, race, creed, nationality, etc., and all of these would contribute to massification of society. Thus, Segundo may have made valuable contributions in positing presuppositions to biblical exegesis, but his hermeneutic circle is incomplete in that he has only a limited presentation of what these presuppositions are.

On the other hand, where he does use masses and minorities, he may be guilty of overuse. Can one, for instance, conveniently divide the world politically into oppressors and oppressed? The view is partially true, but cannot be an adequate category by itself. Moreover, there seems also to be a danger of elitism in the way Segundo uses this category of the minority. For one thing, he seems to think that on the concrete level, the effective minority is the one that operates on Marxist social principles of analysis. It is too exclusive a view of masses and minorities, as we have seen, since the Marxist minority is not totally free from oppressing the masses, and since a minority could operate effectively on other than Marxist social analysis.

An indication of this elitist tendency through a too heavy reliance on Marxist sociology appears in what Segundo expects from the Latin American bishops. He criticizes their support of existing governments as maintaining the status quo, and implies they should take specific political stances based on the Marxist social analysis.[22] This may actually be expecting too much from the bishops, since the social and political analysis is much more complicated than that, and since the Christian message can operate authentically through a plurality of political analyses. Segundo may be correct in criticizing the bishops for maintaining the status quo, but he moves toward elitism in asking them to make a specific Marxist declaration as *the* Christian minority message.

In the last chapter of *The Liberation of Theology* our author gives four expressions of the tension between masses and minorities. He speaks of an ecclesiastical formulation (Christendom vs. little flock or leaven), a socio-political formulation (Marxist-Leninist presentation of the masses), a scientific or biological formulation (Teilhard de Chardin's view of life as an overcoming of inertia in matter), and a biblical response to the other three (e.g., in the concept of *flesh* and *world*). He suggests here again the hermeneutic circle in that the first three formulations suggest what to look for in the biblical text, and the biblical text can speak to the previous formulations. In this particular part of his writings he gives the impression of a wide view of masses and minorities, with the Marxist application simply as one among many. However, in other sections of his works, where he speaks of these formulations, he gives the impression that the Marxist-Leninist social analysis is the practical application of the other expressions of masses and minorities, and is the foundational insight (precondition) that helps uncover the others.[23] In this overuse of one particular social analysis he runs the risk of elitism.

The idea of masses and minorities can tend toward elitism also when Segundo relates them too strictly to numerical categories. The valid concept of masses concerns a qualitative ingredient, massification as the path of least resistance. It is immaterial whether or not massified humanity is a quantitative mass or a small segment of a society, although the process is more generally related to the desire to keep large numbers under domination. In any case, the concept of minority does not have to be linked to quantitative categories. If one can act creatively, decisively and with appreciation of the complexity of motives required, then one functions in a minority capacity. Thus, Segundo's categories are extremely helpful in highlighting the dehumanization of society, but they become elitist when he links them to specific numbers of people.

The concept of minority runs the risk of elitism especially when Segundo speaks of ecclesiology and the problems of mass Christianity. While the desire for numbers may have led to the massification of Christians, it is not necessarily true to say that they can be demassified only by being reduced in numbers. Where does one draw the line? To speak of small numbers seems to make Christianity in the concrete a religion of the few, and discriminates against the numerical masses of society. This is not necessary to maintain the valid point that Segundo makes about massification, even within Christianity.

Segundo does seem to acknowledge the possibility of the minority being a quantitatively large number. He likens this "popular messianism" to Marx's "proletarian messianism," whereby the masses themselves change attitudes and structures. He also says in the same section of his book, "From a more strictly methodological viewpoint, a 'theology of the people' [i.e., the masses with minority traits] would seem to lead us towards a hermeneutic circle that could very well enrich such a theology and keep it vital."[24] Nevertheless, when he gives more extensive treatment to masses and minorities in Christianity, he does not seem to apply this possibility, but treats the minority rather like a quantitative few.[25]

At minimum, therefore, Segundo's concept of masses and minorities runs the risk of elitism if it is not actually guilty of such. Segundo may be conscious of his own ambiguity, for he says, "It is worth noting here that Marxism has never really solved this basic issue either [of masses and minorities], not in an explicit and convincing way at least. . . . So we are left with a major issue that must still be explored."[26]

What we have seen thus far shows the necessity of verification of the first steps of the hermeneutic circle, and also offers modification in what Segundo brings as his analysis of the life situation. We have been trying to apply the "human criteria" for objectivity, the balance of other ideologies[p] and views of life, as we proposed to do at the beginning of this chapter. In what follows we wish to come back briefly to the other criterion proposed earlier, i.e., the need for a true dialectic between text and life experience. We have already mentioned that if revelation is to maintain its aspect of transcendence as well as immanence, then what the Bible says must somehow challenge the life experience as well as being influenced by life experience. We can now reiterate this same point by taking up the distinction Segundo makes between ideology[p] as efficacious means and faith as value system.[27]

Segundo makes a good distinction in contrasting faith and ideology[p] and in saying that faith relativizes every ideology[p]. The difficulty seems to be that he does not allow for this in his concrete applications, when he uses his hermeneutic circle. For him to say that he always begins with social analysis or ideology[p] is to hide the fact that he is making hidden value judgments as to which ideologies to use. What determines that some ideologies are negative and some positive? Why begin with some and not others? It seems that the very use of an ideology[p] is already a value judgment, and, on Segundo's terms, that must come from faith. On the other hand, the full appreciation of faith is influenced by the ideologies operating. In other words, we have much more of a dialectic than Segundo's hermeneutic circle calls for. His methodology gives valuable insight, but it is a partial insight within the dialectic.

We can ask Segundo why commitment to liberation is the entry into the hermeneutic circle. My guess is that he overstates his point precisely because that is the nature of a commitment. He is rightly convinced that the situation of poverty in Latin America—and elsewhere for that matter—is of such proportions that it is intolerable for Christianity to let it continue. He finds that many attempts to solve the problem up to the present have been futile and he sees Marxism as offering a ray of hope—at least a new possibility. Marxism is to be taken seriously, and so Segundo undoubtedly feels it will not be taken at all unless he insists only on that approach.

But what is to prevent us from merely reversing the conflict or inverting the problem? If the difficulty in the past has been that the Bible has been interpreted through the prejudiced optic of the rich and the dominant, what is to prevent the same thing from happening through the poor or dominated? What will prevent their reading the Bible through prejudiced views? It seems to me that it can only be avoided through a dialectic in which faith and the Scriptures themselves relativize any reading of the text, even while life situation determines how one is reading the Scriptures.

This judgment may appear to coopt all that Segundo and liberation theology are trying to accomplish. I hope not. I hope that their commitment still comes through, especially to encourage our own. Nevertheless, commitment is one thing, and academic formulation of a methodology is another. As Segundo uses the term "hermeneutic circle" it is only a geometric figure of speech for stages of interpretation that he does not think can be switched around. As we have been presenting our critique, the "hermeneutic circle" is a genuine statement of the interrelationship of the stages. The fourth step is also the first step in a dialectical relationship. One can really enter on the level of the text or the ideology[p]—or other ideologies[p] for that matter—but each influences the other.

Notes

1. Robert McAfee Brown, *Theology in a New Key* (Philadelphia: Westminster Press, 1978), pp. 106–13.

2. For an overview of Segundo, see Alfred Hennelly, S.J., *Theologies in Conflict* (Maryknoll, N.Y.: Orbis Books, 1979). For an overview of liberation theology, see Brown's book in the preceding note.

3. Karl Rahner, *A Rahner Reader,* ed. Gerald A. McCool (New York: Seabury, 1975), p. 66.

4. Ibid., p. 67.

5. Juan Luis Segundo, *Our Idea of God* (Maryknoll, N.Y.: Orbis Books, 1974), p. 5.

6. Ibid., p. 114.

7. Ibid., p. 86.

8. Juan Luis Segundo, *The Liberation of Theology* (Maryknoll, N.Y.: Orbis Books, 1976), p. 13.

9. Rahner, p. 340.

10. Segundo, *Idea of God,* p. 178.

11. Ibid., p. 49.

12. Cf. Juan Gutierrez Gonzalez, *The New Libertarian Gospel,* pp. 63–66; and Edward J. Berbusse, S.J., "Gustavo Gutiérrez: Utopian Theologian of Liberation," *Faith and Reason* (1975): 67–96.

13. Brown, p. 65.

14. Segundo, *Liberation,* p. 35, n. 10.

15. Tambasco, *The Bible for Ethics,* pp. 65–67.

16. Juan Luis Segundo, "Capitalism-Socialism: A Theological Crux," *Concilium* 96 (1974): 123.

17. Cf. Tambasco, p. 62 and Segundo, "Capitalism-Socialism," p. 105.

18. Cf., Tambasco, p. 136 and Juan Luis Segundo, "The Church: A New Direction in Latin America," *Catholic Mind* 65 (1967): 45.

19. As we have not been concerned with evaluating the Marxism as such, so we abstract here from evaluating Lenin's concept of massification as such or Lenin's interpretation of Marx. We are interested only in Segundo's interpretation of Lenin.

20. Pierre Bigo, S.J., *The Church and the Third World Revolution* (Maryknoll, N.Y.: Orbis Books, 1977), p. 163.

21. Ibid., p. 175.

22. Cf., Tambasco, pp. 83–84 and Juan Luis Segundo, *The Hidden Motives of Pastoral Action* (Maryknoll, N.Y.: Orbis Books, 1978), pp. 37–44.

23. We showed how Segundo builds the ecclesiastical formulation on Marxist social analysis on pp. 78–86. We showed the relationship of Marx to Teilhard according to Segundo on pp. 130–31, n. 42. The biblical response was seen on pp. 146–65. Our critique here would conclude that Segundo has valid and valuable insight in each of these sections, but seems to overstate his case and runs the danger of elitism.

24. Segundo, *Liberation,* p. 236.

25. Cf., Tambasco, pp. 78–86 and especially p. 85.

26. Segundo, *Liberation,* p. 205.

27. Cf., Tambasco, pp. 99–106.

Exodus and Exile:
The Two Faces of Liberation

John Howard Yoder

This article originally appeared in *Cross Currents* in 1973.

"Liberation" and "Revolution" are no longer the dominant slogans in the with-it culture that they were two years ago. If our concern were to join—or to resist—a fad, we would need to test in which churches and cultures the theme is still lively, and to develop a theological critique of faddism. That would not be an unworthy activity, especially since "Peace" is also one of the words recently cheapened in the marketplace.

Yet for now my focus is more perennial. The fad may *formulate* our agenda and sensitize our ears, but the right answer will have to be as old as Israel. The fad may fade or it may bounce back—in Latin America in any case it is not waning—the question is perennial and so must the answer be.

In preparation for the Assembly of the Commission on World Missions and Evangelism of the World Council of Churches, which has since been held in Bangkok, a collection of documents was circulated in March, 1972 under the heading *Salvation Today and Contemporary Experience.* In the Introduction to the collection, written by Thomas Wieser, we read:

> ... the contemporary quest for liberation, whether political, economic, cultural or personal, has for many Christians become the context for the Church's mission and its proclamation of salvation. The biblical story, too, especially in the Old Testament, is to a large extent a story of liber-

ation. A number of interpreters see in this affinity a direct
scriptural support for the present quest, contending that
the biblical meaning of liberation must not be allowed to be
"spiritualized". Others, however, warn that the Bible cannot be used to support what they believe to be a mere temporary political struggle.

The purpose of the following remarks is to foster critical
thought in a context of ecumenical conversation where the statistical
observation, "many Christians believe . . ." often takes the place of
theological discourse about what Christians *ought* to believe. My
good friend Tom Wieser is right; the dominant vogue of "with-it"
theology since the late 1960's has been centered on liberation as the
purpose of God. It seemed self-evident to many that the dominant
biblical image is that of Exodus and that by taking off from the event
of Exodus it would be possible in some broad sense to have a "Biblical Basis" for an especially committed Christian involvement in the
political struggles of our age.

There have been a few thinkers asking careful questions about
this very popular approach. Jose Miguez Bonino for instance has
asked why it should be so obvious that out of the total biblical heritage it should be dominantly or even exclusively the picture of Exodus which becomes illuminating and motivating, without equal
reference to exile, captivity, cross, the giving of the law, the taking of
the land, the scattering of the faithful or other major themes of the
biblical witness. To this observation our meditations shall return.

Another set of critics, thinking on the level of the methodology
of proper theology, have expressed doubts about whether this approach was not a new and questionable form of natural theology, in
the sense that the theologian tags after cultural styles trying to accredit his theology by proving that it can say what other people are
saying anyway. Is not the relevance of a transcendent critique greater
than the "search for relevance" of echoing contemporary styles?

Still another set of critics have been unconvinced about the clarity and solidity of liberation language when tested for its own sake.
Do we really know what that liberating action is in which we should
participate if we were to follow the mandate of Exodus? Are those
particular guerrilla efforts which call themselves liberation fronts

really liberated or liberating? Or are they a new form of cultural colonialism, imposing upon oppressed peoples yet another no less alien, no less self-righteous, no less violent form of minority rule in the name of a Marxist or a nationalist vision of independence? Have liberal democratic, or Marxist, or one-party nationalist movements demonstrated sufficient capacity to liberate that it should be the business of Christians to sanctify those programs by reverberating to them in theological idiom?

But all three of these criticisms—that on the level of biblical selectivity, that on the level of theological method, and the internal critique of the political ideology—have been expressed less sweepingly and less publicly than the liberation rhetoric, with the end result that it still seems useful to face that liberation language in its own right and to test the legitimacy of its claim to be echoing a biblical message.

Since that approach seems to get the most mileage by taking off homiletically from the story of Exodus, my invitation is to honesty in rhetoric. I am not doubting at all the propriety or the fruitfulness of leaping from the biblical language to the present; I am only asking that in that leap there be honesty and there not be unjustified selectivity.

We may take as expressive of the quintessence of the approach of which we speak a fragment of an address delivered by Mr. Poikail John George to the United States Conference for the World Council of Churches at Toledo, Ohio, in May, 1972, on the theme, "Whence and Whither World Council Studies?" This particular quotation is picked out not because it is unique or original but because it is representative, not only of a wide stream of thought and communication but also of an effort to encapsule that stream of thought in an interpretation of the work of the best known interchurch agency for thinking about these matters.

> The cries of God's people everywhere, the continents of Africa and Asia particularly, as well as those around us here at home, have reached the ears of the Lord when he tells us first of all to go and tell the Pharaohs of this world 'Let my people go.' Exodus must come before Mt. Sinai, liberation of God's people must come before communion with God.

The same centering upon the paradigm of Exodus is typical of the "liberation theology" of Latin America; Ruben Alvez or Gustavo Gutiérrez show the same selectivity. The following sample from Alvez will suffice:

> The Exodus was the generating experience of the conscience of the people of Israel. It constituted the structural center which determined their way of organizing their time and space. Observation: note that I am not simply saying that the Exodus is part of the content and conscience of the people of Israel. If it were that, the Exodus would be some information among much other. More than information it is the structural center because it determines the integrating logic, the basis of organization and the interpretation of the facts of the historical experience. Thus the Exodus does not go down as a past experience which took place at some well-defined time and space. It really becomes a paradigm for the interpretation of all of space and all of time.

Our respectfully critical response shall lead us in two directions: First, by staying with the mosaic model itself, we shall test the appropriateness of its application by extension to the revolutionary rhetoric of our day; and secondly, we shall return to the question of Dr. Miguez Bonino; what of the other models?

Our first concern then is with the story itself. Assuming Exodus to be the valid model our authorities say it is, what does it say? What kind of "Revolution" does it represent?

I

FIRST OBSERVATION:
THE EXODUS WAS NOT A PROGRAM BUT A MIRACLE

The exodus experience is a piece with the ancient Hebrew vision of Holy War. The wars of JHWH were certainly lethal, but they were not rationally planned and pragmatically executed military operations; they were miracles. In some of them (and the Red Sea is such a case), the Israelites, according to the record, did not even use arms. The combatant was not a liberation front or terrorist commando but JHWH himself.

The legitimate lesson of the wars of JHWH for contemporary ethics is not that "war must not be sin because God commanded it," bur rather that because God declared and won it entering a war was not a matter of human strategizing and winning it was not an effect of preponderant human power. The Red Sea event is for the whole Old Testament the symbol of the confession that the Israelites do not lift a hand to save themselves. They only trust, and venture out. What the wars of JHWH point to in their fulfillment in Christ is not righteous bloodshed but non-violent non-conformity.

II
SECOND OBSERVATION:
THE EXODUS WAS NOT A TAKEOVER BUT A WITHDRAWAL

The model of revolution most currently called "liberation" in our time is for subject peoples (or more accurately for a minority group acting in their name) to seize sovereignty within the land within which they are oppressed, taking that sovereignty away from a foreign power or from a feudal minority in their own society. This is very strikingly *not* what the Exodus did. Even though the princely figure of Moses would not have made unthinkable an effort to rise up and take over Egypt, as minority groups of invaders and infiltrators did many times in the history of the ancient Near East, this never is suggested as the story is told. Liberation means literally *Exodus:* going out. The only reason there must be plagues and ultimately death is that the hardness of Pharaoh's heart would not permit the Exodus to be peaceful.

It thus appears that if the appeal to the model of Exodus were to be taken seriously as a model rather than whimsically as a slogan, it would point far more clearly to the creative construction of relatively independent counter communities, and less to a seizure of power in the existing society. This countercommunity would be built with the sober expectation that it would call forth a violent reaction by the powers in control, and that in this violent reaction the powers might expose themselves to their own destruction. But the way it is done is very different. Moses was no Bonhoeffer. The old tyranny is destroyed not by beating it at its own game of intrigue and assassination, but by the way the presence of the independent counter community (and its withdrawal) provokes Pharaoh to overreach himself.

III

THIRD OBSERVATION:
THE EXODUS WAS NOT A BEGINNING BUT A CULMINATION

There would never have been a Red Sea experience if there had not previously been the willingness to follow Moses out of Goshen. This was a leap of faith, made in common by the Hebrew people, not on the basis of any calculation of their capacity to destroy the Egyptians, but fully trusting in the transcendent intervention of Yahweh.

Before that there was the fostering of a sense of communal solidarity and vocation as the Israelites had survived through the plagues as an experience of their distinct identity as objects of God's care. There had already been a series of smaller experiences of liberation as a minority people.

Before the experience of preservation through the plagues, there had to be proclamation: preaching of the liberating purpose of God, addressed to both the oppressed and the oppressor, by the preacher Moses who had come from outside the situation with a message from God. That preaching involved a need to accredit (by signs) the status of the prophet; it did *not* involve planning processes to engineer liberation, or predicting either a possible or a utopian design for the liberated state. Its insistence was upon the identity and the saving purpose of JHWH.

Even before there could be a Moses and a people to hear him, there had to be an oppressed community affirming its identity by talking about the Fathers and the God of the Fathers. Moses would not have recognized his mandate, and his brethren would not have heard him, if there had not been a prior common history of recital amidst and despite the bondage. *Goshen is prior to Exodus.* The identity of the poeple, and even in a serious sense the identity of the liberating God himself were dependent upon the confessing community. The God of their Fathers could not have called them to the Red Sea if they had not already been a people under the whips. Peoplehood is the presupposition, not the product of Exodus.

The tragedy of many "liberation fronts" in our time is that the minority which claims to have the right to establish the new order leaps to righteous violence without passing through the experience of creating a supportive people that gives them the right of spokesmanship, or creating a coherent ethos that will permit their own leadership team to work together without recurrent new divisions. To say it another way, to be oppressed together is not sufficient to constitute a people. Nor being a people yet sufficient to be the people of God. Exodus is not a paradigm for all kinds of groups with all kinds of values to attain all kinds of salvation. Exodus is a particular form of withdrawal into insecurity.

Before there could be that preaching there was the overwhelming and solitary experience of the calling of the prophet at Horeb, which in the tradition merges with Sinai.

Before that there was the unique cultural experience that produced the man Moses, in his own personality an amalgam of three cultures, that of the Israelite slaves, the Egyptian court and the desert. As in the New Testament story the bi-cultural identity of the hellenists and of Paul was the key to the missionary opening of the church, so in this case the tricultural identity of Moses is the prerequuisite for the idea and the implementation of the Exodus.

Recent experience demonstrates equally well the dependence of valid freedom movements upon distinctive personal charisma or vocations. In fact such experiences are so tied to the personality of a Gandhi, a King, a Dolci, a Chavez, that mainstream churchmen and ethicists are prone to interpret that personal quality as an argument against either the ethics or the objectives of the movements. Yet both such current experiences and the model of Moses would lead us to affirm that dimension of distinct personal creativity and focus. To take it seriously would mean that both ecumenical administrators and academic ethicists should put their discussion of decision-making processes and their intellectual competence into a framework with more room for the distinct contemporary divine intervention which brings into the scene a man with a catalytic message.

The cultural uniqueness of a Moses reminds us of one dimension where the interpreters of current social change are conscious of the issue but the advocates of legitimate revolutionary violence are usually not. Gandhi was not a Hindu alone but also had a British and South African education and experience. Martin Luther King was not only a representative southern Black Baptist, he also had a doctorate from a liberal Methodist New England school. Whereas liberation movements, especially after the loss of a leader, may gladly appeal to national or tribal or racial identities to provide an audience or even a rationale for revolution, the possibility of true liberation would seem to be dependent upon a leader who is *not* simply the incarnation of distinct tribal cultural drive but who at the same time has been beyond that culture, can project a vision of liberation which includes the wider world, and can communicate the legitimacy of that liberation in a way that the power centers of the wider world cannot permanently close their ears to it. If we are, then, interested in fostering genuine liberation of oppressed peoples, our concern should be less to reiterate the classic moral legitimations of seditious violence, and more to facilitate trans-cultural educational experiences for leaders who *at the same time* would remain identified with their people and become mature and confident participants in the wider world.

Even before Moses, before his vocation could be conceivable and its implementation feasible, there was the memory of the slaves who knew that they were the children of Abraham and Isaac and Jacob and Joseph, who in their time had been in conversation with their own God, so that "the God of the Fathers" was known to them as a living memory in their past.

At this point we must note that Mr. George, in the quotation above, seems to equate indiscriminately the phrase "people of God" with any and all subject peoples. This is certainly counter to the meaning of Exodus, which is the experience of one oppressed and wandering minority, not of any and all suffering peoples. "The people of God" is not everybody.

Not only is "the people of God" not to be equated with any or every nation or any oppressed portion of any nation; it is equally illegitimate in Jewish or Christian theology to talk about "the people of God" at all outside the context of historical relationship to the calling of Abraham. The people of God is an elect people chosen by sovereign divine initiative from among many nations not because of any particular merit (not even because of any particular suffering), only because it pleased the Lord to demonstrate His goodness in that visible way. To transpose the motif of liberation out of that distinct historical framework and thereby also away from the distinct historical identity of the God of Abraham, Isaac, and Jacob, into some kind of general theistic affirmation of liberation, is to separate the biblical message from its foundation. There exists a liberation message only because of the particularity of the God of the fathers; Jews and Christians cannot talk confidently about liberation except in that connection.

Thus peoplehood is not the product of liberation; peoplehood with a history and a trust in the God who has led the fathers is prior to liberation. This has implications for contemporary thinking.

A. One is the awareness that what really makes liberation possible is the cultural fruit of generations prior to liberation which developed in the fiber of their cultural personalities a sense of those values which could then lead them together into new liberating engagement. Several generations of ex-slaves singing Black spirituals are the presupposition of a Martin Luther King. If you want to help liberate the people, it is not a service to tell them that violence is justified; it is a service to help them develop their spirituals.

B. A more negative conclusion to draw from the above observation is that there are times and places where no liberation is possible because no peoplehood has been formed. There are slums and *favelas,* there are perhaps whole racial groups and especially there are refugee cultures who have no songs, no historical self-understanding even as oppressed peoples. In such a context there is no base for liberating change either violent or non-violent. But in such cases the argument for violence is even less fitting. There is

no possiblity of constructing a new people on the other side of the
Sea if peoplehood does not exist in Goshen.

IV
FOURTH OBSERVATION:
EXODUS IS ONLY THE BEGINNING

The slogan "Exodus before Sinai" presupposes that "liberation"
is a single and final event; that is the claim that justifies treating its
violence as a legitimate ethical exception. Yet Sinai was to become
the place of a new bondage. Exodus leads not to the promised land
but to the desert, and in that desert Sinai is the place of a new en-
slavement motivated partly by loyalty to the values of Egypt.

What happened at Sinai was thus first the fall of Israel, unwill-
ing despite the liberation just experienced to be patient in awaiting
the Word of God from the mountain, preferring under Aaron's leading to take things into their own hands. If this has any relation to the
question how we take the initiative in the combat against injustice it
would hardly be in the direction of fostering the authority of any human community to define autonomously and implement violently its
own liberation.

Let this reminder of the golden calf point us to the awareness
that after slavery was left behind everything was yet to be done.

Mr. George in the text I quoted referred to Sinai as the symbol
of the "communion with God" that can come only after liberation.
Yet what happened at Sinai was not "communion with God" in any
such "religious" sense, but rather the formal constitution of Israel as
a community under the law. This consolidation of the community is
part of the meaning of liberation. Not only the divinely chiseled tablets of Torah, but also the common-sensical borrowing from Moses'
father-in-law of a model of grassroots government was needed for the
mixed multitude to become a people. Exodus was the leap of faith
but Sinai was its landing. Historically Exodus was the prerequisite of
Sinai, but morally it is the other way 'round. Liberation is *from*
bondage and *for* covenant, and *what for* matters more than *what
from.*

If Exodus was the prerequisite of Sinai, in terms of movement,

Sinai was the prerequisite of Exodus in terms of motive. It was the reason given to the Egyptians (Ex. 8:2, 20, 26f, etc.). Even before the arrival at Sinai, the column of fiery cloud was a symbol of Sinai leading them. Liberation after the model of Exodus issues in the reconstitution of community around the liberator. This is then another point at which to take the contemporary rhetoric seriously. Can the various "fronts" and "movements" which today call themselves "liberation" point us with any confidence, on the basis of experiences elsewhere or of the inherent quality of their vision, to a constitutive event *following* the "exodus" that will give substance to their separate existence? Or is not what is today called "liberation" sparked and justified only by the wrongness of the oppression it denounces, while sharing with the oppressor many of his ethical assumptions about how to deal with dissent, about the use of violence, about the political vocation of a liberating elite?

So liberation has its post-requisites as well as its prerequisites. It is not a revolution but only a threshold linking two phases of pilgrim peoplehood.

In giving this degree of attention to the fuller dimensions of the Exodus story I am not merely pressing a parable beyond its limits into allegory; I am unfolding the meaning of "story," as illumination of how we understand a God who works among men for their salvation. The primary resources for the Exodus are not located in the money or the weapons or the stratagems brought to bear at a particular point to destroy some tyrant. They are rather the prior developments of an identity, a common story, a sense of community and purpose and a set of expectations as to the shape of the divine initiative, without which the story of the Red Sea would have no frame and no point. It is not too much to suggest that as Christians talk about Exodus and liberation there is still need for the awareness of similar prerequisite dimensions. Clarifying the identity and mission of minorities might then be a better guide even today than efforts to take over the pagan society from above and make it a good.

Parallel to the alternative Exodus/Sinai Mr. George placed the pair liberation/communion. This is to suggest, as we noted, a distinct (and secondary) place for "communion with God," and thereby a replay of the polemic, frequent in World Council circles, against "pietism." But since Sinai is the formation of a community, the polarization in the phrase of Mr. George does not serve for the argumentative purpose which he intends. In order to speak to the present polarity represented by "pietism" on one hand and "social action relevance" on the other, Mr. George has made Sinai something it never was, namely "communion with God" in a "religious" sense. Or to reverse the parable, he has also made piety something it never was. It is a misreading of history to see in the worship patterns of pietism, or of any other group of real cultic concern, an idea of distance from the world that seeks authenticity through heightened separateness. Pietism—and valid sacramental worship for that matter too—celebrates the working of God within history in the creation of community; it is not a self-contemplating mystical exercise.

V

FIFTH OBSERVATION: EXODUS IS AN EXCEPTION

I noted before in an introductory way that the preference of modern preachers for the model of Exodus can be challenged as an unexplained and arbitrary selectivity. Why is there not some broader review of all the great events which Scripture puts in the light of the Word of God at work: the taking of Canaan, the pluralism of the age of the judges, the rise and fall of Kingdom, the dividing of the Kingdom, exile . . . (to stay with the Old Testament)? But the point here to be made is much more than that by concentrating on Exodus something or other is omitted; it is that the elements omitted are *relevant.* Israel's experience with trying Kingship and even empire, and ultimately abandoning them, is part of the lesson of the biblical witness; exile and the abandoning of nationhood as the form of peoplehood are prophetically interpreted as the way of JHWH. Ezra and Nehemiah reestablish the community precisely *without* national sovereignty.

Most relevant to the "oppressed people" theme, and most in tension with the juxtaposition of exodus language with modern guerilla theology, is the fact that over against the paradigm of leaving Egypt and destroying Pharaoh on the way we find in the Old Testament, more often, another model of how to live under a pagan oppressor. It is the way of Diaspora. This is the model taken over by the New Testament Church, and the model as well of two millenia of rabbinic Judaism.

> These are the words of the letter which Jeremiah the prophet sent from Jerusalem to the elders of the exiles, and to the priests, the prophets, and all the people, whom Nebuchadnezzar had taken into exile from Jerusalem to Babylon. . . . Build houses and live in them; plant gardens and eat their produce. Take wives and have sons, and give your daughters in marriage, that they may bear sons and daughters; multiply there, and do not decrease. But seek the welfare of the city where I have sent you into exile, and pray to the Lord on its behalf, for in its welfare you will find your welfare. For thus says the Lord of hosts, the God of Israel: Do not let your prophets and your diviners who are among you deceive you, and do not listen to the dreams which they dream, for it is a lie which they are prophesying to you in my name; I did not send them, says the Lord (Jeremiah 29:1, 5–9).

The exile of Judah had begun, with the move to Babylon of the King, the Queen mother, the temple treasurer, the artisans, and the priests and prophets.

But young Zedekiah, left in Jerusalem to rule the rest, got ideas of liberation. Prophets like Shemaiah encouraged him to believe that Judah was still where the action was. "Don't settle down in Babylon, you'll soon be back." "Jerusalem will again be free." These are the deceiving diviners Jeremiah denounces; these are the lying dreams.

"You'll be in Babylon a long time. Seek the peace of *that* city. Identify your welfare with theirs. Abandon the vision of statehood."

There is only one Exodus in the history of Israel; but on the other hand there are several samples of the way a moral minority can "seek the welfare of the city." This advice of Jeremiah was given in the age of the exile after the defeat of Josiah: but we have the same stance taken by Joseph in Egypt, by Daniel under Nebuchadnezzar, and by Mordecai in Persia and even in a sense by Jonah in Nineveh. Far from destroying the pagan oppressor, the function of the insightful Hebrew is to improve that pagan order so as to make it a resource of protection for the people and viable as a government. He does this in ways which force the pagan power to renounce its self-mythologizing religious claims and to recognize the higher sovereignty that is proclaimed by the Hebrew Monotheist. This Joseph/Daniel/Mordecai model is so characteristic in the Hebrew Bible that we have to claim that this kind of elite contribution to the reforming of the existing order is more often the fitting contribution to the pagan community than any theocratic takeover. The complement to the Exodus of the counter community is not a *coup d'état* by the righteous oppressed, but rather the saving message of the resident minority.

VI
CLOSING THE CIRCLE

Let us return to the last words of our opening quotation from Thomas Wieser. Some want to identify "the contemporary quest for liberation" with biblically understood "salvation in contemporary experience," to ward off "spiritualization." Others don't want the Bible to be used to support a "mere temporary political struggle." We have not been testing the latter position, though it may be pointed out on the basis of our parable that to object that salvation should not be "temporary" is not an argument. According to most other definitions salvation in the form which can be experienced today is also temporary. It would be a more serious reproach that it is "temporal"; i.e., lacking in or denying transcendent depth which goes beyond the present power struggle. This is what Mr. George was trying to safeguard by retaining "Sinai" as symbol of "communion with God" subsequent to "Exodus" as liberation. I personally doubt that either way of safeguarding transcendence above the temporal is adequate or Biblical; either Mr. George's two-step dialectic or Wieser's critique of the "merely temporal."

More important in our present concern, however, is that Wieser's phrasing misframes the criticism of the "liberation" focus as "spiritualizing" or as avoidance of the "political." It will be visible from the above that that is not my criticism at all. It is rather that the "many Christians" in question have borrowed from the Bible an imagery or *language* of liberation, but have avoided learning from the biblical story anything about the meaning of liberation.[1]

The *form* of liberation in the biblical witness is not the guerrilla campaign against an oppressor culminating in his assassination and military defeat, but the creation of a confessing community which is viable without or against the force of the state, and does not glorify that power structure even by the effort to topple it.

The *content* of liberation in the biblical witness is not the "nation-state" brotherhood engineered after the take-over but the covenant-peoplehood already existing because God has given it, and sure of its future because of the Name ("identity") of God, not because of a coming campaign.

The *means* of liberation in the biblical witness is not prudentially justified violence but "mighty Acts" which may come through the destruction at the Red Sea—but may also come when the King is moved to be gracious to Esther, or to Daniel, or to Nehemiah.

From the "Believers' Church" perspective, the "neo-constantinian" approach that blesses a going political movement, and the "spiritualist" approach that downgrades the "temporal" are mirror images. Both use biblical imagery more for window dressing than for content, both avoid seriously dealing with the way in which *pilgrim peoplehood* is projected by the Bible as the shape of salvation in any age.

So let us abandon the spiritual/secular polarity and ask what *kind* of spiritual historicity reflects the shape of liberating grace.

We will be farthest along if instead of following only the pattern of going out into the wilderness—which the Exodus taken alone really was—and instead of dreaming of a theocratic takeover of the land of bondage by the brickmakers—which ideological exegesis has sought to do with the Exodus imagery—we seek more creatively to describe what can best be done by creative minorities in a society they don't control. Let us observe:

- Jesus and his movement;
- Christians in the second century Roman Empire;

- the Jews in medieval Europe;
- the Pennsylvania Dutch in colonial America;
- the Indians in East Africa;
- the Chinese in South Asia;
- the unmeltable ethnics in contemporary America.

The line runs from the ten good men who could have saved Sodom through Paul in his boat saving his captors on the way to Rome.

You know the famous description in the (second century?) *Letter to Diognetus:*

> They reside in their respective countries, but only as aliens. They take part in everything as citizens and put up with everything as foreigners. Every foreign land is their home, and every home a foreign land. . . . They spend their days on earth, but hold citizenship in heaven. They obey the established laws, but in their private lives they rise above the laws. They love all men, but are persecuted by all. . . . They are reviled, and they bless; they are insulted and render honor. Doing good, they are penalized as evildoers; . . . and those who hate them are at a loss to explain their hatred.

In a word: what the soul is in the body, that the Christians are in the world.

We need not bother debating the questionable metaphysics of body/soul dualism to confirm the writer's point about the church/society dualism. What the world most needs is not a new Caesar but a new style. A style is created, updated, projected, not by a nation or a government, but by a people. This is what moral minorities can do—what they have done time and again.

Liberation is not a new King; we've tried that. Liberation is the presence of a new option, and only a non-conformed, covenanted people of God can offer that. Liberation is the pressure of the presence of a new alternative so valid, so coherent, that it can live without the props of power and against the stream of statesmanship. To *be* that option is to be free indeed.

Note

1. Elsewhere Wieser, like Rubem Alvez, shows sympathetic insight into the "people-in-exile" alternative. The "typical" quotations used here should not be seen as representative of their authors' best wisdom.

Toward a Feminist Biblical Hermeneutics: Biblical Interpretation and Liberation Theology

Elisabeth Schüssler Fiorenza

This article originally appeared in *The Challenge of Liberation Theology: A First World Response*, 1981.

To discuss the relationship between liberation theology and biblical interpretation in general, and to ask for the function of the Bible in the struggle of women for liberation in particular, is to enter an intellectual and emotional minefield. One must detect and lay bare the contradictions between historical exegesis and systematic theology, between value-neutral scientific inquiry and "advocacy" scholarship, between universal-objectivist preconceptions of academic theology and the critical partiality of liberation theologies. To attempt this in a short paper entails, by necessity, a simplification and typologization of a complex set of theological problems.

To raise the issue of the contemporary meaning and authority of the Bible from a feminist theological perspective, and to do this from the marginalized position of a woman in the academy,[1] is to expose oneself to triple jeopardy. Establishment academic theologians and exegetes will reject such an endeavor as unscientific, biased, and overly conditioned by contemporary questions, and therefore unhistorical, or they will refuse to accept it as a serious exegetical or theological question because the issue is raised by a woman. Liberation and political theologians will, at best, consider such a feminist theological endeavor as one problem among others, or at worst, label it as "middle-class" and peripheral to the struggle of oppressed people. After all, how can middle-class white women worry about the ERA or the sex of God, when people die of starvation, are tortured in prisons, or vegetate below poverty level in the black and Hispanic ghettos of American cities? However, such an objection against feminist theology and the women's movement overlooks the fact that more than half of the poor and hungry in the world are women and children dependent on women.[2] Not only do women and children represent the majority of the "oppressed," but poor and Third World women suffer the triple oppression of sexism, racism, and classism. If liberation theologians make the "option for the oppressed" the key to their theological endeavors, then they must become conscious of the fact that "the oppressed" are women.

Feminist theology, therefore, not only challenges academic theology to take its own intellectual presuppositions seriously, but it also asks other liberation theologies to concretize their option for the oppressed. Finally, the feminist theologian challenges not only the supposedly neutral and objective stance of the academic theologian, but she also must qualify the definition of the advocacy stance of liberation theology as "option for the oppressed." Her involvement in liberation theology is not "altruistic," but it is based on the acknowledgment and analysis of her own oppression as a woman in sexist, cultural, and theological institutions. Having acknowledged the dimensions of her own oppression, she can no longer advocate the value-neutral, detached stance of the academician. In other words, feminist theologians' experience of oppression is different from those of Latin American theologians, for instance, who often do not belong to the poor, but have made the cause of the oppressed their own.[3] Such an emphasis on the differences in the approaches of different liberation theologies is important. Robert McAfee Brown has pointed out, "What we see depends on where we are standing."[4]

Moreover, the Native American theologian Vine Deloria[5] has cautioned that one way of co-opting liberation theology is to classify all minorities as oppressed and in need of liberation. Christian theologians often add to this that we are all under sin and therefore all equally oppressed: male and female, black, white, and red. In co-opting the term "oppression," and generalizing it so much that it becomes meaningless, the liberal establishment successfully neutralizes specific analyses of oppression and prohibits oppressed groups from formulating their own goals and strategies for liberation. Therefore, it seems to be methodologically inappropriate to speak in generalized terms about oppression or about liberation theology in the singular.

I

THE "ADVOCACY" STANCE OF LIBERATION THEOLOGIES

This insight has far-reaching consequences for the methodological approach of this paper. Instead of asking for the Scriptural *loci* of liberation theology in general, or critically evaluating their approach from a "superior" methodological historical-critical point of view, I have decided to concentrate on one specific issue of contention between so-called academic theology and all forms of liberation theology. The basic insight of liberation theologies and their methodological starting-point is the insight that all theology knowingly or not is by definition always engaged for or against the oppressed. Intellectual neutrality is not possible in a historical world of exploitation and oppression. If this is the case then theology cannot talk about human existence in general, or about biblical theology in particular, without identifying whose human existence is meant and about whose God biblical symbols and texts speak.

This avowed "advocacy" stance of all liberation theologies seems to be the major point of contention between academic historical-critical or liberal-systematic theology on the one side and liberation theology on the other side. For instance, in many exegetical and theological circles a feminist interpretation of the Bible or the reconstruction of early Christianity is not the proper substantive historical and theological subject matter for serious academic theology. Since such a feminist interpretation is sparked by the women's movement and openly confesses its allegiance to it, academic theologians consider it to be a popular "fad," and judge it not to be a serious historical-theological problem for historical-critical scholarship.[6] Since this interpretative approach is already prejudiced by the explicit advocacy position of the inquiring scholar, no value-neutral scientific inquiry is possible. Therefore, no one publicly identified with the "feminist cause" in theology and society can be considered to be a "serious" scholar. Or as one of my colleagues remarked about a professor who wrote a rather moderate article on women in the Old Testament: "It's a shame! In writing this article she may have ruined her whole scholarly career."

The ideal of historical-critical studies that all exegetical inquiry should be a value-neutral and objective historical description of the past overlooks the fact that biblical studies as "*canonical*" studies are already "engaged," insofar as the Bible is not just a document of past history, but functions as Holy Scripture in Christian communities today.[7] The *biblical* exegete and theologian, in distinction from the historian of antiquity, never searches solely for the historical meaning of a passage, but also raises the question of the Bible's meaning and authority for today. The argument that the "hermeneutical privilege of the oppressed"[8] or the feminist interest in the role of women in the New Testament is too engaged or biased pertains, therefore, to all biblical inquiry *qua* biblical inquiry, and not only to the study and use of the Bible by liberation theologians. Insofar as biblical studies are "canonical" studies, they are related to and inspired by their *Sitz im Leben* in the Christian Church of the past and the present. The feminist analysis of the Bible is just one example of such an ecclesial contextuality and of the theological commitment of biblical studies in general.

This fact is recognized by Schubert Ogden, who nevertheless objects to the "advocacy" stance of liberation theology. He argues that all existing liberation theologies are in danger of becoming ideologies in the Marxist sense insofar as they, like other traditional theological enterprises, are "the rationalization of positions already taken."[9] Rather than engaging in a critical reflection on their own positions, liberation theologies rationalize, with the help of the Bible, the positions of the oppressed instead of those of the oppressors. Insofar as they attempt to rationalize the prior claims of Christian faith and their own option for the oppressed, they are not theologizing but witnessing. Theology as a "second act" exists according to Latin American liberation theologians, not "for its own sake," but for the sake of the Church's witness, its liberating praxis.

One must, however, question whether this statement adequately characterizes the "advocacy" stance of liberation theologians. Ogden suggests that the only way theology—be it academic or liberation theology—can become emancipated is by conceiving its task as that of a critical reflection on its own position. He then proceeds to work out a "still more adequate theology of liberation than any of them has as yet achieved."[10] However, he not only fails to reflect critically on the political standpoint and implications of his own process theology, but he also goes on to talk about "women's theology" and to explore the "being of God in himself" as if he had never studied feminist theology.

While Ogden accuses liberation theologians of too "provincial an understanding of bondage," James Cone insists to the contrary that the option for the oppressed should become the starting point of all theology: "If Christian theology is an explication of the meaning of the gospel for our time, must not theology itself have liberation as its starting point or run the risk of being, at best, idle talk, and at worst blasphemy?"[11] Such a provocative formulation should not, however, be classified as mere "rhetoric,"[12] but must be seen as an indicator of serious theological differences in the understanding of the task and function of theology.

This disagreement about the function and goal of theology has serious implications for the way theologians understand the task of biblical interpretation. As a feminist theologian I have taken the "advocacy" position, but do not think that this option excludes "critical reflection" on my own feminist position. Such a critical reflection must not only be applied to the "advocacy" position of liberation theologies, but it must also be extended to the ways exegetes and theologians have construed the relationship between the biblical past and its meanings, and explicated the claim of Christian theology that the Bible has authority and significance for Christians today.

Such a critical reflection indicates *first* that biblical and theological interpretation has always taken an advocacy position without clearly reflecting upon it. Such an advocacy position is not unique to liberation theologies.

Second, in order to reflect critically on the function of liberation theologians' explicit advocacy position in the process of biblical theological interpretation, I have chosen to discuss two concrete examples of liberation theological hermeneutics. This is necessary because it is methodologically incorrect to reduce every advocacy stance and every analysis of concrete structures of oppression by liberation theologies to one common level. I will argue that liberation theologies, because of their option for a specific group of oppressed people, e.g., women or Native Americans, must develop, within the overall interpretative approach of a critical theology of liberation, more adequate heuristic interpretative models appropriate to specific forms of oppression. In short, the biblical interpretation of liberation theologians must become more concrete, or more "provincial," before an "interstructuring" of different interpretative models, and a more universal formulation of the task of a critical theology of liberation can be attempted.

T. S. Kuhn's[13] categories of scientific paradigms and heuristic models, which evolved in the methodological discussions of the natural sciences, provide a conceptual theoretical framework that allows for the advocacy stance of liberation theologies, as well as for their distinctive interpretative approaches. According to Kuhn, a paradigm represents a coherent research tradition, and creates a scientific community. Since paradigms determine how scientists see the world and how they conceive of theoretical problems, a shift in paradigm also means a transformation of the scientific imagination, and thus demands an "intellectual conversion" which allows the community of scientists to see old "data" in a completely new perspective. For a period of time different paradigms may be competing for the allegiance of the scientific community until one paradigm replaces the other or gives way to a third.

The usefulness of this theory for biblical and theological studies in general and for our discussion here is obvious. It shows the conditioned nature of all scientific investigation, and maintains that no neutral observation language and value-free standpoint is possible insofar as all scientific investigations demand commitment to a particular research approach, and are carried out by a community of scholars dedicated to such a theoretical perspective. Moreover, this theory helps us to understand that theological approaches, like all other scientific theories, are not falsified, but replaced, not because we find new "data," but because we find new ways of looking at old data and problems. Research paradigms are therefore not necessarily exclusive of each other. They can exist alongside each other until they are finally replaced by a new paradigm.

II
Paradigms in Biblical Interpretation

The debate around the "advocacy" stance of liberation theology and the "value-neutral" stance of academic theology appears to reflect such a shift in theological paradigms. Since the Bible as Holy Scripture is a historical book, but at the same time claims to have significance and authority for Christians today, theological scholarship has developed different paradigms to resolve this tension between the historical and theological claims of the Bible.[14]

The *first* paradigm, which I will call the "doctrinal paradigm," understands the Bible in terms of divine revelation and canonical authority. This paradigm is concerned with the truth-claims, authority, and meaning of the Bible for Christian faith today. It conceives of biblical authority in ahistorical, dogmatic terms. In its most consistent form it insists on the verbal inspiration and literary inerrancy of biblical writings. In this understanding the Bible does not just communicate the Word of God, but it *is* the Word of God. It is not simply a record of revelation, but revelation itself. As such, it functions as proof-text, "first principle," or *norma normans non normata*. The tension between the historical and contemporary meaning of the Bible can be dissolved by means of allegory, typology, or the distinction between the literal sense and the spiritual sense of Scripture.

The most widely used method is proof-texting, which provides the ultimate theological arguments or rationalizations for a position already taken. The general formula is: "Scripture says, therefore . . ." or "This argument is also borne out by Scripture." The proof-texting method presupposes that the Bible reveals eternal truth and timeless principles which can be separated from their historical expression. Biblical writings are only important for theology insofar as they are a source of "proof-texts" or "principles" which can be taken out of their historical context. Biblical texts function as theological justification for the moral, doctrinal, or institutional interests of the Christian community. Insofar as liberation theology too exclusively and abstractly focuses on certain biblical texts, e.g., the Exodus-texts,[15] certain prophetic indictments against the rich in Luke 4:16–30, or the Last Judgment in Matthew 25:31–45, it could be in danger of submitting to the "proof-texting" or the allegorical method.

The *second* paradigm of historical-critical exegesis was developed in confrontation with the dogmatic use of Scripture and the doctrinal authority of the Church. It linked its attack on the doctrinal paradigm with an understanding of exegesis and history that is objective, value-free, rationalist, and scientific. Modeled after the natural sciences, historical-critical exegesis seeks to achieve a purely objective reading of the texts and a scientific presentation of the historical facts. As objective, scientific exegesis, it identifies theological truth with historical facticity. According to James Barr, in this paradigm:

A biblical account of some event is approached and evaluated primarily not in terms of significance but in terms of correspondence with external reality. Veracity as correspondence with empirical actuality has precedence over veracity as significance.[16]

Although academic historical-criticism has become suspicious of the objectivist-factual understanding of biblical texts, it still adheres to the dogma of value-neutral, detached interpretation. Academic historical-critical scholarship reconstructs as accurately as possible the historical meaning of the Bible, but on methodological grounds it refuses to discuss the significance of biblical texts for the contemporary community of faith. Therefore, academic biblical exegesis must limit itself to historical and literary inquiry, but strictly speaking, it is not a theological endeavor.

It is obvious that liberation theologians must distance themselves from such an understanding of biblical interpretation since they focus on the significance of the Bible for the liberation struggle. However, it is interesting to note that José Miranda,[17] the prolific biblical exegete among the Latin American liberation theologians, adheres to this paradigm. He insists that the historical-critical method is in itself objective, scientific, and controllable. When Western exegetes frequently miss the true meaning of the text, this is not due to the exegetical method, but it is due to the Greek thought which Western exegesis has adopted, and which it must abandon in favor of a Marxist reading of the Bible. However, it is questionable whether Miranda's distinction between Greek and biblical thought can still be maintained, and whether liberation theology can adopt the value-neutral stance of historical criticism.

The *third* paradigm of biblical interpretation takes seriously the methodological insights of historical-critical scholarship, and at the same time radically questions how it conceives of its interpretative task. This paradigm is justified by two developments in biblical scholarship: the methods of form and redaction criticism have demonstrated how much biblical writings are theological responses to pastoral-practical situations and problems, while the hermeneutic discussions have elaborated how biblical texts can have meaning today.

First: form and redaction critical studies have highlighted the fact that the biblical tradition understands itself not as a doctrinal, exegetical, or historical tradition, but as a living tradition.[18] In order to understand biblical texts it is important not only to translate and interpret a text in its immediate context, but also to know and determine the situation and the community to whom the text is addressed.

The New Testament authors rewrote their traditions in the form of letters, gospels, or apocalypses because they felt theologically compelled to illuminate or to censure the beliefs and praxis of their communities. The biblical books are thus written with the intention of serving the needs of the community of faith, and not of revealing timeless principles, or of transmitting historically accurate records. They, therefore, do not locate revelation only in the past, but also in their own present, thereby revealing a dialectical understanding between present and past. On the one hand the past is significant because revelation happened decisively in Jesus of Nazareth. On the other hand the writers of the New Testament can exercise freedom with respect to the Jesus traditions because they believe that the Jesus who spoke, speaks now to his followers through the Holy Spirit.

However, form and redaction critical studies can be criticized for conceptualizing the situation of early Christian communities too readily in terms of a confessional struggle between different theologies and church groups. Such a reconstruction often reads like the history of the European Reformation in the sixteenth century or a description of a small town in America where five or six churches of different Christian persuasions are built within walking distance of one another.

The studies of the social world of Israel[19] and early Christianity[20] emphasize the fact that it is not sufficient merely to reconstruct the ecclesial setting. Christian faith and revelation are always intertwined within cultural, political, and societal contexts. It does not suffice merely to understand biblical texts as expressions of religious-theological ideas or ecclesial disputes. What is necessary is to analyze their societal-political contexts and functions. For instance, it does not suffice merely to recognize the literary form of the household-code, or its theological imperative in the post-Pauline community tradition, if one does not also ask why these communities appropriated this particular form in their societal-political environment.[21] While the doctrinal paradigm understands miracles as proofs of the divinity of Jesus, the historical-contextual paradigm discusses whether they actually could have happened as they are told, and the form and redaction paradigm debates whether they are a religious expression of the time or a genuine expression of Christian faith, the contextual paradigm points out that miracle-faith was widespread in lower classes who did not have money for medical treatment. Miracle-faith in Jesus is best understood as protest against bodily and political suffering. It gives courage to resist the life-destroying powers of one's society.[22]

Second: The hermeneutical discussion is concerned with the meaning of biblical texts. While one direction of hermeneutics seeks to discover the synchronic ontological, a-temporal, ideal, noematic meaning of written texts by separating it from the diachronic, temporal, communicative, personal, and referential speech-event, another direction does not concentrate so much on the linguisticality of the text as on the involvement of the interpreter with the text. The interpreter always approaches the text with specific ways of raising questions, and thus with a certain understanding of the subject matter with which the text is concerned.[23]

The hermeneutic circle conceives of the relationship between the contemporary interpreter and the historical text as a continuous dialogue that corrects the presuppositions of the interpreter and works out the true meaning of the text. At this point, it becomes clear that in this third paradigm dialogical interpretation is the governing model. While form and redaction criticism show that early Christian communities and "authors" were in constant dialogue with the tradition and the living Lord authorizing this tradition, the hermeneutic circle continues this dialogic endeavor in the act of interpretation. Therefore, this hermeneutic understanding can be combined with the neo-orthodox theological enterprise. Or as Schillebeeckx points out: "The apparent point of departure is the presupposition that what is handed down in tradition and especially the Christian tradition, is always meaningful, and that its meaning must only be deciphered hermeneutically and made actual."[24]

In conclusion: All three paradigms of biblical interpretation espouse a definite stance and allegiance to a research perspective and community. The doctrinal paradigm clearly has its allegiance to the Church and its teachings. The norm by which it evaluates different texts and their truth claims is the *regula fidei.* The scientific paradigm of historical-critical exegesis shares in the objectivist-scientific worldview, and espouses the critical rationality and value-free inquiry of academic scholarship. The hermeneutic-contextual paradigm is interested in the "continuation" of the tradition, and therefore advocates a position in line with neo-orthodox theology, a "hermeneutics of consent."[25] It would be interesting to explore which political interests each of these paradigms serves, but this would go far beyond the task and aim of this paper. The explicit advocacy position, however, of liberation theologies threatens to uncover the hidden political interests of existing biblical interpretative paradigms. This may be one of the main reasons why established theology refuses to reflect critically on its own societal-ecclesial interests and political functions.

III
Liberation Theology and Biblical Interpretation

The second part of this paper will attempt to explore critically the position of a theology of liberation within the existing paradigms of biblical interpretation. I will do this by discussing two different hermeneutical approaches of liberation theologies. As case studies, I have chosen the hermeneutical model of Juan Luis Segundo as one of the more sophisticated proposals in contemporary theology, and have placed in contrast to it Elizabeth Cady Stanton's approach in proposing the *Woman's Bible*. Both examples indicate that liberation theologies have worked out a distinctive approach to biblical interpretation which leads to a redefinition of the criteria for public theological discourse. Instead of asking whether an approach is appropriate to the Scriptures and adequate to the human condition,[26] one needs to test whether a theological model of biblical interpretation is *adequate* to the historical-literary methods of contemporary interpretation and *appropriate* to the struggle of the oppressed for liberation.

The Interpretative Model of Juan Luis Segundo[27]

While the hermeneutic-contextual approach advocates the elimination of all presuppositions and pre-understandings for the sake of objective-descriptive exegesis, existential hermeneutics defines pre-understanding as the common existential ground between the interpreter and the author of the text. Political theologians have challenged this choice of existential philosophy, while liberation theologians maintain a hermeneutics of engagement instead of a hermeneutics of detachment. Since no complete detachment or value-neutrality is possible, the interpreter must make her/his stance explicit and take an advocacy position in favor of the oppressed. To truly understand the Bible is to read it through the eyes of the oppressed, since the God who speaks in the Bible is the God of the oppressed. For a correct interpretation of the Bible, it is necessary to acknowledge the "hermeneutical privilege of the oppressed" and to develop a hermeneutics "from below."

Since theology is explicitly or implicitly intertwined with the existing social situation, according to Segundo the hermeneutic circle must begin with an experience or analysis of the social reality that leads to suspicion about our real situation. In a second step we apply our ideological suspicion to theology and to all other ideological superstructures. At a third level we experience theological reality in a different way, which in turn leads us to the suspicion that "the prevailing interpretation of the Bible has not taken important pieces of data into account."[28] At a last stage we bring these insights to bear upon the interpretation of Scripture. However, only active commitment to the oppressed and active involvement in their struggle for liberation enable us to see our society and our world differently, and give us a new perspective for looking at the world. This perspective is also taught in the New Testament if the latter is interpreted correctly.

Segundo acknowledges that James Cone has elaborated such a liberation theological interpretation for the black community. He admits his indebtedness to Bultmann, but he reformulates the hermeneutic circle to include actions:

> And the circular nature of this interpretation stems from the fact that each new reality obliges us to interpret the word of God afresh, to *change* reality accordingly, and then go back and reinterpret the Word of God again and so on. [emphasis mine][29]

It is apparent that Segundo cannot be accused of rationalizing a previously taken position. He does not operate within the interpretative tradition of the doctrinal paradigm. He also clearly distinguishes his own theological interpretation from that of academic historical-critical scholarship by rejecting the biblical revelation-contemporary application model. According to him biblical interpretation must reconstruct the second-level learning process of biblical faith. Faith is identical with the total process of learning in and through ideologies. Therefore, faith should not be defined as content or *depositum fidei,* but as an educational process throughout biblical and Christian history. Faith expresses the continuity and permanency of divine revelation, whereas ideologies document the historical character of faith and revelation. "Faith then is a liberative process. It is converted into freedom for history, which means freedom *for ideologies.*"[30] It is obvious that Segundo does not understand ideology as "false" consciousness, but as historical-societal expression.

According to him, Christian faith is also not to be defined as content, doctrine, or principle, but as an educational process to which we willingly entrust ourselves. "In the case of . . . the Bible we learn to learn by entrusting our life and its meaning to the historical process that is reflected in the expressions embodied in that particular tradition."[31] It is thus clear that Segundo does not work within the overall approach of either the doctrinal or historical value paradigms, but proposes an interpretative model within the hermeneutic-contextual paradigm. He shares with neo-orthodoxy the hermeneutical presupposition that Scriptural traditions are meaningful, and that they can therefore claim our obedience and demand a "hermeneutics of consent." In distinction from neo-orthodox theology, Segundo does not claim that it is the content of Scripture that is reflected in the Bible as meaningful and liberative. It is, rather, in the process of learning how to learn that meaning and liberation are seen.

However, this assumption does not take into account the fact that not only the content of Scripture, but also this second-level learning process can be distorted. Segundo must, therefore, either demonstrate that this is not the case, or formalize this learning process to such a degree that the "advocacy" becomes an abstract principle not applicable to the contents of the Bible. In other words, Segundo's model does not allow for a critical theological evaluation of biblical ideologies as "false consciousness." One must question whether historical content and hermeneutic learning can be separated. Such a proposal also does not allow us to judge whether a text or interpretation is appropriate and helpful to the struggle of the oppressed for liberation. The failure to bring a critical evaluation to bear upon the biblical texts and upon the process of interpretation within Scripture and tradition is one of the reasons why the use of the Bible by liberation theologians often comes close to "proof texting." To avoid such an impression liberation hermeneutics must reflect on the fact that the process of interpretation of Scripture is not necessarily liberative.

The Hermeneutics of the Woman's Bible

While liberation theologians affirm the Bible as a weapon in the struggle of liberation, and they claim that the God of the Bible is a God of the oppressed, feminist writers since the inauguration of the

368 / *Elisabeth Schüssler Fiorenza*

women's movement in the last century have maintained, to the contrary, that the Bible and Christian theology are inherently sexist, and thereby destructive of women's consciousness. A revisionist interpretation of Scripture and theology, therefore, will either subvert women's struggle for liberation from all sexist oppression and violence, or it will be forced to re-interpret Christian tradition and theology in such a way that nothing "Christian" will remain.

Feminist theology as a critical theology of liberation must defend itself against two sides: While liberation theologians are reluctant to acknowledge that women are exploited and oppressed, radical feminist thinkers claim that feminist consciousness and Christian faith are contradictions in terms. When our daughter Christina was born we announced her baptism with the following statement:

> She is born into a world of oppression
> She is born into a society of discrimination
> She is re-born into a church of inequality . . .

The reaction of our friends to this announcement illustrates these objections to Christian feminist theology. Some colleagues and students in theology shook their heads and asked whether we had planned a Marxist initiation rite. Or in indignation they pointed to the privileged status of a girl born to middle-class professional parents. However, a very bright college student (who felt suffocated by the patriarchal environment of Notre Dame and was later hospitalized with a nervous breakdown) challenged me on the street saying: How can you do this to her? She will never be able to be a consciouness-raised woman and a committted Christian. Christian faith and the Church are destructive of women-persons who struggle against sexism and for liberation.

The question which feminist theologians must face squarely is thus a foundational theological problem: Is being a woman and being a Christian a primary contradiction which must be resolved in favor of one to the exclusion of the other? Or can both be kept in creative tension so that my being a Christian supports my struggle for liberation as a woman, while my being a feminist enhances and deepens my commitment to live as a Christian.[32] Insofar as feminist theology as a Christian theology is bound to its charter documents in Scripture, it must formulate this problem also with reference to the Bible and biblical revelation. Since the Bible was and is used against women's demand for equality and liberation from societal, cultural, and ecclesial sexism, it must conceive of this task first in critical terms before it can attempt to formulate a hermeneutics of liberation. While the danger of liberation theology is "proof texting," the pitfall to be avoided by feminist theology is apologetics, since such an apologetics does not take the political implications of Scriptural interpretation seriously.

The debate surrounding the *Woman's Bible,*[33] which appeared in 1895 and 1898, may serve here as a case-study for the *political* conditions and implications of feminist biblical interpretation as well as for the radical critical impact of feminist theology for the interpretative task. In her introduction to the *Woman's Bible* Elizabeth Cady Stanton, the initiator of the project, outlined two critical insights for a feminist theological hermeneutics. The Bible is not a "neutral" book, but it is a political weapon against women's struggle for liberation. This is so because the Bible bears the imprint of men who never saw or talked with God.

First: Elizabeth Cady Stanton conceived of biblical interpretation as a political act. The following episode characterizes her own personal conviction of the negative impact of Christian religion on women's situation. She refused to attend a prayer meeting of suffragists that was opened by the singing of the hymn "Guide Us, O Thou Great Jehovah" by Isabella Beecher Hooker. Her reason was that Jehovah had "never taken any active part in the suffrage movement."[34] Because of her experience that Yahweh was not on the side of the oppressed, she realized the great political influence of the Bible. She, therefore, proposed to prepare a revision of the Bible which would collect and interpret (with the help of "higher criticism") all statements referring to women in the Bible. She conceded, however, that she was not very successful in soliciting the help of women scholars because they were

afraid that their high reputation and scholarly attainments might be compromised by taking part in an enterprise that

for a time may prove very unpopular. Hence we may not be
able to get help from that class.[35]

And indeed, the project of the *Woman's Bible* proved to be very unpopular because of political implications. Not only did some of the
suffragists argue that such a project was either not necessary, or politically unwise, but the National American Woman's Suffrage Association formally rejected it as a political mistake. In the second
volume, which appeared in 1898, Cady Stanton sums up this opposition: "Both friend and foe object to the title" and then replies with
biting wit to the accusation of a clergyman that the *Woman's Bible* is
"the work of women and the devil":

> This is a grave mistake. His Satanic Majesty was not to join
> the Revising Committee which consists of women alone.
> Moreover, he has been so busy of late years attending Syn-
> ods, General Assemblies and Conferences, to prevent the
> recognition of women delegates, that he has no time to
> study the languages and "higher criticism."[36]

Although the methods and theological presuppositions of the
"higher criticism" of the time are rather outdated today, the political
arguments and objectives of a feminist biblical interpretation remain
valid. They are outlined by Cady Stanton in her introduction to the
first volume. She gives three reasons why such an objective scientific
feminist revision and interpretation of the Bible is politically necessary:

    1. Throughout history and especially today the Bible is used to
keep women in subjection and to hinder their emancipation.

    2. Not only men, but especially women are the most faithful be-
lievers in the Bible as the Word of God. Not only for men, but also
for women the Bible has a numinous authority.

    3. No reform is possible in one area of society if it is not ad-
vanced also in all other areas. One cannot reform the law and other
cultural institutions without also reforming biblical religion which
claims the Bible as Holy Scripture. Since "all reforms are interdependent," a critical feminist interpretation is a necessary political en-

deavor, though perhaps not opportune. If feminists think they can neglect the revision of the Bible because there are more pressing political issues, then they do not recognize the political impact of Scripture upon the churches and society, and also upon the lives of women.

Second: Elizabeth Cady Stanton advocated such a revision of the Bible in terms of "higher criticism." Her insights, therefore, correspond with the results of historical biblical studies of her time. Over and against the doctrinal understanding of the Bible as Word of God, she stresses that the Bible is written by men and reflects patriarchal male interests. "The only point in which I differ from all ecclesiastical teaching is that I do not believe that any man ever saw or talked with God."[37] While the churches teach that such degrading ideas about patriarchal injunctions against women come from God, Cady Stanton maintains that all these degrading texts and ideas emanated from the heads of men. By treating the Bible as a human work and not as a magic fetish, and by denying divine inspiration to the negative biblical statements about women, she claims that her committee has shown more reverence and respect for God than does the clergy or the Church. She concedes that some teachings of the Bible, such as the love-command or the golden rule, are still valid today. Since the teachings and lessons of the Bible differ from each other, the Bible cannot be accepted or rejected as a whole. Therefore, every passage on women must be carefully analyzed and evaluated for its impact on the struggle for the liberation of women.

In conclusion: Although the idea of a *Woman's Bible* consisting only of the biblical texts on women must be rejected today on methodological grounds,[38] biblical scholarship on the whole has proven accurate her contention that the Bible must be studied as a human work, and that biblical interpretation is influenced by the theological mindset and interests of the interpreter. Contemporary feminist interpreters, like some of Cady Stanton's suffragist friends, either reject biblical interpretation as a hopeless feminist endeavor because the Bible is totally sexist, or they attempt to defend the Bible in the face of its radical feminist critics. In doing so they follow Frances Willard, who argued against the radical critique of the *Woman's Bible* that not the biblical message, but only its patriarchal contemporary interpretation preaches the subjugation of women.

I think that men have read their own selfish theories into
the book, that theologians have not in the past sufficiently
recognized the progressive quality of its revelation nor adequately discriminated between its records as history and its
principles of ethics and religion.[39]

The insight that scholarly biblical interpretations need to be
"depatriarchalized" is an important one. However, this critical insight should not be misunderstood as an apologetic defense of the
nonpatriarchal character of the Bible's teachings on ethics and religion. It was exactly Elizabeth Cady Stanton's critical insight that the
Bible is not just misunderstood, but that its contents and perspectives
can be used in the political struggle against women. What Gustavo
Gutiérrez says about human historiography in general must also be
applied to the writing of the Bible:

Human history has been written by a white hand, a male
hand from the dominating social class. The perspective of
the defeated in history is different. Attempts have been
made to wipe from their minds the memory of their struggle. This is to deprive them of a source of energy, of an historical will to rebellion.[40]

If we compare Cady Stanton's hermeneutical stance with that of
Segundo then we see that she could not accept his understanding of a
liberative second-level learning process within Christian history exactly because she shares his "advocacy stance for the oppressed."
Cady Stanton cannot begin with the affirmation that the Bible and
the God of the Bible are on the side of the oppressed because her experience of the Bible's use as a political weapon against women's
struggle for suffrage tells her otherwise.

The subsequent reaction to the *Woman's Bible* also warns liberation theologians that a biblical interpretation that resorts too quickly to the defense of the Bible could misconstrue its advocacy stance
for the oppressed. The task of liberation theologians is not to prove
that the Bible or the Church can be defended against feminist or socialist attacks. Only when we critically comprehend how the Bible

functions in the oppression of women or the poor can we prevent its misuse for further oppression. Otherwise, liberation theology is in danger of succumbing to proof-texting. The advocacy stance of liberation theology can only be construed as a rationalization of preconceived ecclesial or dogmatic positions if it does not fully explore the oppressive aspects of biblical traditions. Because of their advocacy for the oppressed, feminist theologians must insist that theological-critical analysis of Christian tradition should not begin with the time of Constantine, but it also must apply itself to the Christian charter documents themselves.

Because of its allegiance to the "defeated in history," a feminist critical theology maintains that a "hermeneutics of consent" which understands itself as the "actualizing continuation of the Christian history of interpretation" does not suffice. Such a hermeneutics overlooks the fact that Christian Scripture and tradition are not only a source of truth, but also of untruth, repression, and domination. Since the hermeneutic-contextual paradigm seeks only to *understand* biblical texts, it cannot adequately take into account the fact that the Christian past, as well as its interpretations, has victimized women. A critical theology of liberation,[41] therefore, must work out a new interpretative paradigm that can take seriously the claim of liberation theologians that God is on the side of the oppressed. Such a paradigm must also accept the claim of feminist theologians that God has never "taken an active part in the suffrage movement," and that therefore the Bible can function as a male weapon in the political struggle against women's liberation.

IV

Toward a Feminist Interpretive Paradigm of Emancipatory Praxis[42]

A critical theology of liberation cannot avoid raising the question of the truth-content of the Bible for Christians today. If, for instance, feminist theologians take fully into account the androcentric language, misogynist contents, and patriarchal interests of biblical texts, then we cannot avoid the question of the "canon," or the criterion that allows us to reject oppressive traditions and to detect liberative traditions within biblical texts and history.

First: Such a need for a critical evaluation of the various biblical texts and traditions has always been recognized in the Church. While the doctrinal paradigm insisted that Scripture must be judged by the *regula fidei,* and can only be properly interpreted by the teaching office of the Church, the historical-critical paradigm evaluated the theological truth of biblical texts according to their historicity. The hermeneutic-contextual paradigm has not only established the canon as the pluriform root-model of the Christian community, but it has also underlined the fact that the Bible often includes various contradictory responses to the historical situation of the Israelite or Christian community.

Since not all these responses can equally express Christian revelation, biblical scholarship has attempted to formulate theological criteria to evaluate different biblical traditions. Such a "canon within the canon" can be formulated along philosophical-dogmatic or historical-factual lines. Some theologians distinguish between revelatory essence and historical expression, timeless truth and culturally conditioned language, or constant Christian tradition and changing traditions. When such a canon is formulated along the lines of the hermeneutic-contextual paradigm, scholars juxtapose Jesus and Paul, Pauline theology and early Catholicism, the historical Jesus and the kerygmatic Christ, or Hebrew and Greek thought. Whereas, e.g., Ogden accepts as such a canon the Jesus-traditions of Marxsen,[43] Sobrino emphasizes the Jesus of history as the criterion for liberation theology. Segundo, on the other hand, is methodologically most consistent when he insists that no contentual biblical statement can be singled out as such a criterion because all historical expression of faith is ideological. In line with the hermeneutic-contextual paradigm, he insists that not the content but the process of interpretation within the Bible and Christian history should be normative for liberation theology. Yet such a proposal does not allow for the insight that this process of expressing faith in a historical situation can also be falsified and serve oppressive interests.

Therefore, a critical theology of liberation cannot take the Bible or the biblical faith defined as the total process of learning in and through ideologies as *norma normans non normata,*[44] but must understand them as sources alongside other sources. This point was already made by James Cone, who pointed out that the sources of theology are the Bible as well as our own political situation and experience. However, the norm for black theology is *"Jesus as the Black Christ who provides the necessary soul for black liberation."* ". . . he is the essence of the Christian gospel."[45]

I would be hesitant to postulate that Jesus as the feminist Christ is the canonical norm since we cannot spell out concretely who this feminist Christ is if we do not want to make Christ a formalized *chiffre* or resort to mysticism. This is the argument of Jon Sobrino, who in turn postulates that the historical Jesus is the norm of truth since *"access to the Christ of faith comes through our following of the historical Jesus."*[46] However, such a formulation of the canonical norm for Christian faith presupposes that we can know the historical Jesus and that we can imitate him, since an actual following of Jesus is not possible for us. Moreover, a feminist theologian must question whether the historical man Jesus of Nazareth can be a role model for contemporary women, since feminist psychological liberation means exactly the struggle of women to free themselves from all male internalized norms and models.

Second: I would suggest that the canon and norm for evaluating biblical traditions and their subsequent interpretations cannot be derived from the Bible or the biblical process of learning within and through ideologies, but can only be formulated within and through the struggle for the liberation of women and all oppressed people. It cannot be "universal," but it must be specific and derived from a particular experience of oppression and liberation. The "advocacy stance" of liberation theologies must be sustained at the point of the critical evaluation of biblical texts and traditions. The personally and politically reflected experience of oppression and liberation must become the criterion of "appropriateness" for biblical interpretation.

A hermeneutical understanding which is not only oriented toward an actualizing continuation of biblical history, but also toward a critical evaluation of it, must uncover and denounce biblical traditions and theologies that perpetuate violence, alienation, and oppression. At the same time, such a critical hermeneutics also must delineate those biblical traditions that bring forward the liberating experiences and visions of the people of God. Such a hermeneutics points to the eschatological vision of freedom and salvation, and maintains that such a vision must be historically realized in the community of faith.

A feminist theological interpretation of the Bible that has as its canon the liberation of women from oppressive sexist structures, institutions, and internalized values must, therefore, maintain that only the nonsexist and non-androcentric traditions of the Bible and the nonoppressive traditions of biblical interpretation have the theological authority of revelation if the Bible is not to continue as a tool for the oppression of women. The "advocacy stance" demands that oppressive and destructive biblical traditions cannot be accorded any truth and authority claim today.[47] Nor did they have such a claim at any point in history. Such a critical hermeneutic must be applied to *all* biblical texts and their historical contexts. It should also be applied to their subsequent history of interpretation in order to determine *how* much these traditions and interpretations have contributed to the patriarchal oppression of women. In the same vein, such a critical feminist hermeneutics must rediscover those biblical traditions and interpretations that have transcended their oppressive cultural contexts even though they are embedded in patriarchal culture. These texts and traditions should not be understood as abstract theological ideas or norms, but as faith-responses to concrete historical situations of oppression. For instance, throughout the centuries Christian feminism has claimed Galatians 3:28 as its magna charta, while the patriarchal Church has used 1 Corinthians 14 or 1 Timothy 2 for the cultural and ecclesial oppression of women.[48]

Third: The insight that the Bible is not only a source of truth and revelation, but also a source of violence and domination is basic for liberation theologies. This insight demands a new paradigm of biblical interpretation that does not understand the Bible as archetype, but as prototype.

A dictionary definition reveals the significant distinction between the words. While both archetype and prototype "denote original models," an archetype is "usually con-

strued as an ideal form that establishes an unchanging pattern. . . ." However, . . . a prototype is not a binding, timeless pattern, but one critically open to the possibility, even the necessity of its own transformation. Thinking in terms of prototypes historicizes myth.⁴⁹

Since the hermeneutic-contextual paradigm has as a goal the appropriation of biblical truth and history, but not its ideological critique, liberation theologians must develop a new critical paradigm of biblical interpretation. T. S. Kuhn has pointed out that such a new scientific paradigm must also create a new scientific ethos and community.

The hermeneutic-contextual historical paradigm allows for the "advocacy stance" within the hermeneutical circle as a presupposition from which to raise questions, but objects to it as a conviction or definite standpoint. However, a new critical paradigm must reject such a theory as ideological. It must, in turn, insist that all theologians and interpreters of the Bible stand publicly accountable for their own position. It should become methodologically *mandatory* that *all* scholars explicitly discuss their own presuppositions, allegiances, and functions within a theological-political context, and especially those scholars, who in critiques of liberation theology, resort to an artifically construed value-neutrality. Scholars no longer can pretend that what they do is completely "detached" from all political interests. Since we always interpret the Bible and Christian faith from a position within history, scholarly detachment and neutrality must be unmasked as a "fiction" or "false consciousness" that serves definite political interests. Further, theological interpretation must also critically reflect on the political presuppositions and implications of theological "classics" and dogmatic or ethical systems. In other words, not only the content and traditioning process within the Bible, but the whole of Christian tradition should be scrutinized and judged as to whether or not it functions to oppress or liberate people.

Finally, the "advocacy stance" as a criterion or norm for evaluating biblical texts and their political functions should not be mistaken as an abstract, formalized principle. The different forms of a critical theology of liberation must construct specific heuristic mod-

els that adequately analyze the mechanisms and structures of contemporary oppression and movements for liberation. On the one hand, too generalized an understanding of oppression and liberation serves the interests of the oppressive systems which cannot tolerate a critical analysis of their dehumanizing mechanisms and structures. At the same time, it prevents the formulation of very specific goals and strategies for the liberation struggle. On the other hand, too particularized an understanding of oppression and liberation prevents an active solidarity among oppressed groups, who can be played out against each other by the established systems. The "advocacy stance" as the criterion or norm for biblical interpretation must, therefore, develop a critical theology of liberation that promotes the solidarity of all oppressed peoples, and at the same time has room enough to develop specific heuristic theological models of oppression and liberation.[50]

In conclusion: Liberation theologians must abandon the hermeneutic-contextual paradigm of biblical interpretation, and construct within the context of a critical theology of liberation, a new interpretative paradigm that has as its aim emancipatory praxis. Such a paradigm of political praxis has, as a research perspective, the critical relationship between theory and practice, between biblical texts and contemporary liberation-movements. This new paradigm of emancipatory praxis must generate new heuristic models of interpretation that can interpret and evaluate biblical traditions and their political function in history in terms of their own canons of liberation.

Notes

1. See Adrienne Rich, "Toward a Woman-Centered University," in *Women and the Power to Change,* ed. Florence Howe (New York: McGraw-Hill), pp. 15–46; and my analysis in "Towards a Liberating and Liberated Theology: Women Theologians and Feminist Theology in the U.S.A.," *Concilium* 115(1979): 22–32.

2. See e.g., Lisa Leghorn and M. Roodkowsky, *Who Really Starves? Women and World Hunger* (New York: Friendship Press, 1977); Diane E.

Nichole Russel and N. Van de Ven, eds., *Crimes against Women: Processings of the International Tribunal* (Millbrae, Calif.: Les Femmes, 1976); Susan Hill Lindley, "Feminist Theology in a Global Perspective," *The Christian Century,* 96 (April 25, 1979):465–469.

3. See, for instance, Gustavo Gutiérrez. *A Theology of Liberation* (Maryknoll, N.Y.: Orbis Books, 1973), pp. 204–205: "A spirituality of liberation will center on a *conversion* to the neighbor, the oppressed person, the exploited social class, the despised race, the dominated country. Our conversion to the Lord implies this conversion to the neighbor." Compare the description of feminist conversion by Judith Plaskow, *Sex, Sin, and Grace: Women's Experience and the Theologies of Reinhold Niebuhr and Paul Tillich* (Washington, D.C.: University Press of America, 1980), pp. 171–172: "The woman who, having seen the non-being of social structures, feels herself a whole person, is called upon to become the person she is in that movement. . . . The experience of grace is not the experience of the sole activity of God, but the experience of the emergence of the 'I' as co-creator. . . . Relatedness to God is expressed through the neverending journey toward self-creation within community, and through the creation of ever wider communities, including both other human beings and the world."

4. Robert McAfee Brown, *Theology in a New Key: Responding to Liberation Themes* (Philadelphia: Westminster, 1978), p. 82.

5. Vine Deloria, "A Native American Perspective on Liberation," in *Mission Trends No. 4: Liberation Theologies,* ed. Gerald H. Anderson and Thomas F. Stransky (New York: Paulist Press, 1979), pp. 261–270.

6. See my article, "Women in Early Christianity: Methodological Considerations," in *Critical History and Biblical Faith in New Testament Perspectives,* ed. T. J. Ryan (Villanova, Pa.: Catholic Theology Society Annual Publications, 1979), pp. 30–58.

7. See my article, "For the Sake of Our Salvation . . . Biblical Interpretation as Theological Task," in *Sin, Salvation, and the Spirit,* ed. Daniel Durken (Collegeville, Minn.: Liturgical Press, 1979), pp. 21–39, for a more extensive discussion of the literature.

8. See Lee Cormie, "The Hermeneutical Privilege of the Oppressed: Liberation Theologies, Biblical Faith, and Marxist Sociology of Knowledge," *Proceedings of the Catholic Theological Society of America* 32(1977); D. Lockhead, "Hermeneutics and Ideology," *The Ecumenist* 15 (1977): 81–84.

9. Schubert M. Ogden, *Faith and Freedom: Toward a Theology of Liberation* (Nashville: Abingdon, 1979), p. 116.

10. Ibid., p. 32.

11. James H. Cone, *God of the Oppressed* (New York: Seabury, 1975), pp. 51–52.

12. See Charles H. Strain, "Ideology and Alienation: Theses on the Interpretation and Evaluation of Theologies of Liberation," *Journal of the American Academy of Religion* (hereafter *JAAR*) 45 (1977):474.

13. See Thomas S. Kuhn, *The Structure of Scientific Revolutions* (Chicago: University of Chicago Press, 1962); Ian G. Barbour, *Myth, Models, and Paradigms* (New York: Harper & Row, 1974).

14. See my article, "For the Sake of Our Salvation . . ." for the development of these paradigms. See also for the general paradigm-shift in biblical studies, Walter Wink, *The Bible in Human Transformation: Toward a New Paradigm for Biblical Studies* (Philadelphia: Fortress, 1973).

15. See, e.g., G. Sauter, " 'Exodus' und 'Befreiung' als theologische Metaphern: Ein Beispiel zur Kritik von Allegorese und missverstandenen Analogien in der Ethik," *Ev Th* 38 (1978): 538–559, although one suspects that his criticism leads to a totally depoliticized interpretation.

16. James Barr, *Fundamentalism* (Philadelphia: Westminster, 1978), p. 49.

17. José Miranda, *Marx and the Bible* (Maryknoll, N.Y.: Orbis Books, 1974). See the discussion by J. A. Kirk, "The Bible in Latin American Liberation Theology," in *The Bible and Liberation,* ed. Norman K. Gottwald and Antoinette C. Wire (Berkeley: Radical Religion, 1976), p. 161.

18. See Norman Perrin, *What is Redaction Criticism?* (Philadelphia: Fortress, 1969): Werner G. Kümmel, *Das Neue Testament in 20 Jahrhundert* (Stuttgart: KBW, 1970).

19. See especially Norman K. Gottwald, *The Tribes of Yahweh: A Sociology of the Religion of Liberated Israel, 1250–1050 B. C. E.* (Maryknoll, N.Y.: Orbis Books, 1979).

20. See, e.g., Leander E. Keck, "On the Ethos of Early Christians," *JAAR* 42 (1974): 435–452; John C. Gager, *Kingdom and Community* (Englewood Cliffs, N.J.: Prentice-Hall, 1975); Gerd Theissen, *Sociology of Early Palestinian Christianity* (Philadelphia: Fortress, 1978); Wayne A. Meeks, "The Social World of Early Christianity," *CRS Bulletin* 6 (1975): 1, 4f.; Willy Schottroff und Wolfgang Stegemann, *Der Gott der kleinen Leute: Sozialgeschichtliche Auslegungen: BD. 2 NT* (Munich: Kaiser, 1979).

21. See my article, "Word, Spirit, and Power: Women in Early Christian Communities," in *Women of Spirit,* ed. Rosemary Radford Ruether and Eleanor McLaughlin (New York: Simon and Schuster, 1979), pp. 29–70; David Balch, *"Let Wives Be Submissive . . ." (Ann Arbor: University Microfilms International,* 1978).

22. See Gerd Theissen, "Synoptische Wundergeschichten im Lichte unseres Sprachverhältnisses," *Wissenschaft und Praxis in Kirche und Gesellschaft* 65 (1976): 289–308; for the interrelation between poverty, violence, and exploitation, cf. Luise Schottroff und Wolfgang Stegemann, *Jesus von Nazareth: Hoffnung der Armen* (Stuttgart: Kohlhammer, 1978).

23. See T. Peters, "The Nature and Role of Presupposition: An Inquiry into Contemporary Hermeneutics," *International Philosophical Quarterly* 14 (1974): 209–222; Frederick Herzog, "Liberation Hermeneutic as Ideology Critique," *Interpretation* 27 (1974): 387–403.

24. Edward Schillebeeckx, *The Understanding of Faith* (New York: Seabury, 1974), p. 130.

25. See especially Peter Stuhlmacher, *Historical Criticism and Theological Interpretation of Scripture: Toward a Hermeneutics of Consent* (Philadelphia: Fortress, 1977), pp. 83 ff.

26. For these criteria, see Ogden, *Faith and Freedom,* p. 26, and especially David Tracy, *Blessed Rage for Order: The New Pluralism in Theology* (New York: Seabury, 1975), pp. 72–79.

27. This whole section is based on an analysis of Juan Luis Segundo, *The Liberation of Theology* (Maryknoll, N.Y.: Orbis Books, 1976).

28. Ibid., p. 9; see also José Miguez Bonino, *Doing Theology in a Revolutionary Situation* (Philadelphia: Fortress, 1975), pp. 86–105, who accepts Professor Casalis' reformulation of the "hermeneutical circle" as "hermeneutical circulation" (p. 102).

29. Segundo, *The Liberation of Theology,* p. 8.

30. Ibid., p. 110.

31. Ibid., p. 179.

32. See my article, "Feminist Spirituality, Christian Identity and the Catholic Vision," in *Womanspirit Rising: A Feminist Reader in Religion,* ed. Carol P. Christ and Judith Plaskow (New York: Harper & Row, 1979), pp. 136–148.

33. Elizabeth Cady Stanton, *The Woman's Bible,* American Women Series: Images and Realities, 2 vol. in 1; reprint of 1895 ed. (New York: Arno).

34. Barbara Welter, "Something Remains to Dare: Introduction to the Woman's Bible," in *The Original Feminist Attack on the Bible (The Woman's Bible),* by E. Cady Stanton, facsimile ed. (New York: Arno, 1974), p. xxii.

35. Cady Stanton, *The Woman's Bible,* 1:9.

36. Ibid., 11:7f.

37. Ibid., 1:12.

38. See, however, Marie Fortune and Joann Haugerud, *Study Guide to the Woman's Bible* (Seattle: Coalition Task Force on Women and Religion, 1975) for a contemporary application; and Leonard Swidler, *Biblical Affirmation of Women* (Philadelphia: Westminster, 1979), who basically follows the same principle.

39. Cited in Cady Stanton, *The Woman's Bible,* 11:200.

40. Gustavo Guitiérrez, "Where Hunger Is, God Is Not," *The Witness* 59 (April 1976): 6.

41. For the conceptualization of feminist theology as such a critical theology of liberation, see my article, "Feminist Theology as a Critical Theology of Liberation," in *Woman: New Dimensions,* ed., Walter Burkhardt (New York: Paulist Press, 1977), pp. 19–50.

42. See the pathbreaking article of Francis Schüssler Fiorenza, "Critical Social Theology and Christology: Toward an Understanding of Atonement and Redemption as Emancipatory Solidarity," *Proceedings of the Catholic Theological Society of America* 30 (1975): 63–110.

43. Ogden, *Faith and Freedom,* pp. 44ff., and his article, "The Authority of Scripture for Theology," *Interpretation* 30 (1976): 242–261.

44. For this expression, see David Tracy, "Theological Classics in Contemporary Theology," *Theology Digest* 25 (1977): 347–355.

45. James H. Cone, *Liberation: A Black Theology of Liberation* (Philadelphia: Lippincott, 1970), p. 80.

46. Jon Sobrino, "The Historical Jesus and the Christ of Faith," *Cross Currents* 27 (1977/78): 437–463, 460.

47. Such a proposal should not be misunderstood in the sense of the *Woman's Bible* approach that has singled out for discussion biblical texts on women. The criterion has to be applied to all biblical texts insofar as they claim authority for today. Such a theological evaluation must also be distinguished from a reconstruction of early Christian history in a feminist perspective. While a feminist reconstruction of early Christian history asks for women's history and heritage, a feminist biblical hermeneutics evaluates the truth-claims of biblical texts for today. Thus both approaches are interdependent but quite distinct.

48. See my analysis in "Word, Spirit, and Power," in *Women of Spirit.*

49. Rachel Blau DuPlessis, "The Critique of Consciousness and Myth in Levertov, Rich, and Rukeyser," *Feminist Studies* 3 (1975): 199–221, 219.

50. Rosemary Radford Ruether, *New Woman/New Earth: Sexist Ideologies and Human Liberation* (New York: Seabury, 1975), pp. 115–132, has called for an "interstructuring" of various models of alienation/liberation.

Biographical Notes

Richard H. Hiers is Professor of Religion at the University of Florida.

James H. Cone is Charles A. Briggs Professor of Theology at Union Theological Seminary.

Jack T. Sanders is Professor of Religious Studies at the University of Oregon.

Richard J. Mouw is Professor of Philosophy at Calvin College.

Philippe Delhaye is Professor of Moral Theology at the University of Louvain.

Hans Schürmann is Professor of New Testament at the Regional Seminary of Erfurt, East Germany.

Edouard Hamel is Professor of Moral Theology at Gregorian University in Rome.

James M. Gustafson is University Professor of Theological Ethics at the University of Chicago Divinity School.

Charles E. Curran is Professor of Moral Theology at The Catholic University of America.

Allen D. Verhey is Associate Professor of Religion at Hope College.

Stanley Hauerwas is Professor of Theology at the University of Notre Dame.

James F. Childress is Professor of Religious Studies and Medical Education at the University of Virginia.

Richard A. McCormick is Rose F. Kennedy Professor of Christian Ethics in the Kennedy Institute of Ethics at Georgetown University.

Alfred T. Hennelly is Research Fellow at Woodstock Theological Center.

Anthony J. Tambasco is Assistant Professor of Theology at Georgetown University.

John H. Yoder is Professor of Theology at the University of Notre Dame.

Elisabeth Schüssler Fiorenza is Professor of Theology at the University of Notre Dame.

READINGS IN
MORAL THEOLOGY NO. 2
THE DISTINCTIVENESS OF CHRISTIAN ETHICS

CONTENTS

READINGS IN
MORAL THEOLOGY NO. 1
MORAL NORMS AND CATHOLIC TRADITION

CONTENTS